The Expanding Prison

The Expanding Prison

David Cayley

The Crisis in Crime and Punishment and the Search for Alternatives

The Pilgrim Press
Cleveland, Ohio

The Pilgrim Press, Cleveland, Ohio 44115

Copublished with the House of Anansi Press Limited, Toronto, Canada

© 1998 by David Cayley

All rights reserved. Published 1998

Printed in Canada

03 02 01 00 99 98   5 4 3 2 1

ISBN 0-8298-1333-0

The mood and temper of the public in regard to the treatment of crime and criminals is one of the most unfailing tests of the civilization of any country. A calm and dispassionate recognition of the rights of the accused against the State, and even of convicted criminals against the State, a constant heart-searching by all charged with the duty of punishment, a desire and eagerness to rehabilitate in the world of industry all those who have paid their dues in the hard coinage of punishment, tireless efforts towards the discovery of curative and regenerating processes, and an unfaltering faith that there is a treasure, if you can only find it, in the heart of every man — these are the symbols which in the treatment of crime and criminals mark and measure the stored-up strength of a nation, and are the sign and proof of the living virtue in it.

Winston Churchill to the British
House of Commons, July 1910

CONTENTS

PREFACE

This book was conceived at a conference held at the Norwegian Academy of Science and Letters in April of 1995. The meeting was convened by Nils Christie, a professor of criminology at the University of Oslo, in the hope of drawing attention to a dangerous political emergency: the swelling numbers of people imprisoned throughout the Western world. In 1993, Christie had attempted to sound a warning with a book titled *Crime Control as Industry: Toward Gulags Western-Style?* The Oslo conference was a further effort to make the world aware of the urgency of curbing the expansion of the crime-control industry.

I first met Nils Christie three years earlier, when I spent several days in Oslo interviewing him for CBC Radio's *Ideas* series. He was pleased with the results — a series of three one-hour programs coinciding with the publication of *Crime Control as Industry* — and we subsequently became friends. This led him to appeal to me to come to Oslo in 1995 and help publicize the proceedings of his conference on prison growth. A year later, in June of 1996, I broadcast "Prison and Its Alternatives," a series of ten one-hour radio documentaries. The programs outlined the reasons for the current prison boom and explored alternative modes of crime control that have been successfully used in countries and communities that have resisted this trend.

"Prison and Its Alternatives" got an enthusiastic response from listeners. Letter after letter from judges, corrections officials, lawyers, members of parliament, prisoners, and interested members of the public indicated widespread dissatisfaction with the status quo in criminal justice and a favourable disposition to alternatives. Based on this encouraging response, I have transformed and expanded the radio series into the present book.

I dedicate the work to Nils Christie, whose friendship inspired it. I would also like to thank Alison Moss, who was the producer of "Prison and Its Alternatives." Her editorial advice and her cheerful attention to numerous other details were indispensable to the project and invaluable to me. My executive producer, Bernie Lucht, also provided generous support. Finally, I thank my wife Jutta for the continuing conversation in which so many of the ideas in this book have been tested and refined.

INTRODUCTION

The prison has always been a doubtful instrument of correction. "In a prison," Samuel Johnson wrote in *The Idler* in 1759, "the awe of public eye is lost, and the power of the law is spent, there are few fears, there are no blushes. The lewd inflame the lewd; the audacious harden the audacious."[1] Johnson's contemporary, Henry Fielding, the novelist and magistrate, made a similar observation. Speaking of the "houses of correction" of his time, he pointed out that "whatever these houses were designed to be, or whatever they at first were, the fact is that they are at present . . . no other than schools of vice, seminaries of idleness, and common bearers of nastiness and disease."[2]

The institution of imprisonment has changed its style many times since these comments were made. During the early nineteenth century, the virtually self-governing jail that Johnson and Fielding knew was replaced by the total regimentation of the penitentiary with its solitary confinement, treadmills, and morals instructors. When this regime was recognized as a source of madness and melancholy, further reforms followed. At the turn of the century, the warden of New York's famous Sing Sing, Thomas Osborne, dreamed of the prison as a democratic community.[3] Later, a medical model prevailed: incarceration as treatment. Today's Canadian prison, with its programs in life skills and anger management, is apparently very different from the dank warren that stood at Newgate in 1750. And yet, Johnson's and Fielding's remarks seem as pertinent today as when they were made. Whatever has changed, prisons still teach vice and foster criminality.

Officially, prisons exist to protect society. A prison term is given to deter someone who has broken the criminal law from doing so again, and to discourage others by his example. But these rationales cannot withstand serious scrutiny. The idea that having been in prison deters people from offending again is refuted by universally high rates of recidivism. The idea that others are deterred is undercut by the fact that crimes meriting incarceration are rarely committed as calculated risks. In the United States between 1992 and 1995, a 43 percent rise in marijuana arrests, and a stiffening of penalties, was accompanied by a considerable increase — by one estimate, a doubling — in marijuana use.[4] Even the commonsense idea that prisons keep dangerous people out of circulation runs up against the persistent difficulty of predicting who will be dangerous in the future. It is obviously prudent to confine certain predatory individuals — Paul Bernardo and Clifford Olson are the universally recognized examples — but it is not so easy in less obvious cases to foresee who will re-offend. Since 1992, for example, Canadian law allows the parole board, under the advice of the Correctional Service of Canada (CSC), to hold an offender deemed "dangerous" until the very end of his sentence rather than giving him the normal "statutory release" after doing two-thirds of his time. The law was intended to allay the public's fear of dangerous offenders; but when a CSC researcher compared the recidivism rates, he found that 37 percent of those on statutory release had re-offended, as compared to only 16 percent of those held to the ends of their terms.[5] In other words, when the CSC and the parole board tried to judge who was likely to re-offend, they got it almost entirely wrong. This finding confirms a number of previous studies showing how hard it is to predict or pre-empt dangerousness. Of course, it might be argued that the lower rate of re-offence among those held to the end of their sentences was a result of staying in prison longer, but this seems to me unlikely. If the threat of re-imprisonment failed to deter those on conditional release, why would continued imprisonment deter those held longer?

Imprisonment, except in rare cases, does not actually enhance public safety. "Research into the use of imprisonment over time and in different countries," say criminologists Norval Morris and David Rothman, "has failed to demonstrate any positive correlation between increasing the rate of imprisonment and reducing the rate of crime."[6] But prisons do undoubtedly do three things. First, they provide a dumping ground for unwanted people. Alexander Solzhenitsyn puts it bluntly in *The Gulag Archipelago* when he describes the rising tide of imprisonment between the Russian Revolution and Josef Stalin's death under the heading "The History of Our Sewage Disposal System." Second, following the ancient image of justice as a scale, they subject convicts to surroundings whose harshness appears to pay them back for, or "balance out," their crimes. And, finally, they signify to the public that Something Has Been Done.

These less frequently acknowledged functions of imprisonment are costly in several ways. First of all, the prison as the bottom rung of the welfare system is extremely expensive. The csc's costs per prisoner are estimated at up to $50,000 annually. The hiring of 1,000 new correctional officers, announced in April of 1998, will increase the ratio of officers to prisoners to 42.7 per 100 and take those costs even higher.[7] Still more important are the costs of the prison as an agent of desocialization. Jim Cavanagh, who served twenty-five years in Canadian penal institutions before becoming a minister with Prison Fellowship Canada, calls prisons a way of "warehousing the problems for X number of years and then bringing them back into society worse off."[8] (Cavanagh's story is told in detail in Chapter 6.) Rehabilitation certainly can occur in prison; but the general effect of imprisonment as a system of ostracization and lifelong stigmatization is to foster defensive and antagonistic criminal subcultures among the inmates. In a vicious circle, the institution intended to make society safer actually makes it more dangerous. The product of imprisonment is a person who will require more imprisonment in future.

Ivan Illich has argued that modern institutions often reach a scale at which they begin to frustrate their own purposes[9]: schools stupefy their students, traffic hampers movement, and medicine becomes a threat to health. The prison would seem to be a prime instance of this law of unintended consequences. And yet, during the last generation, country after country has increased its reliance on this counterproductive tool. In the early 1970s, for example, the state of Texas had about 14,000 people in its jails. Today the number is 140,000, and a capacity of 200,000 is planned for the millennium. The United States as a whole now has more than 1.5 million of its citizens behind bars, four times as many as there were in 1970. If those awaiting trial, on probation, or on parole are added, the total number of Americans currently caught up in the institutions of criminal justice comes to more than 5 million.[10]

The countries of the disbanded Soviet empire have also had large increases in their prison populations. Russia, the current per capita world leader in incarceration, has more than a million people in prison, twice as many as the entire U.S.S.R. had in 1989. If the swelling number of prisoners in the Baltic states and the former Soviet republics were to be combined with Russia's total, the figure would be well on the way to rivalling the estimated 2.5 million people held in the gulags at the end of Stalin's regime. Prison numbers are growing in Eastern Europe as well, and even the Western European countries formerly known for their low rates of imprisonment have seen substantial increases. The Netherlands, which reduced its prison population to an astonishingly low 17 per 100,000 between the 1950s and the 1970s, now has more than three times that many people in custody.

Canada too has followed the trend, with an annual growth of about 4 percent in recent years. By 1995 the number of prisoners in our federal prisons was 15 percent over capacity, which means that most inmates begin their terms sharing a cell originally designed for only one person. According to a recent report from Canada's correctional investigator, this practice produces crowding so severe that it "defies not only any reasonable standard of decency, but also the standards of international convention."[11] Nevertheless, former federal solicitor general Herb Gray has projected a further growth of 25 percent by the year 2000, and a CSC report has even warned of a possible 50 percent increase within ten years.[12]

This startling growth cannot generally be accounted for by any increase in crime. In fact, contrary to what common sense might assume, levels of crime and levels of imprisonment show no regular or predictable relationship. Crime has certainly gone up in the countries of the disbanded Soviet empire; but, in both Canada and the United States, it has gone down for a number of years without any abatement in the growth of prison population — as a recent headline put it, "Crime Keeps on Falling but Prisons Keep on Filling."[13] Many historical cases confirm the fact that crime alone does not drive prison rates. In the Netherlands between 1950 and 1970, recorded crime increased by 300 percent while prison numbers were cut in half.[14] Societies alike in every respect, including the frequency of crime, may still differ dramatically in their rates of imprisonment. In the United States, for example, South Dakota imprisons its citizens at more than twice the rate of its demographically similar neighbour, North Dakota.[15]

Prison numbers reflect political decisions about what constitutes crime and how it should be punished. Neither is self-evident. Certain acts are universally deplored, but beyond this minimum, political societies exercise considerable discretion concerning what they penalize and what they tolerate. In Europe in the Middle Ages you could be executed for blasphemy; today in certain American states you can go to prison for life for selling a little marijuana. Criminologists make various estimates of "the dark figure," or the percentage of technically illegal acts that actually show up in court as crimes, but all agree that it constitutes only a small proportion of the available pool of "criminalizable events." Crime, as Nils Christie has said, is in more or less endless supply.[16] How it is penalized depends on the enactments of legislatures, the practices of the police, the decisions of judges and parole boards, the biases of news media, and the social atmosphere in which all these agencies go about their work.

In the West, in recent years, this atmosphere has been querulous and uncertain. The neoconservative ascendancy in politics is reflected in a renewed emphasis on the individual responsibility of offenders and a rejection of the idea that crime expresses general social conditions. The collapse of communism as an external enemy has produced a new awareness of internal enemies. The emergence of an economy that grows by shedding labour has heightened anxiety about jobs and increased the number of people who find themselves without prospects and without a stake in the current order of society. There have been major moral panics about drugs and about sex crime.

Legislatures, prison administrations, and parole boards have reacted accordingly. Sentences have lengthened, and parole rates have been cut. The prison rate has surged.

I believe that this continuing increase presents a real threat to the decency and civility of the countries in which it is occurring. The ethos of the prison spreads beyond the prison's walls. This is true, first of all, because the violence endemic to prison life returns to the streets with the released offender, setting up the vicious circle of which I have already spoken. But it is also true in a larger sense. Prisons, by definition, are totalitarian institutions. As they take a more prominent part in social control, they acclimatize the societies that rely on them to this totalitarian mode of maintaining order. A prisoner, as the U.S. Supreme Court asserted in 1871, "is for the time being a slave of the state."[17] He has been put in a cage and made entirely subject to someone else's will. The more often this is done, the more acceptable it comes to seem — and the more necessary it actually becomes.

Prisons foster the very behaviour they purport to control, and so justify their own expansion.

The growth of imprisonment also threatens civility by overwhelming feeling for prisoners in the rest of society. The utilitarian political theory that underwrote the development of the modern prison saw the institution as a humane limitation on punishment. Punishment, argued the English philosopher and prison promoter Jeremy Bentham, was "a necessary evil . . . which ought to be admitted in as far as it promises to exclude some greater evil."[18] This philosophy at least recognized what the euphemistic vocabulary of "corrections" often hides: imprisonment is a deliberate and measured infliction of pain on a person.

Today, when crime is discussed, there is often a tang of brimstone in the air, and a disturbing enthusiam for the expansion of penal control, as if punishment were no longer a necessary evil but had become a desired good. Local communities in both Canada and the United States actively lobby to have prisons built in their precincts. Advertisements in correctional journals proudly trumpet the advantages of new technologies for controlling people — from portable electronic tracking devices to surveillance systems that Mitsubishi promises will "meet the growing need in home detention," to automated controls inside prisons that virtually eliminate face-to-face contact between prisoners and staff.[19] Crime control has become a self-justifying growth industry engaged in a thrilling "war against crime," and war imagery has inured citizens to the idea that crime is committed by a special class of moral monsters who deserve no better than they get. Sensitivity to suffering has been dulled, and resistance to imposing suffering has been weakened.

The prison boom is the shadow of the new social order that has been emerging during the last generation. The hallmarks of this order so far have been a general depreciation of the state's capacity to organize or improve society, an increasing polarization in the distribution of wealth, persistent high unemployment, and the liberation of capital from local loyalties and constraints.

Rising levels of imprisonment characterize this new order in much the same way that mass incarcerations have marked earlier periods of upheaval in Western history. In *Madness and Civilization*, Michel Foucault gave the name "The Great Confinement" to that period in mid-seventeenth-century Paris when 1 percent of the population was institutionalized in an effort to control the "masterless men" produced by the first great capitalist revolution and make Paris "safe for the bourgeoisie."[20] Imprisonment also exploded around the turn of the eighteenth century during the Industrial Revolution, when incarceration levels tripled in England and Wales.[21] Today, the dislocation and anxiety accompanying catastrophic change are once again generating big increases in the number of people in captivity. A new class of masterless men seems to be in the making, and the crime-control industry has been called on to restore order and reassure those who have managed to cling to their places in society.

There is, however, a difference between today's prison bulge and the increase at the beginning of the nineteenth century. The great incarceration that accompanied the Industrial Revolution presented itself as a reform. In place of "the spectacle of barbarous and useless torments, cold-bloodedly devised,"[22] a regime of sober, scientific correction was to be created in the new penitentiaries that were then being built. This hope was disappointed, but it was for a time sincerely entertained. No such faith underlies the penal expansion of the last twenty years. The idea of rehabilitation in prison has never seemed less plausible. Imprisonment continues to serve important symbolic and ideological functions, but I doubt if even its most enthusiastic supporters any longer believe that a prison is a good place to try to reform someone.

This disillusionment with the idea of imprisonment as correction contains both a danger and an opportunity. The danger is that contemporary societies will increasingly practise imprisonment in what amounts to a concentration-camp model, and that prisons will simply become holding pens from which nothing more is expected than efficient containment. The opportunity is the possibility of putting in question the way imprisonment currently monopolizes criminal justice.

Current attitudes towards criminal justice have taken shape during a history that stretches all the way back to the twelfth century, when the power to prosecute crime was first claimed by the English king Henry II and a count in Flanders called Philip of Alsace. Before that time, in Europe, in classical Greece and Rome, and almost everywhere else, what we call crime was seen as a private injury done by one party to another, demanding compensation and penance. Constituted authority might arbitrate disputes and enforce settlements, but nowhere did it initiate action or punish offenders. Then, gradually, crime was reinterpreted by the nascent European state as what Herman Bianchi has called "a social heresy," an offence against the state and its law, rather than an injury to a person or to God.[23] The state became the surrogate victim of crime; the injured party receded from plaintiff to witness; and punishment replaced restitution as the proper response to criminal injury.

Today we take the system of criminal justice that evolved on this basis largely for granted. The glorification of the judge as a demigod in robes, the complex procedural rules, the emphasis on isolating and defining criminal acts, the adversarial character of the trial, and the exigency of punishment are all the familiar stuff of a thousand courtroom dramas. But in recent years there has been a growing recognition of the ineptitude of this system in the face of many of the problems brought before it. "What most of us are doing," Ontario Provincial Court Judge David Cole told a Law Union of Ontario conference in November of 1997, "is a lot of routine processing of petty offenders — most of whom are mentally ill. We are getting tired of watching the parade."[24] Yukon Territorial Court Judge Barry Stuart has pointed to the way the criminal justice system feeds on its own failures, absorbing more and more resources as the problems it ostensibly deals with grow worse.[25] Other justice and corrections professionals have also recognized that imprisonment doesn't reduce crime, correct offenders, or give any real sense of agency or acknowledgement to victims.

This dissatisfaction with the existing institutions of criminal justice has led to the creation of a number of new forums in which criminal acts can be dealt with. New Zealand, for example, has produced the family group conference, in which all parties to a conflict involving a young offender seek a resolution in an open assembly moderated by a justice official called a youth justice coordinator. North American Mennonites have pioneered a guided face-to-face negotiation called victim-offender mediation. And Canadian aboriginal communities have submitted criminal cases to sentencing circles, in which all concerned members of the community are invited to contribute to a disposition. Other jurisdictions from Vermont to Norway have introduced local mediation or reparation boards.

All of these forms have certain features in common: they seek noncustodial settlements; they allow both the offender and the victim much more initiative; they are oriented more to peacemaking than punishment; and they try to mobilize the capacities of families, friends, and local communities in correcting offenders and holding them accountable.

All have also proved themselves in practice. New Zealand has radically reduced the number of youth in custody; victim-offender mediation is now successfully used in hundreds of cases a year in Winnipeg, where Manitoba Mediation Services operates Canada's most extensive mediation program; and Judge Stuart reports from the Yukon, where circle sentencing has been widely used, that it has produced "dramatic decreases in the frequency and seriousness of criminal behaviour."[26]

These alternatives to criminal justice are all rooted in the renewal of an old view of justice as peacemaking rather than retribution. They stand, in a sense, outside the "tough on crime / soft on crime," "offender as enemy alien / offender as victim of society" axis on which so much contemporary debate about crime control has turned. Offenders are seen as neither wholly wicked, nor as wholly excusable. It is well known that many of the inmates of Canada's prisons come from a background of poverty and poor education. Many were mistreated as children; many have crippling drug or alcohol dependencies; and an increasing number are mentally ill. Most were offended against before they became offenders, and their mores reflect the models that were available to them. It is also true that they have done things, sometimes very terrible things, for which their liability must be recognized and enforced. Peacemaking justice does not make an either/or of these overlapping perspectives. It insists on accountability, reparation, and reform — but tries to avoid ostracization, stigmatization, and the compounding of old violence with new violence. In this view, punishing those who have never known justice will not make them act justly in future. Justice must be enacted, not simply invoked. Imprisonment will sometimes be necessary in the interests of public safety, but it should be used only when diligent efforts at reform and repair have failed.

This book argues for this new view of criminal justice and warns of an increasingly uncivil society if such a view is not adopted. It is organized in three main parts. Part I looks into the reasons why prison numbers have increased so relentlessly over the last twenty years. Part II examines both the practice and the theory of incarceration as a punishment for crime, and seeks out the historical roots of our commitment to this way of doing things. Part III describes a number of successful alternatives that are in use around the world and outlines the very different approach to criminal justice on which they are based. A concluding chapter looks at the possibilities and the pitfalls of extending the use of these alternatives in Canada and elsewhere.

The criminal justice system in Canada is at a crossroads. Overcrowding will soon demand either a commitment to build more prisons, or a decisive adoption of alternatives. Churchill's "decisive test of civilization" lies before us.

I

The Prison Boom

When I visit countries [where] high incarceration rates are taken for granted as a trend that must continue, I have this feeling of the last days of the Weimar Republic ... I ask myself: when is enough enough? How many people can you execute? How large a prison population can you have before you change the kind of country you live in? ... How many prison camps can we have before my Norway isn't Norway anymore, or your Canada isn't Canada?

Nils Christie, from an interview with Richard Swift,
The New Internationalist 282 (August 1996)

THE EXPANDING PRISON

W hen I was a very young student," Norwegian criminolo-gist Nils Christie recalls, "the professor in penal law asked me if I would try to describe some very sad events in Norway during the Second World War."[1] As part of the Nazi campaign of *Nacht und Nebel*, or night and fog, which was intended to confuse and terrorize their captives, a large group of captured Yugoslavian partisans had been brought to a prison camp in northern Norway. The camp was staffed by several hundred Norwegian guards. Conditions were as bad as in the worst German concentration camps — so bad that in one year 70 percent of the prisoners died. After the war some fifty of these Norwegian guards were found guilty of killing, or severely maltreating, their Yugoslavian prisoners; this was the circumstance that Christie's professor, Johs Andenaes, wanted him to investigate.

Christie began to interview the guards, and it soon emerged that those who had maltreated their prisoners had generally been much more distant from them than those who had treated them more considerately.

One indicator was whether they had seen any pictures. The killers had never seen any pictures, while the non-killers said, oh yes, they showed me pictures of the family and they were sitting on the balcony and looked rather nice etc., etc. . . . The killers said [the prisoners] were dirty: they didn't even take off their trousers when they needed to go to the toilet. The non-killers said they were sick; they couldn't help it. The killers said you could see the lice move on them, and the non-killers said they hadn't been able to wash for months. Infections, dirtiness, misery — these can be interpreted as indicators of badness, or indicators of sickness . . . So . . . the killers . . . built up an understanding of those they later killed, or had already killed, as being outside the framework of ordinary people . . . these were bandits from the Balkans, as the Germans told them . . . Those who had been close to the prisoners [were] able to connect to their own existence, and most of them behaved decently.[2]

The idea that social distance was the defining difference between those who behaved decently and those who did not was confirmed by this story, told to Christie by one of the Yugoslavians:

During one of his first days in the camp he had found a little dictionary, a German-Norwegian dictionary, and at night he had used his ration of oil in making a little lamp, so he had learned to speak Norwegian. And one day they marched out with a Norwegian guard in the front and one in the back. They were building a road up in the North; they still call that road the Bloody Road. The guard in back asked the guard in front, "Do you have a match?" And the man in front said, "No, I have none." And then the Yugoslavian said in Norwegian, "I have a match." And, he said, "From that day my chances of surviving were much greater, much greater." He changed from being a strange, unbelievable animal into an ordinary human being.[3]

Christie came to the conclusion that those who had killed were for the most part "not monsters" but "decent, ordinary Norwegians" who had, in a deep sense, misinterpreted their experience. They had seen the sickness, dirtiness, and incontinence of their prisoners in a completely different way than had the guards who had gotten closer to the prisoners. This experience became the seed of Christie's lifelong study of what he has called "the social production of moral indifference." Willingness to inflict pain, he came to think, varies with our social distance from those who suffer, and breaks all restraint when the sufferers can be defined as belonging to a kind different from ourselves. Where people are relatively close to each other and relatively equal in status, they will have to be "very careful about solving conflicts with power." Where authority is distant and immune from immediate consequences, more punitive solutions become possible.

I begin with this early experience of Christie's both because of his seminal influence on my own thinking and because his sober and thoughtful awareness of what had gone wrong in Norway's concentration camps typifies a mood that was general in Western countries after World War II. The totalitarian state, as Graham Greene told an audience in Paris in 1948, had shown that it is possible to make whole populations accomplices in tyranny by suppressing among citizens "all sense of guilt, all indecision of mind."[4] It had also given many people who would not normally have been exposed to such things direct experience of prisons and concentration camps. This created a certain skepticism about the operations of the criminal justice system. Dutch criminologist Louk Hulsman, for example, grew up under German occupation and then went on to hold various senior positions in the Dutch Ministry of Justice. He identifies the German occupation of Holland as a formative experience for him and for a number of his colleagues.

> There were quite a lot of people involved in making crime policy and doing things in that field who had war experience and some like me who had also had the experience of being imprisoned. I had seen as a kid how unreliable an official system is. I had seen how most of the people in Holland after the German occupation cooperated with the Germans. I had also been arrested by the Dutch police for resistance, and I had seen that you can't trust them. That naturally has an influence, and there were several other people in the Ministry of Justice with comparable experiences.[5]

Memories like Hulsman's engendered a liberal mood in the administration of criminal justice. Fortified by advancing prosperity, it led to a remarkable reduction in prison rates. The Netherlands set the standard, bringing a rate of 90 prisoners per 100,000 of population after the war down to a remarkable 17 per 100,000 in 1975. This change, as I mentioned in the introduction, took place over a period in which registered crime rose by 300 percent. It was accomplished mainly by a steady reduction in the length of sentences. In 1970, according to Louk Hulsman, only thirty-five sentences in excess of three years were passed in Dutch courts.[6]

Many other Western countries outside the Soviet sphere also experienced declines in imprisonment rates during this period. Norway lost 13 percent of its prisoners at a stroke when forced labour for vagrant alcoholics was abolished in 1970. Another large group fell away in 1975 when the youth prison system was abolished.[7] Canada's prison population also declined.[8] In Ontario, a detailed study showed a reduction of about a third between the 1950s and the early 1980s.[9]

Then, gradually, this trend came to an end. In 1967 in the United States, a blue-ribbon commission set up to respond to Senator Barry Goldwater's charges of "violence in our streets" had assured President Lyndon Johnson that "the most . . . important method of dealing with crime is . . . by ameliorating the conditions of life that drive people to commit crimes . . ."[10] Ten years later the broad consensus that this statement had once expressed was under sustained attack. Curiously, one of the most influential challenges came from someone who had been an academic adviser to the commission: Harvard professor James Q. Wilson. In a 1975 book entitled *Thinking About Crime* — which his acolyte and former student John DiIulio says "single-handedly revolutionized the contemporary study of crime"[11] — Wilson argued that the endless harping of liberals on "the root causes of crime" had obscured the moral responsibility of perpetrators. "I have yet to see a 'root cause,'" he wrote sardonically, "or to encounter a government program that successfully attacked it." He continued,

> Wicked people exist. Nothing avails except to set them apart from innocent people. And many people, neither wicked nor innocent, but watchful, dissembling, and calculating of their opportunities, ponder our reactions to wickedness as a cue to what they might profitably do. We have trifled with the wicked, made sport of the innocent, and encouraged the calculators. Justice suffers, and so do we all.[12]

The argument had obvious appeal. By portraying himself as an amateur who had come into criminology "by the back door" and was, therefore, able to assert common sense against the debilitating orthodoxies of its professional practitioners, Wilson made a neat end-run around a well-researched body of opinion in criminology that clearly showed the counterproductive effects of imprisonment. In place of the utopian extravagances of his liberal opponents, he offered "a sober view of man." In calling criminals "calculators," carefully measuring opportunities against consequences, he promised to reinvigorate the theory of deterrence and put criminology back on a solid Hobbesian footing. This held out the consoling prospect of a restoration of civic virtue, and a return of individual responsibility, at a time when many citizens feared that moral boundaries were being erased. Reductions in imprisonment had been brought about by what Dutch criminologist Willem de Haan once called "the politics of bad conscience." By assuring his countrymen that the institution was just, necessary, and effective, Wilson relaid the foundations for what Andrew Rutherford, adapting de Haan's phrase, has called "a politics of good conscience about imprisonment."[13]

The about-face in criminal policy, to which Wilson contributed in the United States, occurred in other countries as well. In the Netherlands, a government white paper tabled in 1985 argued that "the gap between the number of infringements of standards embodied in the criminal law and the number of real

responses to them by the criminal justice authorities has become
unacceptably wide . . . Order must be restored in the affairs of
criminal justice."[14] One of the most important influences behind
the turnaround in Dutch penal philosophy and practice was a
senior public prosecutor called Dato Steenhuis. He suggested
that the prevailing humanitarian ethos ought to give way to a
technocratic production model of criminal justice. The justice
system, he proposed, was no different from a factory or a commercial enterprise.

> The criminal justice company can, in my opinion, be defined as the
> totality of organs whose function, in mutual relationship to one
> another, is aimed at (or responsible for) the maintenance of the penal
> legal order. The different production phases of the company are
> coupled to each other serially, like a car manufacturing factory or in
> a company where, for example, chocolate bars are produced.[15]

The implied comparison between convicts and chocolate bars
epitomized this new, managerial conception of justice. Steenhuis
wanted to see the Dutch criminal justice system improve its
"coverage" of crime by eliminating obstacles to efficient administration and speeding the flow of cases "through the different
phases of the production process."[16] His ideas addressed what he
perceived to be a crisis of public confidence in the criminal justice
system. There was, he said, "an imbalance between what the
government has to offer the individual when he breaks the law
and what it has to offer to the one who abides by it."[17] A more
conservative turn in Dutch politics gave these ideas currency,
and, during the 1980s and 1990s, the Dutch rate of imprisonment
increased steadily. By 1994, new construction was necessary;
today, the country's total prison capacity is five times what it
was in 1975.[18]

Steenhuis and Wilson provided new rationales for imprisonment
at a time when the prevailing justifications were weakening.
Beginning in the 1960s a critical generation of academic crimi-

nologists had produced study after study showing that imprisonment neither deterred crime nor rehabilitated prisoners.[19] The
neoconservative movement in criminal policy shifted discussion to new grounds. Wilson still spoke of deterrence, but the
main object of his concern was clearly "the innocent" who had
been "made sport of" by excessively lenient law enforcement.
Steenhuis, too, emphasized what might be called the "audience"
for criminal justice. What counted, for him, was public credibil-
ity, not the actual effects of incarceration. Imprisonment figured
in the analysis of both men only as the established coin in which
the gravity of offences and the adequacy of the state's response
is measured.

Behind the success of this new approach lay growing public
anxiety about crime. Measurement problems make it hard to
know, from place to place, just how much more crime there really
was, but there was certainly a widespread *feeling* after the sixties
that moral disorder was increasing.[20] There was also fear, in some
elite quarters, of political disorder. A report prepared for the
Trilateral Commission by Samuel Huntingdon and two other
writers in 1975 suggested that the progress of popular mobiliza-
tions like the anti-war movement raised fundamental questions
about "the governability of democracies."[21] On top of these
concerns came the first signs of the economic changes that would
eventually shake the postwar welfare state to its foundation.
The unexpected appearance of "stagflation" sabotaged Keynesian
orthodoxy; trade union power began to wane; and government
debt started its climb to the top of the political agenda. The era
of deregulation, free-market fundamentalism, and the shrinking
state began.

Crime, in this climate, became a lightning rod for anxiety.
Instead of seeking to "ameliorate the conditions of life that drive
people to commit crimes," as Lyndon Johnson's commission had
recommended in 1967, governments now declared war on crime.
The first such war — the war on drugs — was declared by
Richard Nixon in 1970, but it was only in the 1980s that it really

began to fill the prisons in earnest. Even the Scandinavian countries, which had been noted for the mildness of their penal regimes, adopted draconian punishments for drug offences. According to Norwegian criminologist Thomas Mathiesen,

> You now have a situation where you have a possible sentence of twenty-one years for drug-related crime in our penal code. According to the law, the maximum possibility of twenty-one years is supposed to be used for organized criminals. In actual practice, it is, with very few exceptions, used for ordinary drug pedlars, who use drugs themselves and sell and buy a little, and who are then defined as "drug sharks," as they're called in Norwegian. And they spend years in prison.[22]

Drugs have also become a way of displacing less acceptable anxieties. In Norway, many of those imprisoned for drug crime are foreigners. The warden of one Norwegian prison I visited reported that two-thirds of the inmates were there for drug crimes; and of these, 48 percent were foreigners. "Norwegians feel strange in a Norwegian prison," he said. Many of these prisoners are "mules" in the international drug trade. Often they have been arrested at the border and will be deported at the end of their frequently long sentences. All they will ever know of Norway is prison.

Nils Christie calls drugs the snake in Norway's socialist paradise. He has described the old Labour Party prime minister on his walk to work, passing by the grounds of the royal palace where the "druggies" gathered in the 1960s. This was "a really idealistic man, living his whole life, even when he was a prime minister, in a little apartment in the east end of Oslo." How could he account for the appearance of these dissolute and disaffected people at the very moment when the dream of a comprehensive welfare state had been fulfilled? "There were two possible explanations," Christie says. Either there was "something still wrong in the society of the social democrats," or "drugs are so deadly . . . that if you touch them, you're lost."²³ The second explanation was overwhelmingly preferred, and official Norway increasingly committed itself to the view that severe penalization of drugs was the way to regain social control.

The same story has been played out with variations in nearly every other Western country. German criminologist Johannes Feest estimates that a quarter of the sentenced population in all Western European countries are there for drug crime, and another quarter or more are there for offences committed in the service of a drug habit.²⁴ He says that because petty traders in illegal drugs frequently reappear in court, and because judges feel obliged to make succeeding sentences stiffer than the first, drug crime exerts a continual upward pressure on prison rates. In what was then West Germany during the 1980s, for example, there was a concerted effort to reduce prison numbers. This was the result of what Feest calls "a crisis of conscience," touched off when the number of prisoners inched over the symbolic level of 100 per 100,000 in the early eighties. The German bar association convened a widely attended conference on the subject in Bonn and pressed judges and legislatures to seek alternatives to imprisonment for minor crimes. Pretrial detention was also limited on the theory that when "you come into court as a free person, you're more likely to get out as a free person than when you come in as a prisoner."²⁵ Prison numbers fell substantially, reaching a low of 78 per 100,000 in the late eighties. But then they began to rise again, and today they have surpassed their previous high. The reason, according to Feest, was that the effect of escalating sentences for drug crime eventually overcame the effect of the increased use of alternatives to imprisonment.

The "war on drugs" has had many perverse consequences of this kind. Catching, convicting, and imprisoning people for drug crime is immensely expensive. It is futile as a way of combatting drug use, since drugs are as readily available in prison as they are outside it. It establishes an immensely lucrative illegal economy, which leads to a reign of terror on the streets and

tempts entrepreneurs to tap this instant wealth rather than
applying themselves to the economic regeneration of their communities. It excuses political inaction on any problem that can
be blamed on drugs. And it places a grotesquely exaggerated
importance on vice, wasting the moral credit of the law on the
policing of self-abuse.

The war on drugs has also played a terrible role in aggravating
racial conflict in the United States. African-Americans have always
been overrepresented in American prisons. Even seventy-five years
ago, their proportion in prison was double their proportion in the
population. Blacks were also subject to a terrifying "informal"
justice system. "Castration, lynching, and other vigilante-type
actions were characteristically reserved for citizens of color,"
American criminologist Jerry Miller has written. "[They] provided the backdrop and collective memory against which the
formal criminal justice system functioned when it came to blacks."
Black and white Americans have long been caught in what
South African writer Athol Fugard, with reference to his own
country, calls "the blood knot," and the American criminal justice system has reflected this unique entanglement. Nevertheless,
the situation has grown drastically worse since 1970, as the war
on drugs has increasingly taken on the aspect of a covert war on
black America.

Twelve percent of the U.S. population is African-American.
According to the National Institute on Drug Abuse, they use
illegal drugs with about the same frequency as white Americans
— they constitute 13 percent of those who will use illegal drugs
at some point during a given month. But, in 1992 and 1993, they
received 74 percent of the prison sentences for drug crime.
Together with Hispanics they account for 90 percent of prison
sentences.[26] This disparity increases at every stage of the justice
system when it comes to drugs. Thirty-five percent of those
arrested, 55 percent of those convicted, and, as I have already
said, 74 percent of those sentenced to prison in the United
States are black. A similar bias has recently been reported in

the administration of criminal justice in Ontario. The Ontario Commission on Racism in the Criminal Justice System, which released its report in January of 1996, found that 49 percent of black men convicted of possession of a narcotic were sent to prison, as opposed to only 18 percent of whites. It also found such disparities between races to be greatest in the area of drug enforcement.[27]

In the United States, differences in the penalization of cocaine use further illustrate the racial bias of the justice system. Cocaine is available as a crystal rock called crack that can be smoked, or as a white powder that can be inhaled. Crack is associated more with black users, powder with white users. (According to the U.S. Sentencing Commission, blacks are still a minority of crack users, but they are definitely overrepresented, making up about 38 percent of total users.)[28] Crack cocaine users are sentenced far more harshly than powder cocaine users. Until 1990, when the law was struck down as unconstitutional by the state's Supreme Court, Minnesota punished the possession of crack cocaine four times as heavily as possession of the same amount of powder cocaine — twenty years for crack versus five for powder.[29] Under current federal sentencing guidelines, possession of five grams of crack carries a mandatory minimum sentence of five years, while possession of the same amount of powder is a misdemeanour punishable by a maximum of one year. Trafficking in five grams of crack worth $750 now brings the same sentence as selling half a kilogram of powder worth $50,000.[30] These draconian penalties are much more likely to be applied to blacks than whites. In 1995, for example, the Los Angeles Times surveyed crack convictions in federal courts serving the Los Angeles metropolitan area since 1986 and discovered that there had not been a single white person convicted, despite research indicating that whites are a majority of crack users.[31]

In fact, the disparity in crack convictions in the Los Angeles area has become so marked that in May of 1996 the matter reached the U.S. Supreme Court. The case, an appeal by the city's

public defender's office, concerned the fact that in 1994, under a
new federal law mandating minimum ten-year sentences for
selling more than fifty grams of crack, all twenty-four people
convicted were black. Two lower courts had noted "a conspicuous
racial pattern" in the convictions, but the Supreme Court dismissed the case. The court reasoned that racial bias could be
established only if it could be shown that white crack dealers had
received more lenient treatment; since no white crack dealers
had been arrested, there could be no such proof.[32]

The new ten-year minimum sentence for trafficking in trivial
amounts of crack cocaine is typical of a general escalation in the
drug war and the adoption of more and more draconian penalties. Offenders subject to these long sentences will accumulate
in American prisons, adding to the already dramatic overrepresentation of blacks in those prisons. At the moment, the
incarceration rate for blacks is seven times that of whites.[33]
The Sentencing Project, a Washington-based organization that
conducts criminal justice research and promotes sentencing
reform, released a report in October of 1995 showing that on any
given day nearly a third of *all* black American males in their
twenties are under the control of the criminal justice system.[34]

In certain cities the rates are even higher. One survey in
Washington, D.C., found "that on an average day in 1991 more
than four of every ten African-American males ages eighteen to
thirty-five (who were residents of D.C.) were in prison, jail, on
probation or parole, on bail, or being sought on arrest warrants."
A second survey carried out three months later in Baltimore
resulted in the even more disturbing finding that on an average
day 56 percent of all young African-American males were under
some kind of criminal justice supervision.[35] Because these figures
are all snapshots based on one-day counts, they suggest a lifetime
risk of arrest for young black men in inner cities of somewhere
between 80 and 90 percent.

The American war on drugs seems to be animated by the spirit
of the commander in Vietnam who justified the razing of an

entire village by saying that it had been necessary to destroy the village in order to save it. The danger of exposing nearly an entire generation of inner-city black men to the brutalizing influence of criminal justice processing ought to have been obvious, and yet there has been remarkably little sober reflection on these dangers among American policy makers. A few American judges have spoken out. In a recent issue of William Buckley's conservative *National Review*, Robert Sweet, a federal court judge and former deputy mayor of New York, described the discomfort he feels when applying the mandatory minimum sentence of ten years to someone for a minor drug crime. Mandatory penalties for drugs, he has subsequently said, are "debasing the rule of law."[36] But these dissenting voices have generally been hard to hear above the unreasoning outcry for more punishment. Again and again, one hears thoughtful people asking plaintively for nothing more than a rational discussion. The fact that none occurs, according to Norwegian criminologist Thomas Mathiesen, has a lot to do with the expanding influence of mass media.

Mathiesen has been trying for more than thirty years to expose the institution of imprisonment to rational scrutiny. During the 1960s, he participated in the founding of KROM, the Norwegian Association for Prison Reform. The organization brought together prisoners, social workers, academics, and other citizens interested in prison conditions. It was, in part, through their efforts that forced labour for vagrant alcoholics was abolished in 1970, and the youth prison system eliminated in 1979. KROM has also tried to foster a continuing dialogue between interested people inside and outside the prison system:

> We organize a yearly conference on criminal and penal policy . . . [at] a resort in the mountains where we always return. We have tried to make a tradition of it. Participation crosses border[s] within the system. There are lawyers, researchers, social workers, prison people, prisoners, ex-prisoners — the whole range is represented . . . In the early days . . . the prison department refused to come. And

the prisoners weren't there because they would never get furloughs for this purpose, so we had ex-prisoners instead. But gradually this changed. The mass media pointed to the fact that it was illogical of the prison department not to come, and their policy of furloughs changed and now they come in great numbers.[37]

Conviviality as well as discussion is emphasized at these gatherings, which have taken place annually for more than twenty-five years now. "During late evenings and nights," says Nils Christie, who has been an annual participant, "one can see — if one happens to know who is who — prisoners, prison directors, guards, policemen, and representatives of the liberal opposition in heated discussion on penal policy in general and on prison conditions in particular. But they can also be found in relaxed and peaceful talks on the prospects for the next day's cross-country skiing." Under such conditions, Christie adds, "pictures of monsters do not thrive."[38]

This annual meeting in the mountains constitutes what Mathiesen calls an "alternative public sphere." It exerts a benign and calming influence on penal policy by providing a forum in which the activities of the Norwegian Prison Department are exposed to thoughtful criticism. But this influence has been increasingly counteracted by the effects of mass media, most notably television, on Norwegian society. Following the American media researcher George Gerbner, Mathiesen holds that at a certain intensity of media exposure, society enters "something which is equivalent to a new religion."[39] The media environment affects crime policy not by inducing specific changes in behaviour or opinion but by its broad "enculturating" influence.[40] According to the British media critic James Curran,

The modern mass media in Britain now perform many of the integrative functions of the Church in the middle ages. Like the medieval Church, the media link together different groups and provide a shared experience that promotes social solidarity . . .

The two institutions have engaged . . . in very similar ideological "work" . . . The modern media have [for example] given, at different times, massive and disproportionate attention to a series of "outsiders" . . . comparable to the hunting down and parading of witches allegedly possessed by the devil by the medieval and early modern Church . . .[41]

Television, in this sense, is like the automobile, the passenger jet, or any other major technological innovation. The automobile's influence is not restricted to its direct effects in expanding possible destinations; it restructures society. Television, by exalting compact visual symbols over literate and discursive modes of argument, has an analogous effect.

At the conference in Oslo where I met him, Mathiesen illustrated this point with a story. A convicted drug dealer had absconded while on authorized furlough from a Norwegian prison. Much was made of the case in the Norwegian media. The chief of the narcotics police told the largest Olso morning newspaper that the Prison Department was "spineless." The escapee was said to have dined on breast of duck and Cardinal wine during his unauthorized absence. Mathiesen was invited to comment on the case, and he agreed. "My prior knowledge that you are often unable to say much at all on television somehow evaporated," he says. He remembered being flattered by the invitation and "lured into participation" by the "marginal chance" of influencing the discussion. A ten-minute statement was recorded. That evening Mathiesen turned on his television to find that a single sentence — "I am for more liberal prisons!" — had been extracted from the interview and intercut with pictures of breast of duck and Cardinal wine in crystal glasses against white damask. Against his assertion was thrown another single sentence from the director of the Oslo District Prison: "I am for more discipline, though not slavish discipline." His sentence was accompanied by pictures of an American prison in which uniformed prisoners ran in a circle while armed guards in battle dress shouted orders at them. "Two views on prison policy," the reporter concluded.

Experiences like this forced Mathiesen to the conclusion that "principled argumentation based on truthfulness, sincerity, and relevance is now almost impossible in the broad sphere of television and mass media." This is true for at least three reasons: television as a medium of moving pictures undercuts discursive argument; television as a marketed commodity (and public television, too, insofar as it is subjected to "market discipline") favours talk that is familiar enough to "sell"; and television as a religious ritual heightens the importance of symbols at the expense of facts. Thus, the discussion of prisons on television tends to focus on their symbolic functions rather than their actual effects.

One of these functions is the stigmatization of criminals. The more the character of the outlaw is darkened, the more brightly the virtues of the law-abiding citizens shine. The prisoner becomes a scapegoat and his real being is eclipsed by the angers, resentments, and fears of the good citizens, which he is forced to carry away with him, metaphorically, into the desert. "The picture which is given," Mathiesen says, "is the picture of the crook without a conscience, without a culture, who is just a criminal, nothing else but a criminal." Popular stereotypes are consolidated, and the growth of prisons is fostered.

A rational assessment of prisons would recognize that they cost an immense amount, fail to deter wrongdoers, and often make their inmates more desperate and dangerous than they were when committed. Moreover, Mathiesen points out, if they think about it, most citizens recognize these considerations. Public opinion studies consistently show that if people are simply asked what should be done to criminals, answers will tend to be harsh and punitive; but if more detailed questions are asked about actual situations, the answers become more nuanced, more humane, and more sensible. So the destructive effects of prisons are widely understood, but this general understanding can never become effective where the actual institution is eclipsed by its symbolic significance.

British criminologist Andrew Rutherford has observed the same tendencies at work in the United Kingdom.[42] Britain, like Germany, undertook a reduction in imprisonment during the 1980s; but this initiative was undone in the early 1990s by the new, more volatile political climate Thomas Mathiesen has been describing. To understand the story it's necessary to go back to the early years of this century when Britain brought about a dramatic reduction in its rate of imprisonment. It began in 1910 when Winston Churchill, as home secretary, undertook what he described in a memo to his cabinet colleagues as "an abatement of imprisonment." Churchill, who had been imprisoned himself during the Boer War, felt an active sympathy for prisoners; on occasion, Rutherford says, "he would turn up . . . at Pentonville Prison, see a man on the yard, ask for his papers, and, on reviewing the case, grant him executive clemency then and there."[43] Under Churchill's influence, the number of British prisoners was cut in half between 1910 and the early 1920s, accelerating a long-term declining trend that had been going on since the middle years of the nineteenth century, when the first flush of enthusiasm for the newly built penitentiaries had begun to wane. British prisons during the 1930s held only a seventh of the per capita population they had held during the 1830s,[44] and less than a third of the number today.

After World War II, the extremely low British incarceration rate tended to rise gradually, while rates in other European countries were falling. Policy was in the hands of the civil service and was essentially pragmatic and uncoordinated. Politicians, by convention, treated criminal policy as a nonpartisan matter, which was not to be milked for political advantage. By the early 1980s the prison population had increased to the point that Margaret Thatcher's home secretary, William Whitelaw, could speak of "the grave crisis" of the prison system and acknowledge that "a continued increase in the prison population could not be sustained." Whitelaw proposed reducing the prison population by up to five thousand people by moving up release dates for some prisoners, but ran into fierce opposition, first from the judiciary and then from his own Conservative Party. This culminated in what Rutherford calls "a very rough ride" for Whitelaw at the 1981 Conservative Party Conference, and a withdrawal of his proposal.

During this period a remarkably broad-minded and well-informed civil servant named David Faulkner exerted a strong influence within the Home Office. Between 1981 and 1990, he delivered 120 speeches at seminars, conferences, and meetings around the country. In these appearances he managed to convey a frank and realistic account of the limitations and ill effects of imprisonment as an institution, and to suggest principles that could guide a reduction in its use, without ever seeming to pre-empt his minister or exceed his authority. He argued that the problems society experienced as crime were far beyond the scope of the criminal justice system, and he stressed

> the importance of a collective, community-based approach in which the community as a whole accepts some responsibility for offending behaviour and is prepared to do something about it and about the offenders and potential offenders who are in its midst. It should not regard offenders and potential offenders as being some kind of external threat, as people who are different from ourselves and who do not properly belong in our society and against whom we need to raise physical defences or who ought to be contained in their ghettos or failing that in prison.[45]

One of Faulkner's most consistent arguments was that criminal policy should be based on principles, not just on pragmatism. During the third term of Thatcher's government after 1987 he got a sympathetic hearing from his minister at the Home Office, Douglas Hurd. The Conservative Party's election manifesto had already enunciated a policy that called for "a tough legal framework . . . for . . . those who pose a threat to society" together with an attempt to "keep out of prison those who do not." This was followed by a Home Office green paper in June 1988. It argued that, because putting people in custody inevitably had a "criminalizing effect" on them, it would be better in many cases to seek forms of "punishment in the community." These would require offenders to take some responsibility for themselves rather than segregate them at state expense in the exclusive company of other offenders. A white paper produced in 1990 consolidated this view, arguing that, where imprisonment is not justified on the grounds of public protection, "it can be an expensive way of making bad people worse."

Until the end of 1989, when he became foreign secretary, Hurd actively promoted this view, initiating what Rutherford calls a "practice-led revolution" that brought the British prison population down from 50,846 in 1987 to 44,246 in 1993, a 13 percent drop.[46] Just as the reduction in prisoner numbers in West Germany in the 1980s had been touched off by a crisis of conscience, so this decline in Britain, at a time when American numbers were exploding and Canada's climbing steadily, seems to have been the result of the climate of opinion that Faulkner, Hurd, and others had created rather than any specific legislative or administrative fiat. There was, in Rutherford's careful formulation, "a reasonably high degree of congruence between policymakers and practitioners."

The reduction, however, was short-lived. In 1991, while prison rates were still falling, the government brought in a new Criminal Justice Act, which codified some of the reforms already occurring. For example, it directed judges, in most cases, to sentence on the basis of offence rather than record — a second or even a fifth conviction for the same offence did not deserve a sterner sentence than the first. To a considerable extent this was exactly what had been happening — but when the practice was made mandatory, the Lord Chief Justice complained that judges had been placed in an "ill-fitting straitjacket." The climate of public opinion also began to change in the early 1990s. A panic spread about juvenile crime in the wake of the abduction and murder of two-year-old Jamie Bulger by two preadolescent boys in 1993. And, more significant for my purposes here, there was what Rutherford calls "a sea change" among senior politicians within both main political parties. Tony Blair, as part of his campaign to transform the Labour Party into "New Labour," saw an opportunity in the debate over criminal justice. An admirer of Bill Clinton, he took note of how Clinton's administration had co-opted the crime issue. Labour now argued that the victims of crime were its natural constituency and pronounced itself "tough on crime, tough on the consequences of crime." The Conservative Party repudiated its own legislation, amending it in 1993 and again in 1994. Home Secretary Michael Howard announced to the 1993 party convention a view that was diametrically opposed to Hurd's: "Let us be clear," he said, "prison works." Prison rates began a steep rise, surpassing by March of 1995 the previous high point reached in 1987. David Faulkner, who by then had retired from the Home Office to an academic post at Oxford, commented:

> There is now a serious void at the centre of the criminal justice system. There is no clearly understood set of purposes which it is meant to achieve or principles which it is meant to observe, and no effective and acceptable system of accountability for its operation ... Without a greater sense of purpose and direction, the prospect is one of increasing frustration and anger, a spiral of rising crime, increasing severity of punishment and the alienation of a growing section of the community.[47]

British criminal policy, according to Rutherford, has entered a new world. Where politicians and civil servants once made criminal policy behind the scenes according to their sense of the public interest, crime policy has now been politicized and brought to centre stage.

> [There] is a sense among politicians that this issue is too big and too volatile, too potentially damaging but also potentially fruitful, to be

left in the hands of elites and that it can be manipulated and used in a way that can gain a fair degree of political mileage. The genie is out of the bottle now, and it may be very difficult to put back.[48]

Britain's rejection of a reductionist prison policy based on what were essentially political considerations is a parable of what has happened in northern Europe generally since 1980. Both Rutherford and Mathiesen emphasize what might be called a "democratization" of crime policy: how it has become increasingly subject to the influence of mass media, operating at the lowest common denominator of popular prejudice and stereotype, and increasingly removed from the sphere of those, such as civil servants, who are in a position to appreciate the futility of imprisonment as a measure against crime. Criminal justice has been transformed into a "commodity" that allays public anxieties and benefits politicians who make themselves appear responsive to such concerns. Winston Churchill after 1910, and Douglas Hurd after 1987, exercised decisive political leadership on this issue. Churchill's reforms lasted thirty years, Hurd's only five. The difference measures the extent to which governments are now creatures of an endlessly churning and instantly available public opinion.

Crime policy in Canada has been subject to similar forces. The new political volatility of the crime issue first became evident in 1984 when the National Parole Board, in response to public concerns about dangerous people at large, began granting fewer paroles. This started the upward movement in the rate of imprisonment that has led to the current overcrowding of Canadian prisons. Then, in 1986, the federal government passed a law instructing the csc to seek special parole-board hearings for those whose early release might pose a threat to public safety. As I mentioned in the introduction, this law has now been proved ineffective, since research shows that those held longer because they are considered dangerous actually re-offend less frequently than those given parole. But it did add to the prison population.

In 1995, almost 500 inmates were detained to the end of their sentences under this procedure, up from just 100 in 1989.[49] The 1990s have also seen a 50 percent jump in the number of sex offenders in federal prisons. According to Queen's psychologist William Marshall, this represents "an increase in the way the judicial system has responded to sex offenders" rather than an increase in the number of sex offenders in society.[50] There has been a rise, too, in the number of mentally impaired people in prison — a result of the closing of mental hospitals and restrictions on the involuntary committal of the mentally ill. And, finally, the overall length of sentences has increased. In the federal system, for example, median sentence length rose by 6.7 percent between 1992–93 and 1993–94.[51]

Another force driving this steady upward movement in the prison rate during the 1990s is the victims' rights movement, as it has come to be called. This movement, in its organized form, emerged in 1992 with the founding of Citizens Against Violence Everywhere Advocating its Termination, or CAVEAT. The organization was started by Priscilla de Villiers, an Ontario woman whose daughter, Nina, had been murdered the year before.[52] She and her husband drew up a petition to the federal government which asked, among other things, for more careful bail hearings, tighter parole restrictions, greater Crown accountability, and longer sentences for crimes of violence. By the spring of 1993 it had attracted 1.4 million signatures.

This movement has been successful in most of its aims. Its growing political influence can be seen in the recent successful campaign to amend Section 745 of the Criminal Code, the so-called faint hope provision. When capital punishment was abolished in 1977, a mandatory twenty-five-year sentence for first degree murder was instated in its place. However, a provision was added allowing a jury to review the case after fifteen years had been served. A two-thirds majority of such a jury would have the power to make the prisoner eligible for parole, although a regular parole hearing would still be necessary as well. The first prisoners sentenced under the 1977 law became eligible to apply in 1991. Neil Boyd, director of Simon Fraser University's School of Criminology, summarized the results up to the middle of 1995 as follows:

> As of July 1995, 173 murderers were eligible for judicial review, but only 60 reviews of sentence had taken place. In 47 of these 60 cases juries [moved up the offender's] eligibility for parole, but to date only 26 of these people have actually been granted either day parole or full parole. Of these 26 murderers, only one has committed another criminal offence since release, a robbery.[53]

Murderers, generally, are far less likely to re-offend than other classes of convicted criminals. A study of 457 murderers released on parole between 1975 and 1986 showed that fewer than 9 percent committed another offence. Only six of these crimes were assaults and only two were murders.[54] But despite this low recidivism and the cautious way in which Section 745 was operating, the "faint hope" clause became a lightning rod for victims' rights protests. It began in January of 1996 with a rally in the Alberta town of Okotoks. The rally was organized by Darlene Boyd, the mother of a teenage girl who was abducted, raped, and killed by two men in 1982. One of these men committed suicide in prison, but the other would have been eligible to apply to have his parole eligibility advanced in 1997. The tabloid *Calgary Sun* enthusiastically took up the issue, putting the story on the front page five times and including in every edition a clip-out coupon headed "Section 745 Must Go!" A picture of Premier Ralph Klein signing a coupon was shown on one *Sun* cover. Three weeks after the Okotoks rally, a second, larger protest was held in Calgary during which 30,000 signed *Sun* coupons were presented to the visiting federal justice minister, Allan Rock. Rock acknowledged the demonstrators' righteous anger and promised to change Section 745. "On this issue, I've heard people loud and clear," he said. "The status quo with respect to Section 745 is not on."[55]

In December of 1996 Parliament passed amendments to the Criminal Code that altered Section 745 but didn't eliminate it altogether. Under the new rules nobody who has killed more than one person can apply, and the jury must be unanimous for parole eligibility to be advanced. (Although the protesters had wanted the changes to be made retroactive, they were not, because retroactivity would have violated a fundamental legal principle.) The compromise appeared to satisfy no one, however, and, several months later, the issue heated up again when Canada's most notorious serial killer, Clifford Olson, presented an application under Section 745. Some of the families of his victims assembled a press conference in Vancouver, and newspapers reported that the application had "produced a torrent of anguish and anger from families of some of his eleven victims." The *Globe and Mail* centred its story around a large photograph of the grief-contorted face of the mother of one of Olson's victims. The father of another victim commented that allowing Olson to speak would only "tear open the scars."[56] No one remarked that the publicity causing the anguish had in fact been produced by the "745 Must Go" campaign in the first place; Section 745 entitles Olson only to a legal hearing, not to a national audience.

At the moment there is no sign of this campaign's abating. During the run-up to the federal election in the spring of 1997, in an attempt to outflank the Reform Party on the crime issue, Conservative leader Jean Charest made a whistle stop in Prince Albert, where Clifford Olson is imprisoned. He promised to repeal Section 745 in order to prevent "Clifford Olson thumbing his nose at Canadians."[57] Charest might have made this promise with the confident expectation of not having to fulfill it, but his words still demonstrate the pressure he must feel to play to the crowd on this issue. His willingness to bend to ill-considered public opinion is a perfect example of the growing irrationality that Thomas Mathiesen perceives in the discussion of crime today. Section 745, by any rational criterion, represented a prudent, balanced policy. No evidence was brought forward that anyone unfit for early release had ever been granted it under the existing law. The only argument provided against it was that victims in a handful of high-profile, easily dramatized cases might be exposed to painful memories. No one could have possibly believed that Clifford Olson would be released; existing safeguards rendered the possibility almost infinitely remote. At issue was his right to *apply*. Yet the federal government, without counterargument and almost visibly against the justice minister's better judgement, amended the law.

Section 745 was written to mitigate slightly a draconian *mandatory* twenty-five-year penalty in cases where imprisonment past fifteen years could serve no good public purpose. All the amendments will do is unnecessarily increase overcrowding by keeping in jail a few more people who ought to be released. Clifford Olson is a red herring. Consider, for example, the following case, which is precisely the kind the original Section 745 was intended to address. It was described in the *Globe and Mail* in March of 1996.

Leonardo Rocha, a fifty-nine-year-old carpenter, was seeking release after serving sixteen years of a life sentence for the murder of his sixteen-year-old daughter, Leonilde. Mr. Rocha shot the teenager in the back of the head after an argument in late 1979. Moments after the killing, Mr. Rocha also shot one of his sons in the jaw after mistaking him for Leonilde's boyfriend. The Rocha case provided an interesting test of the judicial-review provision. The killing had been about as close to spontaneous as a "premeditated" killing could get (premeditation is one criterion for a charge of first-degree murder) and Mr. Rocha's prison behaviour has been exemplary.

[Jeffrey] Manishen [Rocha's lawyer], . . . adduced evidence before the jury that Mr. Rocha's remaining family members were in favour of his being released — providing an example of why Mr. Manishen maintains opponents of the section are wrong to say the reviews automatically "revictimize" the victims. Testifying in thickly accented English, Mr. Rocha said he simply had been unable to adjust to a society that, in his view, allows teenagers to gallivant in the outside world in defiance of their parents' wishes that they remain at home at certain times. "I was so confused, so out of control," he said. "I felt like my hopes were gone. My family was gone. Things happened that never should have happened." The Brampton jury ultimately elected to permit Mr. Rocha to apply for parole in three years.[58]

There are no typical murders, or typical murderers. But Leonardo Rocha can, in a limited sense, stand for a certain class of prisoner. His crime was an aberration, not a product of settled viciousness. He is contrite and poses no danger to others. The shame and the anguish that the memory of his folly must provoke probably constitute a crueller punishment than the state could ever devise. He has already served eighteen years in prison, which is surely more than enough to denounce his crime. Yet the "745 Must Go" campaign demanded that prisoners such as Rocha remain ineligible even to *apply* for parole, dooming them to add to prison overcrowding and public expense. Victims' rights were pitted against prisoners' rights in a zero-sum contest. The complex problem of prison policy was presented as a matter of appropriate retribution, pure and simple; the costs, moral and monetary, of imprisonment did not enter the case, and neither did the possibility of contrition, forgiveness, or restoration of dignity. The rights of victims were seen to be vindicated only to the extent that the criminal could be made to disappear.

In later chapters I explore other ways in which the rights of victims can be construed, but this call for a more thorough and more assured vengeance is certainly the prevailing definition. Since 1993, it has been represented in federal politics by the Reform Party. During 1996, for example, several Reform Party MPS investigated federal prisons. Their purpose, according to *Western Report*, a magazine sympathetic to Reform, was to expose "the cushy conditions and soothing methods of the jail system."

The CSC, says *Western Report*, "views the more than 14,000 offenders in its charge as incarcerated citizens, not convicted criminals." The story presents highlights from a list of what Reform MP Randy White calls "absurdities." These include free medical care, conjugal visits, and the right to personal property.[59] These are, by implication, what the magazine later calls "criminal-coddling practices." Once it was the central axiom of humane prison administration that the loss of liberty, by itself, is the supreme punishment. "Men come to prison as a punishment, not for punishment,"[60] said Sir Alexander Paterson, an early twentieth-century English prison commissioner. Elements of the Reform Party now seem to reject this standard in favour of more obvious and spectacular suffering.

The absolute distinction that *Western Report* draws between "criminals" and "citizens" seems to be at the heart of the victims' rights or "tough on crime" movement. A criminal, in this view, is exclusively a criminal. To allow him any other attributes, like citizenship or rights, risks condoning the evil he has done. Classical justifications for punishment stretching back to Plato hold that punishment is an honour capable of "wiping out the stigma of crime."[61] *Western Report*'s distinction makes criminality an indelible ontological attribute. Criminals are criminals are criminals; the question becomes not how they can be reinstated in society but rather how can they be kept more or less permanently away from the rest of us, the citizens.

I have tried in this first chapter to make a preliminary sketch of the U-turn that has taken place in crime policy since 1975. This sketch includes details from a number of countries because, despite the huge variations in prison numbers between, say, Norway and the United States, the changes that have taken place seem to have certain common features. Everywhere emphasis has shifted from rehabilitation to retribution, from the culpability of society to the culpability of the offender, and from reasoned policy to symbolic gesture. The expanded reach of visual media; alarms about drugs, sexual deviance, the breakdown of public decorum; and fear that the economic reconstruction of society is creating a dangerous new underclass have all played their part. The result has been a futile attempt to segregate and contain "the criminal." Such a policy might work, "if it were only necessary to separate [evil people] from us and destroy them. But the line dividing good and evil," as Alexander Solzhenitsyn writes in *The Gulag Archipelago*, "cuts through the heart of every human being."[62]

CRIME CONTROL IN THE UNITED STATES

"Trail 'em, Surveil 'em, Nail 'em, and Jail 'em"

In August of 1996, 5,000 jailers gathered in Nashville, Tennessee, for the annual convention of the American Correctional Association. Accompanying their meetings was a trade show comprising more than 600 booths hawking everything from ballistic batons to "the violent prisoner chair."[1] There were promotions for plastic toilet compartments ("I got ten years, but Santana is in here for life"), tear gas ("When you're facing the worst, you need the best"), and body armour ("Don't get stuck with anything less"). The conference brochure called corrections a "Fortune 500 industry" with revenues of $26 billion (U.S.) in 1995. Communities are excited by the jobs this expanding industry promises to create. "Fifteen years ago," says Dick Lewis of the Texas Department of Corrections, "if you wanted to place a prison in a locale, you would have major opposition. Now the turnaround is 180 degrees. They are seeking those prison units. The local media call it the prison derby."[2]

The economic boom in prison services is one aspect of the astonishing growth in the American imprisonment rate over the last generation. To help house the 1.5 million Americans currently in prison, 168 new state prisons and 45 new federal prisons were built between 1990 and 1995 alone, but these were still not enough to accommodate the number of new prisoners. State prison populations remained at 3 percent above capacity in 1995, while federal prisons exceeded their capacity by 24 percent.[3] Forty years ago President Dwight Eisenhower warned his fellow citizens against the growing power of what he termed the military-industrial complex. Today, with the Cold War at an end, a new prison-industrial complex seems to be taking its place as the major threat to democracy and civil rule.

The United States has now exposed so many of its citizens — especially its black and Hispanic citizens — to the brutalizing influence of its prisons that a self-fulfilling prophecy has been set in motion. The more Americans who are manhandled by the criminal justice system, the more there are whose behaviour seems to justify and demand this treatment. Justice grows coarser and more mechanical as it comes to be conceived as a "war on crime." Social problems that have been inappropriately displaced onto the criminal justice system grow worse. Economic and political power concentrates in the agencies of crime control and creates a second circle of self-sustaining growth. These developments, taken altogether, present other Western societies with an example of where the tendencies examined in the first chapter can lead, and so I want to devote my second chapter to this cautionary tale.

The United States has two primary ways of measuring crime. One is through the FBI's Uniform Crime Reports, which are based on reports from local and state police departments. The other is through a National Crime Survey administered annually by the Justice Department since 1972, which measures the number of victimizations and not just crimes of which the police have been made aware. Criminologists therefore generally believe it to be more accurate than the FBI reports. The National Crime Survey rate is approximately twice as high as the FBI rate. During the 1980s, while the number of Americans locked up nearly tripled, the uniform crime reports stayed more or less the same, and the National Crime Survey rate fell (despite an upswing in the late

1980s) from nearly 12,000 crimes per 100,000 of population to about 9,000. Clearly, we have to look to some explanation other than increased crime to explain the American prison boom.

This explanation lies largely in the political and media spheres. A first major step, which I have already mentioned, was the Reagan administration's intensification of the "war on drugs" at the beginning of the 1980s. A second was the adoption in 1984 of the Sentencing Reform Act. This act created a federal Sentencing Commission, which then produced a detailed table precisely correlating punishments with crimes. All the sentencing judge has to do is look up the specific offence he is dealing with in the table. So, for example, if a house has been robbed, the sentencing judge looks up "burglary of a residence" in the table. There he will discover that the "basic offense level" is seventeen. Then he adjusts for the "specific offense characteristics": if the offence involved "more than minimal planning," the offence level is to be increased by one; if drugs were involved, by another one; dangerous weapons advance the level by two; and so on, until the precise sentence is reached. Judicial discretion is eliminated, and the offender is reduced to a set of "offense characteristics."

The position in which this leaves judges was described to me recently by a federal judge from Cleveland. He currently had a young man in front of him, he said, whose crimes were almost entirely products of misadventure rather than any viciousness in his character. Nevertheless, the judge went on, he had absolutely no choice but to sentence this young man to *fifty-four years* of imprisonment. And yet, he added plaintively, "nobody's dead."

Behind this reform there had originally been a good deal of idealism. Many reformers argued that wide judicial discretion at sentencing left prisoners unfairly subject to "therapeutic experts" who had the power to vary the time to be served substantially. This led to a movement to base punishment on the solid foundation of "just deserts" — to make criminals suffer only as their crimes deserved, not according to speculative judgements about their fitness for release or as object lessons to others.[4] Following the principle first enunciated by the Enlightenment philosopher Cesare Beccaria that punishment should be "prompt, necessary, the least possible in the given circumstances, [and] proportional to the crime,"[5] this was generally a push for less punishment, not more. But it was also a plan to turn justice into a great machine, automatically dealing out so much pain for so much blame; and, as such, it was easily co-opted by the growing demand in the early 1980s for more punishment. So when the new sentencing tables actually came to be written, the effect of limiting judicial discretion was to increase sentence length rather than reduce it.

A second effect of the new sentencing regime was to transfer power from judges to prosecutors. With sentencing reduced to reading a table, criminal judges were stripped of the power and the obligation to reach a judgement about the cases before them and transformed into glorified technicians, august experts in the management of trials. The power of prosecutors increased because an offender's sentence was now fully determined by the charge brought against him. And, because prosecutors in the American system are often aspiring politicians, they have generally used their increased power to "get tough on crime." So an idea that had originally aimed at strict limits to punishment became, in the reactionary and unsettled climate of American opinion, a warrant for its expansion. Prison numbers started to explode.

The politicization of crime further intensified during the federal election campaign of 1988. Al Bronstein, who recently retired after nearly twenty-five years at the head of the American Civil Liberties Union's (ACLU) National Prison Project, believes that George Bush won that election by his relentless emphasis on a convict named Willie Horton:

> Willie Horton was a black prisoner in Massachusetts, serving a very long sentence, who was given a furlough, and while on furlough, was alleged to have committed a horrible crime. Now there's some question as to whether he even did that, but that's beside the point. What was portrayed in that Presidential race day after day was the

picture on the television and in the newspapers of this black man who had committed this horrible crime while out on furlough. And going after that on a regular basis, I think, made the difference in that Presidential race. Mr. Bush was elected President; and all of our politicians thereafter began to realize that the way to win elections, which has nothing to do with crime, is to promise to be tough on prisoners, to be tough on criminals, to be tough on offenders, to be tough on ex-offenders. And so, what is going on . . . now . . . is a race to be meaner than the next person, to be more punitive.[6]

The political popularity of "getting tough on criminals" has resulted in attempts in many states to restore the conditions that prevailed in American prisons before the civil rights of prisoners began to be recognized in the 1970s. In 1995, for example, the state of Mississippi reinstituted caning as a criminal punishment, and ordered that convicts once again wear striped uniforms — red and white for maximum-security offenders, black and white for medium, green and white for minimum — with the word "convict" written on the back[7]. Alabama, Florida, and Arizona revived chain gangs, in which uniformed convicts are shackled together with leg irons and chains in a work detail, although Alabama later discontinued the practice.[8] Federal grants to prisoners for post-secondary education were cut off by the 1994 federal crime bill, despite studies showing that higher education reduces recidivism.[9] In some places prisoners have even been ordered to pay for their own incarceration. In 1996, a Missouri circuit court judge ruled that Daryl Gilyard, who is serving a life sentence without parole, must reimburse the state for the cost of his imprisonment, beginning with a back payment of $97,724.61. Other states have imposed lesser charges on inmates.[10]

A number of states have also severely curtailed parole by passing so-called truth in sentencing laws. On September 30, 1994, for example, Virginia enacted a law requiring offenders to serve at least 85 percent of their sentences, doubling prison terms for violent first-time offenders and increasing them for repeat

violent offenders by 300 to 500 percent.[11] According to the state's
own estimates, the number of prisoners in Virginia will double
by the year 2005. Where parole persists, prison rates are being
forced up by stricter enforcement of parole conditions. In California, according to American criminologist Jerry Miller, fully a
third of those in prison are there for a technical violation of
parole or probation conditions — "things like not keeping their
appointments, having a dirty urine [sample], moving without
permission, [or] marrying without permission." Parole and probation services, which were once seen as a branch of social work
whose aim was to keep people out of prison, Miller says, have
now become ersatz police agencies whose officers wear firearms
and pride themselves on how many they get into prison. When
a staff member from Miller's National Center on Institutions and
Alternatives visited the office of California's chief probation
officer, he found mounted on the wall the motto "Trail 'em,
Surveil 'em, Nail 'em, and Jail 'em."[12]

Perhaps the most remarkable example of the move to reduce
prisoners' rights came with the passage of the Prison Litigation
Reform Act in the spring of 1996. This law, in the guise of ending
vexatious lawsuits, went a long way towards ending prisoners'
access to the courts altogether. To understand its significance it's
necessary to go back to the early 1970s, when the death of
forty-two prisoners and guards during the storming of Attica
Prison in northern New York by state troopers, and the wide
dissemination of several books by prisoners, such as Eldridge
Cleaver's *Soul on Ice* and George Jackson's *Soledad Brother*, had
injected the question of prison reform into American politics. Al
Bronstein had just been appointed to head the ACLU's new
National Prison Project, after having directed a litigation project
in the South during the civil rights movement of the 1960s. The
project aimed to advance the civil rights of prisoners, and its first
chance came when Judge Frank Johnson of the U.S. Federal
Court decided to act on a letter he had received from a seventy-
eight-year-old prisoner in Alabama. Bronstein recalls,

basically this letter said, "Dear Judge Johnson, I've been in the Alabama prisons off and on for forty years, and they've never done anything for me. They just make me worse." The judge had been getting a lot of prisoner mail and prisoner petitions about particularly egregious complaints, and he decided that maybe it was time to really look at that. So he took that letter and filed it as a case . . . And . . . he appointed us in that case . . . to represent the court. We would be *amicus* [curiae], a friend of the court but with the rights of a party.[13]

Bronstein and his colleagues went into the case with the intention of getting the court to look not just at individual problems prisoners might face, such as overcrowding, violence, or enforced idleness, but at prison conditions as a whole. They argued that if the totality of these conditions could be shown to be making prisoners worse, that would violate the prohibition against "cruel and unusual punishment" in the American Constitution. Judge Johnson accepted this argument, and in January of 1976 he ruled against the state of Alabama. Conditions in the state's prisons, he said, were actually "dehabilitating" prisoners, and he ordered these conditions improved. The following year a similar judgement was entered against Rhode Island, and for the next twenty years American courts closely supervised prison conditions. As of January 1, 1995, thirty-nine states, plus the District of Columbia, Puerto Rico, and the Virgin Islands, were subject to court judgements requiring them to limit populations and/or improve conditions in some or all of their prisons.[14]

The Prison Litigation Reform Act has now undermined the very basis on which this system of court supervision operated. At the time the bill was passed, twenty states were under what are called "consent decrees." These decrees permit courts to enforce negotiated settlements regarding prison conditions arrived at before a full trial is held. The time, expense, and public embarrassment of a trial are all avoided, and prison administrations are able to address the problems complained of without a formal admission of guilt or liability, which might expose them to further suits. The Prison Litigation Reform Act terminated all existing consent decrees and required that there be a finding of liability — and, therefore, a full trial — before any court orders any relief in future. This all-or-nothing way of doing things will make prisoner suits prohibitively expensive and encourage prison administrations to stonewall rather than face the risks of admitting liability.

At the same time, the act limits prisoners' access to lawyers by drastically limiting the court-awarded "attorney's fees" on which organizations like the National Prison Project depend for their income. Since 1976, the United States has followed the British practice of making the loser pay in civil rights cases. Prevailing parties were entitled to recover the reasonable market value of their fees from losing parties, and to receive continuing payments for monitoring compliance with court orders. In the 1977 case involving Rhode Island's prison system, for example, the National Prison Project continued to receive attorney's fees for their work during the eighteen years it took the state to comply fully with the judgement against it. The new act specifies that lawyers are entitled to recover attorney's fees only for the initial court proceeding where there is a finding that a federal law has been violated, and these fees are capped at the rate paid to lawyers assigned to represent defendants in minor federal cases. This new rate is barely one-tenth of the top market rate that experienced lawyers were previously entitled to charge, and is entirely insufficient to finance the preparation of complex cases. It will undermine the basis on which organizations like the National Prison Project have represented prisoners for the last twenty years and potentially leave them without representation.

The act also limits the power of courts to order emergency relief in cases not yet adjudicated. A recent example of such relief occurred in Pennsylvania when Judge Jan E. Dubois, a Reagan appointee, reacted to evidence of a serious tuberculosis outbreak in Pennsylvania's prisons by granting a "preliminary injunction requiring state prison officials to implement an effective tuber-culosis screening and control program."[15] As a result of that injunction, more than 400 prisoners were found to be infected in just one of the prisons covered by the order. The new act auto-matically terminates such an injunction unless it is made final within ninety days. Making such an injunction final requires that the parties complete discovery, that the court complete the trial, and that a decision be issued — highly unlikely to happen within ninety days in the case of complex litigation. Emergency relief, in other words, may become impossible.

The reason the Prison Litigation Reform Act was brought forward, according to its sponsor, Senator Orrin Hatch, was to "help bring relief to a civil justice system overburdened with frivolous prisoner lawsuits." The press release from Hatch's Sen-ate Judiciary Committee mentions as an example a case from the Senator's home state of Utah in which "an inmate sued demand-ing that he be issued Reebok or L.A. Gear brand shoes instead of the Converse brand being issued." "In another case," the release goes on, "an inmate deliberately flooded his cell, then sued the officers who cleaned up the mess because they got his Pinochle cards wet." "The crushing burden of these frivolous suits," the committee argued, was making it "difficult for courts to consider meritorious claims."[16] It's hard to believe that either of the cases cited took up much of anybody's time before they were dismissed — indeed, the implicit contempt of the Senate Judiciary Committee for the good sense of the American judi-ciary is striking. But even had frivolous suits been a serious problem, the committee's release could only be considered disin-genuous in claiming that such suits were the main target of the act. What this new legislation actually does is systematically weaken the means available for dealing with any and all prisoner grievances. Its effect, according to Al Bronstein, will be to "basi-cally eliminate prison conditions litigation as we know it."[17]

That something more than brands of running shoes or wet pinochle cards is at stake is shown by the example of an institution currently under court order, the Pelican Bay Prison in California. Pelican Bay was opened in 1990 by California Governor George Deukmejian, who called it "a state-of-the-art prison" and "a model for the rest of the nation." This was how the *Los Angeles Times* described it just before it opened:

> Pelican Bay is entirely automated and designed so that inmates have virtually no face-to-face contact with guards or other inmates. For twenty-two-and-a-half hours a day, inmates are confined to their windowless cells, built of solid blocks of concrete and stainless steel so that they won't have access to materials they could fashion into weapons. They don't work in prison industries; they don't have access to recreation; they don't mingle with other inmates. They aren't even allowed to smoke because matches are considered a security risk. Inmates eat all meals in their cells and leave only for brief showers . . . and they exercise alone in miniature yards of barren patches of cement enclosed by twenty-foot-high cement walls covered with metal screens. The doors to their cells are opened and closed electronically by a guard in a control booth . . . There are virtually no bars in the facility; the cell doors are made of perforated sheets of stainless steel with slots for food trays. Nor are there guards with keys on their belts walking the tiers. Instead the guards are locked away in glass-enclosed control booths and communicate with prisoners through a speaker system.[18]

Pelican Bay is an example of the recurring fantasy in American corrections of the "supermax": the perfect, no-touch security machine for managing difficult people. The inevitable effects on both the staff and the inmates were soon evident. Within the first two years of the prison's existence, the U.S. District Court had received more than 300 petitions from prisoners complaining of violations of their civil rights, and eventually a class action suit was heard by Judge Thelton Henderson at the end of 1993. He found that the extreme isolation the prison's design imposed was producing madness in the inmates and brutality in the guards.

Evidence was given that prisoners had stored up their feces in their cells to throw at guards. The guards in their turn had thrown bags of urine at prisoners. Prisoners had been hogtied, caged, and assaulted, their heads bashed into walls and floors while they were shackled, their bodies repeatedly kicked and hit with batons, their teeth knocked out, their jaws fractured, their limbs broken, and their bodies burned with scalding water. "Some of the defendant's comments, actions, and policies," Judge Henderson said, "show such disregard for inmates' pain and suffering that they shock the conscience. . . . Dry words on paper cannot adequately capture the senseless suffering and sometimes wretched misery." In January of 1995 he ruled that Pelican Bay was in violation of the U.S. Constitution, and ordered the parties "under the supervision of a court-appointed Special Master to negotiate a plan to make Pelican Bay meet constitutional standards."[19] A year later a report by a United Nations human rights investigator corroborated Judge Henderson's findings. Conditions at Pelican Bay, and at several other high-tech, high-security American prisons, investigator Nigel Rodley said, were "inhuman and degrading."

Even so, new prisons along the same lines continue to be built. In December of 1994, for example, while judgement was pending in the Pelican Bay case, *USA Today* reported that "the most dangerous inmates in the federal prison system are quietly being shipped to a new ultra-maximum security penitentiary in Florence, Colorado." Prisoners in this "Alcatraz of the Rockies" are to be subject to the same regimen of total isolation and remote control that was tried at Pelican Bay.[20]

Cases like the Pelican Bay suit will have a harder time reaching the American courts in future. And when they do, settlements will be harder to enforce. Special Masters such as the one Judge Henderson appointed to oversee reform at Pelican Bay are hemmed in by several provisions of the act, which limit both their authority and the compensation to which they are entitled. It is possible that the legislation can be successfully challenged on the grounds that the separation of powers prevents the legislature from constraining the courts in their interpretation of the Constitution. The act also appears vulnerable insofar as it singles out prisoners as a special class of litigants and deprives them of rights still available to other complainants in civil rights cases. But so long as it stands, it testifies to the vengeful mood that now dominates the U.S. Congress and exemplifies the new status of prisoners as nonpersons.

The dramatic expansion of prison numbers in the United States has had a variety of consequences. One, as I said at the start, has been to touch off an economic boom in prison services. Another has been to turn the employees of the crime-control industry into a formidable lobby with a vested interest in further growth. The political influence of this lobby can be measured by a study of campaign contributions in California in 1991–92, which found that the California Correctional Peace Officers' Association was the state's second-largest political donor, spending "around $1 million on political contributions for the governorship and the legislature in each electoral cycle."[21] Worst of all has been the continual projection, in politics and the media, of the idea of crime control as a war, and the image of the criminal as an enemy alien. Conceiving crime control in this way subordinates every other consideration to the goal of victory. Judges lose the duty of careful and humane deliberation and become, in Nils Christie's phrase, "tool[s] for fighting crime." Police become careless of civil rights. Prisons become places of internment rather than correction. New techniques of electronic control further alienate prisoners. "Monster pictures are created," Christie says, "just as they are in war."[22]

In a highly differentiated, highly mobile society where wealth puts down no roots and recognizes no boundaries, ties of mutual obligation between classes fade away, and the burden of social control falls more and more on the criminal justice system. Media sensationalism and racial anxieties reinforce this tendency, so that there is nothing to challenge or modify "the monster pictures." The result, in Christie's view, is that people come to accept large prison populations as a necessary and even benign feature of the social landscape. Once the pains of prisoners cease to register, the category of those who do not count tends to expand, and decency and civility suffer. This is so in part because people tend to enact, and therefore seem to justify, our expectations of them, but also because the practice of total control cannot easily be confined to the criminal justice system. It is liable, says Christie, to become a "cancerous growth." The current expansion of the organs of crime control gives him "an unpleasant feeling of being in central Europe during the 1930s."[23]

This "war" on crime, by the estimate of Jerry Miller, is now costing the United States $200 billion (U.S.) annually, and many of these costs are concentrated in a handful of large states.[24] California, in 1980, devoted 2 percent of its budget to corrections. Fifteen years and seventeen new prisons later, the state had six times as many prisoners and was devoting close to 10 percent of its budget to corrections. The outlay for prisons now exceeds the state's shrinking budget for higher education, and the Rand Corporation estimates that by 2002 the prison budget will consume 18 percent of the state's resources.

Part of California's deepening fiscal crisis arises from its "three strikes and you're out" law. Such laws impose life imprisonment upon anyone convicted of a third felony. At least twenty-two states and the federal government have enacted "three strike" laws since the state of Washington led the way in 1993; but only California has actually put the law into serious and sustained operation.[25] Wisconsin has such a law on the books but has used it only once, while Tennessee, New Mexico, and Colorado have never applied theirs. In California, the law resulted from a popular movement, similar to CAVEAT in Canada, which took shape in the wake of two horrible and highly publicized crimes by ex-convicts and ultimately gathered 841,000 signatures on a petition to put the question on the 1994 state ballot. It has already resulted in the imprisonment of 1,300 offenders on third-strike felonies and more than 14,000 for second-strike felonies. However, its status is currently uncertain as a result of a California Supreme Court ruling in June of 1996 that, since prosecutors were exercising discretion as to which felony convictions would count as "strikes," judges ought to have the same authority in sentencing.

So far the law has been applied more to nonviolent offenders than to the violent felons it was intended to put away:

> One of the first . . . third-strike prosecutions was of a twenty-seven-year-old San Diego man subject to life in prison for stealing a piece of pizza because he previously had pleaded guilty to two felonies — robbery and attempted robbery . . . The first prosecution of a woman under the law was for a $20 cocaine purchase she allegedly made nearly fourteen years after her second strike.[26]

"We're worried about Willie Horton, and we lock up the Three Stooges," said Franklin Zimring, a criminologist at the University of California at Berkeley.[27] One study found that almost four times "as many marijuana possessors (192) have been sentenced for second and third strikes in California as for murder (4), rape (25), and kidnapping (24). Eighty-five percent of all offenders sentenced under this law are sentenced for nonviolent offenses."[28] The law also heightens the already exaggerated powers of prosecutors because it is they who determine what counts as a previous strike and whether new cases will be charged as felonies or misdemeanours. So far the law has been applied unevenly. For example, "forty-three percent of the third-strike inmates in the state are African-Americans, though they make up 7 percent of the state's population and 20 percent of its felony arrestees."

The governor of California and other state officials have claimed that the three-strikes law is working because there has been a reduction in the crime rate. Critics reply that this drop in crime began before the bill was passed, and is better explained by demographic changes and falling unemployment. What is certain, however, is the tremendous costs that keeping prisoners for life is going to impose on the state. In states like Louisiana, which initiated the trend towards life sentences without parole twenty years ago, the bills for geriatric care for prisoners are already starting to come due. The Louisiana State Penitentiary at Angola will soon be "the world's biggest nursing home," according to Wilbert Rideau, the lifer who edits the prison newspaper *The Angolite*.[29] Rideau, as Peter Moon described him in a story in the *Globe and Mail*, is a case in point.

> He was a black teenager from a poor background with only an eighth-grade education in 1961, when he robbed a bank in the southwest part of Louisiana and committed his murder. He spent eleven years on Angola's death row, where he discovered the pleasures of reading and ideas, before his death sentence was commuted to life imprisonment . . . In 1976, a reform-minded warden offered him the editorship of a prison magazine to be called *The Angolite*. The warden promised that the magazine would not be censored as long as its articles told the truth. At the time Angola was the most violent prison in the United States. It was poorly managed and rife with brutality — not only prisoners attacking other prisoners, but guards brutalizing convicts . . . From 1972 to 1975, forty inmates were murdered and 350 were wounded in knifings.
>
> Mr. Rideau and his small staff of convicts exposed conditions in the prison in the pages of their magazine and began writing knowledgeably about flaws in the whole correctional system. *The Angolite* went on to win national awards for magazine journalism, influenced major reforms in the state's prison system, and helped change Louisiana's method of execution by publishing photographs that showed electrocution caused severe burns to a condemned man before he died. The state now uses lethal injection.
>
> In the past twenty years conditions at Angola, while still tough, have improved. There has been only one inmate murder in the past eighteen months.[30]

Burl Cain, the current warden at Angola, says that Rideau is rehabilitated and should go free, but he can't release him. Rideau travels under guard to high schools and colleges around the state. He has addressed national conferences in Washington and appeared on radio and television; but, as the law now stands, he'll die at Angola.

It remains to be seen whether crippling costs will finally force the United States into the rational discussion of prison policy that considerations of justice and prudence have so far failed to bring about. In the meanwhile, according to criminologist Jerry Miller,

> what we have now, in the area of criminal justice particularly, is a system designed to ensure that we remain ignorant of people; it's designed to ensure that we don't know them too well because then the categories break down very quickly. I testify a lot in court . . . particularly in capital punishment cases, and it's always amazing to me how the prosecution in these cases dances about the room trying to keep you from saying things that are real, or that are honest or truthful, for fear the jury will be drained of a need to punish. It's an exercise in trying to keep things in very neat categories, and trying in a sense to avoid dealing with reality, which is much more complex than the criminal-justice system allows.[31]

Miller has been involved in the criminal justice field since 1969 when, as commissioner of the Department of Youth Services for the Commonwealth of Massachusetts, he closed all of the state's reform schools.[32] (This story is discussed in detail in Chapter 13.) Today he heads the National Center on Institutions and Alternatives, an organization that has pioneered noncustodial sentencing alternatives. He thinks that in recent years political discourse with regard to crime in the United States has undergone a disastrous over-simplification in which all feeling for the narrative meaning of criminal acts has been driven out by stereotypes, slogans, and bare, unenlightening categories. When a federal court recently made him the trustee of a collapsing child-welfare agency in the District of Columbia, he found that the agency didn't even maintain histories of its clients. There were charges and diagnoses on the files, but no stories that would lend a sense of meaning or continuity. "We are not getting a sense of movement, of texture, of career in people's lives," Miller says. "It allows you to pull yourself back from . . . people . . . and to detach yourself from their lives, and therefore be very manipulative, very judgemental."

During the last generation, Miller says that he has seen every profession involved in the criminal justice field grow steadily more punitive. Probation, for example, was originally about keeping people out of jail. It began with a Boston shoemaker named John Augustus, who went to court and tried to persuade judges to entrust delinquent boys to his care so that he could find them jobs. It has now become an arm of law enforcement, as Miller has seen:

> What we have done is turn to the criminal justice system to deal with a wide range of personal and social and economic problems. And that has had a deadening effect on the democracy, but it's had an even more hurtful effect on elements of our society that you would have hoped would have been insulated against it . . . Now social workers join prosecutors to go out and catch issues of incest. Rather than try to keep families together, or deal with these generally delicate issues within families, they come in with the meat-axe of the criminal justice system, which rips families apart willy-nilly.
>
> It's now a myth that helping professionals [like] psychiatrists, psychologists, [and] social workers are the bleeding hearts that come into court and testify that the [accused] really shouldn't be held accountable. That is not true anymore, if it ever was. Now they come in as arms of the prosecution. They come in talking about responsibility. They withdraw from the case in a clinical sense when crime is involved. And [it's] generally a pretty brutal crew that comes from the helping professions into our courtrooms.[33]

Miller believes that substituting what he calls "the meat-axe of the criminal justice system" for social policy has had disastrous consequences for American democracy. Because in many states a criminal conviction permanently removes the right to vote, "we have succeeded," says Miller, "in disenfranchising a large percentage, if not the majority, of young black men." Worse, he goes on, they have been socialized to the mores of prison life.

> You now have on the streets the warped philosophy of violence that holds correctional settings together. The kinds of behavior that seem meaningless or senseless to the average observer, like drive-by shootings, killing someone over their sneakers or their athletic jacket, those are not senseless at all to anyone who knows prison life. Those are precisely the things that are done day in and day out in a prison. It has to do with status, it has to do with respect in front of your peers. You learn not to open your mouth and say anything unless you are willing to deliver in violence. Now, in prison for the most part, it's confined to . . . fights and maybe a knifing now and then. But on the streets of this country, we've thrown millions of handguns into the mix. Drive-by shootings are performance art. Very rarely would you see a person alone in a car, driving by and shooting people; it has to do with whoever else is riding in the car and demonstrating his ability to be unfeeling and to get back at someone. It's the kind of thing that characterizes day-to-day prison life. And so, we have now on the streets people acting like they're in a prison or reform school, only without the walls and without the limits and with all the handguns that they wouldn't have were they in prison. So, in a sense, imprisonment has resulted in a self-fulfilling prophecy on our streets. You don't have a reputation in many large cities unless you've been to prison. You certainly can't be a gang leader unless you've done time.[34]

Miller's account of imprisonment is precisely the opposite of the one put forward by those who have argued that imprisonment is the answer to the social breakdown that is expressed by crime.

Scholars like John DiIulio of Princeton present imprisonment as both a moral and a practical imperative[35] — moral because it is the only serious way to assert the existence of inviolable social standards, and practical because it averts the expense of the crimes prisoners don't commit while they're behind bars.[36] Crime, in this analysis, is taken for granted as a moral evil to which the criminal justice system merely responds. But, as Miller points out, the reported heartlessness and brutality that seem to justify imprisonment are frequently the *result* of socialization within the institutions of criminal justice in the first place. Criminal justice processing has become the primary "rite of passage" for inner-city juveniles. It should not surprise us that youths whose encounter with "society" is mediated by such hostile and alienating procedures turn out hostile and alienated.

In the United States, the word "crime" often encodes the more troublesome reality of race, and so some of what has happened there has to be understood as the unfolding of a uniquely American predicament. But even so, I think the American experience also offers a generally applicable illustration of the dangers of trying to deal with a social dilemma by transforming it into a question of crime. This transformation, as I have already said, sets in motion a self-fulfilling prophecy. The more problems of idleness, vice, community demoralization, and family breakdown are seen to demand punishment as crimes, the more violent and vicious people become. At the bottom of this descending spiral lurks the monster that DiIulio, with his co-authors William Bennett and John Walters of a new book called *Body Count*, call "the super-predator."

> America is now home to thickening ranks of juvenile super-predators — radically impulsive, brutally remorseless youngsters, including ever more preteenage boys, who murder, assault, rape, rob, burglarize, deal deadly drugs, join gun-toting gangs, and create serious communal disorders. They do not fear the stigma of arrest, the pains of imprisonment, or the pangs of conscience.[37]

This profile, however questionable it may be, certainly reflects the existence of frighteningly violent young people. But it doesn't ask where these quintessences of evil *came* from. The sensational snapshot of the super-predator effaces the vicious circle that produced him. Even where he is acknowledged as the product of a broken community, the forces that broke the community are unlikely to be carefully observed. And this allows more of what caused the problem in the first place to be prescribed as the cure.

The American criminal justice system did not by itself produce the crisis that has put 5,000,000 Americans, and counting, under its control. Its causes are many and complex, including the disappearance of decently paid jobs, resulting from the rapid deindustrialization of American cities; the migration of the growing black middle class to the suburbs; the creation of a lucrative economy in illegal drugs at exactly the moment that other economic opportunities for young, inner-city black men were disappearing; and the breakdown of families. What criminal justice processing has done is to reify *as crime* the problems arising from these circumstances. Crime demands punishment, and punishment initiates the vicious circle that eventually demands more and more punishment.

Whether the United States can break this cycle partly depends on whether the problem can ever be recognized by a political system in which ambitious politicians, highly commercialized media, and a resentful public now all fortify each others' prejudices.

3

PERCEPTION AND REALITY
IN CRIME POLICY

One of the things that makes crime such a volatile political issue is widespread public confusion about both the character and the extent of the problem. This disorientation is fed by a constant infusion of contradictory statistics. For example, the Canadian Centre for Justice Statistics says that since 1991 the youth crime rate has followed the downward trend in the general crime rate,[1] while well-publicized local reports have pointed to alarming increases. One such report appeared on May 15, 1996, when the Toronto police department released figures pointing to "a steady shift toward ever-younger perpetrators of certain types of crimes, most notably those involving theft with violence or the threat of violence." The report claimed that more than 40 percent of those charged with robbery in 1995 had been juveniles, as opposed to 21 percent in 1985.[2] Two days later, a story in the *Toronto Star* revealed that 1985, the year the police had used as a standard of comparison, was the last year in which sixteen- and seventeen-year-olds had been counted as adults.[3] The reported increases, in other words, were almost entirely the result of a change in the definition of youth crime; the comparison was meaningless, as well as wilfully misleading. The *Star* story went on to present research by Anthony Doob of the University of Toronto's Centre of Criminology on the prevalence of youth crime in Ontario. Doob had analyzed Ontario's youth crime figures for 1993 through 1995 and found that, although violent cases increased by 4 percent, all of the increase occurred at the lowest level, and probably reflected a tendency to lay charges for more petty assaults. Doob also found a 4 percent *decrease* in the number of robberies, and a stable rate at the highest level of violence — sexual assault, murder, and manslaughter. He concluded that reported changes in the rate and character of youth crime represent changes in how youth crime is categorized, charged, and sentenced, and not in how youths behave. Lies, damned lies, and statistics.

A few weeks later, the same doubtful numbers became the occasion of a contretemps between the attorney general of Ontario, Charles Harnick, and the chair of the House of Commons Standing Committee on Justice and Legal Affairs, Shaughnessy Cohen. Harnick and Ontario Solicitor General Bob Runciman were before the committee to propose that the Young Offenders Act be amended to allow children under twelve to be prosecuted and youths over fifteen to be routinely treated as adults. As evidence of the rising lawlessness he wanted to stem, Harnick cited the 11,000 charges laid under the Young Offenders Act in 1995. The well-informed Cohen bit back, observing that Ontario was notorious for charging youths with petty offences. "About 4,200 of your offences were Level 1 assaults," she told Harnick. "That is schoolyard pushing." In later testimony, Anthony Doob confirmed Cohen's point, pointing out that only one in fifty-seven youths who commit an offence in Quebec end up in court, while in Ontario the figure is one in seventeen.[4] Outside the committee room, Harnick defended his approach as a reflection of what he hears from the public. "I come at this from the point of view that this is what the public is telling us. We have to be responsive to them."

Unfortunately, citizens are consistently mistaken about the prevalence of crime. This fact was demonstrated by a 1994 federal study comparing what Canadians believe about the prevalence of crime with the actual number of crimes reported to the police or uncovered by victimization surveys.[5] It found a systematic discrepancy. Two-thirds of Canadians believed that crime rates had risen in the previous five years, when in fact they had been stable. Most respondents also believed that homicides were increasing more quickly than any other crime, though the homicide rate had actually remained stable for thirty years and had declined slightly after the abolition of capital punishment (2.7 per 100,000 in 1992 versus 3.06 per 100,000 in 1977); that housebreaking was increasing, although the rate reported to the police had gone down significantly (from 26.3 per 1,000 households in 1980 to 22.4 in 1990); that gun crime was becoming more common, when the percentage of robberies involving a firearm had actually declined (from 37 percent in 1978 to 26 percent in 1990); and they consistently overestimated the parole rate and underestimated the number of convicts sent to prison. "The system is not the lenient joke people believe it to be," the study's author, University of Ottawa criminologist Julian Roberts, told the *Globe and Mail*.[6]

Skewed public perceptions are particularly evident in discussions of the Young Offenders Act. Enforcement of this act is widely believed to be extremely lenient when it is actually quite tough[7]. A recent report for the Justice Department, for example, says that 80 percent of juveniles in jail in Canada are there for property offences or for breaching probation orders. Based on a bill of $12,000 for a sixty-day sentence, the report calculates that Canadian governments are spending $262 million a year jailing juveniles for nonviolent crimes. As a *Vancouver Sun* editorial writer remarked, this is harsh punishment for the taxpayers as well as the youths. The report also noted that, in 1993, 263 kids ended up in secure custody for mischief.[8] According to Judge Heino Lilles of the Yukon Territorial Court, a former law professor at Queen's University and a specialist in young offender law, the Canadian youth justice system, contrary to its reputation, detains in custody 34 percent of all young people adjudicated in court — "much higher than the corresponding figure for youth courts in any Westernized society that I'm aware of," he says. Canada's practice in youth justice, in other words, is the exact opposite of what many of its citizens imagine:

> We like to think of the American system as being a very harsh penal system. And indeed, if you look at overall incarceration rates comparing the American states to Canada, we see incarceration rates in the States overall, for adults and young offenders, being about three times the Canadian rate; however, when we focus just on young offenders, we see a startling reversal in those statistics. The rate of custody use for young offenders in Canada is twice as high as that in the United States. So, the myth or the view, rather, that the Young Offenders Act is soft on young offenders is false, particularly if one views incarceration as the measure of that softness.[9]

In Judge Lilles's view this popular fiction about the treatment of young offenders obscures the real problem with the act: its incoherence. When it was adopted as a replacement for the obsolete Juvenile Delinquents Act in 1984, it was a prefaced by a statement of eight principles. The statement alludes promiscuously to all possible purposes of youth justice from punishment and public protection through to rehabilitation, thus providing judges with a principle for every prejudice. Lilles calls this preface "internally inconsistent . . . indecisive and thus confusing." "In true Canadian fashion," he adds, "we have served up, not a Declaration, but a Compromise of Principles, in an attempt to provide something for everyone."[10]

The incoherence of the act's instructions to judges is evident in the wide variation in sentencing practices that now exists across Canada. Some variation, Lilles says, would be understandable and even desirable, but the current degree of difference can only indicate that, as a national community, we suffer from badly crossed public purposes:

> If you look in northern communities, you find incarceration rates that are three to four times that of other provinces. Alberta will use

incarceration at a rate two to three times higher than, for example, Prince Edward Island. You see similar variation in the number of transfers to adult court, which is a very significant decision made in youth court — that is, when a young person commits a very, very serious offence, usually a homicide, the question is whether or not the young person should be transferred to adult court to be dealt with as an adult or left in youth court — I suppose this is the real test of Section 3 of the Young Offenders Act, the Declaration of Principles. Ontario and Quebec transfer together a handful of young offenders on an annual basis, although the majority of Canada's population is found in those two provinces. The great bulk, the great majority, of young offenders are transferred to adult court in the western provinces, Alberta and British Columbia. So, there's an example and, I think, a dramatic example of the inconsistencies that we find in the practice of the Young Offenders Act. In part, that flows from [its] contradictory aims.[11]

Crossed purposes in youth justice are one of several reasons why Canada puts so many kids in custody. Another, according to Judge Lilles, is the vicious circle that ostracization of "difficult youth" initiates. "By maintaining a high level of incarceration, we introduce more and more youth to the criminal justice system," which just "breeds more crime" and demands more imprisonment in turn. Lilles proposes a "sober recognition that criminal justice processing often increases the likelihood of kids reoffending rather than reducing it." Incarceration rates are also fed by the popular belief, as we saw in Chapters 1 and 2, that punishment reduces crime, a belief seemingly immune to evidence. This belief has the property that anthropologist Max Gluckman attributes to a ritual[12]: it conceals the contradiction between what is meant to happen and what actually does happen, and so, by definition, can never fail. If it rains, the rain dance has been successful. If it fails to rain, we must have danced it wrong and ought to try again. If imprisonment fails to reduce crime, Lilles say, then "everyone falls into line and demands that we get tougher."[13]

What holds us back from youth justice reform is a combination of prejudice and selective attention. A few terrifying incidents, and the very real demoralization and derangement of a small minority of juveniles, are easily stitched together into a net to catch thousands of others who pose no enduring threat. Opportunists in politics and mass media find it easier to inflame popular prejudices than to contradict them. It is a perception that makes the "youth crime problem" intractable. Evidence of the counterproductivity of punishment is abundant, and alternatives that hold offenders to account without hardening their resistance are available. All that lacks, Lilles says, is political leadership.

> We know absolutely unequivocally that, contrary to public belief and expectations, the youth criminal justice system cannot cure delinquency; it does not help dysfunctional families; it does not make our streets safe; it does not make our adolescents walk, talk, and dress like adults. We have lots of experiential evidence within Canada and the States, and we have lots of research evidence that establishes beyond a reasonable doubt that increasing penalties and making transfers to adult court easier does not reduce offending. What it does is it creates an illusion of action. It may be good politics but it's very poor public policy.[14]

The contradiction between sound policy and popular politics is illustrated by the career of the Mike Harris government in Ontario, which has spent its first term in office solving all sorts of problems that it doesn't actually have in order to appear to be cracking down on crime. It began with the closing of the province's halfway house system, which had been in operation for twenty years. The 400 residents of the twenty-five houses were sent back to prison. The halfway houses, operated on contract by nongovernment agencies like the John Howard Society, cost less than $80 per day per inmate as opposed to $130 a day for a provincial institution. Correctional Services Minister Bob Runciman said that a voluntary electronic monitoring system, for which people would be eligible only after a "rigid risk assessment process," would be introduced to replace the halfway houses — a measure he claimed would save $9 million a year. The director of one halfway house, Arthur Stratton of Bunton Lodge in Toronto, said he was "astounded by the fact that somebody believes that personal contact . . . can be replaced by an electronic bracelet."[15]

The Ontario government's next move was to revamp the parole board and tighten the parole system generally. As a result the number of people released on parole fell from 2,700 in 1995 to 1,800 in 1996. This move has increased the median sentence served in Ontario jails from twenty-six to thirty-three days and increased the annual price tag by at least $30 million a year.[16] Then Bob Runciman, who at the time was solicitor general as well as correctional services minister, announced the cancellation of Ontario's twelve bail programs. These programs were set up in 1979 for those eligible for bail who lacked the money to pay for it. The cost of supervising someone under a bail program is $4.05 a day, considerably less than it costs to keep someone in prison.[17] The only explanation given for the cancellation in the letter from the Ministry of Correctional Services was financial constraint. The decision, according to the *Globe and Mail*, "caused the justice community in the province to buzz with outrage from one end to the other."[18] It also produced a certain mystification, since saving the annual $1 million budget of the bail programs would cost the province $25 million in new jail expenses. The cynical explanation put forward by defence lawyer Paul Calarco was that this was a way of extorting guilty pleas from people who would otherwise have to spend weeks or months in jail awaiting a chance to argue their innocence. The government never explained, but under intense pressure it did temporarily reinstate some, but not all, of the bail programs. The question is now being reviewed by an independent consultant.

The Ontario government has also announced plans to replace fourteen ageing provincial jails with two new "superprisons," one with a capacity of 1,000, the other of 1,200. It is currently considering having one of these institutions privately managed. A number of Ontario towns vied for these plums in a Canadian equivalent of the American "prison derby" discussed in Chapter 2. Lindsay and Penetanguishene were chosen. According to Bob Runciman, the new prisons are to be "no frills" institutions, with a stripped-down design that allows them to function with far fewer guards. Arguing that "our goal in the correctional system . . . is not necessarily to improve the quality of life for people convicted of crimes," Runciman boasted that a projected operating cost of $76 per inmate per day would make these the cheapest prisons in North America.[19] Critics countered that large prisons, relying on surveillance-based security rather than personal contact, generally foster violence and alienation. Replacing local jails with large centralized facilities also tends to interrupt ties of family and friendship by making visiting more difficult.

Ontario has also introduced a privately run "boot camp" for difficult sixteen- and seventeen-year-old juvenile offenders and announced plans to privatize the operation of seven secure detention centres for young offenders aged twelve to fifteen by the spring of 1999.[20] The boot-camp idea spread from the United States, where a camp was opened in Georgia in 1983 and in Oklahoma in 1984. Modelled on military training, the camps' appeal stems from the idea that strict discipline is what wayward youths need. By the beginning of 1993, eight American states had a total of nineteen juvenile boot camps in operation — and twenty-seven states had adult boot camps as well.[21] In Canada, Alberta was the first to adopt this model, followed by Manitoba.

The first reports on the Alberta program indicate that it differs significantly from the stereotype suggested by the name "boot camp." The program more closely resembles earlier Outward Bound–type initiatives like Ontario's long-standing DARE program. There are no leather-lunged drill sergeants harassing and humiliating cowed recruits, ordering them to do endless push-ups. The head of Alberta's Young Offenders Branch, Patricia

Meade, rejects the idea that "you have to knock a person down before you can build them up again. These kids have already been knocked down a lot," she says. Instead, the Alberta system takes chronic offenders who have expressed a desire to reform and puts them in a rural camp that combines hard work with life-skills training, counselling, and education. Jim Creechen, a criminologist at the University of Alberta, says that although the Klein government undoubtedly set up the program to appeal to voters, he thinks it has a chance of success because it rejects the illusion that you can "beat common sense into people," selects candidates motivated to succeed, and fosters pride of accomplishment in those who can handle the rigorous life. A follow-up study on the first 140 graduates found only 15 had re-offended after a year and a half — while the recidivism rate for young offenders at urban institutions is closer to 85 percent."[22] Ontario has promised that its program will also avoid "the shout-in-your-face adversary-type system that has been a failure in so many U.S. States," though "it will require military-style uniforms with blue epaulets on white shirts."[23] No research has yet appeared on this program, but perhaps it too will rise above the rhetoric with which it was launched.

The transformation of Alberta's boot-camp initiative into something much better than its advance notices promised is an indicator of the ambivalence that so far has kept Canada from altogether succumbing to an American-style cult of mindless toughness in justice policy. Instead, Canadian policy has tended to yaw equivocally in the political winds, moving now to the right, now to the left. The career of Justice Minister Allan Rock during the first Chrétien government between 1993 and 1997 indicates the pattern. Early in his tenure, Rock introduced changes to the Young Offenders Act that increased sentences and made it easier to transfer sixteen- and seventeen-year-olds into adult court — and therefore, if convicted, into adult prison.[24] He also amended Section 745 of the Criminal Code, as discussed in Chapter 1, and introduced draconian legislation, never adopted, that would have allowed people designated as "high-risk" offenders to be supervised for up to ten years *after* having completed their sentences — and, even more controversially, would have allowed police to monitor electronically someone never convicted or charged if a judge deemed that person dangerous.[25] On the other hand, he introduced amendments to the Criminal Code authorizing "conditional," or noncustodial, sentences, and put forward extremely liberal and skeptical views in testimony before the Commons Justice Committee during hearings on the Young Offenders Act in 1995. He said, for example, that he thinks Canada locks up far too many juveniles for minor crimes, and pointed out that it costs about $100,000 a year to keep a young offender behind bars — up to $300,000 in the Territories; the total bill for detaining nonviolent offenders is about $250 million each year. "Do you want a young offender in custody for three months, shooting pool and smoking cigarettes," he asked the MPS, "or meeting the victim, who can directly confront the offender, and have the offender do work that is meaningful to the victim?" He suggested that the greater part of federal transfers to the provinces for youth justice should go to alternatives, rather than to custody as 80 percent now does.[26]

The same ambivalence is evident in the diametrically opposed policies instituted in various provinces. While Ontario and Alberta have been getting tough, New Brunswick and Quebec have announced plans to close prisons and adopt noncustodial alternatives. I will look into these plans in more detail in the final section of the book. Here I want to emphasize the haze of misinformation that obscures the real world of criminal justice, and the pressure politicians are under to make policy in that haze rather than risk contradicting "what the public is telling us." Crime is often banal and rather stupid. Punishment often makes a bad situation worse. But within the haze of misinformation we hallucinate dramatic misdeeds and decisive responses. What makes a policy of imprisonment for crime so popular, if it is so manifestly ineffective? To this question I turn next.

4

RITUALS OF REPRESSION

In 1992, an American criminal justice policy lobby called The Sentencing Project, in an attempt to "discourage political demagoguery on crime," initiated the Campaign for an Effective Crime Policy. The campaign issued a "Call for a Rational Debate on Crime and Punishment," and sought the endorsement of both elected officials and criminal justice professionals.[1] By "rational debate," the campaign's organizers meant, among other things, submitting the question of whether imprisonment is an effective means of correction to evidence. Eight hundred officials have so far endorsed this call, but the political frenzy surrounding questions of crime and punishment continues unabated. Why has even so modest a goal as a rational debate proved elusive? Is it possible that rationality is not really the issue?

In this chapter I present the analyses of two eminent contemporary scholars, both of whom suggest that imprisonment serves purposes extending far beyond the reach of rational evidence. The first half of the chapter is devoted to sociologist Zygmunt Bauman's theory that high levels of incarceration are a feature of the new social terrain that he calls "postmodernity"; the second half explores Ivan Illich's related hypothesis that the institution of imprisonment can be fruitfully analyzed as a peculiarly contemporary "religious ceremonial."

The term "postmodern" has been used in many different ways

in recent years, sometimes to refer only to shifts in taste. Zygmunt Bauman uses it in a much more comprehensive and paradigmatic sense to sum up an emergent social order that he sees as being as different from the modern as the modern was from the medieval. He has explored the watershed between the modern and postmodern orders in a series of recent books — *Modernity and the Holocaust* (1989), *Intimations of Post-Modernity* (1992), *Post-Modern Ethics* (1993), and *Life in Fragments* (1995) — and, in a 1995 paper titled "From Welfare State into Prison," he has specifically investigated the role of imprisonment in this new order.[2]

Modernity, Bauman says, can be defined as "legislated reason." It arose out of the shattering of the cosmological framework of the Middle Ages and the discovery that "human order is vulnerable, contingent, and devoid of reliable foundations"; society responded to this crisis with "an effort to make order solid, obligatory, and reliably founded."[3] Post-Enlightenment societies projected "order as a task." Classical sociology viewed society as a coherent "social system" — a "principally coordinated" space (to use Talcott Parsons's rendition of Max Weber). Legislative proclamation was believed to hold the key to the smooth and harmonious functioning of this social system. The state was responsible for its regulation.

Bauman believes that this modern dream is fading as the task of coordinating society is gradually transferred from the state to the market. This change is being expressed in two ways that are directly relevant to the question of prison growth. The first is through the generation of a new underclass of disposable people. In modern societies, the state recognized an obligation to all of its citizens; everyone could properly expect to have a part to play in economic life. Even those who were from time to time out of work still constituted a "reserve army" whose labour would eventually be needed again. We have now entered an era in which those who control capital are trying to cut any permanent ties of solidarity or obligation with their workforce. There is no longer any prospect that all the citizens will have a part to play in the economy. Even the pretense that such a thing is possible is now rare. As the head of the International Labour Organization said some years ago, anyone who thinks that everyone on earth is going to get a job is no longer just an optimist, but actually mad. The reserve army of the unemployed has been replaced by a new class of redundant people.

The second reflection of this great change is in the way society is organized. Whereas the maintenance of social order was previously the task of the state, this function has now shifted to the market. The mechanism that integrates and disciplines our consumer society, Bauman says, is seduction. It is the allure of market, and not the exhortation of society, that induces postmodern people to play by the rules. It is the market that elicits effort and apportions rewards. There is, as Peter Drucker has said, "no more salvation by society."

In a society integrated through seduction citizens must be in a position to be seduced — they must have the necessary means, or at least a sufficient possibility of getting them that they are willing to discipline themselves in order to protect their access to desired commodities. But this is not true of that part of the population who have been made redundant, and have no access to the primary form of community that is shared consumption. Baumann explains that

. . . the seduction of the majority by market allurements has to be supplemented by the suppression of the other part of the population, of those redundant, imperfect consumers, people who are of no visible utility, no visible use from the point of view of the circulation of commodities . . . In that, I see the major social-political cause of the appallingly fast-growing number of people who are treated by the law as criminal elements . . . On the one pole, you have this thriving part of the population, using the opportunities offered by the new consumer/market economy . . . On the other hand, you have this waste product of the same development which has to be disposed

of. You can consider the criminal system, punishment system, as a
sort of a sewage pipe or sewage gutters into which the waste products
of society are channeled.[4]

Every type of social order, Bauman says, produces its own
image of the dangers that threaten it. Its fears are "made to its
own measure":

> The image of the threat tends to be a self-portrait of the society with
> minus signs; or, to put it in psychoanalytic terms, a projection of the
> inner ambivalence of the society about its own ways . . . The enemies
> who have laid siege to [society's] walls are its . . . own inner demons
> — the suppressed, ambient fears which permeate its daily life, its
> *normality*, yet which, in order to make the daily reality endurable,
> must be squashed and squeezed out of the lived-through quotidian-
> ity and moulded into an alien body; into a tangible enemy one can
> fight, and fight again, and even swear to conquer.[5]

The danger that haunted the now-waning modern state was
revolution. Its order depended on "legislating / generalizing /
classifying / categorizing." The administration of the state was
both the coordinator and the archetype of these activities. The
counter-order consisted of those "alternative classifiers and legislators" who aspired to rule the state according to a different,
but equally unified and comprehensive, scheme. Totalitarian
communism in this sense was the mirror image of totalizing
modernity. The opposing sides in the Cold War differed in how
they ruled society, but they agreed that it ought to be ruled. With
the collapse of communism as an official geopolitical other,
and with the advance of deregulation of every kind, this agreement has broken down. "The one universal categorical grid has
fallen apart," Bauman says. "Self-aggrandizement is replacing
. . . socially sponsored improvement; self-assertion takes [the]
place of the collective cure for class deprivation."

The emerging, postmodern order is haunted by new enemies.

It fears not a counter-order but the absence of any order at all: chaos. In the new order, no recognizable agency seems to be at the helm. This is recognized even by those we might suppose are in charge. For example, I recently came across these interesting remarks by a minister of the Canadian government. Pierre Pettigrew, then the minister for international cooperation, was addressing a conference on African development in September of 1996:

> Globalization is an invisible, anonymous process, driven by abstract, nonhuman forces and factors. As it bypasses the authority of states, reducing their power, it sets up the marketplace as, in effect, the new god that we must worship, replacing the nation-state. The trouble is, this new god, though it may be more efficient, is incapable of taking a long-run view and can think only in material terms. The state, for all its shortcomings, is made up of people — people whose life experience may give them a long-term perspective and whose children make them likely to have a broad-ranging concern for the future. Furthermore, because the state is run by people, if we don't like what they're doing to us, we can eventually change them. Sooner or later, the state must respond to the demands of the people living in it. However, if we don't like what the market does, we can't repeal its laws. If we storm the bunker of globalization, we won't find a madman there or a clique of conspirators — just an empty space.[6]

An order ruled by an empty space, an order founded on competition, an order whose very existence depends on the incitement of envy, meets its inevitable other in the form of "the criminal." Indeed, Bauman goes so far as to say that "whatever has been registered in recent years as rising criminality" runs "parallel to the falling of the membership of the communist or other radical parties of 'alternative order.'" The criminal is the excluded one who has forced his way into the consumer feast.

Consumer society cannot live without the constant stimulation of desire and without the continual replacement of what was recently said to be good by what is now said to be better. Nor can its inducements be targeted — they must be broadcast promiscuously in all directions. This produces two important consequences. It creates a class of unfulfilled consumers. And it engenders ambivalence even among those who are in some measure fulfilled — because, as Bauman says, once "the lid has been taken off human desires, no amount of acquisitions and exciting sensations is likely ever to bring satisfaction in the way [that] 'keeping up to the standards' once promised. There are no standards to keep up to, the finishing line moves forward . . . with the runner."[7]

The emergence of this new order has been marked by a steady reduction in the prestige and accessibility of those services that once constituted "the welfare state." (I use the term as a broad designation for the type of state that flowered in the Western democracies after World War II, even where the word wasn't explicitly used.) When the welfare state began it was considered a way of creating the conditions for freedom. In Britain, for example, Aneurin Bevan took the view that the National Health Service would be a "one-off" expenditure. You introduce it, everyone becomes healthy, and you gradually have less and less need of it. "The welfare state," Bauman says, "was thought of as an enabling institution, as a temporary measure to provide a sort of safety cushion for people, so that they know they can dare, they can take risks, they can exert themselves, because there is always this safety provision if they fail."[8] Universality was the essence of this type of state. Everyone contributed, everyone potentially benefited. Today this solidarity has given way to "the polarization between the seduced and the suppressed." Social benefits are increasingly seen as an entitlement to permanent crippling dependency rather than a hand back up for those who have unhappily or unluckily fallen. Collective responsibility has been replaced by individual responsibility. The central figure in what John Kenneth Galbraith calls the "Culture of Contentment" is the long-suffering taxpayer who gives and never gets.[9]

The promise of tax reduction is the hallmark of contemporary conservative regimes. The state has been discredited as a redistributor of wealth; those who once benefited from this redistribution have been redefined as social burdens, whom the contented seek to cast off. Only the repressive function of the state has been strengthened.

Thus, Bauman says, the erosion of the welfare state, the precariousness of the global consumer economy, and the disposability of a certain part of the citizenry all underlie the exuberant growth of prisons in recent years. The new order generates criminality by sealing off socially approved pathways to prosperity and respect. But it also, in a deeper sense, *requires* this criminality. The criminal is the "inner demon" of "the fully fledged and all-embracing consumerist society." Imprisonment casts this demon out. It allows the good citizens, who successfully cling to their jobs and regularly trade in their obsolete cars and computers, to send their own fears and misgivings away to prison with the offender. Like the ancient scapegoat over whose head the priest confessed "all the iniquities of the children of Israel, and all their transgressions in all their sins" and who then carried these transgressions "away . . . into the wilderness" (Leviticus 27:21), the contemporary prisoner takes with him aspects of ourselves and our way of life that the main body of citizens prefers to disguise and disregard. Imprisonment, in this symbolic sense, accomplishes a double end. It locks up behaviours that may be more characteristic of the workaday world than most would like to admit; and it justifies our sticking to the straight and narrow by making the alternative "too awful to contemplate."[10]

The psychological mechanisms of projection and displacement that Bauman identifies are, of course, not new. Where his analysis is original is in its demonstration of the snug fit between our bursting prisons and a chaotic social order that has entrusted justice to the market. Insofar as the new order is actually a disorder, a war of each against each in which there are no overriding allegiances, it gives rise to fears that are consoled by the imprisonment of those who appear disorderly. This explains not just the fantastic rise in imprisonment but also the widespread preoccupation with crime. This preoccupation is expressed in a political concern that has grown out of any proportion to actual registered crime, and in a taste for movies, television programs, and journalistic media that place the same disproportionate emphasis on deviance.

Bauman's demonstration that prison growth is a convenient and necessary element of the new order is fairly cheerless; but there is a more hopeful note in his general analysis of postmodernity. In *Modernity and the Holocaust*, Bauman argues that what was quintessentially modern about the Holocaust was its bureaucratic execution, expressed in the carefully graduated procedures by which a unthinkable evil was domesticated and made routine. It demonstrated that in modern societies "there is no moral-ethical power higher than the state."[11] Before the authority of the state, the moral scruples of otherwise decent individuals systematically gave way. Now, imprisonment is a characteristic institution of the modern state — *the* characteristic institution, Michel Foucault argues in *Discipline and Punish*. Its ability to translate the diverse and heterogeneous acts that constitute "crime" into the uniform arithmetic of prison time makes it part of "the one universal categorical grid" by which Bauman defines modernity. But because the postmodern revolution destroys the ethical monopoly of the state, the legitimacy and moral prestige of the prison will suffer. Why reduce all problematic behaviour to the common denominator of imprisonment? Why put the imaginary insult to the state ahead of the real injury to the victim in the administration of justice? These questions take on a new urgency and plausibility in a postmodern milieu. The institution of imprisonment continues to thrive as a warehouse for unwanted people and a psychological safety valve for an unstable social order; at the same time, its legitimacy is undermined and its counterproductivity made more obvious.

The fading of modernity's power of decisive categorization

permits the reappearance of what was hidden by the ethical monopoly of the state — personal responsibility. "Responsibility," Bauman says, paraphrasing Emmanuel Levinas, can be perceived once again as "the essential, primary, and fundamental structure of subjectivity." Postmodernity thus has a dual aspect; it is "the moral person's bane and chance at the same time."[12] The element of ethical opportunity in postmodernity is evident in the widespread experimentation and rethinking that is currently happening on the fringes of the criminal justice system. Many of the alternatives to imprisonment that I discuss in Part III stress personal accountability over the modern notion of a "debt to society" and thus display postmodernity's more cheerful and promising face. Bauman sets in front of his readers not a fate, but a choice.

The second thinker whose work I want to take up here is Ivan Illich. During a long intellectual career devoted to the study of the influence of tools on their users — taking the term "tools" in the large sense of any engineered means to an end — Illich has developed a distinction between what a tool *does* and what it *says*. A computer, to take a current example, can be used to execute various tasks; but it also generates a symbolic aura within which the user defines his own being as, for example, programmed or system-like. Examining only what prisons *do* throws us back on the apparent paradox of an institution that persists despite overwhelming evidence of its counterproductivity as a means of correcting offenders and protecting public safety. Examining what prisons *say* to society allows us to see that they also function on a symbolic level — and that on this level they may succeed all too well.

Speaking in this symbolic sense, Illich interprets the emergence of "gulags Western-style" as "the creation of an experience . . . characteristic for our time."[13] The prison, first of all, is a "nonplace," often hidden from sight and confronting the surrounding society only as a blank or void. In it are housed nonpersons, who have been stripped of their social identity on admission. There they live a featureless existence, punctuated by bursts of terrifying violence. Such a life is a negative quintessence of what everyone experiences in the abstract and impalpable cyberspace of a globalized society. By distilling this experience the prison also estranges it, making it both absent and present at the same time. Illich illustrates this double function by recalling the stone effigies, or *colossoi*, by which the ancient Greeks made the dead present among the living. These figures were not initially of great size; the sense we give to the word "colossal" derives from later antiquity when the gargantuan Colossus of Rhodes came to be considered one of the seven wonders of the world. The *colossos*, as it was studied by the French anthropologist Jean-Pierre Vernant, was a "double," existing on "two contrasting planes at the same time." It was a sign at once of absence and presence, by which "the dead are made present in the world of the living [and] the living are themselves projected into death."[14] A *colossos* was a gateway at which the absence of what had been present, and the presence of what was absent could be signified. It made an invisible realm visible, linking the living with the underworld, but, through "the tension that is to be found at the very heart of the religious sign," it also symbolized all that was "inaccessible . . . mysterious and . . . fundamentally foreign" about that realm.[15]

Prisons, Illich supposes, face society in the same way. They double social existence, facing us with a form of life that is somehow the same and yet utterly different from the one we live. Imprisonment concentrates the modern experience of placelessness or displacement. But at the same time, it somehow relieves people of this experience, making them feel that it is only the prisoners, the criminals, who suffer this disorientation. This double action is characteristic of religious rituals; and Illich thinks imprisonment, finally, is

> a huge ritual which creates a scapegoat, which we can drive out into
> the desert, believing that by loading onto that scapegoat all that we

experience, we'll get rid of it . . . Prisons are the place in which we can face horror too terrible for us to recognize that we are ourselves immersed in it . . . The existence of prisons makes it possible to transform the entire society into a disembodied, disembodying, meaningless, managed, frontier-less, threshold-less place of people with reasonably limited needs, which will be in some way satisfied for them . . . I'm very sure that, within the next five years, some good anthropologist will present prison as the great religious ceremonial by which our society — I'm not saying becomes livable, but doesn't collapse.[16]

Crime is the foundation on which the ritual of imprisonment rests. But, according to Illich, crime takes on a very peculiar colour in a world beyond good and evil. Good and evil are terms of what Buddhism calls codependent origination — they are mutually defining. Christian tradition, following the rejection of the Gnostic heresies, which conceived evil as an aboriginal substance, has defined evil as the absence of good, the way cold is the absence of heat. Cold is a perfectly real experience — we can freeze to death — but in itself it is only an absence, not a positive quality. Evil too can be deadly, but in relation to the ultimate good, it is secondary. Its only meaning comes from what is missing in it, from what ought to have been present. It has no inherent meaning.

This changes, Illich thinks, when the idea of an ultimate good disappears. For most modern persons, including many who esteem themselves religious, there is no good that human beings have not made and cannot modify at will, no good that transcends and defines us. Without this good there can be no evil in the older sense, either. What faces us is something new, something that confuses us by claiming the old name. Illich calls it "crime without evil." It could equally well be called "evil without good," depending on which sense of the term is used. This new entity fills the vacant cultural space that older ideas of good and evil have left behind them. It allows us to name what horrifies and fascinates us, but it lacks evil's inherent reference to good.

Illich believes that part of the current popular fascination with crime is a new awareness of "evil as an entity." He became aware of this new atmosphere during a conversation with a theologian friend who "professionally watches movies." Illich has not watched movies, out of a desire to avoid the consequences of his being, as he says, "too impressed" by them, but he took seriously the view of his theologian friend that a number of recent films, such as *Natural Born Killers*, represent evil as "the only thing that can be talked about as transcendent." He says:

> I began to reflect on the tremendous danger of the secularization of
> evil as a powerful attractor of attention to something which claims
> transcendence, as the explanation for whatever might lie beyond the
> threshold of our reasoning powers or of the amplitude of our hearts'
> willingness to grasp. This would be a return of evil not as grounded
> in the opposition to good and the absolute good, the ultimate good,
> but evil as an explanatory device for depths of the human soul, which
> we can't fathom.[17]

Fascination with evil as the final frontier once good has been exposed as a pious Platonic fraud is not entirely new. In *Crime and Punishment*, Rodion Raskolnikov, Dostoevsky's sardonic portrait of revolutionary nihilism in Russia in the middle of the nineteenth century, is already shown as passing beyond any possible account of his crime as good or evil into a pure will to power.

> I guessed then . . . that power is given only to him who dares to bend
> down and take it. Only one thing matters, one thing: you just have
> to dare! . . . I decided to *dare* and I killed . . . that was the whole
> reason! . . . I decided . . . to kill someone, to kill without casuistry,
> for myself, for myself alone! I didn't want to lie about this even to
> myself! It wasn't to help my mother that I killed — that's rubbish!
> It wasn't to gain riches and power and become a benefactor to

mankind that I killed. Rubbish! . . . And money wasn't the main thing I needed . . . it wasn't so much money I needed as something else . . . I had to know then and as soon as possible whether I was a louse, like all the rest, or a man. Could I step over, or couldn't I? Dare I bend down and take it or not?[18]

The idea of crime as a daring embrace of truth as power also fascinated Michel Foucault and has been with us in many forms since Dostoevsky wrote. But Illich, I think, has identified a change in scale. Nietzsche is no longer the scandal of the intellectuals but the opiate of the masses, who are bathed in the lurid blue glow of visualized violence at all hours. In a world without good, evil is secularized as crime. Crime then becomes a "powerful attractor of attention to something which claims transcendence, as the explanation for whatever might lie beyond the threshold of our reasoning powers or of the amplitude of our hearts' willingness to grasp."

If the world is without any ultimate good, then we are bound to be fascinated by those who assert themselves as their own lawgivers by stepping outside the ungrounded conventions that hem in the meeker citizens. Evil in the old sense, however dreadful, was finally secondary. Crime, in its incarnation as evil after the death of the good, becomes colossal. This makes it a powerful cultural foundation for the ritual of which Illich speaks.

This point is important, I think, because the criminal justice system is focused almost entirely on guilt and punishment. It may have developed in a metaphysical context in which redemption, as well as revenge, was anticipated; but now, as Dutch criminologist Louk Hulsman has said, "we have lost the reward and only get the punishment."[19] Criminal justice institutions now operate in symbiosis with "crime without evil," strengthening the cultural presence of secular evil even as they erect a bulwark against it. Justice without a sense of the good is darkened. The prison as *colossos* manifests this darkness. It is a religious object in which we can both affirm and deny what our world is like.

Ivan Illich and Zygmunt Bauman, in different ways, reveal within the institution of imprisonment deeper, more involved purposes than are ever hinted at in the sentencing decisions of judges. They solve the riddle of why states claiming to be interested only in cost-effectiveness pursue a costly and ineffective policy; but they also suggest that even the most successful demonstration that imprisonment is, in rational terms, a fiasco will not necessarily loosen the institution's purchase on the popular imagination.[20] The institution of imprisonment, and the philosophy of punishment it enforces, are the products of a long evolution. Their powerful appeal to common sense is grounded not in evidence but in history, and this appeal is heightened all the more by unconsciousness of its symbolic and religious dimensions. It would seem, therefore, that any challenge to the institution of imprisonment must get past its aura in order to discover, first, what it actually does; second, how it got that way; and third, how else crime might be addressed. I tackle the first two of these tasks in Part II, and the third one in Part III.

II

Imprisonment and Society

In my beginning is my end . . . In my end is my beginning.

T. S. Eliot, *East Coker*

5

SOMETHING MUST BE DONE

Rationales for Imprisonment

onfidence in imprisonment as a response to crime constitutes what Thomas Kuhn calls a paradigm, or Joseph Schumpeter a "pre-analytic vision." Schumpeter's term is the more expressive because it indicates what such a structure actually does: it provides the basic shape within which understanding will be organized — not what we are looking at, but what enables us to see it in the first place. This is another reason why rational argument cannot prevail against the conviction that imprisonment is an effective means of crime control. The paradigm itself determines what counts as rationality. Belief in the efficacy of imprisonment is self-validating: a fall in crime proves that imprisonment is an effective deterrent; a rise in crime only shows that we need more punishment to achieve the desired effect.

Four justifications are commonly offered for imprisonment: (1) that it prevents or deters crime; (2) that it incapacitates criminals; (3) that it satisfies the demands of justice by denouncing wrong and giving the offender what he deserves; and (4) that it rehabilitates the offender. References to some, and sometimes all, of these rationales are generally found in the sentences passed by criminal courts. In his 1990 book *Prison on Trial*, Thomas Mathiesen makes a systematic critical survey of the existing research relating to each of these rationales and finds that none of them really stands up under serious scientific scrutiny. In what follows I review Mathiesen's findings in my own words, sometimes supplementing his examples with my own.

Deterrence, the first of the "official" rationales, is supposed to operate on both the imprisoned individual and on society at large: the convict is deterred by the pains of imprisonment, which he doesn't want to suffer again; others are deterred by the spectacle of his suffering. There are several difficulties with this theory. Deterrence implies premeditation, but much of what is punished as crime is either not premeditated at all or not considered in the light of possible punishment. The largest study ever to consider the effect of expected severity of punishment on criminal behaviour was carried out in Germany among more than 1,500 young offenders in the city of Bremen. "The study," as Mathiesen summarizes it, "showed that the expected severity of punishment had no effect on youthful criminal behaviour. Neither . . . had the expectation of youth prison."[1] Similarly, there seems to be no correlation between the severity of a nation's drug laws and its rate of drug consumption. In the United Kingdom harsh penalties do not discourage teenagers from smoking marijuana at one-and-a-half times the rate of those in Spain and the Netherlands, where the drug is decriminalized.[2] Finally, high recidivism rates suggest that the experience of imprisonment deters nearly as little as the prospect, probably because of the habituating and socializing effect of learning to live in a prison.

The idea of deterring society in general runs into two main objections, one moral and one practical. The moral objection to punishing someone in order to frighten someone else is that it treats the person punished as a means rather than an end. This objection grows in force because those who are so used are generally from the poorest and weakest sections of society. The second objection is that the hypothesized effect depends on levels of penalization being clearly communicated — which they generally aren't. What the media present to the public as crime is filtered to remove the routine, unnewsworthy dross, so that what gets through are only the dramatically deviant, and therefore highly unrepresentative, cases. University of Toronto criminologist Anthony Doob in a recent essay draws attention to the decision of a Canadian appeal court to increase the sentence of two female drug mules on the grounds that Canadian society wishes to send a stronger message than the lower court delivered that such behaviour will not be tolerated. Professor Doob found the decision reported on the inside pages of the *Globe and Mail.* Do drug runners, he wondered, generally pay close attention to the *Globe*, or other media in which legal decisions are disseminated?[3] Does someone in Thailand who is presented with an opportunity to make some money transporting illegal drugs really consider the current level of penalization for the offence? Are differences in sentencing levels even detected by those to be deterred? The question answers itself.

Tough sentences are addressed, Mathiesen says, "to the resentments of the righteous" rather than to potential offenders, who see in them only instruments of oppression. Excepting only some minor areas like parking, where penalties do seem to have some effect, the preventive effect of imprisonment is felt only by those who wouldn't have committed serious offences anyway. Reassuring those who obey the law is a real and serious function of imprisonment, but it is misleading to pretend that it constitutes crime prevention.

The second justification for prison, incapacitation, involves constraining future acts. There are cases when this is obviously prudent; but, considered in general, the notion of incapacitation offends fundamental legal principles by punishing people speculatively for things they haven't done yet. Most arguments about the incapacitating effect of prison, and the savings to the state that result from taking malefactors out of circulation, are based on averages. You take the average number of offences per offender per year and assume that the offender, were he at large, would be committing that number of offences. This identifies the individual with a statistical and probabilistic construct of his class. It also understands crime as the doings of a discrete and limited class of criminals, and presumes that once you have caught all the criminals there will be no more crime. But if, as most criminologists would argue, arrest and criminal prosecution is a selection process that culls "crimes" from a vastly larger pool of potentially criminalizable acts, then crime cannot be much reduced by incapacitating criminals. Certain kinds of crime can be interrupted by catching the perpetrator — if a rapist who is terrorizing a district is caught and sent to jail, another rapist will not necessarily step forward right away — but there are many other kinds of criminal activity that cannot be controlled in this way. If a drug seller is sent to jail, another drug seller will be found to take his place; and the same will be true in any other criminal enterprise organized enough to involve planning and recruitment.

The incapacitation of individuals depends on predicting their future dangerousness; and dangerousness, in general, is notoriously hard to predict. Mathiesen cites a statement Nils Christie made to the Norwegian Penal Council in 1974 in which he argued that, while it is possible to predict with a fair degree of accuracy that those who have committed traditional property crimes will do so again, the same is not true of those who have perpetrated more serious and frightening crimes. The more serious the anticipated crime is, the more doubtful is the prediction of its likely occurrence. "It must be stated clearly," Christie wrote, "that today we do not have any sound basis for predicting later dangerous behaviour at all . . . If we want to catch a few dangerous people later, we have to lock up a large group which probably would not have committed anything dangerous at all."[4] To my knowledge, no instruments have been developed in the twenty-three years since Christie wrote these words that make predictions of future dangerousness any more certain.

Mathiesen's review of the literature on incapacitation shows that incarceration, in some cases, has a small incapacitating effect; but he concludes that the gain is generally marginal in relation to the fiscal and moral costs of speculative sentencing.

Giving criminals their "just deserts" is the third of the four common rationales for imprisonment. Classical theories of desert were formulated in the Enlightenment by reformers like Cesare Beccaria in order to curb upper-class power to vary sentences by social standing. A revival of the idea of just deserts was launched by the American Friends Service Committee in a report published in 1971 called *Struggle for Justice: Crime and Punishment in America*. A century and a half earlier, Philadelphia Quakers had pioneered imprisonment as forced penitence at the Cherry Hill Penitentiary; now they argued for the abandonment of rehabilitation and the reinstitution of strictly measured punishment scales based on the seriousness of the offence.

The perceived failure of rehabilitation efforts subsequently led to widespread adoption of this approach. The farce of rehabilitation in an institution inimical to it was to be ended; the diagnostic power of experts was to be curbed; and imprisonment was to be refounded on the bedrock of the offender's own deserving. Unfortunately, as Mathiesen points out, pain and power have no absolute zero point on which fair punishment scales can be founded. Historical variation in the estimated gravity of crimes is immense. Blasphemy was once a capital crime, while many of the sex crimes that today cause the most alarm formerly went unrecognized and unpunished. The perceived seriousness of crimes also changes with the perceiver. Mathiesen's own public opinion studies, for example, show that willingness to punish generally decreases as people learn more about a given case. The more nuanced the question, the more compassionate the answer. Absolute punishment scales imply an omniscient perspective that is unavailable to us.

Mathiesen identifies three key weaknesses in the theory of just deserts. The first is that it is "pseudoscientific," pretending through its rhetoric of proportionality, "punishment values," and objectionability that there is some expert way in which the correct punishment for a given offence can be determined. In this sense, it lets a whole new set of jurisprudential experts in the back door while the therapeutic experts are being shown out the front. Second, as I have already discussed, it implies fixed standards where there are none. And, finally, it depends on the pains of imprisonment being in some sense commensurable with the pain caused by crime. But does one really connect with the other? The complaints that are heard when offenders are released, however long they have been held, suggest that prison time is felt to be an arbitrary exaction that never really pays the debt it is supposed to discharge.

The idea that crime demands and deserves punishment has been advanced by a distinguished philosophical lineage stretching from Socrates to C. S. Lewis. Socrates states in the *Gorgias* that "any . . . man who escapes punishment for his misdeeds must be miserable far beyond all other men"[5]; Hegel calls punishment a right and says that an offender "by being punished . . . is honoured as a rational being"[6]; Simone Weil claims that only just punishment can reinstate someone who has committed a crime within "the chain of eternal obligations which bind every human being to every other one;"[7] and C. S. Lewis adds that it is only as crime's desert that punishment can be called just. In an essay attacking what he calls "the humanitarian theory" that crime demands treatment, not punishment, Lewis writes:

> The Humanitarian theory removes from Punishment the concept of Desert. But the concept of Desert is the only connecting link between punishment and justice. It is only as deserved or undeserved that a sentence can be just or unjust. I do not here contend that the question "Is it deserved?" is the only one we can reasonably ask about a punishment. We may very properly ask whether it is likely to deter others and to reform the criminal. But neither of these two last questions is a question about justice. There is no sense in talking about a "just deterrent" or a "just cure." We demand of a deterrent

not whether it is just but whether it will deter. We demand of a cure not whether it is just but whether it succeeds. Thus when we cease to consider what the criminal deserves and consider only what will cure him or deter others, we have tacitly removed him from the sphere of justice altogether; instead of a person, a subject of rights, we now have a mere object, a patient, a "case."[8]

Simone Weil makes a similar argument in *The Need for Roots*, where she calls deserved punishment one of the soul's vital needs. Crime, Weil says, places an offender outside the web of obligations that constitute society. Punishment alone can reinstate him. In the best case, this occurs with the offender's consent; but the offender's dignity demands, in any case, that the state should attempt to reconcile him to the law by exacting the law's price.

> Sometimes it may be necessary to inflict harm in order to stimulate this thirst before assuaging it, and that is what punishment is for. Men who are so estranged from the good that they seek to spread evil everywhere can only be reintegrated with the good by having harm inflicted upon them. This must be done until the completely innocent part of their soul awakes with the surprised cry "Why am I being hurt?" The innocent part of the criminal's soul must then be fed to make it grow until it becomes able to judge and condemn his past crimes and at last, by the help of grace, to forgive them. With this punishment is completed; the criminal has been reintegrated with the good and should be publicly and solemnly reintegrated with society . . . Punishment is a method of procuring . . . good for men who do not desire it.[9]

Weil then goes on to stipulate the conditions that must be met if this need is to be satisfied and "a feeling of justice" awakened in the offender. It is *not* satisfied where "the penal code is merely a method of exercising pressure through fear"; "where everything connected with the penal law" fails to wear "a solemn and consecrated aspect"; where punishment is stigmatizing rather than de-stigmatizing; where the severity of the punishment is dictated by "the interests of public security" and not by "the kind of obligation that has been violated"; and where the police, the judiciary, and the prison administration fail to display a probity in keeping with their public trust. Punishment, to deserve its name, "must be an honour" and must be proportionate to the social situation of the offender so that "the relative degree of immunity should increase, not as you go up, but as you go down the social scale."[10]

Few, if any, of these stipulations can be met in existing prisons. Prisons tend to be violent, exploitative environments that are not felt to be just by their inmates; the selection of prisoners tends to reflect the distribution of social power as much as the distribution of crime; and the generally accepted reasons for their incarceration, like deterrence, make prisoners an object lesson to other citizens rather than ends in themselves. Instead of extending the greatest leniency to those with the least experience of justice in their lives, criminal courts often treat them the most harshly. It is not the powerful who have abused their trust, but the weakest and most vulnerable who are cast as villains in the morality play the mass media present to society as justice. Imprisonment expresses contempt rather than honour, and those who suffer it are often made less rather than more capable of peaceful social existence. Rather than being welded back into the chain of social obligations and recovering their dignity, they are stigmatized as "losers" and degraded socially.

Weil recognizes that in practice this is how criminal justice operates, and admits that coarseness in the administration of justice, the stigmatization of prisoners, and the lack of due proportion in penalties "all make it impossible for there to exist among us, in France, anything that deserves the name of punishment." Indeed, she goes so far as to say that repressive justice that "stops short with the infliction of harm" is the "one . . . thing in modern society more hideous than crime."

Punishment, then, presents a paradox. According to a philosophical tradition that demands to be taken with the utmost seriousness, punishment is indispensable, inasmuch as there are "men so estranged from the good that they seek to spread evil everywhere." But, on the other hand, according to this same tradition, punishment is just only when it is inflicted in a spirit of disinterested and unsentimental compassion, a spirit likely to appear only exceptionally in penal settings, and rare enough even in families and communities. Whomever you punish becomes your brother, say Moses Maimonides in his *Mishne Torah*.[11] Punishment can function as correction only where there is a committed and consequential relationship. Where and how this condition can be met I discuss in Part III of this book; at this point it is enough to say that it can be met only haphazardly in contemporary prison systems.

The ideal of rehabilitation, the fourth rationale for prison, has lost some of its lustre since its heyday in the 1950s, when C. S. Lewis put forward the critique I cited above. But it remains part of the sometimes incoherent mix of motives for imprisonment. A former head of the csc, John Edwards, has said that he thinks prisons ought to "help [prisoners] learn what it means to have good relationships with other people . . . To the extent possible, we should try and provide an environment similar to what we would like them to have on the outside. In effect we're trying to teach people how to live."[12] This certainly implies a measure of rehabilitation, not just the provision of a decent place to suffer. The problem is that the prison environment tends to counteract and neutralize rehabilitation. This is not to say that no one is ever rehabilitated in prison, just that the prison environment as it stands militates against it. Years ago, the warden of the New Jersey State Penitentiary, Lloyd McCorkle, and his director of education and counselling, Richard Korn, analyzed the prison as a social system in an article called "Resocialization Within Walls." "In many ways," they write, "the inmate social system may be viewed as providing a way of life which enables the inmate to avoid the devastating psychological effects of internalizing and converting social rejection into self-rejection. In effect it permits the inmate to reject his rejectors rather than himself."[13] This states the problem very succinctly. An ostracization as total as imprisonment forces the offender to erect defences that make rehabilitation very difficult.

Finally, Mathiesen points out, rehabilitation implies restoration to a former condition or competence. But many prisoners may never have known a condition of honour or dignity to which they could be restored. Furthermore, almost none of the vast resources society assigns to imprisonment are devoted to the reintegration of released prisoners; nor do any rituals mark the restoration of their former status. The stigma remains after the jail is left behind, and the ex-prisoner is always aware of the mark he carries.

This brief review of the four official mandates of imprisonment shows fairly conclusively, I think, that they do not justify the institution. What these mandates do, rather, is provide a cover under which the prison fulfills its less palatable ideological purposes. Mathiesen lists five such purposes: Prison is expurgatory — unwanted people are housed, controlled, and forgotten. It is "power-draining" — feared people are deprived of standing. It diverts attention from big crimes to little ones. It enacts a symbolic drama in which prisoners take on the sins of the good citizens. And, finally, it announces that Something Is Being Done. These ideological functions are important, but hard to face squarely, so they are sheltered from direct attention by the pretense that imprisonment fulfills its official purposes. The public is not told that imprisonment, practically speaking, is a fiasco. Politicians and professionals within the criminal justice institutions avert their eyes, or at least keep quiet in public, because of the price they can be made to pay for seeming to be "soft on crime." The media complete the picture by supplying a steady stream of dramatically unrepresentative vignettes.

Implicit in these unofficial ideological functions of imprisonment are a number of unintentional and often unacknowledged side effects. These arise from the tension between the prison as a useful symbol and the prison as a real social environment in which inmates have to live and staff have to work. Impounding the helpless, the hopeless, the deranged, and the depraved all together in one barren place inevitably creates a powerful, unintended synergy. But judges' sentencing decisions, or politicians' promises to crack down on crime, tend to project an ideal version of the institution and look away from the actual effects that living in prison has on prisoners. They overlook the way the institution abandons the offender to a dog-eat-dog world in which he is apt to form new criminal associations, become further habituated to violence, increase his dependency on external controls, and therefore become even less fit to live in society than he was before. It is this real world of imprisonment that I examine in the next chapter, beginning with an account of one Canadian prison career.

6

THE REAL WORLD
OF IMPRISONMENT

In the fall of 1995, I attended a conference at McMaster University's divinity school called "Crime and Its Victims: A Christian Response." There I met Jim Cavanagh and was intrigued to learn that the courteous and mild-mannered man with whom I was conversing had once been, according to the person who introduced us, "the meanest man in prison" and had served altogether twenty-five years in Canadian penal institutions. Today he's the director of the Kingston chapter of Prison Fellowship Canada, a nondenominational ministry to prisoners and ex-prisoners. I later visited him in Kingston, and he told me his story.

Cavanagh was born in Halifax. His father was "a good provider," but he was also an alcoholic, and when he was drunk, Cavanagh says, "he would beat on my mother, and I would start running the streets to find the hospital where my mother was."[1] He learned to steal food and panhandle for money in order to survive. When he was eight years old he was sexually molested by someone whom he thought had befriended him. "I withdrew more," he says, "and I wouldn't tell anyone and I would strike out at things in society. I'd vandalize cars, I'd vandalize homes that I would break into and steal food from."

By age ten he was in the Shelburne School for Boys, one of the three Nova Scotia reform schools now facing more than 1,250 claims for past physical and sexual abuse. He recalls:

In the reform school, there were adults who were supposed to look after me, give me guidance and help correct me and put me on the right path. But what I learned was that all there was in the reform school was physical abuse, psychological abuse, and sexual abuse. And this hardened me and I withdrew . . . The only ones I associated with and felt I was accepted by were others who were hurting like me. So, then we would form a nucleus and . . . encourage one another and strike back at authority . . . It was a vicious circle. Society's answer to it was just lock them up and punish them. What they were really doing was taking a problematic child and saying we'll warehouse this boy for X number of years in a prison under harsh conditions, and that should change him. Well, it doesn't. It doesn't change anyone. It hardens them worse . . . So, I ended up becoming a career criminal, and I ended up becoming one who didn't care for myself. I hated myself. I hated everyone else, and I felt life wasn't worth living . . . I just gave up.

As a teenager Jim Cavanagh escaped from the reform school, and, while he was out, committed a series of automobile thefts. He was arrested, raised into adult court, given three concurrent three-year sentences, and sent off to the federal penitentiary in Dorchester, New Brunswick, at the age of only fifteen.

When I was being driven up in the car, the one policeman said, "Kid, they'll fix you up there. They'll use you as a woman." And so forth. And he was trying to frighten me. And my response to him was, "The first one bothers me, I'll kill him." But I was scared. Then I started settling in to the prison, and the first prisoner that did stroke my hair and say, "You're a cute kid," and that, I smashed him in the head with a chair. It was in a classroom, and we got in a fight. I poked another guy with a wire that I had made to a point at one end. And the word spread that that kid won't take it, so if you're going to deal with him, you're going to get hurt unless you're going to hurt him first. And others looked at me then and sort of took a liking to me and said, "That kid's got a lotta spunk. He's fighting for himself."

At Dorchester, Cavanagh fell in with men from the Montreal area who taught him "how to safecrack and plan and execute armed robberies." He was in and out of prison several times. During one hiatus, he was able to get a job as freight handler in a dairy factory.

> Then a policeman whom I had had a run-in with earlier in my childhood found out I was working there. He told the employer and he had me laid off and fired. And I had been happy. I wasn't doing any crime or anything when I was working. I felt self-worth. The paycheque was low, but I was happy and I was getting by. My father said, "Well, you'll get another job." And I said, "It'll be the same thing all over again. I've had it." So then I went back to the streets. I picked up the gun, and I went back to that sort of life.

Eventually, during a robbery in Montreal, Jim Cavanagh shot and wounded a police officer, for which he received a fifteen-year sentence. He escaped and was recaptured, which lengthened the sentence. Eventually he ended up in the Special Handling Unit at Millhaven Institution in eastern Ontario. This was in the early 1970s, and Millhaven was then a new maximum security institution, built to house many of Canada's most dangerous prisoners. There, in 1975, he killed a fellow prisoner.

> He was sexually imposing himself on another young prisoner, who I knew, and when I found out about it, I approached him and I asked him to leave the guy alone. I said the guy had enough to do with serving his sentence, and it isn't right, what you're doing. He mouthed off to me and got very abusive. I won't use the language here. And he got off his bed, and he reached into his locker, where a weapon was and he tried to intimidate or threaten me with this weapon. And that made me angry and upset, and I wanted to get into an altercation with him right then and there, but in the back of my mind, I said just wait. And I backed out of the cell, and I let it go for a while.

And then I finally decided after I seen he was still bothering the person. I went and got a weapon and I came back. I confronted him. I gave him the opportunity to say, "Okay, I'm sorry for what I said to you. I'll leave him alone." His choice was, "No, I'm going to do what I feel like I want to do, and that's it." And I said, "That's too bad." And I pulled out my knife, and we got into it and I did kill the man.

When I reflect back on it years later, as a changed person, I believe that I was taking out on him what I couldn't take out on others who perpetrated themselves on me when I was younger. And it's sad because, like, there was nobody to come and claim his body. He had no family members. Nobody. And when I reflect that this man had a messed-up life, like I did, I think it was unfortunate that we locked horns. Due to my anger and his anger, we got into that altercation and I killed him. It's sad.

Years later, Jim Cavanagh was converted to Christianity. It began with a visit from a friend, an ex-prisoner and ex-bank-robber called Ernie Hollands, who had written to say he had "changed his life." Cavanagh says that he could see the change in his friend, and so he agreed to pray for him. Then, one night in 1978, he said a simple prayer for himself and experienced "a warmth that went through my body . . . and shook me up." These experiences continued with tears that were "like a cleansing inside of me."

I knocked on the steel-lined wall and talked to my friend Eddie in the next cell. I said, "Eddie, let me share with you what I experienced." And I told him. And he said, "Jimmy, are you going sideways on us?" In other words, crazy. And I said, "No, Eddie," I said, "I'm not going crazy." I said, "You've known me for years. I'm serving nineteen years federally. I'm under the Lieutenant-Governor's General Warrant for the Province of Ontario" — which is an indeterminate sentence — "I'll probably die in prison here." I said, "You've known me for years." And I said, "I'm in the Special Handling Unit here in

Millhaven and will be for the next three years. Then they'll send me to some maximum somewhere. Do I have anything to gain by lying to you?" And he said, "No, you don't, Jim." I says, "I don't understand it all, Eddie, but there is a spiritual reality that is there. It's for real. I've experienced something," I said, "I believe." And that's when my walk of faith began.

About a year and a half after his conversion, Jim Cavanagh suffered an aneurysm, which left him paralyzed and confined to a wheelchair. He was told he would never walk again, but he forced himself out of his wheelchair in the yard at the Collins Bay Penitentiary, and today he walks with only a cane. He applied for parole, was denied three times, and then was finally released.

Some guard staff and some prisoners apparently made the statement, "Oh, yeah, Jim Cavanagh's got his parole now. He'll lay his Bible down and you won't hear anything more about it." There was one guard who said, when I was going in through the security clearance at one prison, "Jim, keep doing what you're doing. I'm pleased with what you're doing." And he said, "A lot of individuals bet that you wouldn't last six months." And he said, "I took them up on that bet." And he says, "I made big." So, I said, "Well, good for you." And I said, "Well, it's sincere." And I said, "If it wasn't, I would have no reason to come back to the prison." Believe me, when I was approached to go back into the prisons, I didn't want to go back. There's no way I wanted to go back in those prisons, but the motivating factor is my heart goes out to those who are hurting inside.

Out of this sense of obligation, Jim Cavanagh has built a ministry to prisoners and ex-prisoners in the Kingston area. Between his years as an inmate and his years as a chaplain, he's known the institution of imprisonment all his life. He thinks of it, he says, as a way of putting problems off and, thereby, often making them worse. Troublesome people are temporarily gotten out of the way, but only by impounding them in an environment in which they are isolated from the consequences of their acts and in which they must further harden their hearts just to survive. This is not to say that people don't sometimes change in prison — Cavanagh's own story attests to it, and so do many others. But such changes result from remorse, or faith, or an experience of friendship. It is not the prison as such that produces penitence. Consequently Cavanagh thinks that most of the people currently in prison ought to be held to account for their actions outside prison walls. Nothing stands in the way, he says, but prejudice.

> In all the prisons across Canada, there's only a handful in each prison that need to be detained behind the walls. The rest of them can be out in some sort of community-work programs or some alternative things. They don't need to be warehoused. But the thing is you're in a dilemma. You have a lot of people in society who are angry over a lot of issues, so when crime comes into the picture, they're just saying, "Lock 'em up and throw the key away; lock 'em up, throw the key away." And they don't realize that by using that stance and that attitude, they're compounding and escalating crime in Canada. They're making it worse. Instead of saying, "Hey, I'm the taxpayer. What is being done to change these individuals and make them responsible for their actions? And what's being done to help the victim monetarily, and also to restore a relationship between the victim and the offender to find out, hey, why did you do this to me?"
>
> And believe you me, if you talk to a lot of individuals that are in prison for victimizing people on the street, they would rather do anything than face their victim. They'd rather work on a rock pile and break rocks all day than go and face the victim or the family of the victim. And to me, that should be part and parcel of the response to crime. We need to help people to change, first off, and to realize that, yes, there are problem cases but still to ask, "What is the problem making them act out in the way they are? What's led up to this?" And second off, making them accountable, not just warehousing them and saying, "That's your penalty, you're being warehoused."

As I discussed in the previous chapter, the idea that prison is a deterrent presumes that people will refrain from committing crimes in order to avoid the painful experience of imprisonment. But those who are warehoused become habituated and adapted to the institution, and the painful effect of the experience wears off. Pierre Allard, head of chaplaincy for the CSC, says that deterrence might work if offenders were put in prison for a few shocking and fearful days, then had the remainder of their sentence suspended on condition of good behaviour. Doug Call, the former sheriff of Genesee County in northern New York State (from whom you'll hear more in Part III), says that in his experience deterrence works only so long as the threat and shame remain imagined. Once you have been to jail, you have already been stigmatized; and, if you are there long, you have to learn to live there.

Prison is the world of those who feel themselves to have been rejected and ostracized. For this reason, it tends to develop a defensive counterculture — it is an upside-down world, a demonic parody of conventional society in which the rules are reversed. On the way to Dorchester Prison at age fifteen, Jim Cavanagh had to make a conscious and, in terms of his situation, rational decision: if he was to preserve some kind of personal integrity and avoid being exploited and degraded, he would have to become so wild, dangerous, and unpredictable that other prisoners would leave him alone. His decision about how to live in prison was a product of a clear-eyed analysis of his situation — but it also set up a vicious circle that kept him coming back again and again.

According to Monty Lewis, prisons and the world of crime they anchor must be understood as counterfeit communities: a place to belong for people who have not belonged anywhere else. Lewis, like Jim Cavanagh, became a Christian in prison, and today directs the Cons for Christ Prison Ministry in Fredericton, New Brunswick. He has published, along with writer Joanne Jacquart, an autobiography titled *The Caper*, which he gives away as part of his ministry; there are now more than 200,000 copies in circulation. It relates his rebellion against a father who beat up his mother and his descent into the world of alcohol, drugs, crime, and prisons. Many other prisoners, he thinks, can tell a different version of the same story: a futile and doomed search for

the love, acceptance, and discipline that they never had at home. I was told by the most important man in my life I'd never amount to anything, I couldn't be depended upon to do anything, and I'd never be any good for anything. If you can't believe your dad, I don't know who you can believe; so, I went out, and I found a place where I believed I was loved and where I believed there was a value system, because the code of the street and the prison is a value system. I was accepted, and there was a certain amount of discipline there, because you always had to watch out for the police in the activities I was doing. And there is also a hierarchy in the criminal world. I found a place where the crazier I was and the more violent and aggressive, the more recognition I got. I didn't realize that at the time. I'm looking back now in hindsight and seeing how totally blind I was.

You see, the thing about being deceived is, when you're deceived, you don't know you're deceived. And I didn't know I was deceived all those years. But all the while, I was getting accepted, I was growing in the hierarchy of that kind of life, people were looking up to me. I would deal drugs, I was popular, I wore the earring, the high leather boots, the leather coat. And all of those things, I thought, were love. I thought they had value to them. I was accepted and I needed to be accepted. And I went around, like so many in those days, saying, "Well, what you see is what you get, and this is the real me." So, they seemed to be accepting me for what I was. And because I didn't know the real thing at home, I settled for second best.

And I'll tell you: One day I was looking out of the window of my apartment. Lots of drugs, money, music playing, a friend with me. I saw a man and woman walking up the street, and I vaguely knew them and I knew they didn't have very much materially. They had a couple of children. And they were laughing and smiling. And I was looking out the window at them, with a few hundred dollars in my pocket and a few hundred dollars' worth of drugs in my arm, and I said to whoever was with me, "Why are they so happy, when they don't have half as much as I have?" And he said to me, "I hope you don't think they're like that when they get home, because he probably beats his wife and locks the children in the closet." And because that was the only definition I knew of life, I thought, yeah, that must be true for everyone. And so I continued to live that way, and the people I lived with continued to live that way, and what we thought was normal I see today as very abnormal.[2]

Monty Lewis, as he portrays himself in *The Caper*, was a man full of wild rage who left a trail of broken heads and broken bones right across Canada. His career in crime came to an end in 1977, when a brigadier of the Salvation Army visited him in the hole of the London Detention Centre and introduced him to "the One that took me, when I believed that I could never amount to anything, and changed my entire life."[3] The next few years showed him how difficult it can be to change directions.

I wanted to work, but I didn't know how to work, because for thirty-three years of my life, I really had only worked a total of probably eleven months. I was a drug addict for eleven and a half years, put a needle in my arm. I drank alcoholically from the time I was four and a half years of age. What I did for a living was fraud and deal drugs and run bootlegging houses and steal and really try and support a habit.

So, when you went for a job application and were asked, "Where have you lived the last five years?" Well, Bath Institution, Kingston Penitentiary, London Detention Centre, Dorchester Penitentiary, Westmoreland Prison. Every employer is just waiting to have someone like that fill out an application form. "Also list the type of work you've done the last five years." Well, I ran speed houses, bootlegging cans, forgery operations, wrote prescriptions for drugs I was using at the time, stole and robbed all across Canada. Every employer is just dying to get hold of someone like that.

So, these were some of the things I was up against when I came out of prison. I had changed. I knew I had changed. I had a desire not to go back to prison. But in order not to go back to prison, I needed a job, I needed support in the community, I needed a place to live. All of my old friends lived back in the east ends of the cities, with drugs and alcohol. And they're fine people, but they couldn't help me do what I knew I wanted to do.

Monty Lewis got the help he needed from a couple from Belleville, who visited the Kingston Penitentiary as volunteers for Alcoholics Anonymous. They took him into their home when he was released. Another AA connection in Belleville provided a construction job. At first, he says, he hated the hard work, and was so programmed by prison life that he would fall asleep on his shovel at 11:30 in the morning, the hour at which the prison had "locked down" for an hour and a half. He stuck with it, however, and eventually graduated to a much better-paying job at Canada Cement Lafarge in Bath. Later, he married and had children; but, through all this, he never forgot the friends he had left behind in prison, or lost a desire to share his newfound freedom with them. He began visiting prisons and taking prisoners on weekend passes into his home. Jim Cavanagh was one of his first such guests.

Eventually his ministry occupied so much of his time that he quit his job and made his prison work his full-time occupation. Later he and his wife, Lynda, moved their family to Fredericton, where Cons for Christ is based today. They help released prisoners to re-establish themselves in the community, and they look after the wives and children of those who are inside. A recent project is a summer camp for the children of inmates. The camp's cottages were prefabricated by inmates at Renous prison.

Imprisonment, Lewis believes, is part of a culture. He remembers the greeting of an older man when he first arrived at Dorchester Penitentiary: "So, Monty, you finally made it." By the time he got there, he already knew how to live in prison because he had already adopted the inverted ideals that guide prisoners' conduct. Prisons reflect and reinforce these upsidedown ideals by forcing inmates to live on terms of violence, denial, and dependence. This is why people, once incarcerated, so often return; they've adapted to that culture. "If you realize you're going to come back to prison," Lewis says, "you have to come back as a person that can fit back into the system and fit back in with the people that you're going to live with." It's not that people want to live in prison; Lewis himself recalls looking out of his barred window at Dorchester on Christmas Eve, the gentle snow falling, the smoke curling up from the roofs of the houses in the Memramcook Valley down below, and vowing never to return — only to find himself back again the following Christmas. He just couldn't break "the thinking he had" and the associations that reinforced this thinking.

Prison becomes a habit that's hard to break. It removes from people who are poor at making decisions the need to make any decisions at all. In prison you don't even open the door for yourself. A recent houseguest of Lewis's, just out after a long period of imprisonment, even left car doors open once he had climbed out. Lights and hot water were never turned off. The practical details of life — bills, licences, applications, certificates, and forms — can seem insurmountable to former inmates. Public spaces make them feel conspicuous. Mennonite pastor Harry Nigh recalls going to meet a young man just out of the maximum security provincial prison at Millbrook, Ontario.

> I met him in the West End of Toronto. He was having breakfast at this restaurant. There he was at the very back of the room, at the back of the restaurant, in this greasy spoon, his back against the wall. I mean, that would be common because you wouldn't want to have your back exposed to people. And he looked so scared. And I went up to him, and I said, "How's it going?" He said, "I'll tell ya, I sort of miss my cell."

They feel, as soon as they walk out, that everybody knows them. I've been with guys on their first day out, and they seem like they have to explain to people, "I just got out of jail." They feel that it's written all over them, that they are like lepers coming out and they still have the spots.[4]

When he came out, Monty Lewis says, "I thought everybody was looking at me. I believed everybody knew where I came from, and I was full of guilt and shame, because I, like most of the men in prison, was ashamed of the things I'd done."

Prison keeps the offender out of society at the cost of disabling him for life in society. For fourteen years between 1973 and 1987, Harry Nigh was the Ontario director for Man to Man, Woman to Woman (M2W2), an initiative of the Mennonite Central Committee intended to build friendships between isolated prisoners and people on the outside. He says that anyone who enters a prison "with an open heart" will be aware of a powerful pathos. He himself made many friends in prison, and he told me of one man whom he had particularly loved for whom he thought prison was "almost like an addiction."

Prison for him was a place of rescue when the outside world got a little bit too heavy, and he would do the stupidest things just to go back in . . . He even had the judge laughing once, when he told him how he was walking down the street, all drunked up, and his elbow hit the window of a jewellery store and a tray of jewels slid into his pocket. On one level, he didn't want to go back in because he was ashamed and he considered it a sign of his being a loser. But, on another level, prison was a place where he felt he belonged.[5]

Prison, rough as it is, can provide those who have learned to live there with a community, an order, and an anchor.

I think people often subconsciously choose prison, particularly people who have grown up in a culture in which prison has been sometimes seen as a mark of coming of age . . . A lot of . . . men that I've known know the routine, they know the fact that they're going to be fed. There's even the security of the regular counts and so on so that they live in this kind of polarity of hating prison, of not wanting to be a loser, but, on the other hand, when life's pressures build up, particularly when a relationship goes sour, this is one oasis really.

What is tragic about this, for Harry Nigh, is how barren this oasis is.

To be most profoundly human is to be able to love and to be able to feel, to be personal, and those are the things which get deeply buried in prison. Every prison, in my experience, has a consistency of feel. There's a certain kind of consistent role-playing that happens as soon as you go in, that happens with people holding keys and other people wearing prison garb. It seems to me that, as soon as that dynamic is set up, you've got something happening which is dehumanizing. When you have the dynamic of keeper and kept, you have an underlying destruction of the human soul even in the best situations. I'm not a prison abolitionist, but I notice that that is something which happens.

I remember one guard telling me, "When I come in here" — he was a guard at Millbrook Correctional Centre — "When I come in here in the morning, I turn my feelings off." I'll never forget that statement . . . The incidence of personal devastation in the lives of staff has been well documented. Alcoholism and the kind of social devastation that happens to staff is just as severe as it is for prisoners . . . I had staff who were friends of mine. We had correctional officers on our board of directors, for example. I remember listening in tears to one man who was a guard at a prison talking about the suspicion with which other guards treated him because he wasn't hard enough. There's no healing.[6]

The suffering of prison staff is not normally included when the costs of imprisonment are reckoned up. Locking people up gets trouble out of the way, at least temporarily; but the trouble doesn't actually disappear by being put out of sight and out of mind; it's just put in a new place, where someone else has to deal with it. This is what is asked of Canada's various correctional services and their front line, the prison guards. They bear the scars of imprisonment as surely as their prisoners.

Jeff Doucette is a correctional officer and a former head of the Emergency Response Team at the maximum security Millhaven Institution in eastern Ontario. He started there in 1985, after six years in the maximum security federal prison in Edmonton. The emergencies to which his team were called ranged from removing unwilling inmates from their cells — cell extractions, these were called — all the way to full-scale riots. He estimates that, during his sixteen-year career, he has been involved in quelling at least a dozen major riots and smash-ups in which part of the prison had to be retaken from the inmates. He has been exposed to suicide and torture and more murders than he can remember. Eventually the violence and the horror that he'd seen began to take its toll, and in May of 1995 he had to stop work. His bloody memories would no longer give him any rest or any relief. He is now being retrained in the computer field. We met in Kingston at the end of 1995, and he related some of the events that finally made it impossible for him to go on.

> We had an incident: an officer had his throat cut by an inmate. The officer opened the door, and this inmate, my understanding is, had a razor blade melted into a toothbrush. And as soon as the officer stepped out, the inmate just cut his throat and the officer almost died. I was the team leader of the team that went in to take the inmate out afterwards. It was a fairly clean cell extraction. Everything was videotaped. And the last thing I said to my people going in was, "We don't go to court, we're not going to hurt this person." We took him out, and I guess the part that always comes back to me is kneeling in this officer's blood to handcuff this guy. The next time

you go for a response, it's the same coveralls, it's the same boots, and the blood is still on the boots but you're busy with another one.

One other one was a really violent murder: the inmate had his hands tied behind his back and his feet tied together. He was trapped in a cell by another inmate, and he was stabbed forty-two times. Another officer was just starting his range walk, and he heard the screams and went down. And, of course, you can't open a door by yourself, especially if there's two inmates and one has a knife and he stood and watched the whole murder. And there was just nothing he could do to stop it. I can remember going into J-Unit, and as soon as the barrier opened I could smell the blood. And then I got to the corner of 1-K, and this inmate that had been murdered had been taken out into the corridor, a narrow corridor, and it was just pure blood. Probably twenty feet. This inmate had lost everything in that corridor. And to get to the staff, which was the reason I was there, I had to walk through this. Then I got there and saw the looks on the faces of the staff there. I can still remember walking around the corner and looking at one fellow I had worked with for years. He's a friend — and he's got that thousand-yard stare, and, you just know, he's lost. You don't know if you can get him back. We spent till five o'clock in the morning talking to all the staff that were right on site, and I spent till five in the morning talking to this one officer. Even today he's affected by that.

. . . You try and put [these things] away, you try and keep distracted, you try and keep busy, you try and do a lot of things. But for myself, the best way I can describe it is that, at its worst, you're waking up with nightmares. I used to have this film that played. It was like I was watching a screen in front of me, and I'd be talking to you, and it would be through all these bodies and blood and situations. And these played non-stop, fifteen years of them. And you can't function all that long. You sleep two hours a night, because the nightmares are bad, and when you wake up you just sit and smoke cigarettes or something, because you're not going back to sleep. That's just not an option at the time, right? It's easier to be awake, I guess. And it doesn't take too long before you're exhausted.

Thank God, I've got a really supportive wife. I don't know how she's stuck with me through this, but, thank God, she has. When you come home with this stuff and someone says, "Well, how was your day?" you can't talk about it. And if you try and talk to your wife or your spouse, you know, they're not going to understand it. So, you just sit there and you just go, "I know I'm having a problem with this, I don't think anybody else is, because no one else is showing it." So, you withdraw and you just push them away. Then there's guilt feelings, because you're not handling it well, you're not communicating. Depression's a big part of it a lot of the time.

We went to Ottawa, and my wife calls it "Our Tenth Anniversary in Hell." It was right in the midst of all this stuff. And I can remember in the midst of that, telling her, "I think it would be easier if I just walked away right now, because I can see the pain I'm causing. I don't know why I'm causing it, it's just there, and it would just be easier if I just walked away." Which devastated her. And friends? Well, friends don't really understand either, do they? Let's say you get involved in a situation at work where maybe you've used force, or it's been really bloody or there's been a murder and whatever. You come home, and, no, you don't want to go to the mall; no, you don't want to drop over to the Jones's for the evening. Your mind's just in a whole different spectrum.

And the worst problem is that, when you've worked there ten, fifteen, twenty years, whatever, you take that as normal. That's your normal daily fare. I've had a chance to sit back and look at it, and it's not normal . . . At the end of it, my doctor booked me off. I was pumping adrenalin twenty-four hours a day, severely depressed, just nonfunctional. I spent a lot of time with a really good psychologist, who explained to me about post-traumatic stress disorder, and I was given a lot of homework to do on it. When I started reading the material, it was like looking in the mirror. I thought, "There's a name for this. Thank God."

There's people in institutions you don't walk up behind and touch, because they turn around fighting, and that's just the startle response. And I was like that. You're wired all the time. You can't get down. And it goes right to the point where you're numb inside. If you don't numb out to this stuff after the years, you don't live with it, I guess. I've talked to officers who'll say without any emotion, "Well, my little girl fell down and broke her arm," just like, oh, it's another situation, let's get on with it. So, you numb out, but I guess the side effect is that it carries over to your family and friends and to everybody else.[7]

Jeff Doucette was not your average prison guard. He had one of the toughest jobs in what might be Canada's toughest prison. But he thinks that there are plenty of other officers who've been through something like what he experienced, and he thinks that too many of them have felt that they had to deny or suppress their suffering. He's now trying to do something about that in the Kingston area by setting up groups in which guards can talk out the things that have happened to them. In one such group, for officers from the Collins Bay Penitentiary, he found that a number of his colleagues were still preoccupied by an incident that occurred more than fifteen years ago.

In 1978, there were two staff members killed. My understanding was one of them was pretty well decapitated. They were just very ugly murders, and a lot of staff were involved. Some of those staff members are drinking themselves to death, some are just in complete denial, some are suffering from severe depression. I don't know how many marriages have broken up. There are just a lot of ramifications from that event, and they're still ongoing. They don't go away.

And I think one of the reasons they don't go away goes back to what post-trauma is. It's an event that overwhelms you, but it's not recorded in regular memory. It goes into an adrenalin-based, chemically based memory. And the only way you can get rid of that is to integrate it back into regular memory, and there's a few processes that can do that. The group format is very, very powerful. It's just people sharing common experience. That takes the pressure off. And it's interesting: you sit there with a peer, and you say, "Well, this is how I felt, and that scared the hell out of me." And they go, "I thought I was the only one that was scared." And you start to take the power away from the situation.

I know with one group that we were running, at the start of the group, those individuals talked very seriously about how they'd contemplated suicide because it didn't seem like there was any other way out of what they were feeling. When we started off, there were people sweating, they were wringing their hands and just very, very tense. And at the last meeting I was at, they were sitting back and laughing and relaxed. The black humour was gone. It was just peers sitting down that had done something together. You could see the difference in the people. And one thing I'd like to say about these people is, if they didn't care, it wouldn't mean anything. If they didn't care how they did their job, if they didn't care about other people, if they didn't care about a lost life, then it wouldn't mean anything, would it? So, it's the officers that care that generally run into a lot of problems, depending on what they get involved in.[8]

Canadian prisons are violent places — unusually violent places, even for prisons. One CSC study in 1990 found that, when compared to forty American states, Canada's federal prisons had the highest seven-year mean rate of prisoner suicide and the fourth-highest rate of homicide.[9] (Comparisons to European jurisdictions are even more unfavourable.) Prisoners in Canada's jails are also frequently victimized by other inmates. The *Canadian Journal of Criminology* reported a survey of criminal victimization involving 117 male federal prisoners at all three security levels. Nearly 42 percent of the respondents reported having been personally victimized at least once in the last year, and more than 60 percent of these incidents involved physical assault.[10]

Both these studies were carried out by sociologist Dennis Cooley. They form part of a larger work, called "Social Control and Social Order in Male Federal Prisons," which Cooley submitted to the University of Manitoba as his doctoral thesis in sociology in 1995. The question of how prisons actually work fascinated sociologists publishing between the 1940s and the early 1960s — Gresham Sykes's 1958 *The Society of Captives* is a classic example — but in recent decades critical criminology has focused much more on the social significance of imprisonment. Foucault's influential *Discipline and Punish*, for instance, was much more interested in the prison as the archetypal modern institution than as an actual working society. Cooley has tried to revive the tradition of empirical study by undertaking what he believes to be the only recent extensive broad-scale academic research in Canadian prisons.

One of his most interesting findings is that the famous "inmate code" no longer functions in quite the way it was once supposed to do. The inmate code, as reported by Gresham Sykes and Sheldon Messinger in 1960, consisted of five maxims that maintained "honour among thieves": (1) Don't interfere with others. (2) Refrain from arguments. (3) Don't exploit inmates. (4) Don't weaken. (5) Don't give respect to guards or the world they represent.[11] Sykes and Messinger found that this code, while not accepted by all, did tend to enhance solidarity and reduce violence among people whose rejection of external control and lack of internal control could easily result in a war of each against each. Yet Cooley says that in the prisons he studied he found no evidence that most prisoners subscribed to this code. What he found instead was a set of "informal rules of social control," only partially overlapping the old inmate code. He formulates these rules as follows: (1) Do your own time (mind your own business). (2) Avoid the prison economy. (3) Don't trust anyone. (4) Show respect. The inmate code emphasizes solidarity; Cooley's rules show a tendency towards isolation and atomization, as well as towards cohesion. They create an environment that he characterizes as "partially unstable." "The prison," he says, "is neither in a constant state of turmoil nor in accord."

The prison's partial instability is reflected in what Cooley calls "an overwhelming lack of loyalty and solidarity among the prison population." Many of his informants attributed this feature of prison life to the prevalence of "ratting," or informing on other prisoners. Cooley leaves moot the question of whether the CSC as a matter of conscious policy relies on informants as a way of maintaining control of its prisons, and also sets aside as undecidable the question of how different it actually was in the "old days"; but he reports statement after statement from older inmates indicating their belief that prisoner solidarity has broken down. Here are several:

> I thought I came back to a solid prison, but this place is loose. There are too many PC [protective custody] cases and they think they can get out by rolling over someone — which is true! They get out of here faster, they get to camp [minimum security] faster. Guys like me who admit what they did but don't want to make anyone else's life worse don't get out. They don't need to approach inmates, [the inmates] go to them. But a lot of people are stupid enough to let other inmates know stuff about themselves . . . Then they run straight to the administration.

> In the old days you knew where you stood. Guards and inmates all stood behind each other. You either stood with us or you didn't. Now you don't know these things. You get into a beef and the guards don't see. The next day there are twenty kites [messages sent to the administration] because guys want to go to camp [minimum security] or on a day parole . . . That's how they run the place.

> . . . "Don't talk to the man" doesn't apply any more. There is heavy controversy over the code. Being in a medium [security prison], you have to participate in programming. You can't really live by the code because if you do you won't get parole . . . In here staff have to break down the code or they couldn't run the prison — divide and conquer.[12]

Inmates gave different explanations of what had happened. Some pointed to a change in the character of convicts, saying that "true criminals" had been increasingly replaced by a totally different breed whose offences were related to drugs and who neither knew nor respected the old rules. Others stressed the administration's role in breaking down prisoner solidarity by rewarding and protecting informants. But there was a wide consensus that something had changed.

The "solid" prison of yesteryear, to the extent that it existed, was not necessarily a good place. The old code disguised crime as class war and blocked rehabilitation by denying the legitimacy of punishment. It dealt with the crushing rejection imprisonment represents by turning the tables on "the man." The new order represents a gain in control by the administration, but aggravates instability in the prison. This instability is in turn reflected in the high rates of victimization found in Canadian prisons. As far as much of the public is concerned, this is of no importance, since criminals, by definition, can deserve no sympathy as victims; but it nevertheless raises the question of whether convicts can really be expected to give up violence, denial, and mistrust of the good in an insecure and exploitative environment where they are undefended against violence themselves. Prison officials can make a sincere effort to improve this environment; some prisoners will reform in spite of it; but its fundamental features persist. So, in the end, we have to face the question: What can we reasonably expect from such a place but more crime?

7

GOD IS HIMSELF LAW

I argued in the previous chapter that imprisonment fails to fulfill its assigned mandates and generates costly and undesirable side effects. The obvious next question is: How did such an institution come to monopolize the social response to crime? I propose two tentative answers to this question. The first is that, in modern societies, infractions of the criminal law have come to be seen primarily as violations of the good order of society, rather than as violations of persons. Such infractions therefore demand exemplary punishment, rather than such forms of penitence and restitution as might mollify the victims, make good their injuries, and allow the offender a practical means of rehabilitation. The second is that imprisonment during the last two hundred years has become so completely synonymous with deserved punishment that any other response seems like temporizing with evil, and trivializing the harm that has been done. In the next chapter, I retrace the historical steps by which the institution came to exercise such domination; but here I want to explore the cultural matrix that gives such an approach to crime its plausibility in the first place.

The idea that crime demands prosecution and punishment seems no more than common sense to us today. But it cannot be found in Western society before the twelfth century, when modern conceptions of law first made their appearance. Ancient

Roman law treated most of what we call crime as a civil matter. There were no public prosecutors and no special criminal trials. "Punishment was the exception and compensation was the rule," says Dutch historian and jurist Herman Bianchi.[1] This fact is often overlooked, Bianchi says, when we claim Roman precedents for our legal practices. Because popular wisdom has it that our social structures have evolved from classical models, and that this evolution has unerringly preserved the best of classical practices, we miss the novelty of Western legal ideas. In the Roman world, *crimen* did not mean crime, in our sense, at all, but a charge, a private complaint of one citizen against another. Crime demanded compensation. The state, through the office of the *praetor*, had an interest in seeing that a settlement was reached and its terms adhered to, but there its interest ended. Punishments, which were often cruel and barbaric, applied to slaves, enemies, and political opponents and were in the realm of "public law" — the state's proclamation of its right.

This emphasis on compensation is evident in the etymology of the English words "pain" and "punishment." "Pain" comes from Latin *poena*, from the Greek *poine*, meaning "the compensation value to be paid in order to resolve a criminal conflict." "Punish" is from *punire*, meaning "to see to it that the duty of *poena* is fulfilled." "To the Roman legal mind," Bianchi says,

> the law did not serve to express moralistic emotions but rather to overcome them. Romans used law to modify the moralistic concept of guilt into the legal concept of debt — *culpa* into *debitum* . . . With few exceptions we find compensation and penitence to be the normal solutions in ancient societies to crime conflicts, whereas revenge or retaliation was a deviance from the norm. To be sure, in old chronicles, legends, and epics from many parts of the world we hear the bards praising their admired heroes who take revenge against their enemies . . . But . . . heroes, however much glorified, have always been rare. Retaliation was the exception, and even a hero was expected to accept compensation if it was offered by the offender.

In many cultures we come across many devices to avoid revenge and punishment . . . Only if no compensation was offered, if all other endeavors had failed, could retaliation take place . . . It is an anachronism to believe that retaliation was the common law of ancient times.[2]

Compensation for crime also predominated among the Germanic peoples of Europe before the twelfth century. The institution of the blood-feud existed, but its operation was limited by laws and customs intended to bring parties in conflict to a settlement. Village assemblies, or *moots*, heard disputes and issued *dooms* (judgements). Detailed schedules of compensatory payments were established for cases of criminal injury. Ethelbert of Kent, the first Christian king in England, promulgated a written law code around 600 A.D. in which the four front teeth were rated at six shillings each, the neighbouring teeth at four, and the back teeth at one. The variety of misfortunes that might befall other bodily members was also enumerated and a price set for each. In the contemporaneous code of Rothari, the king of the Lombards, the prices to be paid for murder depended on the status of the victim: twelve hundred shillings for a free man, fifty for a household servant, twenty for a slave. Death was to be imposed only when an unfree man murdered one who was free. According to legal historian Harold J. Berman,

> the institution of fixed monetary payment payable by the kin of the wrongdoer to the kin of the victim was a prominent feature of the law of all the peoples of Europe prior to the twelfth century, and indeed of every Indo-European people at some stage of its development, including the peoples of India, Israel, Greece, and Rome. It is also an important part of the law of many contemporary societies.[3]

The conversion of Europe to Christianity did not at first alter the tradition of "folk law." Christianity infused it and softened some of its asperities, Berman says, but did not change its fundamental structure.

The basic law of the peoples of Europe from the sixth to the tenth centuries was not a body of rules imposed from on high but was rather an integral part of the common consciousness, the "common conscience," of the community. The people themselves, in their public assemblies, legislated and judged; and when kings asserted their authority over the law it was chiefly to guide the custom and legal consciousness of the people, not to remake it . . . Law, like art and myth and religion, and like language itself, was for the peoples of Europe in the early stages of their history not primarily a matter of making and applying rules in order to determine guilt and fix judgement, not an instrument to separate people from one another on the basis of a set of principles, but rather a matter of holding people together, a matter of reconciliation. Law was conceived primarily as a mediating process, a mode of communication, rather than primarily as a process of rule-making and decision-making.[4]

The style of law Berman describes — law embedded in social life rather than embodied in special legal institutions — began to give way to a recognizably modern legal system during the eleventh century. The seminal event, he says, was the Gregorian Reform, or Papal Revolution. It began in 1073 when Gregory VII capped several decades of clerical agitation for the "freedom of the church" by ascending the throne of St. Peter and proclaiming "the legal supremacy of the pope over all Christians and the legal supremacy of the clergy, under the pope, over all secular authorities."[5] The church, before this time, had suffused the social order and claimed no separate existence. Ecclesiastical affairs, like other matters of state, had been the concern of prince and bishop alike, after Charlemagne's time, spiritual and temporal authority were merged in the person of the Emperor.

The aim of the Gregorian Reform was to disentangle the church from society and establish it as a distinct legal entity standing over and against "the world." Gregory announced his purposes in 1075 in the *Dictatus Papae* (Dictates of the Pope) — twenty-seven terse and grandiloquent sentences asserting that the pope alone may "depose and reinstate bishops" (a right that at that time belonged to kings); that the pope "may depose emperors"; and that "to him alone is it permitted to make new laws according to the needs of the times."[6] Not all of Gregory's aims had been accomplished by the time the Concordat of Worms defined the new relations of church and state and ended the fifty-year war his assertion of supremacy had touched off — in England the question wasn't finally settled until after Thomas à Becket's assassination in 1170 — but the first characteristically Western revolution had been set irreversibly in motion.

"The Papal Revolution," Berman says, "gave birth to the modern state — the first example of which, paradoxically, was the church itself."[7] The church became an independent, hierarchical public authority executing its own laws through its own administrative machinery — even raising its own armies. (Urban II, Gregory's successor, launched the first crusade in 1095.) The clergy, in claiming a special responsibility for the care of souls and a special mission to regulate and reform society, became Europe's first professional class. Their new status was reflected in a change in the definition of sacraments. Augustine had defined sacraments as "signs of the grace of God," a potentially unlimited category. But Peter the Lombard in 1150 limited the sacraments to seven and added the radically new idea that a sacrament could be "a cause of the grace that it signifies."[8] A sacrament was now effective *ex proprio vigore* (by its own force), so long as it was correctly performed by an authorized person. The outlines of a new confidence in both technology and bureaucracy can be discerned in this change.

The reformed church aspired to what would later be called "the rule of law." Gregory's claim in his *Dictates* that he had the right "to make new laws according to the needs of the times" was already strikingly modern in its presumption that law is not codified custom but is an evolving body of precepts adapting itself to changing circumstances. The monk Gratian's *Concordance of Discordant Canons*, published around 1140, introduced system into the church's mass of canons, or rules. Canons were not previously distinguished from the moral exhortations, liturgical formulas, and theological doctrines[9] with which they were interlaced in the church's teaching. Now they were sorted, analyzed for contradictions, synthesized, and arranged in a hierarchy. Bureaucratic and legal norms replaced older codes of honour and personal loyalty. Canon law began to acquire the properties of the modern legal institution: a distinct sphere of operation, professional staffing, its own body of learning, a complex interaction between the law and its commentary, the possibility of evolutionary advance according to an internal logic, and the claim of supremacy over politics.[10]

Along with the disembedding of law from society went a new conception of justice. Folk law had been concerned with the satisfaction of honour by reparation. Now crime came to be seen as something more than a wrong demanding recompense. Justice itself demanded vindication. Because crime was "a defiance of the law itself," punishment must be imposed "as the price for the violation of the law."[11] The honour of the law overshadowed the honour of the victim. Crime had always been seen as violation of God's law as well as of other persons, and had always demanded penance as a visible sign of contrition; but until the eleventh century it was not seen as offending any embracing political order. In the same way, sin "had formerly been understood to be a condition of alienation, a diminution of a person's being . . . a separation from God and neighbour; [but] now it came to be understood in legal terms as specific wrongful acts and desires."[12] Accordingly, God's law was to be encoded in human statutes, which exacted a specified price for every wrong. Each sin had to be paid for by temporal suffering commensurate with the crime.

This new conception of sin was evident in the doctrine of purgatory, which emerged around the time of the Papal Revolution and, in Berman's phrase, "legalized life after death."[13] The gravity of each sin was assessed by canon lawyers, and the appropriate period of purgation prescribed. What is interesting about this innovation is not the old idea that God judges souls, but the new one that earthly lawyers and judges can. The Gospel of Matthew (16:19–20) has Jesus say to Peter, "I will give you the keys of the kingdom of Heaven; what you forbid on earth shall be forbidden in heaven, and what you allow on earth shall be allowed in heaven." This doctrine was now taken to extraordinary lengths in the idea that the jurisdiction of the church, and of the pope specifically, extended to the trans-mundane realm of purgatory. Not only did the church assign purgatorial suffering; it also exercised the power to stay it. "The Council of Clermont under Pope Urban II," Berman says, "granted the first 'plenary indulgence,' absolving all who would go on the First Crusade from liability for punishment in purgatory for sins committed prior to their joining the holy army of crusaders."[14]

In the doctrine of purgatory, Dutch jurist Louk Hulsman sees a forerunner of today's criminal justice. Present practice, he says, is "a true copy" of this teaching.

> The theologians [who] invented Purgatory . . . had to have a precise measure. You might have, for example, a thousand days to burn in Purgatory, but by certain prayers, you could reduce the number if you did them in the right way. If such a prayer was good, then you might get 300 days less. So, all that was very measured. And to measure it, naturally, you had to have clear names for those sins, so every sin had its own box, its name. And they described very precisely for every box what were the physical elements of that sin and what were the psychological and moral elements . . . God . . . knew everything and could see inside you. Your intention was an open book for him . . . and when you died it was exactly clear: perhaps you had to go immediately to Hell, but perhaps you still had a chance to go to Heaven, but then you had to spend 3,000 days in Purgatory. That was the system, and that is exactly the system of criminal justice.[15]

Hulsman believes that contemporary criminal justice systems preserve in displaced form the presumption of medieval theologians that God's will can be described and expressed in omniscient legal institutions. Criminal courts treat crime not as a conflict in search of a solution but as a moral fault requiring reprobation. Events are reconstructed without reference to their meaning for the people involved; what matters is to reach the absolute objective meaning of what has occurred, to assign it to its appropriate "box," which will dictate the punishment. (The federal sentencing tables in the United States, described in Chapter 2, reduce this approach *ad absurdum*; so does the current requirement in many North American jurisdictions that police lay charges following complaints of domestic assault, whether or not the complainant wishes to proceed.) Conflict is reified as *crime*, and the categories and subcategories of crime that fill out the 300-odd pages of the current Canadian Criminal Code are assigned an absolute existence beyond the reach of those actually affected by the conflict.

A second close resemblance between canon law and contemporary criminal justice lies in the emphasis placed on assessing degrees of guilt. "A large section of the Canon law," says historian Gerald McHugh, "was concerned with the criminal and disciplinary sanctions of the Church." He continues:

> The Canon law taught that punishment of offenders was appropriate only insofar as they were morally guilty of offenses. By definition punishment could not simply be the infliction of some evil on an offender — it had to be the infliction of an evil justly incurred because of guilt. Hence in assessing penalties the Church courts were greatly concerned with the relative degree of guilt of each offender. In determining guilt, Church courts would consider both the action of the offender — "*actus rea*" — and whether or not he/she had a "guilty mind," evil intent — "*mens rea*." No offender could be subjected to punishment unless he/she were morally guilty by virtue of sinful intention.[16]

This close interrogation of mental and spiritual states produced many subtle distinctions, and in some cases a real gain in fairness;

but it also produced a lasting emphasis on intentions over results, and on reprobation over repair in criminal proceedings. The question in criminal law has remained not "What is to be done?" but rather "How much punishment does this person deserve?"

Through canon law the church also arrogated to itself the power to prosecute crimes, a power that had not existed in previous law codes. In Rome, as we have seen, the civil power took no initiative in most criminal conflicts. Courts enforced judgements and served as referees ensuring "equality of arms" between the parties, but claimed no power to prosecute or to continue cases beyond the wishes of the aggrieved party. In fourteenth-century France there still existed the institution of *égale prison*, which required an accuser to submit to imprisonment himself if he wished the accused to be guarded.[17] This equality of accuser and accused disappeared when church courts assumed the right of prosecution, and the Inquisition — another institution of the Papal Revolution period — began actively to seek out heresy. Heresy had been made a crime as early as the reign of Theodosius (379–395), who proclaimed laws classifying non-Christians as "madmen . . . condemned as such . . . to suffer divine punishments and . . . the vengeance of that power which we, by celestial authority, have assumed."[18] But the prosecution of heresy intensified after Gregory IX instituted the papal Inquisition in 1231. According to Herman Bianchi, the Inquisition provided a paradigm that later passed over into secular criminal proceedings.

> In ancient Rome, *inquisitio* (Latin for "the search for evidence and guilt") could, generally speaking, be used only against slaves, not against free citizens. The Holy Roman Church, as self-appointed keeper and guardian of Roman traditions during the Middle Ages, wanted for political reasons to make the religious life and dogmatic opinions of the faithful an object of inquisitory examination. The idea that one could be an object of examination had until then been alien to free people . . . In an inquisitorial system there is no equality

between prosecution and defendant. Repressive systems begin when the accused is no longer equal to the prosecution . . . An entirely new notion in Western culture was gradually taking root, conceiving all crime no longer as a conflict between citizens but as a conflict between the state and the accused, just as religious beliefs were no longer considered a matter between God and man but between church/state and man. What heresy had become to the Roman Catholic Church, crime became to the state and its rulers. Crime was no longer viewed as a regulable conflict but as a social heresy, the state's business.[19]

Yet another consequential idea that took shape during the Papal Revolution period and later influenced secular justice was the doctrine of the Atonement. This doctrine is summed up in the Anglican *Book of Common Prayer*'s formula that Christ's crucifixion was "a full, perfect and sufficient sacrifice, oblation, and satisfaction for the sins of the whole world." British theologian Timothy Gorringe has explored its formative influence on penal practice in a recent book titled *God's Just Vengeance*. He begins by asking why so many mild and even saintly Christians have seen no contradiction between "the ministry of reconciliation" (2 Corinthians 5:18) to which they are called and the violent penal regimes that their church has blessed. Even today, for example, survey research in the United States finds professed Christians more favourable to capital punishment than citizens not so identified. He finds the answer in the idea that God required the death of his son as "satisfaction" for humanity's disobedience. "That the answer to violence in the community is the violence of sacrificial death is taught to Christian society by its faith," Gorringe writes. "Criminals die to make satisfaction for their sins as Christ died for the sins of all."[20]

It is a complex and subtle question whether this idea is justified by scripture, and I cannot do justice to Gorringe's rich and nuanced discussion of it here, except to say that he thinks on the whole it is not. There is barely a hint in the synoptic gospels, or in the Acts of the Apostles, of the doctrine of a Fall that needs to be redeemed by sacrifice; and even in Paul's letters, where Christ is said to be he "whom God hath set forth to be a propitiation through faith in his blood" (Romans 3:25), Gorringe finds no evidence that Paul thought Christ's death was expiatory in a legal or juristic sense. In Christ's crucifixion and resurrection, Christians die to the power of sin and move into a new community with "the ministry of reconciliation" (2 Corinthians 5:18). In fact, the judicial murder of Christ denounces law and reveals it as "the strength of sin" (1 Corinthians 15:56). It is only in the eleventh century, with Anselm of Canterbury, that legal and juridical metaphors came to dominate the church's understanding of the Atonement.

Anselm was born in Italy in 1033 and studied in the schools of Bologna and his native Pavia, where an excited rediscovery of Roman law was then under way. He headed the Abbey of Bec in Normandy and later became Archbishop of Canterbury. In his book *Cur Deus Homo* (Why the God-Man?), Anselm set out to prove by reason alone — *Christo remoto* (Christ aside) — that the sacrifice of the Son of God was the only possible means by which atonement could be made for human sinfulness.[21] To do so he drew from his legal training the Roman concept of *satisfactio*, which "referred to compensation to an injured person other than by direct payment." Humanity, through Adam and Eve's disobedience, had dishonoured God by failing "to render God His due." Since righteousness is God's nature, He cannot treat evil as good without violating His nature. "It is not fitting," Anselm says, "for God to pass over anything in His kingdom undischarged [because then] there will be no difference between the guilty and the not guilty, and this is unbecoming to God."[22] It follows that satisfaction must be made for mankind's disobedience; and, since the offence is against an infinite Being, so the satisfaction must be infinite. Nothing mankind could offer would suffice. Only Christ, who is both human and divine, can fulfill this demand. The image of God, as Adolf von Harnack described it in his *History of Dogma*, is of "the mighty private person who is incensed at the injury done to His honour and does not forego His wrath till He has received an at least adequately great equivalent."[23]

Anselm founded the central tradition of Christian thinking about the Atonement; but, as time went on, an even greater emphasis came to be put on the specifically legal character of mankind's redemption. For Anselm, as for Thomas Aquinas later, "concern for justice is [still] a concern for the integrity of both the social order and the cosmic order which it mirrors." Sin dishonours God by "disturb[ing] the order and beauty of the universe."[24] By John Calvin's time satisfaction was discussed in an explicitly legal and penal context. "Divine wrath, and vengeance, and eternal death" lie upon us, Calvin says, "a deserved curse obstructs the entrance [to heaven], and God in His character of Judge is hostile to us." This divine hostility is overcome only when Christ assumes the guise of a criminal and accepts our due punishment.

> When he is placed as a criminal at the bar, where witnesses are brought to give evidence against him, and the mouth of the judge condemns him to die, we see him sustaining the character of an offender and evildoer . . . Our acquittal is in this — that the guilt which made us liable to punishment was transferred to the head of the Son of God (Isaiah 53:12). We must especially remember this substitution in order that we may not be all our lives in trepidation and anxiety, as if the just vengeance, which the Son of God transferred to himself, were still impending over us.[25]

Calvin gave satisfaction theory its most terrible expression — "wherever Calvinism spread," Gorringe says, "harsh punishment followed" — but, for all that, he still spoke for what became the mainstream of Christian thinking. Christianity underwrote court proceedings through the swearing of oaths on the Bible, though Jesus had taught his followers in the Sermon on the

Mount to swear no oaths (Matthew 5:33–37). Prison "ordinaries" sanctified capital punishment by preaching from the scaffold. Archdeacons like William Paley insisted that hanging was a perfect analogy of divine justice, since "the retribution of so much pain for so much guilt . . . is the dispensation we expect at the hand of God."[26] And when reformer Samuel Romily introduced a bill to reduce the number of capital offences in 1811, its defeat was aided in the House of Lords by the votes of six bishops and one archbishop.[27] "The suffering Christ," Gorringe argues, ought to have been "an icon of the wickedness of judicial punishment," but instead "became the focus of its legality, and of the need for the offender to suffer as he did. An image of torture provided the central construal of the cultural space within which punishment took place . . . it created the 'structure of affect' which guided thinking about punishment."[28]

The idea of redemption as "a legal transaction" expressed an age in love with law and confident that even God must be constrained by his own righteousness.[29] "God is himself law, and therefore the law is dear to him," began the first German lawbook, the *Sachsenspiegel,* or "Mirror of the Saxons," published around 1220.[30] "The land shall be built by law," said the first Scandinavian lawbook around the same time.[31] Law, Harold Berman argues persuasively, became the root metaphor of the age that lasted from Anselm's time to ours.

Berman ends his masterful history of the origins of Western law with a quotation from Octavio Paz: "Every time a society finds itself in crisis, it instinctively turns its eyes towards its origins and looks there for a sign."[32] A backward glance today yields just such a sign. It reveals, first of all, that "the rule of law" throughout most of Western history was nourished from religious and cosmological roots. Its vitality derived from its being felt as an expression of the true and God-given nature of things. When, in the twelfth century, Gratian prepared the ground for modern law by drawing the canons of the church together into one harmonious and evolving body, he arranged law in a hierarchy in which custom was to yield to enactment, enactment to natural law, and natural law to divine law.[33] Today, enacted law is no longer fed from these great tap roots. Religion has become private, and law merely expedient. Under the influence of "abstract and superficial nationalisms," the integral qualities of the Western tradition are neglected in favour of a parochial emphasis on national traditions. The living faith that the law once embodied has left behind only a shell — functional, convenient, necessary certainly, but without that compelling awe that once invested the operations of the penal system and allowed Christian ministers to bless the gallows and the jail. "Western legal institutions," Berman says in summary, "have been removed from their spiritual foundation."[34]

This uprooting and desiccation of the Western legal tradition suggests that it is time to rethink it. Postmodern societies that cynically persist in a system whose metaphysical roots lie withered and exposed will only put off a reckoning with their own growing shadows. Looking back to the watershed between folk law — integral, embedded, local, and limited — and formal law — systematic, autonomous, professional, and universal — allows us to see what we have lost as well as what we have gained. Whether the communal dimension of justice can be recovered is a question I take up in Part III, when I examine alternatives to prosecution and incarceration as responses to crime. In the next chapter, I look into the history of the prison in order to understand how this particular institution came to embody and then to monopolize the social response to crime.

A PERPETUAL SOLITUDE
AND SECLUSION

Imprisonment as a regular response to crime made its appearance around the end of the eighteenth century, and, just as the criminal law had grown from canon law, so the new penitentiaries drew their shape and syntax from monasticism. Enemies have always been detained, of course, but the prison as an instrument of reformation and deserved punishment originated in Christian monasteries. As early as the sixth century, one of the Fathers of the church, St. John Climacus, describes, in his *Holy Ladder, or Steps for Mounting to Heaven*, an annex to a monastery near Alexandria that had already existed for two centuries:

> It was about one mile distant from the great monastery and was called "The Prison." It was a place from which all human consolations were banished. No smoke was ever seen to issue from it. There was neither wine, nor oil, nor food, except bread and very simple vegetables. There the prior sent those who, after taking the monastic vows, had fallen into some notable sin. They were not lodged together; they lived apart, alone, or at the most by twos. And they remained imprisoned there without ever going out, until God had given the prior a sure sign of each one's reconciliation. [1]

At the time of Charlemagne, according to eminent Benedictine scholar Dom Jean Mabillon in his *Reflections on the Prisons of the*

Monastic Orders, "the harshness of some priors went to such an excess (it seems difficult to believe it) that they mutilated the limbs and sometimes struck out the eyes of those of their monks who had fallen into considerable errors."[2] Mabillon, who lived between 1632 and 1707, was so appalled by the harshness of the monastic prisons of his own day that he investigated their history, leaving his *Reflections* among his unpublished papers when he died. The complaints that the monks of Fulda made to Charlemagne, he says, led the Council of Frankfurt in 794 to condemn such tortures and return monasteries to more moderate discipline. An assembly of priors held at Aix-la-Chapelle in 817 "ruled that in each monastery there should be a separate habitation, *domus semota*, for the culprits, that is, a heated chamber and a workroom . . . They also forbade the exposure of these poor creatures in a naked state, to be whipped before the rest of the monks, as had previously been the practice."[3] This reformed regimen, however, didn't last.

> In the course of time, a frightful kind of prison, where daylight never entered, was invented, and since it was designed for those who should finish their lives in it, it received the name of *Vade in pace*. It appears that the first person to invent this horrible form of torture was Matthew, Prior of Saint Martin des Champs, according to the story of Peter the Venerable, who informs us that this superior, a good man otherwise, but extremely severe against those who committed some error, caused the construction of a subterranean cave in the form of a grave where he placed, for the rest of his days, a miserable wretch who seemed incorrigible to him.[4]

Matthew's example was imitated by other priors, and solitary confinement became in time routine in some places. Mabillon states that in his own time

> the prisoners of some monastic orders have . . . few or no visits or consolations, rarely a mass, never an exhortation; in other words, a

perpetual solitude and seclusion without promenades in the open, without movement, without amelioration . . . without consolation, unless one calls consolation a hasty word by a jailer who brings their food or by a superior who asks about their health without really acquainting himself with their needs and without seriously thinking of the means which would be necessary to make them return to God, or without inspiring them with a true spirit of penance.[5]

The isolation of prisoners, in Mabillon's view, was contrary to Christian teaching. He was willing to accept that "in secular justice the principal purpose in view is . . . to instill fear into the criminals, but in ecclesiastical justice . . . the spirit of charity, compassion, and mercy should rule."[6] Moreover, he thought that this style of punishment was as likely to destroy the sanity of its victim as to restore his spirit:

May no one say that it is good for them to be left alone in order to get time to think about their conscience and seriously reflect upon the sad state into which they have precipitated themselves. Far from . . . such a long, violent, and forcible imprisonment contribut[ing] to make them examine their conscience, they are usually incapable of feeling the charm of the state of grace under such conditions, nothing being more opposed thereto than the excess of sadness which overwhelms them and causes them to sigh under the burden of their past sins and even more in the just apprehension of the consequence which they foresee arriving to them, the complete loss of their reputation in a Company where they find themselves engaged . . . By experience, one knows but too well that it is sufficiently hard to pass only a few days in silence and spiritual exercises which are voluntarily done . . . And then one imagines that poor wretches, overwhelmed by shame and sorrow, could pass entire years in a narrow prison without conversation and human consolations? Yet one finds judges . . . who frequently cannot stay in their chambers even a few days, pronounce against them a penance of several years, not to mention other punishments accompanying that penance. Truly it makes one sigh to see so much deception and so little justice.[7]

Mabillon's rueful *Reflections* were published fourteen years after his death, but appear to have had no influence. No English translation was made until twenty years ago, when Thorsten Sellin published the text from which I have been quoting. The monastic prison, in due course, became one of the models for the modern penitentiary.

The first prison in which this lineage was clearly visible was Philadelphia's Walnut Street Jail, erected in 1790 and designed to impose an explicitly penitential discipline on offenders. Prisons previously had been used for enemies, and for persons awaiting trial or execution of sentence, but rarely for punishment. Punishment in the early modern period meant the whipping post, the stocks, or the branding iron — when it didn't mean the gallows. There were 78,000 hangings in England during the reign of Henry VIII; and, as late as 1803, a thirteen-year-old boy was hanged for stealing a silver spoon.[8] The first recognizable precursor of the penitentiary was the Elizabethan bridewell, or house of correction, "the first European institution in which men were both confined and set to labor in order to learn 'the habits of industry.'"[9] In 1703 at Rome, Pope Clement authorized the creation of the St. Michele Reformatory for delinquent boys. Workhouses and debtors' prisons were also known, but there was no institution that aimed at anything like total control of its inmates. "The large debtors' prisons in London," historian Michael Ignatieff says, ". . . were self-governing, self-financing communities, subject only to the loose and occasional tribute exacted by the keepers. Debtors' wards in jails also enjoyed a large measure of self-government, since the keepers were forbidden to limit debtors' access to the outside world or infringe upon their privileges."[10] Nor did prison architecture facilitate surveillance and control. On the contrary, according to Ignatieff, it "encouraged the flowering of inmate subcultures . . . Newgate [in London] was a dark, damp warren of wards, yards, privies, and staircases nowhere affording authority a clear vantage point for inspection and control."[11]

Two currents of thought can be discerned in the creation of the familiar modern prison. The first was the Enlightenment's revulsion at what the Italian philosopher Cesare Beccaria called "the spectacle of barbarous and useless torments, cold-bloodedly devised."[12] Arguing with "that geometric precision which the mist of sophisms . . . cannot withstand,"[13] Beccaria proposed the simple utilitarian principle that "for a punishment to attain its end, the evil which it inflicts has only to exceed the advantage derivable from the crime."[14] The purpose a political society has in punishment, he maintained, is to "prevent the criminal from inflicting new injuries on its citizens and to deter others from similar acts." It can best accomplish this purpose by punishments that are "prompt, certain, and inflict the least [possible] torment on the body of the criminal."[15] Beccaria believed that "one of the greatest curbs on crimes is not the cruelty of punishments, but their infallibility." Forgiveness, therefore, though it may commend the person who extends it, is "contrary to the public good" because it "foments a flattering hope of impunity."[16] Justice should be as merciful as possible, but it must above all be punctual, predictable, and in precise proportion to the offence.

Jeremy Bentham, writing in England, took a very similar approach. He too hoped "to perfect the proportion between punishments and offences."[17] Reasoning "upon the principle of utility," he argued that since "all punishment in itself is evil . . . it ought only to be admitted in as far as it promises to exclude some greater evil." Punishment, therefore, should consist only in what is necessary to "outweigh the profit of the offence."[18] To this end, he outlined precise rules by which punishments could be calculated. He said, for example, that, owing to differences in sensibility, "a punishment which is the same in name will not always . . . produce . . . the same degree of pain." Therefore, "the quantity [of pain] actually inflicted on each . . . offender" should be adjusted so that it corresponds to "the quantity intended for similar offenders in general."[19] Likewise, he suggested that for offences that were less likely to be found out, punishment "must be increased, in point of magnitude, in proportion as it falls short in point of certainty."[20] Drawing on the same materialist psychology as Beccaria, and displaying the same faith that people will behave as rational calculators in a regime that appeals to this faculty, Bentham was confident that he could assign precise values to pain and pleasure, apprehension and remorse, and thereby "augment the total happiness of the community."[21]

At the same time that Bentham and Beccaria were denouncing the cruel extravagance of public tortures and executions, civil authorities were beginning to wonder whether these displays were more likely to excite a morbid prurience than to deter offences. In London, for instance, condemned criminals were taken through the streets by cart to the public gallows near Marble Arch that William Blake called "Tyburn's bloody tree." "This ostensibly solemn ritual," Michael Ignatieff says, ". . . was taken over by the crowd and converted into a thieves' holiday and poor people's carnival."[22] So, in 1783, "the sheriffs of London and Middlesex abolished the processional altogether and ordered that future executions should take place in front of Newgate [Prison, where the condemned were held]." What should have been a terrifying spectacle, they said, had become a travesty.

> It has long been a subject of complaint that our processions to Tyburn are a mockery upon the aweful sentence of the law and that the final scene itself has lost its terrors and is so far from giving a lesson of morality to the beholders that it tends to the encouragement of vice. No man who had been an eye-witness to it can deny the justice of the censure. The day on which some of our fellow creatures are doomed to be Examples of Terror to evil Doers and to Expiate the Offences of an Ill-Spent Life by an Ignominious Death is too often considered by the vulgar of this city as a Holiday; and the Place of Execution is more frequently resorted to with the

strange Expectation of satisfying an unaccountable Curiosity than with a Sober Solicitude for Moral Improvement . . . The whole Progress is attended [by] an indecent levity . . . The crowd gather as it goes, and their levity increases till on their Approach to the Fatal Tree, the Ground becomes a Riotous Mass, and their Wantonness of Speech breaks forth in profane Jokes, Swearing, and Blasphemy.[23]

The feeling that public punishment had become both barbarous and ineffective led to a gradual increase in the use of imprisonment. "Before 1775," Ignatieff reports,

imprisonment was rarely used as a punishment for felony. At the Old Bailey, the major criminal court for London and Middlesex, imprisonments accounted for no more than 2.3 percent of the judges' sentences in the years between 1770 and 1774. These terms of imprisonment were short — never longer than three years and usually a year or less — and they were inflicted on a narrow range of offenders — those convicted of manslaughter, commercial frauds, perjury, combining against employers, or rioting.[24]

Even in these cases, imprisonment was imposed only when the offence was deemed relatively minor. Infractions judged more serious were still punished with transportation or execution. By 1830, the prison rate had trebled.[25]

The second important contribution to the invention of the prison we know today was the movement to reform the internal character of the institution. In England the beginnings of this reform can be dated from 1773 when John Howard, a Quaker of independent means, became the high sheriff of Bedfordshire. Howard was appalled at conditions in the Bedford jail, and at the system of prisoner fees that made jailers the clients of their captives; so he undertook an extensive investigation of penal practices both in Britain and in continental Europe. This led to the publication in 1777 of *The State of the Prisons*, a work denouncing the squalor, idleness, and immorality prevalent in the institutions he had observed. He recommended the creation of penitentiaries that would be in every respect the opposite of existing institutions. Prisons, at the time he wrote, still possessed elements of self-government and connections with the surrounding world. Such places still exist where governments cannot afford to pay for the maintenance of prisoners under conditions of total control. Raúl Zaffaroni, a former judge, and now a professor of law in the University of Buenos Aires, has described one such institution in La Paz, Bolivia:

> The prison is like a ghetto. The state is represented by so few persons that their control is largely symbolic. Prisoners establish their own authority and establish economic relations between the prison and the outside. It's not very difficult to go out of the prison but it is even less difficult to get in, and everybody goes into the prison to visit and to buy and sell things. Children are in the prison. Women are in the prison. It's like a poor neighbourhood. Sometimes things that are produced by the prisoners are sold outside and then the prisoner goes to the city with an official and they come back to the prison together at night. Sometimes they're both drunk because they spent the money that they obtained. Prisoners are selected from a poor neighbourhood and, at last, the prison becomes a new poor neighbourhood.[26]

European prisons of the eighteenth century were not, of course, identical to this institution in present-day La Paz; but Zaffaroni's description gives a sense of what may have made such institutions livable, despite their conditions. What Howard noticed about them, however, was their moral squalor. Where they ought to have encouraged moral reformation, they seemed to him to offer instead new inducements to idleness and vice. What were ostensibly institutions of the state were ruled rather by an "inmate netherworld . . . with its own officers, its own customs and its own rituals."[27] What he proposed therefore was a wholesome, sanitary institution where labour, religious instruction, and solitary reflection would combine to produce penitence. A statute enacted by Parliament in 1779 under Howard's influence authorized the building of such institutions.

This statute was never really put into effect, and the penal utopia Howard imagined was never created. But ideas to which he and his fellow reformers first gave currency, though they were coarsened in practice, did begin to suffuse the emergent prison system. Supervised labour, religious instruction, and solitary confinement all became part of new penal regimens. Solitary confinement, for example, was used in the new penitentiary at Gloucester, where Kyd Wake was imprisoned. Wake was a printer sentenced in 1796 to serve five years for "hissing and booing the King as he drove in his carriage from St. James Palace to the opening of Parliament." His wife, Ignatieff relates, raised money by selling "an engraving [in which] Wake stand[s] downcast in his cell in his ill-fitting blue and yellow prison uniform." Below his image appeared this appeal to the citizens of Gloucester:

Five years confinement, even in common gaols, must surely be a very severe punishment; but if Judges or Juries would only reflect seriously on the horrors of solitary imprisonment under penitentiary discipline! If they allow their minds to dwell a little on what is to be locked up, winter after winter, for sixteen hours out of the twenty-four, in a small brick cell — without company — without fire — without light — without employment — and scarcely to see a face but those of criminals or turnkeys. No friend to converse with when well; or to consult with, or to complain to, when indisposed! Above all — to be subjected to a thousand insults and vexations, almost impossible to be described, and therefore scarcely to be remedied; but by which continual torment may be, and often is, inflicted. If they would but consider what an irreparable misfortune it is to have a once considerable portion of life so wearisomely wasted; they would surely be more tender of dooming any man, for a long time, to such wretchedness. It is a calamity beyond description, more easily to be conceived than explained.[28]

The punishment endured by Kyd Wake was probably not what John Howard had imagined when he called for solitary reflection as an element of penitence, but such isolation came into increasing use nonetheless. (In a parliamentary debate on solitary confinement, one Whig MP said that "the late Mr. Howard was certainly one of the worthiest men who had ever existed; [but] if he had been one of the worst, he could not have suggested a punishment of a more cruel and mischievous description."[29]) By 1842, when the penitentiary achieved its definitive form with the opening of Pentonville Prison in London, enforced solitude had been carried to such lengths that "before stepping out on the catwalk, the convict donned a brown, spade-shaped mask with holes for his eyes."[30] This prevented him from recognizing or being recognized by his fellows. In fact, during a period that was first set at eighteen months, then reduced to twelve, and finally nine months, all newly admitted prisoners were forbidden any contact with each other whatsoever. They worked alone at benches in their cells and exercised alone in tiny individual yards. This inhuman discipline was epitomized by the chapel, which Ignatieff calls "the brain of the penitentiary machine":

> It was divided into hundreds of boxlike compartments big enough for a body, ranged underneath a pulpit. The file of men halted at the chapel door. A duty warder went to a number machine and began to crank. When the convict's number appeared on the board, he stepped out of file and moved along the rows until he reached his box and closed the door behind him. The chapel filled with the sound of the rumbling of convict boots and the slamming of box doors. Perched on high chairs sat warders who swept the chapel with their gaze, looking for gestures among the mass of heads below them.[31]

Some years before Pentonville was built, Jeremy Bentham had published a work with the lengthy title *Panopticon or the Inspection House, containing the Idea of a new Principle of Construction applicable to any Sort of Establishment, in which persons of*

*any description are to be kept under inspection and in particular
to Penitentiary Houses, Prisons, Houses of Industry, Work-Houses,
Poor-Houses, Manufactories, Mad-Houses, Lazarettos, Hospitals
and Schools: with a Plan of Management adapted to the Principle.*
Bentham's "new principle" consisted in a "most effectual con-
trivance for seeing without being seen." The inspector, for whom
the inspection house was named, was to be located at the focus
of an ingenious architecture, which French historian Michel
Foucault describes as follows:

> At the periphery, an annular [circular] building; at the centre, a
> tower; this tower is pierced with wide windows that open onto the
> inner side of the ring; the peripheric building is divided into cells,
> each of which extends the whole width of the building; they have
> two windows, one on the inside, corresponding to the windows of
> the tower; the other, on the outside, allows the light to cross the cell
> from one end to the other. All that is needed, then, is to place a
> supervisor in a central tower and to shut up in each cell a madman,
> a patient, a condemned man, a worker, or a schoolboy. By the effect
> of the backlighting, one can observe from the tower, standing out
> precisely against the light, the small captive shadows in the cells of the
> periphery. They are like so many cages, so many small theatres, in which
> each actor is alone, perfectly individualized and constantly visible.[32]

Bentham apparently intended this monstrous fantasy of the
Panopticon as a commercial proposal and lobbied for a contract
to build such an institution. In this his hopes were disappointed;
but through the design of its chapel and exercise yards, and the
provision of inspection holes through which warders could keep
each cell under surveillance, Pentonville came very close to
Bentham's idea of "seeing without being seen," as well as to his
intention of substituting the will of the inspector for the unreli-
able wills of the inmates. According to Ignatieff, the prison's
endless, empty silences produced madness, depression, and suicide as often as they produced reformation.

By the time Pentonville swung open its gates in London in 1842, similar institutions already existed in North America. It was the novelty of its penitentiary system that first drew Alexis de Tocqueville to the United States in 1831. He was particularly interested in the Eastern State Penitentiary, opened on Cherry Hill in Philadelphia in 1829. In Pennsylvania, as in England, the Quakers had been influential in the prison reform movement; the Cherry Hill prison epitomized their hope that a properly designed and regulated institution could engineer penitence. How this was to be done was set out by the new penitentiary's "morals instructor":

> The utmost that can be claimed for any reformatory system of punishment is its predisposing influence to serious reflection . . . The power of Divine Grace we know can effect a change in the heart of any man under any circumstances, and God always works by means adapted to the end; but so long as "evil communications corrupt good manners"; the association of evil men places an almost insuperable obstacle to moral improvement of the already corrupted. The separation of convicts removes that obstacle.[33]

At Cherry Hill, seven cell blocks radiated from a central administrative hub. Each cell opened onto its own enclosed exercise yard. The inmate worked and ate in his cell and saw no one but the warden and the morals instructor. This was called "the separate system," as distinct from "the silent system" practised at the model penitentiary opened at Auburn, New York, four years earlier, where the inmates worked together but were forbidden to communicate with each other at any time.

In Canada the creation of a penitentiary was first contemplated in 1831 when two members of Upper Canada's House of Assembly, John Macaulay and Hugh Thomson, both of Kingston, were commissioned to investigate the feasibility of such an institution. Thomson concluded that there was no contradiction involved in adding penitence to the more fundamental objective of terrifying offenders and edifying the rest of the citizenry.

> A Penitentiary, as its name imports, should be a place to lead a man to repent of his sins and to amend his life, and if it has that effect, so much the better, as the cause of religion gains by it, but it is quite enough for the purposes of the public if the punishment is so terrible that the dread of a repetition of it deters him from crime, or his description of it, others.[34]

The Kingston Penitentiary was opened in 1835. Like Pentonville and Cherry Hill, it is still in operation today.

The penitentiary came into being through a strange alliance of religious enthusiasm and rational utilitarianism. It appealed to an age that was alarmed by revolution, industrialization, and widespread social dislocation with its promise to restore and enforce social discipline; and it revealed the deeply ambivalent character of this new age. Alexis de Tocqueville and his collaborator Gustave de Beaumont noticed this double character in their research on American prisons. "While society in the United States gives the example of the most extended liberty," they write, "the prisons of the same country offer the spectacle of the most complete despotism."[35] Michael Ignatieff locates this same double character within the "two personae" of Jeremy Bentham, who was an advocate of parliamentary reform on the one hand, and the deviser of the Panopticon on the other. To Ignatieff, these two characters were "not contradictory, but complementary. The extension of rights within civil society had to be compensated for by the abolition of the tacit liberties enjoyed by prisoners and criminals under the *ancien régime*. In an unequal and increasingly divided society, this was the only way to extend liberty and fortify consent without compromising security."[36]

Sociologist Zygmunt Bauman, in a book simply titled *Freedom*, agrees that Bentham's commitment to civil rights and his championing of totalitarian prisons were indissolubly linked:

> Bentham was fully aware that the purpose of securing the safety and
> the smooth reproduction of social order cannot but sediment two
> sharply opposed yet mutually conditioning and validating social
> modalities, one having a total freedom as its ideal horizon, another
> striving towards total dependence.[37]

Total dependence perfectly expresses the condition of the prisoner in the new penitentiaries of the nineteenth century. The United States Supreme Court ruled in 1871 that a prisoner "not only forfeited his liberty, but all his personal rights except those which the law in its humanity accords him. He is for the time being a slave of the state."[38] The prison, in a sense, occupied the Enlightenment's blind spot. Although the American Constitution asserted that men were naturally endowed with certain "inalienable rights," these rights could be alienated when a citizen was successfully prosecuted by a "legal" institution. "Nature cancels itself out," Herman Bianchi concludes, "if its laws can be suspended."[39]

The utopian hopes that animated the creation of the first penitentiaries have long since faded; but, two hundred years later, the institution of imprisonment continues to monopolize the social response to crime. Increased use of prisons in recent years seems to argue that its hegemony in the field of criminal justice is now greater than ever. Yet, at the same time that this increase has been occurring, the legitimacy of the institution has been challenged as never before. This challenge has been both practical and theoretical: alternative forms of correction and restitution have been put into widespread use, and new conceptions of criminal justice have been put forward. In Part III, I look into both the theory and practice of these emerging alternatives. But first I want to look at how recent developments in the science of criminology have prepared the ground for them. This is the subject, then, of the next chapter.

9

A SEA CHANGE

As Michel Foucault points out in *Discipline and Punish*, the birth of the prison was also the birth of the science of criminology. Impounding everyone successfully prosecuted for crime in one place delimited criminality as a category and created the possibility of an inquiry into the common characteristics of criminals as a class. Imprisonment turned the criminal into a stable and available object of investigation, and thus gave criminology its subject matter. The new science at first took this subject matter for granted. How could it question the data that grounded its pretension to be a science in the first place? Cesare Lombroso at the end of the nineteenth century went so far as to suppose that there existed a distinct criminal species, an atavistic type discernible by certain cranial measurements, which he called "criminal man." This extreme style of positivism was later renounced, but criminologists generally continued to take the artifacts of the criminal justice system as givens well into the twentieth century.

This changed during the 1960s, and in some cases earlier, when criminologists began to ask more penetrating questions about how the fundamental categories of criminology are actually constructed. Crime began to be treated not as a naturally occurring phenomenon, but as something selected and shaped from an effectively inexhaustible supply of eligible acts. Labelling theorists noted how youngsters diagnosed as delinquent tended to adopt and embellish this identity, turning the mark of their shame into the badge of their honour. Other critics focused on the way mass media amplify the discretionary power of police and other criminal justice authorities to determine who or what will be considered significantly criminal at a given moment. American media critic Gaye Tuchman, for example, described the role of the New York City Police Department in defining crime:

> The New York City police have a special wire service that goes to all of the major news media within New York City . . . Sometimes stuff that comes over the police wire will be . . . about new kinds of crime waves. At one point a couple of years ago, the New York police invented a crime wave against the elderly. They kept putting more and more news, more and more stories about crimes against the elderly on this wire, in part because the unit within the police department that dealt with crimes against the elderly needed more appropriations. So the police wire managed to help in the creation of a crime wave. And, by accepting the police's definitions of crime, including what's an interesting crime or what's a boring crime, or what's an important crime, what's a trivial crime, the news media are all helping to maintain the police as an important social institution with the right to define crime. That police wire does not carry stories about corporate crime, nor does it carry stories about illegal take-overs or tax fraud. It carries stories about an old lady who got mugged or a nine-year-old kid who stole a car.[1]

In her book *The Persistent Prison?* Canadian criminologist Maeve McMahon calls this more self-conscious stance "critical criminology"; I will adopt her term, and much of her analysis, in what follows.[2] Critical criminology's skepticism about the institutions of criminal justice was reinforced by events in the 1960s and early 1970s: an unpopular war in Vietnam, the civil-rights movement, widespread sympathy for national liberation struggles throughout the world, and major riots at Attica Prison in northern New York State and the Kingston Penitentiary in Canada. The four-day Kingston riot ended with an outburst of terrifying bloodlust in which "fourteen diddlers, rapos, and stool pigeons" were tortured, mutilated, and, in two cases, executed by the rioters[3]; but at Attica Governor Nelson Rockefeller ordered a full-scale assault on the revolted prison. The resulting battle in which forty-one people died before the prison was retaken, produced much more heroic and dignified images of the forty-one prisoners in the public mind. Widely read books like George Jackson's *Soledad Brother* and Eldridge Cleaver's *Soul on Ice* also advanced the idea of the incarcerated criminal as a political prisoner.

This sense of the prison system as an arbitrary and oppressive institution undermined its claim to be a place of treatment and rehabilitation. An article titled "What Works: Questions and Answers about Prison Reform," published in the American journal *The Public Interest* in 1975 by researcher Robert Martinson focused this new skepticism, playing "a pivotal role in shifting perspectives on rehabilitation."[4] Martinson and his colleagues surveyed more than 200 studies carried out between 1945 and 1967 and concluded that, with few exceptions, efforts at rehabilitation had no effect on the rate at which ex-convicts re-offended. The gist of the article, although Martinson didn't say it himself, was often subsequently formulated as "nothing works."

It was in this atmosphere that Foucault's book *Discipline and Punish: The Birth of the Prison* appeared in English in 1978 (it had been first published three years earlier in France). The effect was characterized by Camille Paglia, with shrewd hyperbole, as "academic cocaine"[5]: exhilarating but ultimately anaesthetic. Foucault begins by contrasting the public tortures, mutilations, and mortifications practised in the *ancien régime* with the total control exercised in the modern prison. The purpose of the first, he says, was to inscribe the power of the sovereign on the offender's body for all to read. Once justice had been scourged or seared into the offender's flesh, this purpose was fulfilled and finished. Methods of punishment were cruel, sensuous, and transparently theatrical. The nineteenth-century prison, on the other hand, aspired to remake the very soul of the offender. Its discipline was so diffuse and so total that justice was never done. Punishment as correction was "an interrogation without end . . . a file that was never closed," and even where it was lenient it was a "calculated leniency . . . interlaced with a ruthless curiosity."[6] This ruthless diagnostic gaze produced new forms of knowledge, which, in turn, produced new ways of exercising penal power. Foucault portrays this modern dialectic by which power and knowledge continuously refine and magnify each other's operations as utterly inexorable. It acts not in some obvious, limited, and therefore resistible, way, but more in the manner of the seeping of water, or the growth of roots; obstruction only opens new pathways. Modern penal discipline, he says, penetrates "into the very grain of individuals." By the very perfection of this intimate invasion of its subjects, the prison reveals itself as the quintessential modern institution, the prototypical expression of "a carceral continuum." "Is it surprising," Foucault asks, "that prisons resemble factories, schools, barracks, hospitals, which all resemble prisons?"[7]

The genius of *Discipline and Punish* lies in its account of the intimate and inseparably interfused relations between knowledge and power. Once the criminal is made available as an object to which "political technology" can be applied, power multiplies its effects "through the formation and accumulation of new forms of knowledge." These new forms of knowledge, in turn, generate powerful new techniques, as "the formation of knowledge and the increase of power regularly reinforce one another in a circular process."[8]

The more lenient this operation appears, the more insidious it actually is. "Although the universal juridicism of modern society seems to fix limits on the exercise of power," Foucault says, in fact it operates "on the underside of the law a machinery [of surveillance] that is both immense and minute."[9] This machinery, because of its minuteness, is capable of endless expansion and transformation. Efforts at reform only refine and extend its domination. Moreover these "systems of micropower . . . supported by tiny, everyday physical mechanisms,"[10] by operating on "the underside of the law," tend to escape detection and dissolve resistance.

Discipline and Punish was a rhetorical *tour de force*, as well as a penetrating contribution to the sociology of punishment. It became, according to David Garland of the University of Edinburgh, "a central reference point" in criminology and exerted an influence so pervasive that it threatened "to eclipse . . . other more established traditions."[11] Talking about punishment and classification without Foucault, criminologist Stanley Cohen wrote in 1985, "is like talking about the unconscious without Freud."[12] But, for all this, Maeve McMahon thinks that the book left critical criminology in a theoretical cul-de-sac. "The emphasis on the decentralization and dispersal of power," she has written, produces an image of society in which there is no coordinating political centre that could conceivably be challenged or changed and therefore "yields a receding possibility of resistance."[13] The exclusive emphasis on the mechanics of power also leaves aside the question of whether power is being applied legitimately or illegitimately. This omission, finally, has the effect of rendering all power equally illegitimate, and making a beneficial application of power unimaginable.

Foucault's writings dramatized the situation of the solitary Nietzschean outlaw. He was fascinated, for example, with a murderer of the early nineteenth century named Pierre Rivière, a man who had murdered his mother, sister, and brother. Rivière, according to one of Foucault's biographers, James Miller, was "a paragon of primitive sadism." Foucault and his students published a book about Rivière's case in 1973. According to Miller, Foucault believed that labelling such men as "criminals" or "madmen" was a defensive tactic designed to "defuse the terror" they inspire and thus to drain off their "power."

[Foucault] thought that Rivière's acts merited neither therapy nor confinement. Rather — in his words — they warranted "a sort of reverence." "The most intense point of lives, that which concentrates their energy," he wrote, "is precisely where they clash with power, struggle with it, and attempt to use its forces or escape its traps." Through this struggle, and through "sacrificial and glorious murders," a man like Rivière became a "lightning-existence," illuminating the "ambiguity of the justifiable and the outlawed," revealing "the relation between power and the people, stripped down to essentials: the order to kill, the prohibition against killing; to make oneself kill, to be executed; voluntary sacrifice, ordained punishment; memory, oblivion." Rivière, in short, was a "tragic" hero — just like Sade, or Artaud. His murders, like his memoirs, were an admirable work of art . . . Rivière's memoir, [Foucault] declared . . . was "so strong and so strange that the crime ends up not existing anymore."[14]

Someone for whom even so horrible a crime as Rivière's dissolves in the aesthetic splendour of its execution was unlikely to put forward a positive political program. Foucault's influence, McMahon says, caught academic criminology up in the endless circle of deconstruction, "like the proverbial spider caught in its own web." "Once one adopts the analytical position that power has no centre," she writes, "and that mundane micro-powers are equally the locus of control, then critical criminologists can find themselves theoretically well-equipped, but with no political place to go."[15]

McMahon discovered the dimensions of this predicament for herself in the course of doctoral research she undertook in the early 1980s at the Centre of Criminology at the University of Toronto. Her thesis supervisor, Richard Ericson, had argued in a monograph titled *Decarceration and the Economy of Penal Reform* that the adoption of community-based "alternatives" in Ontario had not reduced incarceration, which had remained stable or even tended to increase.[16] The argument fit in with other studies purporting to show that "net-widening," or expansion of the number of people caught in the net of penal control, was a likelier consequence of attempts to correct offenders in the community than was decarceration or a reduction in the numbers imprisoned. It fit in as well with the prevailing Foucaultian consensus on the expansiveness of penal power. McMahon set out to show how attempts to create alternatives to penal control only end up ensnaring more people in the net, and how the relevant policy makers accounted for this effect, only to discover that imprisonment *had* actually gone down significantly in Ontario. Finding this out took some digging, because the data were complex, but she eventually established that, through the use of community-based correctional programs, Ontario had reduced imprisonment by about a third from the 1950s to the mid-1980s. This unexpected finding proved unwelcome to some of her colleagues.

> The first time I presented the data was about 1985 or 1986 at a conference in Montreal . . . I was still in the midst of some of this research, so it wasn't a very polished presentation . . . but I did get up and . . . produce my data and say, "Contrary to popular belief, the rate of imprisonment in Ontario now, proportionate to the population, is far lower than it was thirty years ago . . ." And basically what happened was that I wasn't able to finish that presentation because some of the other criminologists at that conference were so outraged that I would even try to claim that prison population had decreased. So, I think that's one sign of how much certain notions [had] become assumptions rather than conclusions.[17]

McMahon went on to publish these findings in *The Persistent Prison?* The Ontario experience, she argued, indicated that decarceration was possible, even though critical criminology under Foucault's influence had argued that in principle it wasn't. It was time, therefore, to overcome "the stance of suspicion," to recognize that "substantial decarceration can be observed in many places," and to accept that "the use of alternatives is by no means synonymous with expansion of penal systems."[18]

The consensus by which McMahon was shouted down in Montreal no longer exists in the same monolithic form that it did in the 1980s. But the effects of its pessimism and "internally defeatist logic" are still being felt. As the optimistic politics of prison reform gave way to principled pessimism, McMahon says, the political field was left by default to a technocratic, managerial ethos. The prison, having lost its pretension to treat or rehabilitate its inmates, was left as a holding institution. Advanced electronics were incorporated in sophisticated new systems of monitoring and control. Privatization of prisons was instituted in the hope of greater "efficiency" in the management of unwanted people.

These simplistic managerial responses to crime have thrived, at least in part, McMahon believes, because they have not been subject to sustained public challenge by the majority of her colleagues. There has, however, been one recent school of thought within criminology that has approached the problem of power in a more robust and realistic spirit. She calls this perspective "abolitionism," although "reductionism," the less dramatic term used by English prison reformer Andrew Rutherford, might be more accurate.[19] Abolitionism, by McMahon's definition, is a fundamental challenge to the way imprisonment monopolizes criminal justice. It criticizes the use of imprisonment as the normal and expected response to wrongdoing; seeks other ways of signifying serious disapproval; and advocates reducing imprisonment to a minimum, whose level can be estimated in theory but only finally determined in practice. But because many "abolitionists" are not finally opposed to detaining certain dangerous people in the interests of public safety, the term is inherently confusing, imprecise, and potentially divisive; and some whom McMahon would include in this school avoid the name for this reason.

However, with this proviso, abolitionism is a recognizable movement, whose members have been meeting every two years since 1981 at an International Conference on Penal Abolition. In

Europe the godfathers of this movement are four men whom I've
already quoted extensively: Nils Christie and Thomas Mathiesen
of the University of Oslo, Louk Hulsman of Erasmus University
in Rotterdam, and Herman Bianchi, the retired dean of the law
school at the Free University of Amsterdam. McMahon admires
their defiance of the nihilistic and defeatist logic that she asso-
ciates with Foucault's influence. Foucault himself, as we have
seen, sought a tragic illumination through the cruelty and intensity of his "clash with power." His less heroic followers tended
to subside into tense academic resignation, reduced to proving
that anything less than an impossibly total resistance to the
imprisoning logic of modernity was doomed to co-optation. The
abolitionists, in McMahon's view, are more willing to take a
realistic view of power, more willing to enter into dialogue with
the existing system, and more willing to make limited practical
proposals.

> Abolitionists [have been] relatively comfortable with the idea of
> engaging power, and with advancing proposals for exerting it in
> alternate ways. Perhaps it is this comfort with power which helps to
> explain why, although abolitionism is among the most radical of
> critical criminological perspectives, its adherents have also been
> among the most willing to dialogue, not only with those being dealt
> with by penal systems, but also with criminal justice policy makers,
> practitioners and reformers. Overall, abolitionists have most satis-
> factorily addressed issues of values underlying current practices, and
> have pointed to the possibilities of doing things otherwise.[20]

This willingness to engage in dialogue and advance constructive proposals, while still maintaining a root-and-branch critique
of penal ideology, is evident in the career of Thomas Mathiesen.
As noted in Chapter 1, Mathiesen is one of the pillars of the
Norwegian Association for Prison Reform, or KROM, which
represents both prisoners and free citizens interested in exposing the prison system to public scrutiny. Through its newsletter,

through regular public forums, and through an annual retreat, KROM has consistently tried to shape public spaces where prison policy can be discussed and arguments can be unfolded and exchanged across social and professional boundaries without the requirement to be brief, dramatic, and entertaining that the mass media now impose on most public discussion. Mathiesen has been prominent in these efforts without foregoing his view that imprisonment is "a fiasco" and ought to be abolished as the normal response to criminal wrongdoing. His argument for penal abolition emphasizes the superior uses that could be found for the vast sums now spent on incarceration, and so illustrates what McMahon says about abolitionists being willing to advance proposals for "exerting [power] in alternate ways."

> Think of what we could do with that money, spending it on three important things: first of all, on the offender side, using sensible kinds of alternatives, which exist: conflict resolution of a civil kind; community services; a whole string of treatment arrangements outside the context of the prison system . . . The second third of the billions saved [would go to] the victims. Today the victims don't get anything out of the system . . . Not money, not their health back . . . You could construct a whole new system, escalating compensation to the victim instead of escalating imprisonment to the offender; shifting the parameters completely, not focusing on the offender but focusing on the victim . . . Then the third part of those billions, I think, should go to communication with the public to explain all of this and to keep explaining it over many years. It would have to be a major cultural change obviously. But . . . I can see how we could come relatively close to abolition without endangering anyone.[21]

Of course, there is no immediate prospect of such an abolition. Established institutions have sometimes disappeared suddenly and unexpectedly, but public opinion is hardly running in favour of penal abolition at the moment. Meanwhile, Mathiesen thinks abolitionists should work to cap prison populations. Implementing alternatives without capping prison numbers invites "net-widening," by allowing alternatives to become mere supplements. First a ceiling must be established — in Norway, he suggests, it can safely be set at a quarter of the current number of prisoners — and then alternatives must be developed "as a consequence of that ceiling."[22]

The three elements of Thomas Mathiesen's strategy for abolishing imprisonment — a non-penal framework for offenders, increased attention to victims, and an engaged community — all fit a pattern of change that has been pointed out by Australian criminologist Pat O'Malley. In a 1995 lecture on "Criminology and the New Liberalism," O'Malley argued that changes in criminological thinking have to be seen in the context of a "sea change in political rationality" that has gradually taken shape over the last twenty years.[23] The hallmark of this "new liberalism" is the disappearance of the quintessentially modern idea that "society" is a unified and consistent entity. In its place, new liberalism sees an irreducible plurality of ways of life and modes of thought, incapable of being coordinated, or even conceived of as a single field. Modernity, as the era of "the social," was defined by two certainties: first, that the nature of society as such could be grasped, and second, that its character could be systematically improved by the legislative enactments of national states. The followers of Karl Marx were extreme, but not untypical in believing they had uncovered the "objective laws" by which society develops. Criminology, as a subdiscipline of sociology, shared in this confidence. Criminologists knew that crime expressed underlying social conditions, which it was their vocation to uncover, and they knew that a transformation of society would have to precede any fundamental change in the character or frequency of crime.

This era, in O'Malley's estimation, is now coming to an end — and as it ends, it reveals itself to us with a new clarity. At the height of modern confidence that society was a real, regular, and perfectible entity, it was possible to speak of the shaping action of "social forces" and the normative power of social laws. Today, thinkers as diverse as Margaret Thatcher and Jean Baudrillard concur in proclaiming the end of society in this modern sense. Baudrillard speaks of "the death of the social"; Thatcher states in her memoirs that "there is no such thing as society." (This remark has often been quoted maliciously, but it is clear from the passage in her memoirs where it appears that she intended to denounce the confusion of society with the state, rather than to deny the importance of social relations extending beyond family and community.) The fact that this unlikely pair concur says to O'Malley that new liberalism is neither an emanation of the right, nor a misplaced confidence in free markets as moral arbiters, but a new worldview comprehending a wide spectrum of possible political positions.

New liberalism emphasizes autonomous, empowered individuals and communities, rather than the collectivities that comprise social forces. The new liberal politician employs the state to dismantle the state, and deprecates compulsory state initiatives in favour of the creation of supportive frameworks for voluntary action. Within criminology this emphasis is evident in three tendencies. The first is the new prominence of victims. Offences were formerly understood to have been committed "against society" — it was the offender and the social determinants of his act that interested the criminologist. In a sense, the persons actually injured were incidental. Now, new thinking about criminal justice sees the victim as the moral centre of the proceedings and the victim's concrete injury as both the substance of the offender's debt and the only real hope of his reformation. The second and related emphasis is on the personal responsibility of offenders. The social character of crime is not ignored, but personal accountability is seen as the only way to redress the offence and reform the offender. And, finally, there is a new emphasis on community initiatives, rather than state action. This emphasis is evident, for example, in the recent book *Take Back Your Neighborhood: A Case for Modern-Day Vigilantism* by the chief justice of the Supreme Court of West Virginia, Richard Neely.[24] In this book he points out that expanding professional policing beyond certain limits would cost a lot, endanger civil rights, and probably fail to solve the problem of unsafe neighbourhoods anyway because police currently devote only about 2 percent of their time to patrolling, and citizens don't necessarily want more proactive policing. He argues, therefore, for a revival of the still extant common-law right of citizen arrest, claiming that only the citizens who live there can finally make a neighbourhood safe.

O'Malley calls the worldview that comprehends these ideas new liberalism, rather than postmodernism, among other possible names, because he wants to portray it as a form of political rationality. To see what is happening as political, he says, is to see it as contestable. Postmodernity, on the other hand, suggests the emergence of an entirely new epoch, or historical stage, and therefore something too vast and inevitable to be contested. What he wants to contest is the co-optation and distortion of this new order by the political right. Defining it instead as a broad form of rationality reveals the dialectical tension between communitarianism and free-market liberalism within this order. Recognizing this tension allows for the retrieval of what was worthwhile in the heritage of the left, while at the same time freeing the left from the feeling that it has no alternative but to fight a futile rearguard action on behalf of the failing institutions of the welfare state. A criminology oriented to victims, communities, and personal responsibility, in O'Malley's view, can retrieve the kernel of "the social," while at the same time overcoming an outworn tendency to define political progress exclusively in terms of the action of a unitary state.

Maeve McMahon believes that criminology reached an impasse under the influence of Michel Foucault. In a sense, Foucault reduced "the social" to its final absurdity, by portraying its influence as so total and so tyrannical as to reduce the possibility of political action to a solitary and hypervigilant paranoia. Pat O'Malley indicates that, while this was happening, and while the right was seizing the high ground from the demoralized left, a new criminology was also emerging. Mathiesen's approach is typical in its emphasis on individuals, communities, and hand-crafted alternatives to sweeping state action. It fits the broad paradigm of new liberalism in its attempt to recapture justice from the institutions of the state, but it in no sense belongs to the callous sink-or-swim school of market liberalism currently in the ascendant. In Part III I examine in more detail a range of criminal justice alternatives that move decisively out of the theoretical impasse Maeve McMahon has identified and into possibilities within this new liberalism that twenty years of neoconservative hegemony have tended to obscure.

III

Some Promising Alternatives

We assume that we can detect, pursue, indict, prosecute, and punish the criminal and still retain toward him the attitude of reinstating him in the community as soon as he indicates a change in social attitude himself . . . But control of crime by the hostile procedure of the law, and that of control through comprehension of social and psychological conditions, cannot be combined. To understand is to forgive and the social procedure seems to deny the very responsibility which the law affirms . . . On the other hand the pursuit by criminal justice inevitably awakens the hostile attitude in the offender and renders the attitude of mutual comprehension practically impossible.

G. H. Mead
"The Psychology of Punitive Justice"
The American Journal of Sociology 23: 577–602

CRIME CONTROL
AND COMMUNITY

In old Europe, before the erection of modern legal systems, says historian Harold Berman, law was "an integral part of the common consciousness, the 'common conscience' of the community."[1] In village assemblies with half-remembered names like *palaver* and *moot*, the peoples of Europe addressed violations of law or custom. Today, the word "palaver" denotes profuse talk, and "moot" a point that cannot be satisfactorily settled. The change in the meaning of the words hints at how thoroughly time has been capitalized and justice professionalized during a millennium of modernization. In medieval and early modern Europe, people still felt that criminal conflicts were their business; and, since they often worked no more than ninety days a year, they had plenty of time to palaver.[2] With the advent of industrialized labour, people were left without time to get involved in lengthy dispute settlements and so learned to rely on the institution of public prosecution. Justice, in today's telling phrase, began to be *delivered* to the citizens.

Once the Western world's autonomous, professionalized legal systems were established, their superiority was taken for granted for a long time. Informal, community-based modes of justice were not included within the realm of law at all. The colonial subjects of Western imperialism were considered to be "lesser breeds without the Law," in the words of Rudyard Kipling.[3]

What American anthropologist Al Hoebel called "the law ways" of non-European peoples did not register as law at all. Justice administered outside formal legal institutions came to be known entirely by its failures and degenerations: the lynch mob, the generations-old feud, the night-riding vigilante.

During the last generation, this situation has changed. Within what Pat O'Malley calls new liberalism, and Maeve McMahon identifies as abolitionist criminology, a re-evaluation of the role of community in criminal justice is under way. One of the texts most frequently cited by those engaged in this rethinking is an article Nils Christie published in 1977 called "Conflicts as Property."[4] In it, Christie discusses the shadow cast by formal justice. Community, he says, is made from conflict as much as from cooperation; the capacity to resolve conflict is what gives social relations their sinew. Professionalizing justice "steals the conflicts," robbing the community of its ability to face trouble and restore peace. Communities lose their confidence, their capacity, and, finally, their inclination to preserve their own order. They become instead consumers of police and court "services," with the consequence that they largely cease to be communities.

Christie's argument turned the prevailing view of legal history — that professionalization equals progress — upside down. He pointed out that when conflict is co-opted by professional experts, people lose "opportunities for norm clarification":

> Lawyers are . . . trained into agreement on what is relevant in a case. But that means a trained incapacity in letting the parties decide what *they* think is relevant. It means that it is difficult to stage what we might call a political debate in the court. When the victim is small and the offender big — in size or power — how blameworthy then is the crime? And what about the opposite case, the small thief and the big house-owner? If the offender is well-educated, ought he then to suffer more, or maybe less, for his sins? Or if he is black, or if he is young, or if the other party is an insurance company, or if his wife has just left him, or if his factory will break down if he has to go to

jail, or if his daughter will lose her fiancé, or if he was drunk, or if he was sad, or if he was mad. There is no end to it.[5]

Christie goes on to itemize a whole series of other losses that occur when lawyers monopolize justice. The offender loses "the opportunity for participation in a personal confrontation" where he might "receive a type of blame that would be very difficult to neutralize." The victim is unable to pursue his desire for understanding. Stereotypes around "the criminal" go unchallenged, and public anxieties that might be reduced by more thorough knowledge go unallayed. All these losses make clear the hidden cost of professionalization and establish the grounds for a more realistic accounting of the costs of justice.

Law, in Christie's estimation, is a cultural institution, a vehicle for what Northrop Frye called "primary concern." The acts that we hold apart from ourselves as "crimes" and attribute to an alien tribe called "criminals" are often the most vividly human of predicaments. They are a unique disclosure of the conflicts and tensions underlying social life, and they may sometimes offer a unique opportunity to resolve these conflicts. "Could anything be more important," Christie asks, "than that those who have been hurt get a chance to say so, and that those who have been hurting them would really listen, would really explain why they did it, and really hear what other people thought about it?"[6] These questions point justice back in the direction of the old communal institutions that I mentioned at the start of the chapter. What matters to Christie is that the case have a hearing in which the participants and the circumstances become fully known. "It is not necessarily an ideal that justice be swift and simplified," he says. "You can see, in a lot of anthropological studies, how court proceedings take lots of time . . . If you really see the total complication, you build in some very strong inhibitions against delivering pain."[7]

In Christie's view, these inhibitions weaken as soon as criminal justice systems come to be seen not as "arrangements for ethical debate" but as machines for fighting crime. His response to this danger has been to try to "civilize" justice, both by increasing the civility of its procedures and by moving as many legal imbroglios as possible from a penal to a civil framework. Wherever an offence is not so terrible that anger and grief cripple the relevant community's response, there exists a possibility of converting the wrong into an obligation to those who have suffered from it. Apology, compensation, service, and a change in the offender's behaviour may all be involved in the discharge of such an obligation. In 1992, for example, Christie's native Norway established Municipal Mediation Boards as an alternative to criminal prosecution. The announcement of these boards from the Norwegian Ministry of Justice acknowledged Christie's influence by stating that he could "rightly be called the father of Mediation Boards in Norway." Mediators are lay people from the community whose mandate is to assist "parties in conflict" to find a settlement in circumstances in which one party has "caus[ed] damage, loss or other violation." They are not "authorized to determine [the settlement's] content."[8]

Norway's Mediation Boards belong to a class of new community-based institutions that have recently appeared around the world as alternatives to criminal prosecution. In this chapter I examine several of them. The first case I want to look at is an innovation that has turned New Zealand's Youth Court into "the brightest star in the justice firmament today," according to one of its judges, Peter McAloon.[9] In 1989, New Zealand's Labour government enacted the Children, Young Persons and Their Families Act, which brought into being a new forum in which to address youth crime called the "family group conference." Family group conferences replace court hearings and allow everyone concerned in a given case to express an opinion about it and contribute to a disposition.

The origins of this initiative were mixed. As an effort to shift responsibility from state to community, it was certainly part of the Labour government's "over-all ideological push to privatize and cut back on social spending."[10] But it responded as well to demands from the Maori minority for a youth justice procedure that was less hostile and more closely related to traditional Maori practice. It also addressed widespread concerns about the exclusion of victims from criminal justice proceedings generally; about the number of relatively minor problems preoccupying the attention of youth courts; about the fact that courts are often ill-equipped to deal with the types of problems brought before them; and, finally, about the considerable overrepresentation of the Maoris in New Zealand's courts and custodial institutions.

Whereas Canada's Young Offenders Act mandates an incoherent mix of rehabilitation and punishment, leaving judges free to interpret it according to their liking, the Children, Young Persons and Their Families Act establishes a clear preference for restorative, noncustodial, community- and family-oriented dispositions over criminal prosecutions. This allows the police, the courts, and other concerned agencies to align and coordinate their efforts. The police are encouraged to exercise discretion, issuing "street warnings" for minor offences, perhaps bringing the offender to a police station together with the parents for more formal cautioning, and even arranging modest informal sanctions such as an apology or personal service. Judge Heino Lilles of the Yukon Territorial Court, who spent a year studying youth justice reforms in both Australia and New Zealand, reports that "during 1990, the first full year of operation of the act, almost 75 percent of apprehended young offenders in New Zealand were warned and diverted by the police, a 35 percent increase from five years earlier."[11]

Where charges are laid and not contested, most cases are referred by the youth court to family group conferences. Cases that are tried in court may also be referred to family group conferences for sentencing. Such a conference must be convened within twenty-one days of the offence by an official called a youth justice coordinator. The coordinator mediates between the police, the victim, the offender and his or her family and ensures that everyone concerned is present at the conference. A coordinator may either facilitate the conference herself, or deputize "a respected member or elder of the offender's extended family." Marie Sullivan, manager of Youth Justice Services for the city of Auckland, says that it is her experience that when a nonprofessional guides the conference, "the victims' needs are attended with more grace and sincerity than when the professional facilitates."[12]

Matt Hakiaha, a Maori youth justice coordinator, visited Canada in 1995 and described to me several of the cases with which he had been involved. He estimated that he had facilitated about a thousand conferences at that point, of which only a handful had had to go back to youth court because a settlement couldn't be found. The first case he told me about involved four youths who had broken into a school, done some drinking, and then accidentally set a fire, which they could not control and which ended up doing extensive damage.

> The whole family group conference in this case took about three days. The first day was mainly focused around feelings, feelings of animosity, where teachers, where parents were saying, "Look, you burned our school down, and our kids have to be catered for now, and they can't be, so they've had to build temporary classrooms." I've got quite a clear picture in my mind of these four offenders. They were sitting there, so unmoved, so unemotional. And then this young girl walked up with the scrapbook that she had kept in her classroom, and it was half-charred. About one-half was just burned to a crisp, and the other half was charred. And she came up and sat in front of these four boys . . . and she said, "This is all I've got as a remembrance of my brother, because this scrapbook is photos of my family and a photo of my brother, and he died not so long ago, about a year ago, and that's all I've got now." And then you saw the tears trickling down the faces of these four boys.
>
> The impact that was made by the victims was amazing. And I wonder whether a court would do that. I wonder whether a court process would allow this emotion to come out. And in this case, it

meant that the offence was personalized to the offenders. It meant that they were able to take ownership of the offence. And it meant also that they could deal with their own feelings about it.[13]

Once everyone has had their say about what the events in question have meant to them, a family group conference must reach a settlement satisfactory to all concerned. The family of the offender is encouraged to take the lead in proposing a solution. In this case, the offenders obviously lacked the means to pay for the half-million dollars' worth of damage they had caused. So, they were asked to write letters of apology to the students and teachers of the classrooms that were destroyed, to the Ministry of Education, and to the school board. They were also asked to apologize in person to the school principal, the teachers, the board, and the pupils. And they were required to help build the school a new playground, working every Saturday and Sunday for six months. This plan was not at first embraced by the four boys.

> Initially there was resentment: "I'm not going to do this, I don't want to do this." And I said, "Well, young men, the other option we have is that I hand it to the court, and the court will deal with you, and it means that you could spend some time incarcerated. I don't know what it could mean; but I suspect, and my experiences have taught me, that you could be incarcerated." But it was interesting; the families said, "No, they're going to come, and we will come with them. They're our children. We will be responsible for our children, and either their father or I will be down here with these children."[14]

The parents made good on this promise, and every Saturday and Sunday for six months, while the boys worked on the playground, one of them was there. When the work was completed there was an unveiling ceremony. Because they were successful in this project, Matt Hakiaha says, they were "looked on as heroes." None of them has come to the attention of the police again.

Family group conferences seek nonpunitive dispositions, but often make quite strenuous demands on offenders. For example, Matt Hakiaha recalls a case in which a young man called Shane had to give up his car as a result of having stolen and wrecked someone else's car.

> When they got to the family group conference . . . Shane apologized to the victim and to her family. But then the victim said, "No, you're going to hear how this has affected me. Number 1: I've got a daughter who's asthmatic, and when my daughter has an asthma attack . . . I've got to wait for an ambulance. In the past, I could take my daughter to emergency in our own car. Number 2: I've got a son who plays soccer, okay? Now, he can't go because he can't go to training and he can't go to games; we're now reliant on other team members or the neighbours. Number 3: I can't do my shopping. I can't shop for our family because you've taken our car." And Shane at that stage became a blubbering mess . . . He started to own the offence in its entirety . . .
>
> At the family group conference, it was decided by the family, Shane's family, Shane's mum and dad and Shane, that he would give up his car for the victim . . . Shane said to me later on that he would prefer to have gone to prison for two or three months, because then he would have his car back and still there. There was the embarrassment that came upon Shane because he had to tell his friends that he lost his car because of the theft of another car. Also, friends saw Shane's car being driven by another owner, so Shane had the . . . embarrassment of, "Shane, why is that . . . lady driving your car?" And Shane had to say, "Oh, you know the car I took? Yeah, well, that's the owner, she got my car."[15]

Inducing this kind of shame and embarrassment, Hakiaha says, is a traditional Maori response to antisocial acts. He related the myth of a shaman who was thought to be using magic to destroy people's crops. It was forbidden to shed the blood of such a person, so he was taken to a desert island and abandoned there.

However, the shaman was able to use his power to summon a whale to bring him home on its back. On the way, he passed his abductors returning in their canoes. "Shall I kill them with one flick of my tail?" the whale inquired. "No," the shaman said, "let their shame be their punishment." The saying has passed into Maori culture as a proverb.

In the eight years since it was introduced, family group conferencing in New Zealand has produced results that justify Judge McAloon's accolade. It has radically reduced the number of youths in custody and the number of court appearances by youthful offenders. This has in turn drastically reduced the costs of the system. According to Judge Lilles, "In 1985, in New Zealand, there were 4,397 young persons in youth institutions at a cost of $206 million. Six years later there were 939, at a cost of $113 million. In addition, the overall system costs have also been significantly reduced, as the number of youth and children appearing in court decreased from between 10,000–13,000 each year to 1,800 in 1993."[16] This reduction in costs has been accompanied by an increase in the effectiveness of youth justice. Before 1989, Lilles reports, about a third of the orders made by youth court judges were not carried out. In contrast, very few family group conference agreements have been purely nominal. The involvement of family and community, and the voluntary, consensual character of the agreements that are entered into, make execution of the conference's decision a matter of honour and thus increase the likelihood that agreements will be effectively supervised and carried out.

Canada currently sentences about 30 percent of those tried in youth court to custody. In the first full year the new system was in operation in New Zealand, researchers found that a representative sample of 100 youths were dealt with as follows:

- 75 were warned by the police and diverted out of the system
- 15 were dealt with by family group conferences
- 10 appeared in youth court

- 5 were subject to court orders
- 2 were subject to residential or custodial orders.[17]

Family group conferencing, needless to say, is not perfect, and does not guarantee happy endings. Lilles cites a 1993 study showing that victim participation was still only about 50 percent, and that of these only about half reported themselves satisfied, while a third said they felt worse as a result of participating. Satisfaction among police at 91 percent, and among the young offenders themselves at 85 percent was much higher. The victim finding shows room for improvement, but still compares very favourably to how victims evaluate court proceedings. Marie Sullivan points to the "powerful silence" that often follows from a victim's presence and says she hopes that, as the program becomes more established, more victims will be willing to participate. "I always regret a victim's absence as a healing opportunity lost," she says.

> By focusing on the needs of victims or healing *their* need to be restored to the feeling of being in control of their own lives . . . the young person and her/his family when proposing a plan to deal with the matters can offer a creative, constructive solution. The best solution is that proposed by the young offender, through his family, having taken into account the requirements of the victim. Constantly in my work, where the behaviours and situations of our young people, many jobless and uneducated, have the potential to induce a depressing effect on my own outlook on life, I am affirmed in my belief in the innate goodness of people by the common sense, the compassion and the cooperation of victims. A conference without victims present lacks the power (and consequently the effectiveness) of a conference where they are present.[18]

Family group conferencing is also in use in Australia in the small city of Wagga Wagga in New South Wales. Lacking the statutory mandate and the infrastructure provided by the federal act in New Zealand, the police department in that city initiated family group conferences as part of the exercise of their common-law power of cautioning. A state government white paper has now proposed adopting this way of doing things throughout the state. Lilles reports that Wagga Wagga has had the same excellent results in offender participation — for example, 93 percent of agreed-upon compensation is actually paid — and a much higher rate of victim participation and satisfaction. This may be because "restitution to the victim is given the highest priority" in this system, and secondary victimization — such as the embarrassment of a sister at a brother's offence — is also stressed. In Wagga Wagga, "nearly all young offenders offered to impose tougher demands on themselves than the victims thought appropriate. Victims often found themselves arguing the case for leniency, with the result that offenders viewed victims in a different light."[19] The opportunity afforded to the victim to display magnanimity rather than demand vengeance potentially offers healing to both parties — it liberates the victim from anger and the offender from denial by allowing them to switch positions.

Family group conferencing has had a lot of attention in criminal justice circles over the last few years. Mark Umbreit and Howard Zehr, who have both been involved in victim-offender work for a long time, wrote recently: "Rarely has a new criminal justice idea received such quick exposure and interest from audiences as widespread as activists, professionals, and the general public. No other restorative justice approach has so quickly brought such numbers of law enforcement officials 'to the table' as active stakeholders in the restorative justice movement."[20] Real Justice, an organization based in Bethlehem, Pennsylvania, is vigorously promoting the use of the Wagga Wagga–style of conference in schools as well as by police departments. It has already trained hundreds of police officers and school personnel, including some RCMP and Canadian municipal police officers.

One Canadian community that has adopted this approach is

the town of Sparwood in the Crow's Nest Pass in British Columbia. The change was initiated by a local lawyer, Glen Purdy,
whose practice had involved representing a lot of young offenders
— usually the same ones again and again. "It would be a rare
occasion," he says, "when I would deal with a young offender
only once." He goes on

> The system provides little impact on a young offender either one way
> or another. The young offender has little or nothing to do with the
> court process. His lawyer will ensure, unless he's going to be giving
> evidence on the stand at a trial, that the young offender will say
> nothing, if possible; he will have no contact with his victim. It is the
> way that the adversarial system is designed, to essentially isolate
> the offender as much as possible — that's a defence counsel's job in
> many cases — and to present that young offender to the court in the
> most positive light possible. The system is divorced completely from
> the offending behaviour and the impact that such behaviour might
> have had on a victim.[21]

Shielding young offenders from their communities and from
any sense of the consequences of their actions was a position
Purdy found extremely frustrating; so he was receptive when a
judge from nearby Cranbrook passed on a paper by Heino Lilles
on family group conferencing.

The idea made sense to Purdy, and so he took it to the head of
the Sparwood RCMP detachment, Jake Bouwmann, and asked,
"Could *we* do things this way?" Sergeant Bouwmann, as it
happened, was also disaffected with the youth justice system.
Before his appointment to Sparwood, he had been a watch
commander in a larger centre, where he and the police officers
working under him had felt that youth justice was a revolving
door. "Every shift," he says, "you heard the same frustration of
the policeman coming in and receiving a call to a young-offender
complaint and feeling, 'Well, why am I doing this, 'cause nothing's going to happen anyway, and the kid will be back on the

street, and the same thing will happen again tomorrow, and I'll have to do it again.'" So he told Glen Purdy that he was willing to try.

In New Zealand, as I mentioned above, family group conferences are authorized by statute, while in Australia they are convened under the common-law authority of the police. Purdy and Bouwmann seized on this second, immediately available, option in Sparwood. Juveniles who came to the attention of the RCMP were given a choice: if they didn't admit wrongdoing they could be charged and tried in court; but, if they admitted guilt, they could avoid being charged and tried altogether so long as they were willing to submit to the recommendations of what came to be called a "resolution conference." Bouwmann and Purdy decided that they would exclude, at least at first, major crimes of violence. In the event, they had none, and, during 1995, the first full year of operation, all of the forty-three young offenders arrested agreed to attend resolution conferences.

Because many of the incidents the police investigated involved multiple offenders, eighteen resolution conferences in total were held during this first year. Dispositions have generally involved some combination of apology, restitution, and personal service. The youth who stole from a clothing store was required to make it up to the owner by doing unpaid work in the store. What has generally been most remarkable, Glen Purdy says, has been the part victims have played in the correction of offenders.

> After they get over the emotional aspects of it, it happens on a very frequent basis that the complainant or victim wants to be and is directly involved in assisting the youth. It brings the two parties together in quite an interesting way. They both become more human to each other . . . which is something that doesn't occur at all in the traditional court system. The victim and the offender rarely meet. So, what this process does is humanize [the conflict] and personalize it for all parties, and we think that has quite a significant impact on not only the youth but the victim as well.[22]

Court proceedings, in Howard Zehr's apt caricature, are about "establishing blame and giving out pain."[23] They operate in a complex framework of rights, and they focus almost entirely on who did what to whom and how much pain the perpetrator should be made to suffer as a consequence. The causes and consequences of the events in question, the meaning these events had for those involved, and the restoration of civil peace, are all largely outside the ambit of the court's consideration. Resolution conferences, on the other hand, bring these social considerations to the fore. They permit everyone involved to speak without restriction about how they see a given incident, which allows feelings of anger, but also of contrition and forgiveness, to come into play. Jake Bouwmann, for example, was particularly impressed by the resolution of a case in which two girls had quite severely beaten another girl. The victim had been hospitalized, and one of her assailants had then gone to the hospital and threatened her life. More bad blood between the families was then created when the victim's mother wrote a letter to the newspaper in which she blamed the mother of one of the attackers for not properly caring for her daughter. Twenty-six people were involved in this conference, and it ended, Bouwmann says, in a moving scene of public reconciliation.

> It was guaranteed nothing you would ever see in court, at least I've never seen or heard anything like it in my service. The disposition had been arrived at, and the victim's mother walked over to the mother of one of the [offenders], and they hugged each other, and they were crying, and they were apologizing to each other for things that they had said to one another. And they walked out together.
>
> I had never, in my service, seen anything so effective. Not only was it a learning experience for me, but it was a learning experience for both the victim's parents and the [offenders'] parents. They had always seen their children as good kids, and now they had seen this side that really wasn't that nice. But, during the conference, they had realized that there was still a lot of good in these kids and that they

couldn't just be thrown away and that they had to be dealt with, and that they had to work . . . There's no doubt in my mind that, if the victim and the offender should meet, walking in the mall, that there would be no animosity, just because of the resolution.[24]

Jake Bouwmann adds that resolution conferences like this have also changed both his attitude as a policeman, towards young offenders, and their attitude towards him, increasing respect on both sides.

Programs like Sparwood's have been in operation for too short a time to permit any definitive conclusion about recidivism. But it appears so far that a resolution conference and its homemade disposition are much more likely to provide correction for a young offender than a court sentence. For youngsters in trouble a court is apt to appear as just one more pompous authority; and they are likely to affect indifference to the court's power, as well as to any sermons that may be preached at them from the bench. A resolution conference is an informal proceeding in which it is much more difficult for a youngster to avoid facing the harm he has done. Consequently, Jake Bouwmann says, an offender is much less likely to treat it as a big joke.

Crime and its consequences are inherently dramatic, and whatever response the community makes will also have a dramatic structure. Courts are imposingly theatrical, but what they tend to dramatize is the power and glory of the state in the person of the judge. A resolution conference, on the other hand, is theatre by the community for the community. It is not, after all, the judge's store that has been robbed or the judge's daughter who has been beaten up. Court proceedings dramatize an injury to the law — a concept that is generally too abstract for a youth to grasp; a resolution conference faces an offender with the real victims of the crime. It is, therefore, much more likely to inspire contrition and reform in young offenders, as well as to dispose others to try to help them.

So far Glen Purdy has chaired resolution conferences on a

volunteer basis. He has not sought any special funding for the program because he fears that such funding might come with strings. It would be good, he says, if they had access to the assessment and follow-up services on which courts can rely; but he is unwilling to jeopardize the primacy or the independence of the community in this regard. The key to correction, he thinks, lies in the involvement of the community from which the problem arose in the first place, and this community cannot be truly involved unless it is free to respond without bureaucratic constraint.

Purdy is now trying to extend the use of resolution conferences to cases of adult offending. Meanwhile, the reputation of the work he and his colleagues have done has spread widely across Alberta and British Columbia. When I was first put in touch with Purdy by Heino Lilles in early 1996, I had the impression that Sparwood's program was unique. In the fall of that year, several months after I had broadcast an account of it on *Ideas*, Purdy wrote to say that he already knew of sixteen communities in B.C. and several in Alberta that were attempting something similar.

The final instance of community justice that I want to examine in this chapter is the sentencing circle, a forum pioneered in Canadian native communities, and closely related to the youth justice initiatives already discussed. Thrashing out problems in a circle must be as old as human society, and many aboriginal cultures are permeated by imagery of "the sacred hoop," but the first formally defined use of circle sentencing in a criminal case occurred in 1992. The presiding judge was Barry Stuart, a veteran of the Yukon Territorial Court, who had been appointed to the bench in the summer of 1978 and spent a number of years during the 1980s as a land-claims negotiator. In the dock was Philip Moses, a twenty-six-year-old chronic offender with forty-three previous convictions, who pleaded guilty to carrying a baseball bat with the intention of assaulting an RCMP officer.[25] The Crown asserted that "the community" wanted him sent to jail, a sentence that the circumstances and his record seemed to warrant. "As the plane waited to take us home," Stuart recalls, "I adjourned for a few harried moments to compose a sentence that would give the community its wish." During this interval, questions that had been forming in him for many years suddenly came to a head.

> Where was his family? Did he have any friends? No one but the Crown, who didn't live in the community, had advanced this request [for a jail term]. I was not suspicious that the request was fabricated, but was curious to hear from the community. I realized that most of what I knew or thought I knew about the offender came from people who didn't live in the community. Any gaps in my understanding were filled in by the usual assumptions the experience of being a judge readily provides. I did not have the input of the people who knew him and who would be the most directly impacted by the sentencing: his community, family, and friends. I certainly didn't know what they thought might happen when he came back to the community after I had done "my job" of sending him to jail for a year or more. What could we do then, but wait until someone suffered at his hand in a manner that enabled the justice system to once again legally remove him from his community. The futility, expense, and insensitivity of mindlessly and without direct community input sending the offender yet again to jail, pressed me to do something else.[26]

Stuart decided to put the case over until the next month. When he resumed, he reconfigured his court as a circle and invited the people who could answer his questions to be present. In this circle, Moses' family and friends made it clear that they were willing to aid in his rehabilitation; and, on this basis, Stuart suspended sentence and ordered two years' probation, with the requirement that Moses live with his family and be treated for alcoholism.[27] Moses responded to the sentence by successfully changing his life.

The reputation of this first case spread quickly, and other

communities were soon eager to try circle sentencing as well. Harold Gatensby, who went on to play a prominent part in the development of this idea, remembers Judge Stuart coming to his community of Carcross shortly afterwards.

> When the judge came to the community, he asked for a meeting on justice and said, "We want to try out this circle that they had done in Mayo." And I said without hesitation, "Yes, we want to do it in Carcross." And he said, "When would you like to have another meeting about it?" And I said, "Let's do it today," because it was a court day. "Well," he said, "we're not ready." I said, "Let's do it today, we'll start right now." And I encouraged the other people, and we agreed to go ahead with it.[28]

Harold Gatensby's enthusiastic haste arose from his own experience. Growing up as a Métis, he had felt accepted neither in white nor in native society. At the mission school in Carcross where he was sent when he was eight, the native children called him and his brother "the little white boys" and beat them up, and "took out a lot of their grievances" on them. Later, when he went to school in Whitehorse, he was "the no-good-for-nothing native person." Confused about who he was, he learned to live by his fists, and remembers "getting roughed up by the RCMP quite often." At fifteen he was raised into adult court and sent south for a year to the federal penitentiary at Fort Saskatchewan. He was so young that he recalls spending the five dollars he was given on leaving the prison for firecrackers.

Harold Gatensby continued to be in and out of trouble for a number of years, serving another year-long stint at the new Whitehorse Correctional Centre and many shorter spells for drinking and brawling. Then one day he was taken by his brother to a sweat lodge ceremony; he felt like he had "just made it back home after a long and hard journey." He knew that he had finally found what he had spent a big part of his life looking for. He and his brother became helpers in the sweat lodge ceremony, and eventually began to perform it in the Whitehorse jail. This led to further involvement with the justice system and further reflection on its perverse consequences for native communities.

So by the time Barry Stuart turned up in Carcross with the idea of circle sentencing, Harold Gatensby was ready. He remembered the alienation he had felt when he was in court himself: "my heart just about leap[ing] out of my throat, my hands . . . sweating . . . everybody . . . an expert but me." He knew that jailing people only "makes you mean, makes you bitter, [and] teaches you to be dishonest," since he himself had learned how to forge cheques and crack safes in prison. He had pondered the unfairness of having outsiders make the decisions the community would have to live with, as ex-prisoners returned home rejected, isolated, and volatile. And he knew the virtue of a circle.

> I had been cornered in my life. Perhaps I did it myself. A lot of help from the institutions, what I call heartless institutions. But I'd been cornered. And when I started to learn about a circle, I realized that you cannot corner the human being in a circle, that there is an equality about a circle, that all of life around us [is a circle] — the Earth is round, the trees are round. [If] you burn a fire in the middle of winter, it doesn't matter if you stack it up square, it's going to . . . melt the snow in a circle. I started to see something very powerful in this circle.

The case they tried that first day in Carcross involved a relatively serious offence by a persistent offender. For the first time in his life he "had to listen to the consequences of what he had done in the community." Court, formerly, had been at best a show one could go and watch. Now, community members got involved and confronted the accused directly. The crime would normally have called for a jail sentence, but the circle instead demanded that the offender perform service in the community. The offender was quite talented as a carver and painter, so he was told to work with children at school, and also told to set a fish net and clean and donate his catch to elders in the community. A support group was created with whom he was to meet regularly.

The sentence initially demanded much more from the community than a jail term would have. Harold Gatensby had to help this man find a boat and a fishing net; he had to meet with him regularly; and he had to swallow some of the extravagant hopes inspired by that first circle when the man began drinking again. But, four years later, fully aware that circle sentencing is not a panacea, he retains his enthusiasm for the idea and serves as the "keeper of the circle" in Carcross. The name reflects the ceremonial aspect of circle sentencing. "We start off with a prayer," he says. "We invite the Creator, we invite the ancestors, we invite help. We humble ourselves to them, say[ing], 'We can't do this alone. Please, be with us.'" All members of the circle are equal in terms of the opportunity to talk and the requirement to listen. A turn to speak is signified by a feather, a talking stick, or a rock that circulates during the hearing. This is used, he says, "to hold the direction," and to remind each speaker of his obligation to talk from the heart and to the point. The judge, the Crown, and the defence participate as equals in the circle but retain their special functions. A disposition is arrived at when a sentencing plan achieves consensus, which is defined not as unanimity but as an agreement to which most consent and to which no one is urgently or unalterably opposed. If consensus cannot be reached, or if the judge is unwilling to accept the plan it produces, sentencing responsibility reverts to him.

For Harold Gatensby the importance of circle sentencing lies in the fact that "it gives people a chance." The offender is exposed to the consequences his acts have had for others in a context that fosters and supports penitence. When offenders undertake to reform, they do so in front of witnesses who will be disposed to hold them to their word. And, even when backsliding occurs, the community is still strengthened by its having said, in Gatensby's words, "this is not the way our people are, this is not the way we're meant to be, this is not the way we want to live." There have certainly been disappointments and setbacks, but Gatensby is continually heartened and renewed by the feeling that he is participating in a renaissance of native ways that is going on all over North America and that has to do, finally, with the recovery of a dignified way of life, not just with the criminal justice system.

Circle sentencing is now used extensively throughout the Yukon. In Whitehorse, the federal and territorial governments have funded the Kwanlin Dun Community Justice Project to work with offenders and victims going through circle sentencing. (The Kwanlin Dun First Nation is the name that has been adopted by native people of all tribal backgrounds living in Whitehorse.) Offenders who have admitted guilt, are "motivated and willing to commit to a wellness or healing plan," and can name at least two community members willing to support them are free to apply to the Kwanlin Dun Circle Court. More than two hundred circles have now been held. In other communities, preparing for the circle and following through on its recommendations still depends more on volunteers. In the only study made so far of recidivism by "adults processed through the Kwanlin Dun Community Circles," Judge Stuart and Rosemary Couch, the director of the Kwanlin Dun Commuity Justice Project, found "dramatic decreases in the frequency and seriousness of criminal behaviour. Among offenders who had committed an average of almost twenty criminal offences throughout their lives," they say, "their rate of serious offences after being involved in the circle dropped 80 percent in comparing the same period before and after the circle."[29]

This result is impressive; but, in Barry Stuart's view, it falls far short of stating the full benefit of circle sentencing. He writes,

> The success of the circle cannot be measured solely by what happens to offenders who go through the circle, but must also embrace what these offenders do to change the lives of other offenders. In the Yukon, offenders who have been through the circle and changed their lives have worked "outside the system" to change many others.

Based on discussions with both circle participants and their "recruits," a study of this extension of the circle is warranted. My guess is that twice as many success stories are generated by the work of offenders and their support groups on others whose lives involve repeated offences. The impact is particularly profound when one considers [that in the past] many of these people when they emerged from jail influenced their friends to join them in crime . . . Now they work on expanding their "circle" of friends [who have] cease[d] committing crimes.[30]

Circle sentencing also fosters an art of citizenship that goes far beyond the outcome of individual cases. It allows people to take back capacities that have been, in Nils Christie's words, "stolen" by the criminal justice system.

I think the most important thing to develop in any community is resolving conflict. Whatever the nature of the conflict is, if a community goes through a process in which they can be empowered to resolve the conflict, they're going to get a greater sense of being able to trust each other, to move with each other and get an understanding that they can make a difference . . . Whether it's municipal problems or health problems or criminal problems, I think that's the case. And I think I'm seeing many people who are coming out of the circle-sentencing process with a better understanding of how to use the consensus-based skills in their home situation, in the workplace and in the community generally.[31]

Finally, circle sentencing addresses the culture shock that many natives experience in the courts. Courts generally expect punctual, forthright responses that go very much against "the ethic of noninterference" that pervades many native cultures. The term comes from the late Claire Brant, a Mohawk psychiatrist, who used it to describe unwillingness to criticize or confront another, reluctance in praising or blaming another, and diffidence in showing anger or even in making eye contact in certain situations.

When native people follow this ethic in criminal justice settings, their behaviour is regularly interpreted as passivity, indifference, or uncooperativeness.[32] I don't, of course, mean to suggest that other Canadians feel right at home when facing criminal charges — but only that the discomfort experienced by natives is compounded by the court's requirement that they behave in ways that are felt to be unbecoming and, ultimately, unethical. Circle hearings solve this problem by creating an unforced and unhurried setting in which people can more freely participate.

Because the influence of community sentencing is expressed in such a variety of ways, Barry Stuart, Rosemary Couch, and Harold Gatensby all argue that the process itself is as important as the outcome of individual cases. Beyond the successes they have enjoyed, what really counts is the gradient they believe circle sentencing is helping to establish towards capable communities and a regenerated culture. They are pursuing a vision of justice as something good in itself and not just an instrumental effort to reform the "justice system." Failures from which people learn can sometimes be as important as success. Not every broken individual can be mended, and "sometimes," Stuart says, "the impact of circles is . . . not evident until years later."[33]

Circle sentencing, like any other mode of administering justice, is open to abuse. Formal justice miscarries when bureaucratic and professional interests supersede what is right; community justice has to be safeguarded against the rivalries and prejudices that beset community life. To guard against this danger, Stuart believes that communities should start small, building competence and confidence with cases that can be handled without undue risk of division of opinion. He also believes that police, Crowns, and judges involved with community justice have to be alert for abuses and ensure that circles are not dominated by "powerful local voices" in cases "involving vulnerable victims, such as women and children."[34] "Charter rights, statutory provisions, and all the fundamental principles of justice," he continues, "must be retained. Some aspects of this body of law may be waived by participants, but [this] must be clearly done on record and [is] best done after legal advice."[35]

Circle sentencing is a hybrid, an attempt to crossbreed the community's emphasis on solidarity and accommodation with the rights and protections that are the strength of the formal system. It differs from normal criminal court proceedings, according to Stuart, in the way that it "seeks to move beyond positions to uncover the parties' underlying interests." If the Crown, for example, seeks a jail sentence, the circle will probe the nature of this interest. Is it to punish? Protect the community? Deter others? Jail serves these interests poorly. Perhaps there are other ways to serve them. Negotiation, innovation, and continuous adjustment are substituted for the mechanical application of prescribed penalties.

Such an approach faces formidable obstacles in moving from the margins into the mainstream. The deeply entrenched myths that sustain the existing system ensure, as Barry Stuart says, that "good news in criminal justice rarely travels far."[36] He lists five such myths: (1) all criminals are the same and demand the same treatment; (2) only punitive sanctions work; (3) the public demands harsh punishment; (4) only professionals can deal with crime; and (5) there is nothing citizens can do. The entrenched character of these myths shields from public view two salient facts: first, that the justice system has extremely high social and financial costs, and second, that it grows fat on its own failure, claiming ever more resources as crime and public disorder increase. "In no other area of public tax funds expenditure," says New Zealand Youth Court Judge Michael Brown, "do public monies get less scrutiny in terms of positive effectiveness than in the area of penal policy."[37]

Circle sentencing has been initiated in the Yukon, Stuart says, "without changes to legislation, to administrative or financial arrangements and without coordinated support from justice agencies. It has evolved on its own momentum."[38] This has been both an advantage and a disadvantage. On the one hand, as the

Carcross experience illustrates, the spontaneous and improvised way in which circle sentencing has emerged has given wide scope to a frustrated passion for justice that was waiting to be expressed. On the other hand, Stuart believes, "it spread too quickly; grew too fast . . . [and] over the next five years what was skipped over in the beginning had to be built in."[39] What is needed now is both financial and policy support from governments and justice agencies. The RCMP, for example, maintains a policy of regularly transferring its officers. This practice conforms to the prevailing idea that justice should be blind, detached, and free of local loyalties; but it means in practice that the police are always relative strangers to the communities in which they work. In Stuart's view, there needs to be more continuity. Communities ought not to have to be constantly educating new justice officials, especially as the vast majority will arrive deeply convinced that, as professionals, they know best. There also needs to be better support for local volunteers, he says, so that too few people don't end up carrying too much of the burden of preparing for and executing the decisions of circles.

At the moment, according to Stuart, "there is widespread enthusiasm within government for community justice alternatives," but as yet "there is . . . no government willing to invest adequate resources in designing and developing the infrastructure and training necessary to reap the full potential of community justice."[40] This will change only if community justice comes to be seen as a true alternative to existing practice in many cases, not just as a marginal supplement to the established way of doing things. This requires relevant comparisons that factor in both the full benefit of community justice in preventing crime and building social morale and the full cost that the formal crime control industry imposes through lengthy incarcerations, broken families, and the cycle of violence that prison perpetuates. For these comparisons to be made, Stuart says, "vastly improved 'justice information' is necessary." Otherwise the public will remain unable "to evaluate what formal justice systems and community-based alternatives offer, and thereby what use each can serve."[41]

Timely ideas often have multiple origins, and this seems to be the case with circle sentencing. Judge Stuart's decision in *R. v. Moses* in 1992 was the first time circle sentencing was formally described; but similar ideas were appearing around the same time in other places as well. As early as 1959, the first judge of the Territorial Court of the Northwest Territories, John Sissons, drew on customary law in imposing a sentence of banishment in the Keewatin.[42] Judge Cunliffe Barnett of the British Columbia Provincial Court imposed the first of many unorthodox sentences arrived at in consultation with the community of the accused in the case of Frank Brown in 1978. In the Northwest Territories in 1990, the Dene Cultural Institute established the Dene Traditional Justice Project. Under the direction of anthropologist Joan Ryan, a team of Dogrib researchers investigated how justice had been done in the era before residential schools, permanent settlements, and circuit courts when the people still lived on the land. Their findings were published under the title *Doing Things the Right Way*, a translation of the Dogrib phrase that comes closest in meaning to the English word "justice."[43] The research has led to a number of initiatives that return responsibility for justice to local communities.

One of the most developed and dramatically successful of these native justice revivals is taking place at the southeastern tip of Lake Winnipeg in the adjacent communities of Manigotogan, Aghming, Seymourville, and Hollow Water, which I will refer to collectively as Hollow Water. In the mid-1980s, these communities began to face up to epidemic levels of alcoholism and of incest. In a survey administered at a workshop on sexuality in 1988, two-thirds of the sixty people who were present said that they had been sexually abused as children and one-third admitted to victimizing others in turn. The figure is astonishing, although it is consistent with the result of a survey taken by the Canim Lake Band in British Columbia, in which more than half of band members said that they had been sexually exploited as children.[44] In Hollow Water, a group of social workers, who called themselves the Community Resource Group, mobilized the community to deal with this buried history. This group, which represented the various human service agencies that were working in the community, had come together two years earlier when its members began to share their own stories with one another. One of them, Burma Bushie, who works for the Manitoba Department of Child and Family Services, has said that at the outset only two of them were fully sober. Their willingness to be open with one another, their recognition that "when the sharing took place within a circle of those with whom we felt safe, we began to heal ourselves,"[45] and the growing sense of how widespread incest had become in the community, led to the creation of what they called "community holistic circle healing."[46]

Community holistic circle healing is an alternative to conventional criminal justice processing for sexual offenders. It operates through a protocol negotiated with the Manitoba Department of Justice that allows for diversion and noncustodial sentencing of suitable "victimizers . . . in sexual assault offences." The approach the community has taken is based on the view that the standard procedure of charging, trying, and jailing offenders is counterproductive for at least six reasons: (1) "Judgement and punishment . . . belong to the Creator. They are not ours." (2) Judgement and punishment suppress rather than promote healing. (3) Adversarial court proceedings, which pit victim against victimizer, isolate the offender, revictimize the victim, and prevent the emergence of a more holistic perspective. (4) People charged with violent acts are free in the community awaiting trial for months during which they are technically not guilty and are held to no account. (5) Offenders frequently return from jail more dangerous than when they went in, a condition aggravated by the idea that they have somehow "paid for their crime" and become innocent again. (6) Jail is a particularly dangerous place for sexual offenders, which further promotes silence and denial.[47]

Based on this understanding, Burma Bushie says, Hollow Water has begun to deal with disclosures of sexual abuse within the community:

> We know our families, we know our history. We can quickly validate disclosures. And we insist that we be the ones to do confrontations. Police don't have the relationships and the history to be able to tell if a person is in denial or is actually not guilty. So, we insist that we do the confrontations. We call them confrontations for lack of a better word. But basically we take the disclosure, and we go and ask the offender, "Did you do this?" We explain that they have the option to go with the regular court system, which is go to court, deny and take your chances. Or you can take responsibility, we'll support you through the system, we'll be there all the way through.[48]

Offenders who choose this route are diverted from court while they participate in circle healing. This involves both traditional practices and contemporary therapeutic techniques. It is *not*, the healing team stresses, an "easy way out" or a way of "getting away with it." "We see it rather as establishing a very different line of accountability between the victimizer and his or her community. What follows from that line is a process that we believe is not only much more difficult for the victimizer, but also much more likely to heal the victimization, than doing time in jail could ever be."[49] Sentencing is delayed while a "healing contract" is worked out with the victimizer. Burma Bushie continues

> Once a guilty plea has been entered, we ask the courts for four months to do our own assessment of the victimizer's commitment. We know that initially, when he says, "Yes, I did this," he's under pressure, he's afraid, all kinds of things are in play. So, we ask for four months, because we want to know, Is this person serious about his healing? And, when we say healing, we're talking initially about five years, and that's just a beginning. So, we ask the courts for four months.

And in that four months, we prepare the victimizers and the victims for what we call the Special Gathering. The Special Gathering is the sentencing circle, and that's when sentence is passed, and the whole thing is open to the community. So, in the four months, we sit with the offender, and he tells us, in as much detail as possible, what he's done. It's important that he start to take responsibility for what he's done and that he start telling community members about what he's done.

The next circle is with his family. In lots of cases when a family member is charged with sexual assault, if that person is in denial, then the whole family goes into denial. And so, it's important that the offender begin to tell his family what he's done so that no group denial is possible once he starts to take responsibility.

The other circle is with his victim. It's time for the victim to tell the offender what they've gone through with the impacts on his or her life.

And then the fourth circle is, of course, the sentencing circle, where the court party comes in, and the whole case is open to the community. The community has the opportunity to come and respond to the victim directly, to the offender directly, and they have the opportunity to make recommendations to the judge for sentencing.[50]

Where the offender has undergone this procedure in good faith, the sentence does not involve jail, but rather keeps the offender in the community.

The work of the Hollow Water circles has been observed by Rupert Ross, an assistant Crown attorney in Kenora who has researched aboriginal justice alternatives for the federal Justice Department's Aboriginal Justice Directorate.[51] He reports impressive results and, like Barry Stuart, emphasizes that these results embrace the entire community and not just the individual offenders.

They have dealt with a total of forty-eight sexual offenders, and five of those people ultimately went to jail. They wouldn't participate in the healing program, and they went to jail. Forty-three of them worked with the team, and only two of them ever went into a repeat of their behaviour. The other forty-one remained in the community, remained in the healing program, remained in their jobs, remained a part of the outside life, with no recidivism. This is over a ten-year period. And that's a record which, I suspect, cannot be matched anywhere in the other system.

What has happened is that, when the team ultimately comes before the Western court for sentencing at the end of their process, they are presenting the court with an alternative to jail, which Crown attorneys and judges and the police have uniformly found far more promising, far more attractive than simply sending somebody off to jail, because it promises a process where there can be a full understanding of the harm of the behaviour that was done, a process where all of the parties involved in these webs of relationships are brought back to notions of respect for each other. And it promises a return to peace and order in the community for the benefit of everybody. It is a community healing program. It's not just focused on offenders or victims.[52]

Native Canadians are currently many times more likely to be imprisoned than their fellow citizens. In Ontario, natives are 2 percent of the population and 7 percent of the prisoners in provincial jails. In Manitoba, they make up 12 percent of the population and 47 percent of the prisoners. In Saskatchewan, where 11 percent of the citizens are native, they're 72 percent of the prisoners. The story is the same in our federal prisons, which house those serving sentences of two years or longer. Natives are 3.5 percent of the Canadian population, but they account for 12 percent of male federal prisoners and 17 percent of females.[53] Worse, Statistics Canada figures released in February of 1998 show that the proportion of aboriginal prisoners admitted to federal penitentiaries has increased by 6 percent since 1991. This represents the thin edge of an aboriginal baby boom that is now reaching maturity. It is one of the surest laws of criminology that young men commit more crimes than other segments of the population; so as the population of young aboriginal men continues to increase over the next ten years, the csc foresees "dramatic increases," amounting possibly to a doubling in the proportion of their prisoners who are native.[54]

Under these circumstances, finding alternatives to the revolving door of the criminal justice system is obviously urgent. The recent Royal Commission on Aboriginal Issues claims that aboriginal nations have a right "to establish and administer their own systems of justice, including the power to make laws within the aboriginal nation's territory."[55] This complete legal sovereignty is unlikely to be conceded in the foreseeable future; but even the generally conservative *Globe and Mail*, in its editorial comment on the commission's report, recognized that "no justice system will be successful if it does not have the respect of the majority" and admits that "such respect is lacking among Canada's first nations" for the current system. The *Globe* is unwilling to accept an aboriginal right to make laws superseding the Criminal Code, but it argues that "it is within the spirit of the Canadian Constitution to permit first nations their own police, judges, courts, trials, interpretations of the law and sentences under Canada's criminal law . . . and perhaps to create civil law of their own."[56]

Whether such a system can be brought into being will depend, as Barry Stuart said earlier, on whether governments are willing to move alternatives such as the ones described in this chapter from the margins into the mainstream. But there is another question with which I would like to conclude this chapter. When New Zealand adopted the family group conference, it took an approach drawn from Maori tradition and applied it to the whole society. In Canada the related practice of sentencing circles has so far been seen as an "aboriginal justice alternative" rather than as a practice fit for all. This has led *Western Report* magazine to claim that Canada is moving towards "racially segregated justice."[57] The charge is tendentious, but still partially apt.

The move to establish a separate aboriginal justice system does suggest a questionable belief that culture is the horizon of justice. The word aboriginal has a definite meaning in the context of European conquest; but this meaning tends to hide the fact that no human being is any more or less aboriginal, in the word's largest sense, than any other human being. Europe achieved an unparalleled understanding of "right," in all the senses of that weighty word, but at a tremendous cost. Cultures grown from different roots now offer to redress a lost balance between justice as right and justice as restored community. It seems to me that New Zealand shows Canada the way to honour native tradition by embracing it rather than merely conceding it toleration.

II

RIGHTS AND RESERVATIONS

In this chapter, I look at some of the controversies that have recently attended the adoption of sentencing alternatives in aboriginal communities. Most of these controversies, one way or another, turn on conflicts between individual rights and community rights; by examining them, I hope to shed light on the general question of how the prerogatives of community are to be harmonized with the requirements of law in a reformed justice system.

A number of criticisms have been made of circle sentencing and of its underlying premise that justice should be healing rather than punitive. First of all, healing justice has been challenged on the traditional grounds that crime inherently deserves punishment and, therefore, any attempt to set punishment aside trivializes the evil that has been done. Second, circle decisions have been criticized as straying too far from expected norms of punishment, and several have been overturned by appeal courts on this basis. Finally, women's groups have argued that endowing ill-defined and easily manipulated notions of "community" and "tradition" with legal authority can easily worsen the situation of those who are already weak.

How difficult it can be to evaluate the idea of healing justice can be made clear by a story that Kenora assistant Crown attorney Rupert Ross heard in court and retells in his book *Dancing with a Ghost*:

A young man had severely beaten his wife in an alcoholic rage, breaking her jaw with punches as he held her to the floor with a knee on her neck. The community leaders (all of whom were male) spoke of the young man's sincere efforts to deal with his alcohol and anger-control problems. They advised that he had not touched alcohol since the night of the assault, that he had been of great help to his family and that he felt very strong shame about his acts. They asked that we not take him to jail, preferring that he remain in the community so they could continue to assist him as he tried to change his life. It was my position, accepted by the judge, that such a beating required a jail term if only to send a message to other men that they could not permit their anger to express itself in physical violence . . . After the young man was sentenced to jail, he was escorted outside by the court officer. They then had to wait before boarding the police plane while family members rushed home to collect some things for his trip out. As they waited, they were slowly surrounded by a small crowd of about fifteen people, *all of whom were women*, most of whom were elderly. They kissed the offender and whispered in his ear. There were some quiet tears, a couple of photographs were shyly taken, and then he was led away. There was absolutely no sentiment of "he got what he deserved" or "good riddance."[1]

Ross says he spent a long time pondering this tableau and others like it, and turning over alternatives in his head. Did the hugs and kisses signify forgiveness, or just a defensive effort to mollify a dangerous man who would be coming back? His conclusion eventually was that neither alternative is quite apt because native society lacks the concept of blame, with its implication of individual responsibility. What the individual expresses through crime is something more like a state of possession than a conscious individual act, and what he requires is healing rather than punishment. This interpretation moves matters right outside the Western framework, in which the portrait of the individual as completely determined by external forces has been accounted a denial of morality, and has been seen as underwriting both political and therapeutic tyrannies.[2] But aboriginal societies, Ross argues, even in their present state of broken and partial assimilation, constitute a radically different thought-world that only becomes perceptible as the observer learns to bracket his own assumptions. It must follow that standards appropriate to one cultural milieu cannot readily be applied in another.

This argument has not been accepted by many native women who prefer to remain in a framework of rights than to trust the promise of a revived culture. They reject the image of homogeneity, unanimity, and solidarity implied in terms like "culture" and "community" because they believe this image obscures and even helps perpetuate the inferior status of women in native societies. "The struggle by aboriginal women in Canada for sexual equality rights," writes Teressa Nahanee of the Native Women's Association of Canada, "has been pitted against the collective aboriginal desire for self-government for two decades."[3] In the specific area of criminal justice alternatives, the question of sexual equality rights is a question of whether women are adequately safeguarded in contexts where their victimization may be hidden under a veil of communitarian rhetoric. One of the organizations that has been most vigorous in putting forward this question is Pauktutit, the Inuit Women's Association. Pauktutit has been complaining for some time about what its members see as a pattern of very lenient sentences imposed by northern judges in sexual assault cases. Several of these cases are worth examining before we come to the question of alternatives.

- In 1984, in the community of Baker Lake in the Northwest Territories, three men were found guilty of the statutory rape of a thirteen-year-old girl, resulting in pregnancy. The girl had an intellectual disability, and, in the judge's opinion, "may not have completely understood what was going on," but "did not object to the intercourse." The judge found "that the morality or values of the people here are that when a girl begins to menstruate she is considered ready to engage in

sexual relations." The defendants, he went on, "did not consider their actions 'wrong' until confronted by the police and
the Criminal Code." Each man was sentenced to a week's
imprisonment. The sentence was revised on appeal to four
months, but the appeal court made no comment on the judge's
understanding that group sex with a thirteen-year-old with an
intellectual disability did not seriously violate Inuit cultural
norms.[4]

- In May of 1988, a young man was convicted of sexual assault
  in the Supreme Court of the Northwest Territories. The case
  as the presider, Judge de Weerdt, described it in his judgement
  was as follows: "The woman told the young man that she did
  not want to have sexual intercourse and yet he went ahead in
  spite of her crying and telling him that and try[ing] to push
  him away. He told her that he had sold his soul to the devil
  and that she would die if he did not complete the intercourse."
  The judge acknowledged that the assault was serious, and
  was aggravated by the death threat that accompanied it. He
  pointed out that the offender could be sent to "a penitentiary
  in southern Canada, which is a place where murderers and
  sexual perverts go," and "not a good place for an Inuit." Then
  he gave a two-year suspended sentence.[5]

- In July of 1989 in Cambridge Bay, a drunken thirty-five-year-
  old Inuk man broke into the homes of two women in the
  middle of the night. In the first case, Judge Richard reported
  in his judgement, a nineteen-year-old girl "was awakened
  when Mr. G.A. was pulling off her sweat pants and panties.
  The offender himself had his pants off. He struggled with her
  and held her down with his hands. The offender fondled
  her vaginal area with his hands, in fact there was digital
  penetration. The complainant . . . resisted him and called out
  for members of her family. When her brother came down-
  stairs, the offender fled." In the second case, he broke into
  the house of a twenty-nine-year-old woman, and when "she
  resisted his advances and asked him to leave the two of them

struggled and the offender said, "I could beat you up and rape you." The offender than fondled the complainant by touching her in the crotch area underneath her nightgown and panties. The complainant yelled out, and when her son came, the offender apologized . . . and fled from the house." The judge took note of the fact that the offender was "of previous good character," had supported his wife and three sons without social assistance, and was "an accomplished hunter." He suspended sentence and ordered 300 hours of community service.[6]

These were three of a number of cases that members of Pauktutit pointed to in an appearance before the House of Commons Justice and Legal Affairs Committee on February 28, 1995. What the judges in these cases professed to be doing was recognizing the different cultural mores of Inuit, trying to keep Inuit out of southern penitentiaries where they would likely become far more dangerous to their communities than they presently are, acknowledging acquired merit, and taking into account the mitigating effects of drunkenness and subsequent contrition. But the Pauktutit delegation argued that "the pattern of sentencing in sexual assault cases involving Inuit discriminates against Inuit women's equality rights and rights to security of the person as provided for in the Canadian Charter of Rights." They claimed that lenient sentences for sexual assaults had to be understood in a context in which "women and children are silenced and are not believed when they speak about their abuse" and that "when they do speak out, these women are then blamed in some way for the assaults they have sustained." The Pauktutit presenters continued:

Based on our experiences, we know that when women inform the police of abuses or sexual assaults they have suffered, and when charges are laid against another community member, the community may or may not support the victim. It depends on who the member is. In many cases in which women have had charges laid against men for sexual abuses they had sustained as children, the women are isolated and ridiculed by their communities for bringing these cases forward. In specific incidents we have documented, not only have women not been given support but they also have been threatened and intimidated for participating in the court process as witnesses.[7]

In a presentation to the RCMP made a year earlier, Pauktutit member Patricia Kemuksigak of Happy Valley–Goose Bay claimed that "in some communities wife assault is so common that people see it as normal."

In this context, Pauktutit argued, lenient sentences had to be understood as denying women justice, and telling violent men that what they had done was not, in the last analysis, all that serious. The committee's chairman, Warren Allmand, tried to make the point quite clear as the hearing concluded. "So you do want tough sentences," he asked, "and you do want the offender removed from the community, even if the offender is the supporter of the family." "Yes," replied Martha Flaherty, the president of Pauktutit, "but that's not to say we want to ignore and not help the abusers. We want to help everyone in the community." What she meant by this, it was clear from earlier testimony, was that conditional sentences for abusers would be acceptable to Pauktutit "if and only if there are programs for abusers and services for victims of abuse run by specially trained, permanent members of the community."

In their testimony before the House Justice Committee, Pauktutit also stressed the threat they see in a hasty and unsupervised adoption of "community-based alternatives to imprisonment," which, they suggested, "can pose very serious risks for victims and others within our community." Ottawa lawyer Mary Crnkovich has served as a consultant to Pauktutit's Justice Project, which has looked at the likely effects of alternatives on Inuit women. The risks of which Pauktutit warns were vividly represented for her by the first sentencing circle ever held in the far northern Quebec region known by its residents as Nunavik.[8] She was present at the hearing, which took place in 1993 and involved a man charged with assaulting his wife. He had already been convicted on this charge three times before and had been to prison. The judge, Jean-Luc Dutil, decided on his own initiative to try a sentencing circle. The organization of the circle was carried out by the community's mayor and "appeared to be left to the day of the event," Crnkovich says. In his opening remarks the judge cited as his precedent Barry Stuart's judgement in the Philip Moses case, which is detailed in Chapter 10. He adverted to "the imprudence of excessive reliance on punishment as the central objective in sentencing," stated his intention "to share power with the community," and told the circle that the purpose of the hearing was "to help [the accused] get a fresh start." Neither he nor the community had any prior experience with this format. Mary Crnkovich was mainly interested in what happened to the victim.

> She clearly was uneasy about this whole process. She indicated that she was told by her husband that she was to participate. When I asked her where she wanted to sit, she said that he had asked her to sit beside him. In the time that I spoke with her, he was always very close by. So, if at any point, she wanted to indicate any kind of concern or fear or doubts about what was going on, it would have been very difficult, I think, for her to do that.[9]

At no time, Crnkovich says, did the circle hear from the victim in her own words, nor was there any discussion about the harm she had suffered. The emphasis was on the offender, and how to help him.

> That circle deliberated for a period, I think, of about three to four hours. During that time, what was considered initially his problem became their problem. That was the terminology that was used by the participants in this circle. And they ultimately decided that what would be best is that the couple come on a weekly basis and talk to

three individuals that the group had identified to act as counsellors. These individuals that were identified were not identified because of any expertise they had in dealing with abuse, but just because they were individuals that, the circle thought, the couple could best talk with. And that was the determination of the circle, and the judge suspended sentence and said he would go with that — this was in May — and then the following October, he would return and meet with the couple and discuss how things were working out.[10]

Things didn't work out at all well. The counselling group fell apart. The man, who had been ordered to abstain from alcohol, resumed drinking and beating his wife. Later he was found guilty of a sexual assault on his wife's sister and sent back to jail. The whole proceeding, in Crnkovich's view, was a perfect illustration of how alternatives can be abused in the absence of other supports. Her impression was confirmed when she received a call from an Inuk prisoner who said, "I hear you can get me a sentencing circle. I want out." After explaining that he had called the wrong person, she talked with this man and concluded that what he had heard about sentencing circles was that they were "a quick way out of jail."

Mary Crnkovich summarized her reservations about the vogue for criminal justice alternatives in a presentation to a conference of the Canadian Institute for the Administration of Justice in Banff in the fall of 1995.[11] There she criticized the assumption, which was evident, for example, in Judge Dutil's opening remarks to the Nunavik circle, that "the community" is a relatively homogeneous unit. This assumption overlooks the fact that even relatively small settlements are segmented by such considerations as wealth, gender, family connections, inherited or acquired authority, and so on. Unless these inequalities are acknowledged and attended to, they can easily undermine the equality with which the pursuit of a common good is assumed to endow a sentencing circle. She expressed particular concern about the way in which the assumed homogeneity of the community submerges the identity of the victim in the collective, persuading her to comply with the consensual "community" interest rather than insisting on her injury, her satisfaction, or her safety. This dynamic was evident in the logic of the Nunavik circle, where discussion of "his" problem modulated into discussion of "their" problem, with the implication that the assaulted wife shared in the responsibility for the husband's violence. This problem is acute where communities have not acknowledged a general problem of violence against women. When eruptions of that violence are then dealt with in a "community" forum, a victimized woman is required to speak in a context where her voice is denied. The double message is inherently mystifying.

A second difficulty lies in the tendency to define "community" in strictly local terms. A place is not always a community. For many native groups, a settled way of life is no more than two or three generations old. Old family rivalries persist in the new circumstances and are complicated when the new political structure created by elected band councils is overlaid on older patterns of influence and authority. The assumption that there is an identity of interest in these circumstances is questionable. Moreover, there are nonlocal forms of community that are constituted by some wider common character or interest. Pauktutit, as the "community" of Inuit women, is an example. "The term 'community,'" Crnkovich argues, "should not be used to exclude groups not physically located within the community that provide support to more marginalized individuals within the community."

The idea that circle sentencing is a reinstitution of tradition she finds equally problematic. "In the context of Inuit culture," she told the Banff conference, "I am not aware of anything so exact or complete as a traditional justice 'system' or traditional justice 'practice' that you can immediately identify and implement." In any event, she goes on, "the contemporary concept of community with related and unrelated Inuit and Qallunaat [the Inuktitut term for whites] living together in communities that can vary in size from 150 people to 1,500 has no traditional basis for Inuit." The conflicts and disorders people face in these new circumstances are quite different from those that were formerly known. So, while "there are well-known formal and informal traditional practices of social control, such as a shaming song, individuals fighting one another, challenges of strength, ostracization, banishment, or, in very rare cases, killing," it is not clear that these practices are any more helpful or pertinent today than the stocks or pillory would be to European Canadians.

Inuit share the "ethic of noninterference" common to other aboriginal societies. A Pauktutit publication called *The Inuit Way* supposes that this is because "in a situation where people are forced to live very close to each other at times for extended periods, attempts are made to minimize points of conflict and abuses of others' rights . . . this belief causes Inuit to often feel a certain degree of discomfort when exercising authority over other Inuit . . . Inuit are uncomfortable responding to direct questions concerning other people and their motives."[12] There was, in addition, an informal rule that "punishment must not cause more problems than the initial infraction." What reluctance to interfere and reluctance to generate new problems must have meant in practice, Mary Crnkovich supposes, was that those more critical to the survival of the group must have been dealt with more leniently than those who were not, so that "what the individual did [was] less important than who the individual [was] that did it." The supposition that Inuit are reluctant to judge is confirmed by the low rate of convictions among men accused of sexual offences who face jury trials. When this reluctance combines with a disposition to defer to powerful people who are somehow identified with the interest of the community as a whole, the obstacles faced by sentencing circles are obvious.

Under the assumption that justice alternatives are somehow part of the aboriginal right of self-government, Crnkovich says, they are being implemented without adequate planning, supervision, or support. Local justice committees are struck "without people really knowing the purpose of the committee . . . There

are no guidelines, no standards . . . The government isn't providing any kind of training or any kind of screening mechanism
to find out who it is that's participating in the community."[13] She
says that Pauktutit has heard "many complaints" about individuals "who have abusive behaviour or other types of conduct that
would be unacceptable," participating in justice committees. She
also cites a case in which members of a justice committee pressured
a woman to withdraw a complaint against a prominent member
of the community and "made her life and her family's life quite
miserable."[14] In the guise of fostering aboriginal self-government,
she concludes, federal, provincial, and territorial governments are
"abdicating [their] responsibility to those people who don't have a
voice and don't have any kind of power within the community to
ensure that they're not abused further."[15]

Finally, Mary Crnkovich and Pauktutit question the extent to
which sentencing circles per se really constitute an alternative. If
all that really happens is that a judge makes a qualified extension
of his sentencing power to a small consultative group within the
community, they ask, in what sense is this an alternative? Again
the question is raised as to whether sentencing circles can be
more than a cosmetic solution unless systematic attention is also
paid to underlying social problems.

Neither Pauktutit nor Mary Crnkovich has spoken against
alternatives as such — only against the perverse consequences
they are apt to have in the absence of other changes. It is difficult,
therefore, to know how far their critique applies in cases in which
other changes are also occurring. Hollow Water, for example,
seems to offer an example of exactly the kind of community
mobilization that Pauktutit says would be necessary to make
alternatives effective. The hopes of the Dene Traditional Justice
Project are also explicitly predicated on the broader goals of
overcoming alcoholism, incest, and sexual violence rather than
imagining that community sentencing per se can make much
difference. From the Yukon, the stories of Harold Gatensby and
Barry Stuart convey a sense of ripeness for change that contrasts

with the top-down introduction of a sentencing circle in Nunavik as an academic exercise in "community empowerment." Judge Stuart has drafted a lengthy paper on "Building Community Justice Partnerships" in an attempt to specify the conditions under which such partnerships can function justly, and the formal and informal sectors can become mutually correcting. In British Columbia, Cunliffe Barnett, a Provincial Court judge who has worked with sentencing circles, has disbanded circles that functioned in the way Pauktutit fears and reinstituted normal court proceedings. (See Chapter 13 where Barnett's work is discussed in more detail.)

It is easy to mock the routine operation of the justice system as it mechanically retributes so much punishment for so much guilt; but it is good to be aware that it could change for the worse as well as the better. Where alternatives express an achieved community capacity they are likely to do more good than a remote and retributive justice system. Where they are introduced as cheap justice, or simply as a way of unclogging the courts, or as a means of indulging aboriginal communities that demand self-government but are not yet capable of justly exercising it, there is reason to fear, as Pauktutit does, a fall to a worse condition. It is alarming, for example, when one hears governments say that they intend to clear such and such a percentage of current business out of the courts — the B.C. government recently announced that they would like to see 30 percent of current court business dealt with by alternative means — because it suggests that neither considerations of justice nor the proven superiority of alternatives are dictating the decision, but merely convenience.

Between 1992 and 1995 Rupert Ross travelled "from one end of the country to the other" on secondment to the Aboriginal Justice Directorate, exploring aboriginal justice initiatives. He is enthusiastic about much of what he discovered and believes that the experiment in nonpunitive justice that is going on at Hollow Water, for example, exemplifies a new "healing paradigm." But he also reports having seen examples of the abuses Pauktutit is criticizing:

> I have seen communities which put forward what were described as healing programs for violence in the home and for sexual abuse, and it's my own view that some of them amounted to little more than abuser protection plans, where nothing really was going to be done to change the dynamics of what led up to the original offence. I don't have answers on this, but I can only mention some of the things that I would look for in order to evaluate whether something is sincerely and fully within the healing paradigm.
>
> I would look, for instance, at any program that only dealt with the offender as one that was not responding to this other way of looking at things. [A program that fits the paradigm is one] that considers all the people in a relationship with the offender and spends at least the same amount of time on victims, if not a great deal more, than on the offenders, but at the same time, extending that to all of the other people who are involved. If I didn't see that breadth of analysis, I would be suspicious that this was something put in place just to make it easier for the offender.
>
> I would also look at whether or not the program was going to be one where a group of people were essentially going to be telling parties what was going to happen in their lives as opposed to putting themselves [forward] as facilitators [for] the parties [in] creating their own solutions.
>
> If I saw systems where essentially people were going to be playing the Western role of judges, making all the decisions and telling people what to do, then I would wonder whether or not this was within the healing paradigm. I'd also look for whether or not there was a strong representation of women on the group that was going to be doing the facilitating.
>
> In aboriginal communities, I would also be looking to see whether or not there was good representation from all the various families within the community to avoid the potential for one family maintaining a position of power or abuse over other families.[16]

B.C. Provincial Court Judge Cunliffe Barnett has also proposed guidelines for the use of circle sentencing.[17] In a presentation to a conference on "alternative dispute resolution" in 1995, he suggested, first, that the judge must not abandon basic legal principles — for example, the hearing must be recorded and open to any member of the public. Second, he felt that the initiative must come from within the community. This was fundamentally what was wrong with the Nunavik circle: the initiative came from the judge. Third, the judge must be familiar with the community. Barnett offered an example of what happens otherwise:

> In 1991 a Supreme Court justice sitting in Smithers had to sentence a young native woman for manslaughter; she had killed her husband. The judge decided to hear comments from any community member who wished to speak and was then told that the dead man had been a fine fellow and that the accused woman was a horrible person. The judge, who did not "know" the community at all, did not sense that he was only being told part of the story. The dead man had status within the community but the accused woman came from elsewhere and after she killed her husband, she was ostracized. Nobody told the judge that she had been an abused and battered wife for many years. So she received a harsh sentence (which was ameliorated in the Court of Appeal).[18]

Finally, there are cases that are not appropriate for any form of alternative sentencing. Barnett mentions a case he heard in the fall of 1994:

> I had to sentence a man for a series of sexual offences. His lawyer urged that the court travel to the remote reserve community which was home to the man and his victims and that a circle sentencing session happen there. I was not sure, so I adjourned the case while an experienced probation officer travelled to the community and interviewed people there. When the probation officer's report was filed, it became apparent that the community wounds created by this

man's offences were still too raw: he was not ready — neither was
the community. He was sentenced to two years' imprisonment, to be
followed by three years' probation. But it is a term of the probation
order that he participate in a healing circle when the time is right
and I said that I would be pleased to be there also, if I was invited.[19]

Observance of the criteria that Barnett and Ross propose will
depend, finally, on the articulation of a sensitive relationship
between the organs of community justice and formal justice. This
will inevitably require judges to be judicious, a desideratum that
I don't think can be avoided in an alternative system any more
than in the present one. Despite Pauktutit's fear that government
is abdicating its responsibility, there is evidence of this judicious-
ness in the willingness of the formal system to overturn circle
decisions where appropriate and to guarantee women's rights.
A case in point is the 1995 decision of a sentencing circle in La
Ronge, Saskatchewan, to banish convicted rapist Billy Taylor for
one year to an island in Lake Wapawekka, about sixty miles
southeast of La Ronge. Taylor had at first denied the charge
against him but was found guilty when a doctor's examination
corroborated the victim's story. The sentencing circle decided
that he was to live in a trapper's cabin and be allowed a two-way
radio for emergencies, traps, knives, an axe, fishing equipment,
and food staples like flour, but no firearms, bow and arrow, or
boat. Signs were to be placed at a two-kilometre radius around
the island warning that anyone approaching would be charged.
The victim participated in the circle but afterwards said she had
been pressured into doing so and was not impressed by her
attacker's contrition; "He always said 'I'm sorry' after he hurt me.
He sounded exactly the same in the circle," she said. Other critics
suggested that it would be quite easy for the offender's friends to
visit him during his banishment, and quite impossible to prevent
them from doing so.[20] The decision was overturned on appeal,
and Billy Taylor was sent to prison.

Similarly, in the case Mary Crnkovich mentioned in which

members of a local justice committee made a complainant's life miserable, the judge, in fact, refused to divert the case as the committee wished. So, alongside the unfortunate example of the Nunavik sentencing circle, there is also evidence that cautious supervision is being exercised. Mistakes are an inevitable concomitant of experimentation; but, so long as supervision continues and the dialectic between the existing system and its alternatives is maintained, the failure of the existing system has to be the standard against which alternatives are evaluated. "Alternative sentencing," Judge Barnett emphasized in his Vancouver presentation, "will not rehabilitate every offender, heal all the wounds in any community, or cure all the ills of the criminal justice system. It is a concept that is still evolving. There are pitfalls that must be avoided. Sometimes the results will seem disappointing. But when it is done with an appropriate measure of caution and somewhat sparingly, I believe that the results can be meaningful and cathartic for all concerned."

FROM GUILT TO OBLIGATION

Victim-Offender Mediation

I n 1974 in the small town of Elmira, Ontario, north of Kitchener-Waterloo, two young men got angry and drunk and
vandalized twenty-two different homes and business establish-
ments in one night. They were convicted, and probation officer
Mark Yantzi was ordered to do a presentence report. Yantzi was
part of an occasional informal study group in which he and other
criminal justice professionals and volunteers in the Kitchener-
Waterloo area discussed questions of justice. He presented the
case to this group and said that, in his view, the best thing for
the community would be to have the offenders meet their victims.
Dave Worth, who now heads the Mennonite Central Committee
of Ontario, was also involved in these gatherings. He enthusiastically took up Yantzi's suggestion and asked whether there was
any reason in law why a judge could not make such an order.
Yantzi thought not, so they agreed to present the idea to Judge
Gordon McConnell on the day of sentencing. The judge, Dave
Worth recalls, rejected their recommendations.

> So we went back out and sat in the back of the courtroom. It was
> May the 4th in 1974 in the old courthouse in Waterloo, upstairs
> courtroom. The sun was shining; it was a beautiful day. We're sitting
> in the back, kind of discouraged because it wasn't going to happen.
> Then when the case was called, the judge said, "Now I'm ordering

a further three-week remand." And he said, "I'm ordering you two young men to go with Mr. Yantzi and Mr. Worth there, and I want you to meet your victims and bring me back a report on the damage they've suffered." And the Crown attorney, Bill Morrison, turned around and looked at us like, Now, what have you guys done? And we looked at each other and said, "Now what have we done?" Because we really didn't know.[1]

Worth and Yantzi met the two young men in the early evening on an Elmira street corner. With none of them quite sure what would happen next, they began to ring the doorbells of the victims.

In twenty-two different victims you had twenty-two different responses. Everything from the guy who'd had the tires on his new Volvo slashed, all four of them. The Volvo was six weeks old. And these guys rang his doorbell and said, "Ah, um, well, ah, you remember your Volvo that had the tires slashed?" "Yeah." They said, "Well, we're the guys that did it." "Yeah?!" They said, "Yeah, and the judge has told us we've got to come and find out what the damage was." And this guy was about ready to plow them in the face, and if it hadn't been for Mark and I there, he probably would have. And it went from that all the way to the older woman who was a secretary for the Baptist church. They had kicked in the radiator of her car and caused several hundred dollars' worth of damage. And she said, "Oh boys, come in, come in, let's sit down. I'm going to get you something. Would you like some cookies and something to drink and talk about it?" And everything in between.[2]

After two nights, restitution agreements had been reached with all the victims. In some cases, money was to be paid; in others, the offenders were to work for the victims, helping the owner of a boat in which they had kicked holes to patch the fibreglass, and welding back the cross they had broken off a church sign. Yantzi and Worth reported back to the judge, and he gave the offenders three months to carry their agreements out.

At the end of the three months we went back around and did the same circuit, and it was very different. This time they rang the doorbell, walked right up there and said, "Remember us? We're back. Here's your certified cheque for a hundred dollars. Let's shake hands." And the comment from the victim that still sticks with me after all these years was this one woman who said, "Look, we live in Elmira. It's a small town. We both shop in the same stores on Main Street." And she said, "Look, when you see me on Main Street, don't go crossing the street to avoid me. Come right up to me, shake my hand. Because we're clean now. I don't like what you did, I don't appreciate it, I'll never appreciate that. But as far as I'm concerned, you owe me nothing. We can be friends."[3]

What happened in Elmira in 1974 was the first instance of what has come to be called victim-offender reconciliation. It repeated a very old pattern; but it was the first time in the annals of contemporary criminal justice that a court had ordered such a remedy. Modern criminal justice has stressed the aggrandizement and edification of the state, rather than the satisfaction of victims. Assuming the power of prosecution in criminal cases was one of the ways in which modern states built up their power. Victims, until very recently, were pushed to the side. They had no part in the prosecution of cases and no right to be kept informed about the proceedings. The restoration of their health, dignity, or property was unlikely to figure in the sentence. Instead, the state, through its criminal courts, presented itself as the surrogate victim.

Crime, as American Mennonite writer Howard Zehr has noted, has both a public and a private aspect.[4] The private aspect is the meaning the act has for those involved, most notably the victim and the community. The public aspect is the act's exemplary significance for the wider society. Both aspects are real and important, but philosophical and criminological rationales for punishment stress this public aspect exclusively. The offender is to be punished in order to fulfill the abstract requirements of justice, or in order to furnish an example of consequences to the entire body politic. "A Punishment," Thomas Hobbes says in *Leviathan*, "is an Evill inflicted by publique Authority . . . to the end that the will of men may be thereby the better disposed to obedience."[5] The victim's harm matters only insofar as it constitutes part of this general significance.

This marginal position has begun to change in recent years as victims have acquired a new salience in criminal justice proceedings. A number of North American jurisdictions have enacted legislation entitling victims to compensation and full information about cases concerning them. In many cases they are entitled to participate in both sentencing and parole hearings, as well as to be informed of the release of the offender. Victims' organizations like CAVEAT (which is discussed in detail towards the end of Chapter 1) have had considerable influence on public policy. This integration of victims into the workings of the justice system has ended many of the indignities formerly suffered by citizens harmed through crime. But so far, it has also tended to shore up and strengthen existing ideas of criminal justice rather than challenge them. The victims' rights movement has spoken out of deep anguish, and has denounced real injustices; but it has also definitely tended to polarize discussion of criminal justice. CAVEAT, for example, runs billboards and magazine advertisements in which stereotyped prisoners glower menacingly through bars. The caption reads, "The Easiest Way Out Is Through a Crack in the System." The implication seems to be that endless prison sentences are the only real way to protect the community against crime. The interests of victims and offenders are seen as inversely related, with more respect for the one inevitably producing less respect for the other.

The victim-offender mediation approach that grew out of the Elmira experiment in 1974 has grown up in parallel with the victims' rights movement and shares some of its aims, but it differs fundamentally in its view of justice. The question of justice, according to Dave Worth, is comprehensive. It asks, "How are we going to live together?" It must therefore involve both offenders and victims in a struggle for reconciliation and revival. It cannot neglect the rights of victims, but neither can it become so preoccupied with what CAVEAT calls "protection of society" that offenders come to be seen as unintelligible aliens who have forfeited all right to human consideration.

Victim-offender reconciliation is based on the idea that both parties in a criminal act have a common interest in setting what has gone wrong right again. In the Elmira case, if Judge McConnell had not seen merit in Dave Worth and Mark Yantzi's idea, the victims would never really have known what it was that had happened that night, and the offenders would have faced only the arbitrary exaction of a judge rather than the actual consequences of what they had done. This is the very paradigm of life in a highly bureaucratized and professionalized society. Crime is an affair of police, lawyers, insurance companies, and jailers. Everyone is spoken for; no one speaks for himself. The system abets the offender in his natural desire to avoid facing the harm he has done by presenting him only with hateful surrogates, who intensify his sense of oppression and allow him to go on pretending that he is the victim. The victim can only feel that he has been singled out by an arbitrary and uncivil "out there," his path crossed by an unintelligible story with no connection to his own. Both are left without any opportunity to come to grips with what has happened.

Bringing victim and offender together addresses the personal meaning of criminal acts rather than their exemplary public significance. In this it seizes the main opportunity both for the reformation of the offender and for the healing of the victim. If contrition is possible for the offender, it is the victim's suffering above all that is likely to trigger it. If healing and reconciliation are possible for the victim, then it is the humanization that occurs when an offender acknowledges and tries to atone for what he has done that is most likely to bring it about. In this respect each holds the key to the other's liberation from the continuing thrall of whatever violence has occurred. A crime, by expressing a condition of carelessness, desolation, or abandonment, also offers an opportunity to address this condition, and perhaps in some cases even cries out for this attention. Neglecting possible opportunities to restore peace stores up future violence.

Dave Worth and Mark Yantzi's successful experiment in Elmira in 1974 led to the establishment of a victim-offender reconciliation program under the auspices of the Mennonite Central Committee in Kitchener-Waterloo. The idea soon spread to other places. Howard Zehr was involved in one of the early projects in the United States. He was struck by how creative people often were, both in holding offenders to account and in absolving them of their debt when they had fulfilled their restitution agreements. He recalls one such case.

> Two young men had broken into and . . . vandalized this factory. They had taken fire extinguishers and just sprayed them all over the place, and they put . . . several hundred people out of work for a day while it was cleaned up.
>
> We brought a foreman together with these two kids, and he read them the riot act. He told them about all the people they had harmed and so forth, had one of the guys in tears before he was done. And then he said, "Well, I'd like you to clean up the mess, but we've already done it. But there is an empty lot next door. I'd like you to clean that up, and I'd like you to meet the people you put out of work."
>
> It wasn't very easy for them, but they did it. And on the last day, he said, "I'd like you to bring your bathing suits along." And he took them to the owner's house, and they had a nice party and they had a meal. And then they had themselves a ceremony, and they burnt the contracts. The kids were so proud of themselves. They knew that they'd done something wrong, but they also knew that they'd faced the people they'd wronged and they'd done something about it. And their grades literally went up dramatically in school as a result of it.[6]

This case, with its improvised ritual, displays many of the hall-marks of successful victim-offender mediation. The victim is able to make fully known the nature and extent of his injury and to express his feelings about it. What will subsequently happen can then be determined by the victim's situation as he experiences it, rather than by a restrictive legal charge. Following this, the offender's guilt is modulated into a set of precise obligations by which he can restore his good standing. In successfully fulfill-ing these obligations, the offender may do more than simply discharge his debt — he may also gain in pride, dignity, and confidence. The case can then truly be declared closed. The victim has been satisfied on his own terms; the offender has been released from his debt and reinstated in the community. Both have a sense that justice has been done.

Victim-offender mediation is still used in only a small fraction of the cases suitable for this approach; but it has been relatively widely used in some places. Mark Umbreit of the University of Minnesota told a Victim-Offender Mediation Association Con-ference in 1996 that he is aware of more than two hundred such programs now operating in the United States.[7] In Canada the largest initiative is in Winnipeg, where Manitoba Mediation Services may receive 1,000 referrals in a year and end up medi-ating up to 400 cases. The organization was founded by the Mennonite Central Committee but now operates independently on the basis of court referrals. A case of theirs was recently reported in a compendium of criminal justice alternatives titled *Satisfying Justice*, published by the Ottawa-based Church Council on Justice and Corrections. In order to show how such mediation works, the mediators' account of the case is given below.

> The young people involved were at a party. Most of the persons had been drinking heavily. An argument broke out between several people. When the victim left the party, the accused persons followed him. The victim, Stan, was beaten, and then stabbed several times

with a knife. Stan, who was very traumatized by the incident, is a quite articulate seventeen-year-old attending school and working part-time.

The accused included the following: Terry, a fourteen-year-old, charged with attempted murder and possessing a weapon dangerous to the public peace; he is in a dating relationship with the victim's sister. Kelly, a thirteen-year-old, charged with common assault. Larry, a fourteen-year-old male, charged with attempted murder; Debbie, a nineteen-year-old female, charged with attempted murder, aggravated assault, and possessing a weapon dangerous to the public peace. She is the single parent of a two-year-old daughter.

Initially only Terry's charges were referred by the Crown Attorney. Stan, along with his mother, agreed to meet in a mediation session with Terry. Stan indicated that he has many unanswered questions about what had happened. Terry and his mother agreed to participate in this meeting. However, Terry arrived alone for the meeting indicating that his mother had decided not to attend. In this initial meeting, Stan indicated that he wanted all of the persons involved present so that the unclear details could be unravelled. Because everyone had been drinking heavily, many of the details seemed fuzzy . . . The need for accountability of the persons responsible for hurting him was very important to him. Terry, while being quite noncommittal about his role, agreed to come to a second meeting.

Getting that second meeting together was a challenge. The Crown Attorney was somewhat reluctant to refer Debbie (the adult) to the program because of the severity of her charge. Because the victim requested a mediation with her, the Crown agreed to the referral, indicating that a stay of proceedings would not be entered . . . Debbie was an extremely shy, withdrawn woman who had very limited skills in expressing herself. At times, it was questionable whether she understood the process. The other youths agreed to participate in the meeting. Their parents were encouraged to be part of the process; however, they did not attend the meeting.

On the evening of the meeting the two mediators were wondering if everyone would show up. The lives of these youths were very unstable, with little support from their families. The chairs were arranged in an elongated circle, with the mediators at one end. The three charged youths arrived without their parents; the nineteen-year-old came with her two-year-old child. The victim also came alone. Stan began. He related events . . . He had been at a party. After some quarrelling, a fight broke out. Everyone started beating up on him. He tried to run away but he was chased down the street and grabbed by several persons. Events after this were rather blurred. He remembered running home and noticing blood running down his shirt. He could not get into his house and he collapsed on the porch. His girlfriend discovered him in the early hours of the morning . . . He had lost a considerable amount of blood by this time, and was in critical condition. He had been stabbed four times. He required sixteen sutures, as well as a drain tube in his right arm. Shortly after this incident his girlfriend left him. He lost his summer job because he was unable to work for several weeks. In addition, he had received threats from the accuseds' friends. They were blaming him for the court proceedings and were wanting to "get him."

Storytelling for the others was difficult. One major problem was an accurate retelling. Alcohol had been a major influence in the incident. For some, it was difficult to tell whether it was convenient to "not remember" or whether they genuinely could not relate all of the details because they were intoxicated. Kelly had a very difficult time speaking. He asked to speak to Stan alone. He expressed extreme regret for his involvement. Because he had been present only for part of the event, he genuinely was unsure as to what had transpired. He indicated that he wanted to do whatever he could to resolve things with Stan.

Larry remembered more of the details. He recalled that Stan had got into an argument with a female at the party and had been pushing her. Several people had seen this and had wanted to intervene. They began beating him. When Stan left the party, they followed him. They grabbed him as he was jumping over a fence. Terry had a knife and stabbed him. Debbie then took the knife and stabbed him three more times. Larry indicated that he had been an observer but he was willing to take responsibility for his involvement in any way possible. Terry was very quiet. He basically went along with what the others repeated. He did not verbally express his feeling and did not show remorse for his involvement.

Debbie had an extremely difficult time expressing herself. She met alone with Stan twice during the evening. She cried through most of the meeting, keeping her head down. Her communication was limited. At one point, she said she was very sorry about what had occurred. It was a breakthrough in the meeting with Stan. He accepted her regret, and both felt relieved that they could express those feelings. This was particularly important because Debbie's friends had been very hostile towards Stan and had been harassing him.

It was clear that Terry, Larry, Kelly, and Debbie wanted to resolve this situation with Stan, but really did not know what to do. Stan indicated that he had to pay an ambulance bill, that his clothes had been damaged, and that he had lost wages as a result of this. He felt that they should take responsibility for these costs. The mediators asked all of the parties to jot down things that they would like to see included in an agreement. From their hesitation, it was clear that some of them likely had difficulty with writing skills. (Two of them printed their names on the agreement form.) Kelly, who had been only minimally involved in the incident, suggested that they all equally share the costs. It was a moving moment. Stan was very accepting of this offer, and everyone agreed. Stan verbalized that he would know that they were sorry for the incident if they followed through on their commitment to reimburse him for his bills. Debbie also gave assurances that there would be no further threats to Stan or his family, and that she would convey this to her friends.

All of the accused had limited financial means. Debbie was on social assistance. All of them completed the payments as agreed, with the exception of Kelly. He was several months late with his payment. In the follow-up discussion with Stan, it was evident that the mediation had been significant for him. The payments were a symbolic yet tangible sign that the accused persons had taken responsibility for their actions. Stan was receiving counselling through his school because the event had been extremely traumatic for him. Mediation was a part of the healing process for him.

The court was notified about the results of the mediation. When the youths completed their payments, the charges against them were stayed. Debbie pleaded guilty to a lesser charge and received a conditional discharge with two years supervised probation. Her sentence was influenced by her participation in the mediation. While it was extremely challenging to do the casework on this referral, the mediation has lingered in the minds of the mediators as a particularly significant example of the power of the mediation process in the journey towards accountability and restoration of relationships.[8]

The nature of Stan's injuries, and the substantial jail terms that could have resulted from the charges, made this a fairly serious case. The Crown's initial reluctance to refer Debbie suggests that mediation is still unusual in such a case. In most places, courts have tended to restrict the use of mediation to property crimes of the type seen in the cases described by Dave Worth and Howard Zehr, and to more minor cases generally. But, among some of those involved in this work, there has been a feeling all along that attention to the victim-offender relationship is all the more desirable in more violent and frightening cases. Dave Worth, for example, recalls a visit to Kitchener-Waterloo by Herman Bianchi, the Dutch criminologist (whose work is examined in Chapters 7 and 17), during which he commented that what they were doing with property crime was all very well but they really ought to be working with murders and other cases where healing was most necessary and most lacking.

Mennonite minister Dave Gustafson has taken up this challenge. Gustafson directs Fraser Valley Community Justice Initiatives in Langley, B.C. Since 1981, he and his colleagues have been mediating cases referred to them by the courts. The 1,600 cases they have handled since then have generally involved incidents like robbery, common assault, and fraud rather than crimes more deeply damaging to the victim. But in 1989, they decided to undertake a study of the feasibility of victim-offender reconciliation in these more serious cases. They began by trying to ascertain how many offenders would be willing to meet their victims. This involved a review of all the people placed in federal institutions in the Lower Mainland of B.C. during the last six months of 1988. Of the forty-two who had committed violent crimes, only three said no. Gustafson's team then identified the victims in these cases and asked them if there was anything they wanted from these offenders. Again the response was encouraging. The victims didn't necessarily want to meet the offenders right away, but they were unanimous in feeling that they hadn't been heard and that the trouble hadn't ended with a court hearing and a jail sentence.

Gustafson and his colleagues proceeded to set up a pilot project that was funded by the csc in 1991. Cases could be initiated by either victims or offenders, or they could be referred by interested parties like the parole board, prison chaplains, case management officers, victim service agencies, and so on. When a case was referred, the project staff investigated it and proceeded to a meeting only if they were convinced that the offender was sincere and the victim was equal to the occasion. Nearly two-thirds of all cases initiated were eventually screened out, because a victim could not be located, or one party was unwilling, or staff judged the victim or the offender unfit for such an encounter. In every case where meetings were held or other connections were made, all participants reported satisfaction. A consultant's report on the project for the solicitor general found that "there was unanimous support for the program from all victim and offender respondents interviewed."[9]

Some of these meetings were dramatically helpful to victims. What they got out of the program, Dave Gustafson says, were the three things victims generally want: an explanation of why the crime occurred, a recognition by the offender of the harm he has done, and an acknowledgement from the offender of his responsibility for that harm. Just these three things, even where there was no further reconciliation, were often enough to release people from fears and compulsions that had tormented them for years. Gustafson related one such case to the third International Prison Chaplains' Association Conference in Aylmer, Quebec, in August of 1995. It was initiated by a group of seven women who had been the victims of a masked rapist, who was subsequently imprisoned. Two of these women eventually decided that they wanted to meet the offender. Gustafson gave the first woman the pseudonym Cher.

> Cher was awakened and assaulted beginning at 4:11 a.m. She knew that because there was a digital clock radio on her mirrored dresser which she had struck and accidentally turned on in her struggle. For nine years, she had been unable to sleep between three and five a.m., the hours during which her subconscious mind unmercifully reminded her, night after night, that she was at risk. For nine years she had been unable to use a mirror, to comb her hair or apply her makeup. The worst of it, for her, was that having been a music lover, the joy of music had been stolen from her. Any form of music broadcast — radio, the background music in a supermarket or an elevator — created a traumatic association for her that she would have to flee. Her nights were haunted by the spectre of this offender, and her daytimes were little better, even after he was convicted, and incarcerated. If anything (and despite some therapy) the bogeyman was growing larger.[10]

The second woman, whom Gustafson named Erin, had been attacked in the mailroom of her apartment building. She was pregnant with twins at the time and, two weeks later, suffered a miscarriage. Erin's contact with the offender began with an exchange of videotapes, one of the techniques the project used to begin a relationship without immediately risking a face-to-face encounter. She then decided to go to the institution to meet him. On the eve of this meeting she collaborated with Dave

Gustafson on an article. "To write the final chapter on this era of my life," she wrote,

> I'll need to meet with him face to face. I have dozens of questions that were never touched on in the justice process. I need to ask him "Why?" and "Why me?" And I need to be open to his humanity, his pain, to see if we can find some new freedom for us both . . . I'd like to ask him, "What was all your pain about, and why was it that your rage was turned out on others . . . ? "Just relax," he said, "and you'll survive . . ." "Well, someone didn't survive — my twins lost their lives." I want to see how he responds to the news of the loss of my babies. I want him to have to deal with my pain and his responsibility for the consequences. It may sound funny, but I don't hate him. Maintaining anger for the rest of my life will just eat away at me. My need is to dialogue with him — hold him to account.[11]

Dave Gustafson accompanied Erin and Cher to the institution in British Columbia where the offender was imprisoned. For ten hours over two days, both women met with him. The atmosphere of these meetings was so powerful, Gustafson said, that he felt "as though I was on holy ground." Lawrence, as Gustafson has named the offender, answered their questions and listened respectfully to what they wanted to tell him. The difference this made to Cher became clear to Gustafson as they drove back to their hotel after the second day of meetings.

> We had driven for about fifteen minutes when I suddenly realized my car radio was on. "Oh, no!" I thought, and my hand went surreptitiously to the controls to lower the volume and quietly turn it off. As I did, I caught a glimpse of Cher in the rearview mirror. Tears were tracking down her cheeks, and she said, "Turn it on, Dave — I have my music back." She reported to us that she slept, like a baby, through the night that night, and, with rare exceptions, since. The monster of her nightmares was no more. He had been unmasked, and her truth as an innocent victim validated by the very

one who had caused the harms. As in scores of other cases over the years, this became a therapeutic watershed for Cher. She went on to graduate from a highly regarded technical institute with high honours, and is now a sought-after computer consultant and systems analyst.[12]

The meeting was equally satisfactory for Erin. "For the first time in many years," Gustafson reports, "[she] feels as though she is finally flourishing." Lawrence also recorded his reaction to these encounters. He said that, while he had begun to learn "victim empathy" during his treatment in prison, "hearing what I am responsible for from the person I victimized was more devastating and difficult than all my previous experiences. In my opinion, for an offender who has moved out of his denial, and is at the place in his own therapy where he can truly hear and feel the pain, there is no harder reality than such an encounter." He commended the courage of the two women and acknowledged "the gift I received through their courage."[13]

So long as offenders remain in prison it is difficult to assess claims that they have changed; but it seems clear that, if they are going to reform, their victims hold an important key. They carry with them the evil that offenders have done, and they are uniquely able to make offenders aware of this evil. No one is likelier to kindle repentance in an offender's heart. Jim Cavanagh, the prisoner-turned-minister whose story is told in Chapter 6, says that an offender fears nothing more than his victim.

> I know from past experience that one of the hardest things for an offender is to face the victim they hurt, because they feel bad. They would rather not see that person. And, to me, they should be confronted with the victim, and the victim should be able to be in control, where they won't lash out at the person, but say, "Do you know how bad you hurt me? This is what I felt like." Because then they become conscious of the feelings the victim is going through;

otherwise, they're not in touch with the reality of what the victim is suffering and has felt.

I'll give you one example: a prisoner took the life of his girlfriend, and the girlfriend's sister was a Christian. And years went by, and she eventually got to visit in this one prison when a special function was going on. And she approached a prisoner in that prison and said, "Do you know this man named so and so?" And the guy said, "Yeah, I know him. He's over there." And this guy was a very rowdy, tough character. And she walked over to him, and she says, "I want you to know I am the sister of the person that you killed, and I want to tell you that I forgive you for what you did to my sister." And he told me later that that was such a shock and an impact on him that it brought about a change in him. It was just like somebody hit him in the head with a hammer, to have somebody come up and say, "I forgive you for what you did to my sister and the hurt that it caused me. I'm a Christian and I forgive you." This man has turned around today, and, I believe, if that incident hadn't happened, that man would still be maintaining that hard-core, angry, antisocial attitude that he had in the past. But today that's changed tremendously.[14]

The debt an offender owes a victim is more palpable than the debt he owes society, and therefore more good can potentially come of it. But there is tremendous resistance to an approach to justice that stresses the relationships created by crime. There seem to me to be two main reasons for this. First it allows even the most depraved of offenders a human status that many citizens are unwilling to concede. To grant them this status requires us to separate the evil from the evildoer and to acknowledge that we have some potential connection to it. How much easier, as Solzhenitsyn says in *The Gulag Archipelago*, to believe that all evil is confined within certain evil people and that it is "necessary only to separate them from the rest of us and destroy them." The second reason, I think, is solicitude for victims and a reluctance to expose them to further hurt. Ostracization promises to contain the evil at a safe distance.

Both these reasons are refuted by Dave Gustafson's work. He has shown that healing requires recognition that a relationship between victim and offender exists. This relationship cannot be unmade by distaste for its violent and arbitrary origins. It will continue to reverberate, but often in a mystified form in which both parties console themselves with thin and unnourishing stereotypes. The most common comment that the project evaluator heard from both victims and offenders was that the mediation had made things more real. This was often all that was necessary to free victims from memories that had held them captive.

Gustafson and his colleagues are still unusual in their view that victim-offender contact is appropriate in more serious cases; but there are other instances of such contact being initiated with successful results as well. Wendy Keats, who took part in a pilot victim-offender meditation project called MOVE in Moncton, New Brunswick, in 1993 relates this story.

Elizabeth had been extremely traumatized by the armed robbery during her shift at the convenience store. The crime scene had been absolute chaos. The masked robbers had screamed death threats as they held her captive with a knife to her throat. She had wet herself from sheer terror. Even months after the robbers had been caught, life did not return to normal. Word had got out about her fear-induced loss of bladder control, and customers and coworkers teased her mercilessly afterwards. Not only did she have to cope with fear and shame, but past traumas in her life returned to haunt her. She became ill with bulimia and lost eighty-five pounds. Insomnia kept her awake night after night. Friends and family quickly became impatient with her. "Look, you didn't get hurt. Let it go. What's your problem?" Elizabeth herself couldn't understand the unrelenting torture. Why did she suffer nightmares every time she closed her eyes for a few moments? Why couldn't she resume her life? As her health deteriorated, her marriage broke down and her relationship with her children changed dramatically.

Meanwhile, Charles, the twenty-one-year-old offender, was serving five years for the offence in a federal institution. He had been raised in a violent environment by a family deeply involved with drug and alcohol abuse. His string of surrogate fathers were mostly ex-offenders and addicts themselves. He and his sisters were victims of continuous abuse and poverty. He had committed minor offences as a juvenile, but this was his first serious crime. To him, the offence was the result of an extremely bad acid trip. Completely out of his mind on booze and drugs, Charles had no idea of the trauma caused by his actions.

Charles first learned of Elizabeth's situation when he became aware of her insistence that the court allow her to submit a victim impact statement. She had not been invited by the courts to submit a statement as she was not identified as the victim. The convenience store was. As Elizabeth fought for her right to somehow be included in the process, her anger and frustration grew. She was terrified that Charles and his accomplice would come back to get her as they threatened they would. She was isolated from her family and friends by this time. She was frightened, emotionally haggard, and physically sick.

Finally, after two years and many counselling sessions, Elizabeth realized that she had to find a way to "let it go." She realized that, in order to do that, she had to try to find the answers to the questions that had haunted her. So when Charles's parole hearing came up, she travelled by bus for four hours to the institution . . . alone and suffering from pneumonia. During the hearing, Charles turned around and tried to say something to her, but victims and offenders are not allowed to speak to each other during these hearings, and he was cut off. Back on the bus, she kept wondering, "What did he want to say to me?"

At this point, she contacted the National Parole Board with a request for a face-to-face meeting and they referred her case to MOVE. I was the assigned mediator. When I first met Elizabeth, I asked her why she wanted to meet her offender. "I cannot live like this anymore," she said. "I have to get the answers to my questions.

I have to find out whether he is coming back to get me or my family. I have to tell him how I feel. I have to look him in the face and tell him how he has changed my life." All valid reasons for mediation. And so I went to see the offender.

Charles was amazed by Elizabeth's fear. "Doesn't she know I wouldna' never hurt her? Don't they give them convenience store clerks some training that tells them to just hand over the money and nobody will get hurt?" he asked incredulously. "Doesn't she know that every robber says, 'Don't call the cops or I'll come back an' get ya?' That's just the way it's done. Gee, I'm really sorry about this . . . I had no idea." Without hesitation he agreed to meet with Elizabeth to try to do whatever he could to make up for what he had previously thought of as just a bad night . . . too drunk . . . too stoned . . . and one for which he felt he was the only one paying a heavy price. By this time, Charles had been in prison for two years and it was no picnic. He slept with a knife under his pillow because there were so many stabbings going on around him. Like Elizabeth he lived in daily fear.

The mediation was arranged to take place in a room within the prison itself. Neither of them slept the night before . . . each racked with doubts and fears. By the time the two of them came together, face to face across a thirty-inch-wide table, they were both peaked with emotion. However, the controlled process of mediation soon took its effect and the storytelling stage began. Elizabeth said everything she had been thinking for the past two years. Charles listened intently, and when it was his turn, he answered most of her questions as his own story unfolded. As the dialogue continued, they started to chuckle about a detail. This broke the tension and they really started to talk: face to face and heart to heart. They had shared a violent experience, albeit from different perspectives. A relationship had been formed that night that, until now, had been left unresolved.

Elizabeth got the answers to all of the questions that had haunted her that day. She learned that Charles had never intended to come back and harm her, and that he was genuinely sorry for what he had done. They struck an agreement about how they would greet each other on the street when he is released from prison and returns to their home town. As they finished, they stood up and shook hands. "You know," Elizabeth said, "we will never be friends, you and I — we come from different worlds, but I want you to know that I wish you the best of luck and when I think of you I will hope that you are doing okay. I forgive you."

Leaving the prison, I asked her how she felt. "It's over. It's closed. It's done." Five months later, she tells me that she has not had even a single nightmare since. "I don't feel like the same person anymore. There is no more fear. It's just gone. I have learned from Charles's case manager that he is doing well. Staff feel it was a maturing experience for him and that there is a much better chance of him responding to rehabilitative treatment and taking life more seriously. No guarantees. He's twenty-three years old. My own guess is that he will never forget this experience, and that it will have a profound effect on future decisions."

After the mediation, Elizabeth requested that a letter be sent to the National Parole Board. She no longer wants to be used as a reason to keep Charles incarcerated. "If they want to keep him in prison, that's their business, but I don't want it done because of me. For me, this matter is over. I am healed."[15]

Elizabeth's experience is arguably the heart of this whole case — her suffering the most important consequence of the crime, her persistence in seeking a resolution its only saving grace — but she will hardly appear in its formal record. Criminal justice remains largely a contest between the state and the offender, *Regina v. So and So*, as we still name our law cases. At the moment, victim-offender mediation operates at the margins of the criminal justice system as a useful therapeutic tool for victims and as a way of getting minor cases out of clogged courts. But it is based on principles that could revolutionize that system, principles fundamentally different from those that currently structure criminal justice practice.

Howard Zehr, in a book called *Changing Lenses*, has explored these principles. "Throughout the criminal justice system," he says, "the wounds and needs of both the victim and the offender are neglected. Worse yet, the injuries may be compounded. Throughout this process, the phenomenon of crime becomes larger than life. Crime is mystified and mythologized, creating a symbol that is easily manipulated by politicians and the press."[16] The centre of this system, in Zehr's view, is the assessment of guilt and the assignment of punishment, "establishing blame and giving out pain," in his pithy phrase.[17] Court proceedings are about discovering the guilty, protecting the innocent through guarantees of due process, and making sure that suffering proportional to the deed is imposed on the offender. They are not about repairing the wrong that has been done, consoling those who have been injured, or trying to arrange an outcome that will restore peace and avoid a repetition.

Criminal justice procedure is oriented primarily to facts, not interpreted meanings. It focuses on the unalterable past, not on the present or the future, where a saving change might be hoped for. It leaves the participants out, except as they are useful in establishing the facts. It is majestically authoritarian. The offender is told what will be done to him at all points, which militates against his taking any responsibility for himself. It is abstract and impersonal. The offence is considered to have been against society, or against the law, concepts that are likely to mean little to offenders who are estranged from society and disaffected with conventional authorities. And it is adversarial. The offender is taught to look out for himself and distance himself from the consequences of his acts. He is guilty only when the state can prove it. "It's a system," Howard Zehr says in summary, "that has completely lost our foreparents' idea that when you wrong somebody, you create a liability, you create an obligation."

Many of these aspects of the formal justice system are at times necessary. There are cases where the facts are disputed, and an adversarial trial must be held. There are cases where truly

dangerous people need to be confined in the interests of public
safety. The problem lies in making such circumstances the norm.
As Kenora assistant Crown attorney Rupert Ross says, "We
put moose hunters who shoot out of season into the process
geared to deal with Paul Bernardo."[18] Giving remote, adversarial
procedures a monopoly on justice makes enemies by allowing
offenders no way out. Even the pains of imprisonment that are
prescribed for them don't really settle their debt. Their shame is
so total, Zehr says, that the temptation is strong to claim it as
their honour.

> The shame that our criminal justice system reflects is a stigmatizing
> shame. It says that . . . what you did is bad, but you are also bad, and
> there's really nothing you can do — you can serve your time in prison,
> for instance, but that will not remove the burden of that shame from
> you. You will always be an ex-offender. So, what do you do? You find
> other people who have been shamed also, and you hang out together.
> That's the root of delinquent subcultures. You convert shame into a
> badge of respect.
>
> I was interviewing a lifer, serving a real life-sentence [life without
> parole] in a Pennsylvania prison . . . and we got into talking about
> shame and respect. He'd been in there twenty years. I said, "When
> you were growing up in North Philly, what gave you shame and what
> gave you respect?" And he said, "Well, what gave me respect is
> what you would think should give me shame." He said, "It was when
> I mugged somebody, when I stole from somebody, when I attacked
> somebody, that made me proud." He said, "I remember my first
> arrest. I rode through my community in the back of that police car,
> and it was the proudest moment of my life. I had become a man."
> . . . That's what stigmatizing shame does.[19]

In such an upside-down world, enduring prison time is just
one more token of respect. In fact some would argue that the
bad-is-good philosophy that prevailed in this prisoner's world
probably began in the prison in the first place. But whether

a hostile crime-control system generates antagonistic criminal subcultures or is generated by them is finally academic; once both are established they become mutually reinforcing and chase one another in a classic vicious circle. The question is how to get out of the circle. Howard Zehr believes that the way to do it is to make negotiated settlement the normal way of doing justice and resort to more hostile and adversarial procedures only when this more benevolent approach manifestly fails.

Victim-offender mediation is one paradigm of this restorative justice. Normal criminal justice practice dwells so entirely on guilt that it fosters denial and repudiation in the offender. Victim-offender mediation treats guilt as an opening to a possible solution. It allows an offender to accept responsibility because it offers a way of discharging this responsibility. Crime becomes "larger than life," as Howard Zehr says, because problems, not solutions, are the primary resource of the criminal justice system. Unforgivable acts and irredeemable faults fill the horizon. Mediation throws the emphasis onto the good and allows the case to take shape as a search for a solution. Debt modulates into a tangible obligation, and successful discharge of the obligation erases the stigma and builds a new relationship.

13

WORKING WITHIN
THE SYSTEM

When Cunliffe Barnett began practising law in Prince Rupert in the early 1970s, he was shocked by the harsh and careless justice he saw meted out to natives. At that time, in many of the smaller and more remote communities of British Columbia, justice was still administered by lay judges, prominent citizens without legal training who might be chosen for the job by the head of the local RCMP detachment.

> Some of the things that I saw while I was in Prince Rupert truly horrified me. I would be sent over sometimes by the attorney general to the Queen Charlotte Islands as Crown counsel to appear in court and to tell the local lay judge that the attorney general did not want young native boys raised into adult court to be sentenced as criminals for very minor offences. And I would hear the judge say, well, he could care less what the attorney general wanted, he was going to send this boy to prison so that he would learn a trade and become a good citizen. And some of those court cases were held in the RCMP corporal's office, and boys would be sent off to jail for long periods of time for truly minor offences. This happened not just in the Queen Charlotte Islands, which I saw, but in many, many other communities around the province. That was one of the things that, I suppose, impelled me towards becoming a judge.[1]

Barnett was appointed to the British Columbia Provincial Court in 1973. He worked out of Williams Lake but often held

court in remote communities that other judges were reluctant to
visit. In 1974, as a favour to another judge, he visited the coastal
town of Bella Coola about 300 miles north of Vancouver, where
judges had been regularly cancelling their scheduled visits. There
he learned that the neighbouring community of Ocean Falls was
even more badly served and had a big backlog of cases. Many of
these cases were from Bella Bella, an island reserve policed from
the mainland. Defence witnesses in these cases, he learned,
had to come over to the mainland in small boats, a crossing that
could be quite dangerous during rough winter weather. Crown
witnesses were transported by the police. He decided to hold
court in Bella Bella as well, and it was there, in 1978, that he
imposed on a young boy named Frank Brown a sentence that
became a landmark.

Frank Brown was only fourteen, but he came from a troubled
background . . . He'd had some troubles with the police before and
then he got charged with what was really a very serious armed
robbery. There'd been a gun involved, and Frank, at age fourteen,
had been the leader . . . It was very clear that, unless something
stopped what seemed to be an inevitable headlong rush to a jail cell,
that Frank was going to wind up as a career criminal. And he had
the potential to be a very threatening and dangerous person as a
criminal. People in the community of Bella Bella, however, could see
— better than those of us in the legal system, I'm sure — that
Frank had a lot of potential, which they were hoping could be
channelled in a different direction . . . When it became very obvious after that armed robbery that Frank was going to jail, people
from the community met outside the courtroom, and they talked
about things that could be done to keep Frank away from jail.
And the result was that Frank's uncle and some other community
leaders came into the courtroom and asked whether I would consider
making an order sending Frank to a remote island, which was
actually one of the band's reserves, [where] Frank would spent a
period of time . . . by himself. His uncle was working on a salmon

enhancement project at the time, and that work took him to the island pretty well every day . . . So Frank was isolated but not abandoned.[2]

Frank Brown spent eight months on the island fending for himself, and it changed his life. He was never in trouble with the law again, and he eventually became a leader in his community, reviving the art of building oceangoing canoes and other traditions of his Heiltsiuk people. In 1990, he gave a feast to thank those who had helped him on his way. Masked dancers re-enacted the spiritual transformation he underwent during his banishment, and Cunliffe Barnett was honoured for his foresight and courage with the gift of a ceremonial paddle.

The turnaround made possible in Frank Brown's life by Judge Barnett's willingness to listen and take chances is an example of what courageous people can do within the existing criminal justice system to reduce unthinking reliance on imprisonment. Chapters 17 and 18 focus on formal alternatives to court proceedings; here I want to look at what several creative and dedicated people have done without formal change. In Judge Barnett's case, there were many more decisions reflecting the principles he followed in his judgement of Frank Brown: avoidance of prison sentences on the grounds that they are likely to confirm and reinforce an emergent criminal identity, consultation with the community, and an effort to draw on applicable cultural traditions. An example is a case he tried in the winter of 1994 in the small community of Nazko. It concerned a man in his thirties called David who was accused of sexually molesting a young girl.

I remember the day pretty well, because it took hours for the community hall to get heated up with the little woodstove, and I was suffering with a bad cold. But we stayed there a good part of the day and held court in the community hall seated in a circle. Most of the people who came to court in the community hall that day were . . .

mothers. And there were some teenagers there, and there were some men, quite a number of people considering that we were there during the day and it is a small community.

I learned that it was true that David had gone into this little girl's home while she was there alone with her blind grandmother and that David had sexually assaulted this little girl, whose cries were heard by a neighbour. I learned all that. But I also learned that David has the mind of a boy perhaps six years old. David is a man afflicted with fetal alcohol syndrome. When his mother was carrying him, she was drinking heavily . . . But he was not regarded in the Nazko community as a frightening, bad man. He was regarded as a very simple man, a gentle man. He used to babysit for a number of families. He used to watch over children on the playground. He used to do chores for elders.

The people of Nazko wanted me to know that they were very afraid that, if a judge sent David to jail for what he had done, because that would be the normal response of any judge, the people of Nazko felt that his life would be destroyed and that he would come back to the community, which was the only home he had ever known, in all likelihood, having been victimized and probably having learned things in prison that would make him dangerous in the community. They did not want David to go to jail. What they wanted was for the community to know of David's situation, and by holding court in Nazko, everybody in the community came to understand just what David had done. They wanted David not to continue to have access alone to little children, because clearly there's a danger there. And they wanted me to order that arrangements be made for David to get some very basic education about sexual issues, because here was a man over thirty with the sexual drives of an adult but the mind of a child.

In the end David did not go to jail. A probation order was made that had the conditions in it that the community wanted. And I've kept track of David's situation, at least a little, since then, and I continue to be told it was the right thing. There haven't been any further incidents.[3]

Judge Barnett is aware that sentencing in consultation with the affected community can be risky. "You're testing uncharted waters," he says, "and you're going to make mistakes." A case of spousal assault that he recently heard in Anahim Lake illustrates the danger. He was persuaded to hold court in a community circle, as he had in David's case; but he observed during the course of the hearing that the circle appeared to consist very largely of friends and relatives of the accused. When he commented on this fact, another member of the circle, who was then the band manager, allowed that this might be true. Sentencing was adjourned on that occasion; and, before the circle was reconvened, Judge Barnett learned that the person who had spoken in support of his view that the circle was biased and unrepresentative had been dressed down and made to suffer in his job as band manager by a powerful member of the band council. He discontinued the circle and expressed his displeasure.

> Circle sentencing is an expression by judges and others in the system to place an enhanced measure of faith in persons within communities, most often in aboriginal communities, and to present an opportunity for persons in those communities to offer more meaningful input, to offer constructive suggestions, and hopefully to help the judge find a better way of sentencing people, than sending them to gaol, the thing that we traditionally do.
>
> But if circle sentencing is to work, people have to be free to come into the courtroom, which may be a community hall or a band office serving as a courtroom. They have to be free to come into that place and speak their minds. And hopefully, they will be brave enough to speak in such a setting, and will speak forthrightly and honestly.
>
> When people in Anahim Lake know that if they say the wrong thing they will be hauled on the carpet before Mary William [the band councillor], that is simply absolutely intolerable. It pollutes the court process, and I cannot continue the circle in that circumstance . . . Sentencing is adjourned to continue [in the courthouse] in Williams Lake . . .[4]

Attempts like this one to manipulate community-centred justice do not invalidate such an approach, in Judge Barnett's view, though they may invite a healthy skepticism. He knows that communities that are factionalized and dominated by certain families do not automatically produce justice just by having decisions referred to them, but he believes that the only fair way to evaluate alternatives is to measure them against the existing way of doing things.

> I've made mistakes, or I have done things which in hindsight appear to be mistakes. But then I've sent people to jail and watched that person come out more angry, more violent, a bigger threat to the safety of other persons, and go back to jail, come out and go back again. Jails are very much a revolving-door syndrome for many persons who go there. And if there is a sensible way to avoid a jail sentence, then I think that courts should take the time to explore that possibility. But nobody should think that alternative procedures are going to work in every case and rehabilitate every person who is sentenced in some alternative way.[5]

In his readiness to seek alternatives to imprisonment in consultation with the families and communities of accused persons, Cunliffe Barnett has been willing to face the contradictions that are bound to beset any effort to straddle the divide between the abstract realm of law and the concrete interests that compose communities. These two domains are of different kinds; but in sound judgement they must interact in ways that can never quite be formulated in advance. Barnett has given an example of how formal justice can be taken into informal settings and submitted to consultation, correction, and advice without losing its independence or integrity.

Nils Christie tells a story of what happened when the Communist Party took over the government of Poland after World War II and all the old judges were replaced by party functionaries. The change, he says, produced a "fantastic increase" in the number of prisoners.

It was not so important that [the new judges] were Party members but that they belonged to another social stratum. It meant that they did not have the varied social experience of the old elite. This is difficult to say and might easily sound snobbish, [but] the old judges belonged to what they called the "intelligentsia" of Poland. And they had their connections to authors, to actors, to those working in the newspapers, those working with words, and often the bohemians, people who were in a way breaking down borders and creating variation, showing possibilities of variation. And if you know that from your own life, or at least from your own circles, you will have maybe a bit less difficulty identifying with those in trouble. But they were kicked out and [replaced by] this new group of conformist party members [who] were vulnerable to political influence [and] blind to variations in human life.[6]

The moral Christie draws from this story is that justice will always require judgement, and judgement will always depend on the range of the judge's understanding and imagination. Cunliffe Barnett has displayed these qualities in his judgements, and, by his efforts, shown what critiques of the criminal justice system may sometimes overlook: people, not systems, carry out justice; and people with the character and intuition to know how and when to temper justice with mercy may sometimes do more within existing structures than lesser people could accomplish within even the most ingenious alternatives.

A second remarkable reformer-from-within whose work demonstrates what a resourceful individual can accomplish is American Jerry Miller, currently head of the National Center on Institutions and Alternatives in Alexandria, Virginia. In the summer of 1969 Miller was teaching social work at Ohio State University when a personnel bulletin passed his desk inviting applications for the top spot in the juvenile justice system of Massachusetts. A colleague to whom he showed it suggested that, since Miller was always talking about how youth justice ought to be reformed, he should put his money where his mouth was and apply. "Almost as a joke," Miller says, he sent in a résumé and was invited to Boston for an interview. He made no effort to be politic since he didn't consider himself a serious candidate for the job; but what he hadn't initially realized was that the search committee was looking for someone to shake up a department that had recently been embarrassed by scandal. In some of its institutions boys were still strapped, spread-eagled to bed frames, or confined naked in concrete isolation cells, called "tombs." Within a month of his interview Miller had been offered the job.[7]

He took the position with no concern for how long he would last in it — if you want to change a system overnight, he remarked later, you'd better be ready to leave in the morning — and began introducing changes in the state's ten institutions for delinquent youth. Solitary confinement and bed restraint were eliminated, and the kids were allowed to wear their own clothes instead of standard institutional issue. Many of the staff resented even these moderate changes, and he soon found himself with a full-blown revolt on his hands.

> We had one strike, for example, in which staff, as they left, threw the keys to the place down the hallway and told the kids to do whatever they wanted. We had staff at the detention centre give crowbars to kids, and then leave, and then come back an hour later and say, "Are you still here?" That sort of thing. So these were the kind of "subtle" things that happened. They flew the flag upside down at the administration building at the largest institution, as a sign of distress from Central Office, which was my office; [and] posted escape maps on the bulletin board, saying on the bottom "free copies given here" — all of this encouragement to act out and cause problems, and some kids went with it.[8]

At one point things got so bad that it became necessary to go completely over the heads of the staff at the Shirley Industrial School. Kids were running away "in groups of ten and twelve and passing each other in the woods at night." So Miller brought in one of the few colleagues in whom he had confidence, and this colleague ran the school in association with the kids.

> What he did was to identify about a dozen kids that he trusted and they ran the place with him . . . He had them going around the place and checking this and checking that, and letting him know what was happening in this cottage or that cottage, and basically we had to rely on the more mature youngsters among us to hold the place together during that very difficult period.[9]

This staff revolt continued through most of Miller's first two years. At one point Department of Youth Services employees rallied on the steps of the legislature, carrying signs and banners saying things like "Miller Lets Delinquents Run Free," "Training Schools in Chaos," and even "Miller Condones Free Sex." Miller continued to try to reform the administration of the institutions he had inherited, but he eventually realized that none of his reforms had a chance of outlasting him unless he could effect more permanent changes.

> The staff had been there forever. They were civil-service-protected, although very few had ever seen a civil-service exam — it was primarily a political patronage department — and I think they were waiting me out. They could tolerate my craziness around reforms within the system, but it was very clear that when a new governor came in or I left that it would go right back to what it was. So we just decided at one point to go for broke and just close the places. I didn't really tell the governor, but my naïveté really served me in good stead, because had I known then what I know now I probably would have gone over and told him, and then we probably wouldn't have closed anything. He was a very good man, Frank Sargent, but he had a lot of hangers-on, political types around him, and they would have said, well, governor, you better not do this, you better sound that out, or you better pass this by such-and-such a

committee, and it would have been down the tubes very quickly. So we decided to close them, and we did. Over a three, three-and-a-half-year period we closed ten institutions, moved all the kids — well, not all, as I recall, all but forty — into community-based programs. The forty were kids with us on very, very serious crimes of violence and we set up small ten- or twelve-bed units for them. And there was not that much to-do about it, it went really rather smoothly. We had more controversy during the time we were trying to reform the institutions internally.[10]

Miller followed the principle that "every dollar attached to a person in an institution should follow them to the community at least for the length of time they would have been in the institution." This allowed him to avoid the fiasco of many mental-health deinstitutionalizations in which the patients were dumped into the streets while the money stayed on the hospital grounds. In Pennsylvania where he worked later, Miller says he witnessed situations in which "as the number of patients went down, the number of employees working on the grounds of state hospitals went up." In Massachusetts, there was a brief period after the inmates had been transferred to community settings when many institutions remained open and fully staffed; but Miller got the consent of the governor's office to reassign money from personnel to programs as people resigned or retired — turnover was then over 20 percent a year — and he was able to arrange for staff to transfer to community programs without losing their state benefits. Short-term grants from the federal government made up shortfalls during the transition.

When I arrived there, about 90 percent of our budget — maybe closer to 95 percent of our budget — was in institutions, in running institutions and staffing them. By the time I left, about 75 percent of our budget was in the community programs. We still had about 25 percent in our central office and in the state facilities, but basically we were able to turn that around. If you can get the money out with the kids, then it's very hard to get it back. When I came there the state employees that ran the institutions were the vested interest in the Legislature to keep things as they were. My successors would have found it very hard to move back to institutions because they would have had to take the money away from Catholic charities, or Jewish welfare or child-welfare agencies in the community. So we built a counter-lobby, if you will, with our community-based programs.[11]

The transition to community-based programs took a couple of years to complete. New options had to be improvised as they went along, but Miller says he approached this challenge in a fairly relaxed spirit because he was convinced that nothing could be worse than what had been happening in the institutions. Nearly the first piece of research he had seen when he joined the department was an in-house study done at the Lyman School for Boys that showed that "the longer a boy stayed at Lyman the less likely he was to make it on the street." With the exception of the handful of kids whom they thought truly dangerous and kept in custody, Miller says that he "could have opened the doors and let everybody go home and we would have had a little less crime than if they were subjected to our treatment for a couple of years."

The alternative they tried first was group homes, although Miller says that he thinks, in retrospect, that that was a mistake. The group homes were better than the institutions but still not all that good.

It turned out the very best programs we came up with were the programs that we backed into from crises. We ran out of placements for the kids, and then I started saying to staff: well, see what you can come up with, try to find someone that'll take a kid, or can you take him? We're not going to go back to the institutions, see what you can come up with. And they began recruiting people and paying them just to keep one kid out of trouble, kind of on the run, and that turned out to be the very best program, the one that we had planned the least and backed into . . . You hired someone, you paid them a full salary, and their job was to keep one, two, maybe three kids at most out of trouble, sometimes showing up four or five times a day, having the possibility of taking the kid into their own home if things were falling apart in the kid's home, having that kind of a flexibility in terms of backup for residential care, and that turned out to be the very best kind of program.[12]

From the very beginning of Miller's efforts at change, the Massachusetts experiment was monitored by researchers from Harvard University's Center for Criminal Justice. When Miller moved to close the institutions the focus of this research effort shifted to the community-based programs. The first results from this study, in 1975, showed no overall decline in recidivism or repeat offences, but marked declines in regions where the community programs Miller considered the best were in place. Later studies found lower rates of recidivism throughout the state, as well as a remarkable decline in the percentage of adult prisoners who were alumni of juvenile corrections.

For those kids where we were able to design the program to fit the kid there were dramatic differences. The Harvard study showed that, where it was well-implemented and there was someone on each kid's case and they worked hard with them, you could have really a fairly dramatic effect on the possibility of the kid getting in further trouble. But you had to sustain that . . . It's very clear that with a lot of the kids involved in the more serious offences, to use a medical analogy, you have to deal with it almost as you would a chronic issue rather than an acute or trauma issue. That doesn't mean you have to be involved in long-term treatment; but you have to have put in place, or have found or identified, a support system within the community, or the family, or relatives, and the kid has to know when to reach out and get a little help before things deteriorate. It's just like someone with diabetes, or epilepsy, has to learn to recognize the triggers, or when things are deteriorating, or when their blood sugar is off and they'd better get in and do something about it.

It's very, very similar, and it isn't that one needs particular professional care at such times, it's just that you need to reach out, you need to have something available, and there really needs to be some caring person — I don't know how else to say it — a person to follow this strand, to be there. It can't be a series of agencies or doors, or places to go to for help; you really need a person, someone you can call at night, someone you can talk to when you have a problem, and just that kind of stability to shepherd one through the maze of social-service and other agencies. I think the programs that we set in place in Massachusetts that even approximated that were the programs that worked the best.

And if I were doing it again, I would not have RFPed — as they called a Request for Proposals — for group homes or treatment programs; I would have RFPed kids: I would have said, we have Johnny Smith, who needs help with his education, he needs to live with someone who'll provide this-this-this; who would like to come and offer this? Who can offer help for this person? Here's how we see, and he sees, his needs, or she sees her needs. And I think that could be well done; I mean, the information systems and computerization and all would allow for that. You could in fact do that, then tailor the programs, tailor the supervision and all to the vicissitudes of each kid.[13]

Behind Miller's principle of individual treatment is the idea that even self-discipline is learned in relationship. "The Latin *disciplina*," he says, "comes from *discipulus*, the word for a disciple of a revered person." Self-control is rooted in the desire to be like someone who has this quality. The totalitarian control prisons exercise over inmates cannot be internalized in this way without self-annihilation.

Jerry Miller left Massachusetts in 1973 to take over the Department of Children and Family Services in Illinois. He had successfully closed the reform schools and established durable and effective alternatives; but he knew that his days in Massachusetts were numbered because of the political enemies he had made.

His changes, however, lasted; and, by 1991, when Miller published *Last One Over the Wall*, a memoir of his Massachusetts experiences, the state still locked up fewer teenagers than any other American state.

After a brief tenure in Illinois, Miller moved on to Pennsylvania, where he became a special assistant to Governor Milton Shapp. Pennsylvania law then allowed juvenile courts to send young offenders to adult prisons without benefit of adult trial. One such prison at Camp Hill then held nearly 400 juvenile prisoners, who had been sent there on the grounds of "dangerousness." Most were confined to their cells twenty-three hours a day. Shortly after Miller arrived in the state, one of these boys, sixteen-year-old Bobby Nestor, was found hanged. Nestor was there because his mother had found the roach of a marijuana cigarette in the pocket of his athletic warm-up jacket. She had consulted the local police chief, whom she knew, and he suggested having Bobby arrested and jailed on the grounds that this would give him a salutary scare. While he was in the detention centre, he ran away with an older boy. This made him a *bona fide* delinquent, for which he was sent to Camp Hill. There his boyish looks exposed him to sexual pressure from older inmates, culminating in his rape. His death was presumed a suicide, though the possibility of murder was also raised and never really resolved.

Miller read of the boy's death "in a nearly hidden notice on the inside pages of the *Harrisburg Patriot.*" He immediately drove to the prison, which is located just across the Susquehanna River from the state capitol, and began investigating. This led to a report to the governor, who was already concerned about the presence of juveniles in adult prisons, and created enough stir that Miller was able to have them removed. He did it, first, by having the state's attorney general declare the practice of sending juveniles to adult prisons unconstitutional, and then by having all the kids re-examined and returned to juvenile court for resentencing. This provided what Miller calls "an experiment in diagnosis." A year before Bobby Nestor's death all the kids in

Camp Hill had been classified by a panel of "probation officers, youth workers, judges, psychologists, psychiatrists, and social workers." These experts had been assembled by the governor as the initial step in his effort to get juveniles safely out of Camp Hill. The panel had classified 95 percent of the kids in Camp Hill as requiring maximum or medium security institutionalization. Miller then convened a similarly composed panel, only this time he gave these experts alternatives and encouraged them to devise the best possible plan in each case. The second group of diagnosticians judged that only forty of the four hundred boys at Camp Hill needed to be in secure settings.

> [The] year before [they] had only two options: either probation, which was inadequate supervision, or prison. There was nothing in between. By offering a . . . spectrum of services — Outward Bound Programs, there was all sorts of things we had in there, probably seventy-five different kinds of programs — by offering the diagnosticians that array, that smorgasbord of options, and then guaranteeing them that we weren't going to put them at risk, that we would guarantee that we'd put the kids in one or another of the plans they devised, all the diagnoses changed. It just opened them all up. Diagnosis in the area of criminal justice is primarily determined by the risk at which diagnosticians think they are putting themselves, so they tend to be very, very conservative, unless it's their own kids or their neighbours' kids. Then they can get pretty open and decent.
>
> When we have a system as we have now in this country, which relies so much on imprisonment, it stultifies that whole field that deals with people. Everybody gets very narrow in their conceptions of what offenders are all about. If we had a system of a wide range of options, then our view of everybody in those options would change dramatically.[14]

The individualized plans that came out of this second diagnostic go-round were then presented in juvenile court and the boys were resentenced. Judges generally proved amenable when faced with well-worked-out alternatives. "The conclusion was obvious," Miller writes. "The treatment options in the mind of the diagnostician determined the diagnosis of the person being evaluated."

As in Massachusetts, the deinstitutionalization of the Camp Hill kids was carried out without incident. Later the individual plans drawn up for their resentencing became the model for a much wider application of the idea of alternative sentencing proposals. This initiative began after Miller had left Harrisburg and established the National Center on Institutions and Alternatives, which mainly consulted with state governments about deinstitutionalization. One day Miller got a call from a woman in Harrisburg who had known a member of his staff there. Her son was in trouble. Could Miller help? He listened as she told a strange and tangled tale. Her son, she said, had been lazy and refused to get a job, so she had sought advice from the local police chief, who was a friend. He suggested she have him arrested for trespassing. The reason was the same as in the case of Bobby Nestor — to scare him. He was arrested in his bed at five in the morning and taken off to jail. During the few days he was there, he met a federal prisoner being temporarily held in the local jail. A couple of weeks later this man showed up at the boy's home and suggested they go out for the evening. The evening involved housebreaking, gun theft, and a wrecked car. At its end, the boy was left drunk by the side of the road while the man drove off to New York in a stolen car with the boy's girlfriend. The boy was then charged for his part in the evening's mayhem and was facing a fair amount of jail time.

Miller talked the case over with his colleague, Herb Hoelter.

> We said, why don't we do what we did with the Camp Hill kids? Neither one of us had ever been in an adult court at that point; I had always been in the juvenile area. So we put together a little package. We would have him come down here and work for us; we would have him in some kind of therapy; we would file regular reports with the court; we would make sure he wasn't drinking and went to AA

meetings. And we did a whole little plan and went up there and presented it — a rather conservative court — and the judge went with it: didn't send him to jail, sent him right down here.

Well, while we were sitting there — I remember very vividly — there were seventeen people sentenced that morning and afternoon, in that court; and what you saw was a parade of tragedy. They'd come in for sentencing, they'd all been found guilty a couple of weeks before, and they were being sent off to the county jail or the state prison, willy-nilly. Now and then a mother would come and beg, you know: "Can he come home?" or, "He's a good boy," or whatever. But our case was one of the heaviest or more serious ones of the day, yet the judge let him come with us. And it didn't have to do with any influence: I didn't know the judge and I don't think he knew me.

And, riding back, we said, if we had been there and done little plans for each of these seventeen people, probably fifteen of them wouldn't have been sent anywhere. So we said, let's try that and see what happens. We looked through the newspapers, literally, for a case that would be difficult and have some symbolic value. And the first case was of a kid in [what was] ostensibly [a] drunk-driving incident, up at Fort Mead in Maryland, driving a pickup truck with ten friends in the back, hit a tree, all ten were killed going around a corner. Ten deaths, one survivor — the driver, a seventeen-year-old boy. And it wasn't drunk driving. They'd been to a party, they'd had a little marijuana, but it was a very dangerous curve and it turns out there had been a lot of accidents on this particular curve at night in this place.

We prepared an alternative plan, and the plan involved his losing his driver's licence — literally, as I recall, for life, I don't think he'll ever get it back; that he have alcohol treatment if he needed it — he didn't need it, but we got him in a program anyway; that he would do three years of twenty hours or thirty hours a week (which is virtually all his leisure time, evenings and weekends) of unpaid community service, working with a shock-trauma unit, handling horrible accident cases or learning about that; that he maintain a full-time job, et cetera, et cetera. He was so traumatized by it when we would interview him in our offices, you couldn't mention the accident — he'd faint. He would just fall right on the floor, you couldn't talk about it with him.

Obviously some of the parents wanted him sent away forever; I mean, they wanted him killed. But a colonel, an army colonel and his wife, who lost their only two children in this accident — a teenaged boy and a girl — came forward and said they didn't see any reason to destroy this other kid behind their tragedy. And so we got them and we got two or three others of the surviving families to support our plan when he went to court, which they did — came in and testified for it. And the judge went with it. The kid, incidentally, eventually went on to become a medical technician. So we did that, we were pleased with that.[15]

The next case Miller and Hoelter took on was an arson charge against three kids who had burnt down a high school, causing $6 million damage. They offered their services free to the kids' lawyer and worked out a demanding regimen of community service and reparations payments of $10,000 each, to be paid over a ten-year period, and the court again accepted the plan, which was successfully fulfilled. From there they went on to a number of "regular street-crime cases," sometimes facing derision and incredulity from judges and prosecutors but often winning them over with the well-documented and well-considered plans they put forward. Miller estimates that, by now, he and his colleagues have crafted more than 12,000 such alternative plans. If alternatives were routinely available to courts, he says, the national prison population could be immediately cut by at least a third.

Sentencing is just done very, very poorly. That's because for the most part it's done by lawyers, and they're only interested in whether you're guilty or innocent or whether they can find a technicality to win on appeal. They're very poor at sentencing; they don't like to deal with a guilty client. They're like doctors with a terminal patient. That part of the criminal-justice procedure, which to the individual

is the most important — How many years am I going to go away?
— is handled in a very offhanded fashion, very little thought gone
into it, et cetera, et cetera. It's almost malpractice, what you see
happening.[16]

In Chapter 2, I quoted Miller's views on the quadrupling of the
American prison population during the same years that he was
demonstrating so convincingly that alternatives were available,
affordable, and practicable. His remark that the United States is
"about to go down the toilet" makes his distress clear. In his 1996
book, a *cri de coeur* about the corruption of American justice
called *Search and Destroy: African American Males in the Criminal
Justice System*, he relates his publisher's reluctance to publish so
bleak an essay without the addition of a mollifying final chapter
offering suggestions for change, and his own reluctance to conclude
with a sunny list of "alternatives" when his experience had taught
him that the demonstrated successes he and others had had in
safely reducing imprisonment were, ultimately, beside the point.

> It's not that I don't know or couldn't propose effective options.
> They've always been there for the taking. In thirty years' association
> with corrections . . . I've watched alternative programs come and go
> with the wind. Many worked; some didn't. The point is, it really
> didn't matter . . . The justice system was there to fulfill other purposes
> — some symbolic, some venal. As University of Michigan sociologist
> Robert Vinter found in his studies of juvenile correctional programs
> a quarter-century ago, whether or not a rehabilitative program
> gained official sanction was unrelated to its efficacy. Successful
> programs regularly disappeared from state and local budgets. Indeed,
> when it came to programs like state-run reform schools, the less
> successful they were, the greater the likelihood they would be made
> permanent fixtures of the juvenile bureaucracy.[17]

Miller did ultimately list the policy proposals his publisher
wanted, but with the proviso that "without major political

changes in [the United States], none of this is likely to happen."
This is an honest and heartfelt appraisal from someone who
knows in his bones how easily "the scent of the hunt" drives out
reason in crime policy. Against it I would say only that the record
of Miller's own accomplishments remains a story that offers both
fruitful principles and an inspiring example to those who continue to attempt reform.

The third story that I want to tell in this chapter concerns not
just an individual but a whole community that has harnessed its
existing crime-control institutions to a new vision of justice. The
community is Genesee County, which lies between the cities of
Buffalo and Rochester in northern New York State and com-
prises some 60,000 people living in the town of Batavia and the
surrounding countryside. Its move towards what county officials
now proudly call "Genesee Justice" began in the early 1980s with
a controversy over the future of the local jail. The existing
building had been built in 1902 and its decrepit condition had
recently attracted a lawsuit. The county's elected sheriff was
urging construction of a new facility with an enlarged capacity.
He was opposed by a group of citizens who argued that the
county needed not a bigger jail, but a new way of doing justice.
At the election for sheriff in 1981, a member of this group,
attorney Doug Call, declared his candidacy. Even his supporters
initially gave him little chance of success against an incumbent
from the dominant political party running on the popular issue
of enlarging prison capacity; but he was determined to offer the
voters an alternative. He argued first of all that a new and bigger
jail would inevitably attract more prisoners.

> When you build them, you fill them. It's a natural sequence. If the
> space is available, you fill it up. And you run the risk that you'll see
> lower-level offences coming into jail, because the least risk to the
> system is to send somebody to jail. And then when something
> happens, the judge can say, "I did my duty. I sent him off to jail,"

and the D.A. says, "I did my duty, I advocated jail." You commonly see prosecutors running for political office with ads of slamming jail doors. The real orientation of the system is to put people in jail . . . That's the safe route.[18]

Call told the voters that, even though prison might be a convenient way for public officials to give the appearance of prudence, it is also a costly, irrelevant, and unnecessary response to many of the circumstances in which it is used.

I said that we needed to make offenders responsible, first, to their victims. They're the third party to the system that really has not been made a party. I said that we needed to make offenders responsible to their communities and have them do work for us, and that we needed to make offenders responsible to themselves and have them do something about their lifestyles . . . I just asked people, "Do you want to pay for [offenders] to go to jail . . . or do you want them to pay their victims, to perform work in the community, and to straighten up their lifestyles? Which is it that you would choose?"[19]

The generally conservative voters of Genesee County unexpectedly chose the alternatives that Doug Call was proposing and elected him sheriff by a sizeable margin. He put the question of what to do about the jail on hold and set about introducing the new practices he had promised. He established a new Community Service and Victim Assistance Office headed by Dennis Wittman; and with the cooperation of District Attorney Robert Noonan and County Court Judge Glenn Morton, community sentences were increasingly substituted for jail sentences. Within a few years it was clear that a larger jail would not be needed, and the county legislature agreed to renovate the existing building instead. Today the jail is managed by a committee involving all participants in the local criminal justice system, and the jail population is kept substantially below the building's capacity. This has meant that the Genesee County jail population has

remained stable or fallen during a period when numbers elsewhere in the United States have often doubled and even tripled.
For example, a demographically similar neighbouring county,
which did build a new and larger jail during the same period, now
has twice as many prisoners. Genesee County, on the other hand,
earns an income in excess of half a million dollars a year from
renting the surplus space in its jail to governments with more
prisoners than places.

The main alternative that Call and Wittman introduced was
community service. Since 1981, nearly 3,000 offenders have performed more than 200,000 hours of unpaid work in the community
rather than sitting in jail at public expense. There are 107 agencies
in the county, ranging from the hospital to the highway department,
that are willing to take on offenders as workers. People sentenced
to community service have cleaned cages at the animal shelter,
built cobblestone fireplaces for the county park, and refitted the
plumbing at the Boy Scout camp. A crew of fifteen completely
restored an old town hall. Agencies that take people on refer to
them as volunteers rather than offenders, which reduces the stigma
and the unwanted visibility that might otherwise be attached to
community service. The result has been that some offenders have
continued with their agencies even after discharging their sentences because they appreciated the respect they were shown.

One of the keys to the success of this program has been strict
enforcement. When community sentences are given without
adequate supervision, the idea can easily be trivialized. I know
of young offenders in Toronto who worked off community-
service hours by playing pool because no one at the recreation
centre where they were sent had the time to find them something
to do. In Genesee County, according to Dennis Wittman, he and
his colleagues have made sure that a community sentence is taken
just as seriously as a jail sentence.

> Every week we check with [the] agency. If there has been a problem
> — and there have been a few problems, not many — the beauty of

us working with the Sheriff's Department, a police agency, is that we can send a patrol car out to that site within a minute, two minutes, and be there. What impression do you think an offender has of a uniformed officer showing up at a site saying, "We hear there may be a problem here." Lots of accountability. And . . . what does that say to the agency? That this works . . . We don't want someone that's giving us a jam job or someone that's just drifting around and not really pulling their weight when it comes to duties that are being requested of them.[20]

Strictly enforced community service avoids the stigma that attaches to being in jail while returning benefits to the community. Automatically locking offenders up, rather than first asking for recompense, imposes the cost on the community rather than on the offender. Jail time settles the moral debt that is created by a crime only abstractly, by imposing compensatory pain on the offender. It rebalances the scales of justice in theory; but, in practice, it does nothing for the victim or the community except impose the additional costs of the offender's maintenance while he is in jail. It also ostracizes the offender, rather than reconciling him, which then exposes the community to further harm on his release. Community service, on the other hand, allows offenders to be held to real account, while at the same time putting them in a valued, rather than a despised, relation to the community.

"Genesee Justice" has changed the place of imprisonment in corrections, making it a last resort, rather than a regular response to every serious offence. Doug Call, now retired as sheriff and back in private practice as an attorney, says that prison should be used only where alternatives are unavailable because prison is an effective deterrent only so long as it isn't used. He explains:

After three weeks in jail, people are pretty well adjusted to it. They don't fear it anymore. If you keep them from coming to jail, there's that fear component that stays alive, that I don't want to go there, and to not have to go there, I will do things. But if I've been there four and five times, hey, I'm going to opt for going to jail and not community work or going to school or going to alcohol counselling or doing something for my victim. That takes a long time. I'll just go over, sit in a jail, get my three meals a day, and then I'll get out and do my own thing and nobody's on my back. How many times have I heard offenders say, "I just want everybody off my back." And I think society loses when they just send them the easy way, which . . . is . . . to sit in a jail cell for six months and go back out on the street and nobody's on their back.[21]

Doug Call's successful promotion of the idea that jail is "the easy way" shifted Genesee County out of the sterile "hard on crime / soft on crime" dichotomy that currently polarizes debate about criminal justice. Instead of accepting the prevalent idea that an unacceptable leniency is the only alternative to custody, it demonstrated the possibility of a third way: accountability without the counterproductive alienation and expense involved in imprisonment. In Genesee County a conservative electorate has shown itself quite satisfied with this approach and has repeatedly reelected those associated with the policy. Elsewhere in the United States the cry for more jails continues; but the Genesee County experience makes one wonder to what extent the demand for policies that are "tough on crime" is less a call for vengeance than a frustrated demand for accountability.

Another aspect of Genesee County's criminal justice revolution has been the increased prominence of victims. It has often been said that crime victims undergo a double victimization: the first as a consequence of the crime, the second at the hands of the criminal justice system, which frequently allows them no standing in the case, except perhaps as a witness. Genesee County has tried to insure that this doesn't happen. Dennis Wittman's Victim Assistance Program has offered victims support, information, and a part in the disposition of the case. This is more than a token effort — one manslaughter case in his files lists 205 contacts with a particularly hard-hit family. Wherever possible, meetings are arranged between victims and offenders, so that victims can ask questions and express their feelings about what has happened. Victim satisfaction has become an important consideration in sentencing; and, in some cases, dispositions are actually arrived at during pretrial victim-offender meetings. In January of 1983, for example, a tractor-trailer passing in a no-passing zone killed a motorist coming the other way. The driver of the truck met with the victim's family before the trial, and, together with the judge, they agreed on a nonjail sentence involving probation, community service, and a donation to the fire department where the dead man had worked. At sentencing the judge stressed the satisfaction of the victim's family as the key element. "To punish the defendant for the sake of vengeance alone is not appropriate," Genesee Family Court Judge Charles Graney said, "especially since the victim's family has found it in their hearts not to demand vengeance and because the defendant is truly repentant."[22] What Dennis Wittman calls "victim-directed sentencing" has been used in many subsequent cases.

Much of the recent rhetoric from victims' rights groups has emphasized retribution, calling for longer jail terms and tougher parole conditions. Genesee County has stressed victim-offender reconciliation and has increasingly extended the concept even to the most serious cases. The first such case in which reconciliation was tried occurred in 1984 and involved a sniper shooting in the village of Leroy. An eighteen-year-old boy, Matt Mooney, high on drugs and alcohol, took aim with a high-powered telescopic rifle at two boys across the street. His shots seriously wounded both boys and nearly killed one when the bullet lodged near his spine. The sniper then turned the gun on himself but missed.

Dennis Wittman initially worked with the victims, but when they asked him who was supervising Matt Mooney, then free on bail, Wittman began to meet with him as well. The judge permitted the case to be slowed down while a series of meetings and community consultations were held. More than a year after the shooting, Matt Mooney met with the victims in a church situated near where the crime had occurred. All three boys expressed feelings of hurt, anger, and confusion. Then, according to Dennis Wittman, one victim extended his hand to Mooney. "I will never forget what you did to me," he said. "You almost killed me, and I could've killed you for it. But I can forgive you." The other victim was less willing to forgive, but he did agree that it would be better to have the offender reform than to seek vengeance.[23]

Following this meeting, Dennis Wittman set up a second conference between Mooney and six prominent local citizens. They focused on the role of drugs and alcohol in the crime and said that they would support a predominantly community-based sentence only if these problems were addressed, not just in Mooney's case but in the wider community. Sentencing was eventually delayed for eighteen months. During that time Mooney also took drug and alcohol treatment and did unpaid community service. When the case finally came to trial, he was sentenced to nine months in the local jail, a lot more community service, and what the judge called "educational deterrence." Had he been tried eighteen months earlier in the heat of the passions stirred up by his crime, the sentence could have been up to thirty years in state prison — the maximum allowable for such an offence.

The "educational deterrence," as Dennis Wittman relates, involved visiting local schools.

> Matt had to go out and make speaking presentations . . . at seven different school districts. And Matt was a very introverted person. He did not have a good vocabulary, he did not have a good education, and he sensed it. But the thing that people could sense in Matt was his sincerity. Even though he felt he didn't amount to much as a person, he was making a sincere effort in his life. People read that right off the bat.
>
> After he was sentenced, one of his speaking engagements was with the presiding judge in front of the Rotary Club in Batavia. All your businessmen and merchants and all the big, to-do people in the community were there. Matt got up, and you could have heard a pin

drop. The kid was speaking right after the chief judge in the county, who can put people in prison for life. This little kid, eighteen years old, gets up there and starts telling his story, and you could hear the nervousness in every sentence. And the people applauded him as loud as I've ever heard anyone applaud.

When I went with Matt to different high schools, it got to the point where the kids who were involved in alcohol abuse and drug abuse, they'd ask the teacher, and they'd ask, "Mr. Wittman, could you please leave the room so we can talk to Matt one on one?" He had more to offer those kids than most certified people in the field. Why? Because he was their age, he had been down the road, [and] he was coming back up the road the right way.

And to this day — and it's been nine or ten years — Matt is still sober, he's married, he has a family, he's working, he has not been in any further trouble. So some people are worth the risk. That's the moral of the story.[24]

Matt Mooney's was the first case put on what came to be called the "felony diversion track." In cases where guilt is admitted, proceedings are slowed down, conditions are imposed, and sentencing is delayed until there has been an opportunity to assess the offender's good faith. A total of 130 serious cases have now been dealt with in this way, and 127 of the offenders involved have successfully fulfilled the conditions imposed on them. One of the keys to this success, Dennis Wittman says, has been his department's ability to connect offenders with community sponsors, and the willingness of citizens to step forward in this capacity. Community sponsors are volunteers willing to support and encourage the person in trouble. Wittman says that they have proved particularly helpful and necessary with juvenile offenders.

I've sensed, in the twenty-seven years I've been in this, especially with young people, that they want someone to be consistent with them. Am I worthy of someone's time? A lot of young people don't think that they're worthy of anybody's time. You don't have to go to

Harvard Law School to understand that what human beings need is to feel appreciated, worthy. You've got to put time in, be there for them, listen to what their concerns are, look for the constructive things they're doing. We've had a number of these sponsors say . . . that these relationships have continued after the diversion, they don't stop there. And we have heard young offenders say, "For the first time, someone took a genuine interest in me."[25]

Community sponsorships are one of the ways in which offenders are supported, but also assessed, during their diversion period. By the time this period is over, a dossier exists that allows the sentencing judge to make a much more careful and intelligent disposition than is normally possible. This is why County Court Judge Glenn Morton is such a strong supporter of Genesee Justice. He agrees with Jerry Miller that sentencing is often the weakest link in the criminal justice chain and feels he's become much more able to give deserving people a break, because they now appear before him with what he calls "a track record."

In the old process, you have two attorneys arguing the potential of a defendant in plea bargaining or at sentence, with nothing to go on but a little presentence report. Judges do a lot of educated guessing, and I can tell you that when they do this guessing they're more inclined to opt for protection of the community than take a chance with a defendant.

With this diversion program, you have an individual who has a track record, an experience record, where the judge can see over a year's period of time how he's been able to rehabilitate himself, whether he can, whether he's got the potential for it and whether or not there's going to be any community protection based on his ability to continue that in the future . . . The judge has this greater sense of information as to when to give a defendant a break. And they're more apt in those cases to go for rehabilitation, to keep those people in the community, keep them out of prison, see if you can't really do something with them.

Judges are not born experts; they are just good people that diagnose situations. And garbage in, garbage out. So, if you give more information, you're going to get a more intelligent decision. It's started to make the sentencing phase of a case as sophisticated . . . as the guilt phase.[26]

Judge Morton's enthusiasm is also shared by Genesee County District Attorney Robert Noonan. Like Morton, he's an elected official, and therefore also necessarily sensitive to any suggestion that he's jeopardizing public safety. Popular election of judges, sheriffs, and district attorneys in many parts of the United States is sometimes said to foster "hang 'em high justice," but it hasn't worked that way in Genesee County. Robert Noonan says that one of the reasons alternatives have succeeded has been the high level of cooperation within the local justice system that has resulted from their decision fifteen years ago to try to control the jail population.

We have a number of players in the system who probably get along a lot better with each other than the adversarial players do in other systems. And we have worked together to screen out people who didn't need to be in jail for pretrial detention, when possible. We have worked together to try to break the cycle of criminal conduct by repeat offenders, because sending them back to jail time and time again doesn't seem to do much in that regard. And we have, when possible, tried to figure out alternatives to putting somebody in jail, because of the cost savings and because of the hopeful change in the life of the person that you're dealing with. Naturally, like any other system, when we have somebody that needs to be dealt with in the fully adversarial system, we do that as well . . . We prosecute our violent criminals the way other people do. But where many criminal justice loops work in a mode in which the presumptive disposition of a case is jail, we work in one where the presumptive disposition is not jail and then we send people to jail only if we really have to.[27]

A change in the "presumptive disposition of a case" is potentially more revolutionary than it may sound, especially if it is accompanied by the diligence Dennis Wittman and his colleagues have shown in fostering reconciliation and establishing viable alternatives. So long as jail remains an automatic response to the variety of circumstances that are lumped together as "crime," it is quite impossible to know how many prisoners might have safely discharged their debt and resumed their place in society without imprisonment. By changing its "presumptive disposition" to "not jail" and then using imprisonment only sparingly and as a last resort, Genesee County has begun to demonstrate that criminal justice can satisfy victims and still very often reclaim offenders.

The final case I want to discuss in this chapter moves from the level of a single community to an entire country but still stays within the theme of what dedicated people can do within the received forms of criminal justice. The country is Finland, the only European state whose prison population has consistently fallen during the last twenty years. When this reduction began, Finland stood out from its Nordic neighbours by its considerably higher prison population. Today, its rate of imprisonment is the same as Sweden and Denmark's. Finnish Director General of Prisons K. J. Lång, explains the reasons for the initially high rate as follows:

> . . . the number of prisoners has very little to do with crime. The number of prisoners is rather caused by the general situation of confidence in society and of the political equilibrium. The political turbulence during three wars, the right-wing movements of the 1930s and the criminalized communist movement (of that time) have all led to a greater use of imprisonment in Finland than in any other Nordic country . . . We got accustomed to a high punitive level with long sentences for various crimes . . . Finland had throughout the 1970s three times as many prisoners as Norway. Not because

Finland put three times as many persons in prison, but because each prisoner was kept in prison about three times as long in Finland as in Norway.[28]

What made the Finnish prison rate go down so dramatically was concerted action by a compact elite in the judiciary, the prison service, the relevant government ministries, and the universities. Lång, who has been director general for nearly thirty years, and of course belongs to this elite, says that their views were first formed during their education at the University of Helsinki in the 1960s.[29] There they studied with a group of modernizing professors who were intent on moving the focus of legal studies from "law in books to law in life." This meant presenting a realistic portrait of legal institutions, emphasizing their *actual* operations and effects rather than their ideal, theoretical character. Lång says that he has retained a lifelong preference for narrative, rather than statistical, sociology and acquired, as a result, a large library of prison memoirs. He and his fellow students also came to feel, as their professors did, that Finland's high rate of incarceration had become a national embarrassment. This generation then assumed high offices at a young age, for demographic reasons peculiar to Finland. K. J. Lång was twenty-five when he was appointed director of prisons. Others were appointed to the Supreme Court while still in their thirties; their opposite numbers in neighbouring Sweden were often a whole generation older.

In its efforts to reform the penal system, this group was able to take advantage of the power and prestige traditionally enjoyed by the Finnish civil service. Patrick Tørnudd, who has analyzed declining prisoner rates in Finland, says that "the Nordic countries can generally be characterized as fairly expert-orientated, and Finland has been said to be the most expert-orientated among the Scandinavian countries."[30] This habit of leaving things to the experts abetted criminal justice reform once a new "ideological constellation," as Nils Christie calls it, was entrenched.

Reform was also aided by the fact that crime has never been a big issue in Finnish politics or in Finnish media. "We haven't had any criminal justice lobbyists in the parliament, or in the political sphere," Lång says, "and the media have been very calm." In some countries, more than half of the respondents in opinion polls name crime as the country's biggest problem. When a poll was taken in Finland for a report made by the government to the parliament, only one percent of the respondents named crime as an issue of dominating importance. Another advantage, Lång thinks, was the remembered suffering of many of Finland's citizens in the country's wars. Widespread experience of the "suffering you can have through the control system" made it "easy for us to argue through the years . . . for a more relaxed way of controlling people."

The number of prisoners was reduced by both administrative and legislative means. The prison service exercised its power of early release (conditional release after half the sentence is served is entirely an administrative question in Finland). Some offences were decriminalized altogether, and others were exempted from penal sanctions. Before 1972, for example, ordinary theft was always sentenced by imprisonment; now it is sentenced by a fine. Fines, generally, have been expanded, as have community-service orders. Judges have been extremely skeptical of imprisonment as a method of crime control. This has produced "a very different way of selecting people to prisons than we had in the fifties and sixties," with conditional, or suspended, sentences now much more common.

One of the reforms of which Lång is proudest is the reduction in the number of youngsters in prison. By determined action Finland's officials have brought the number down and down, until today there are only ten boys under eighteen in prison in Finland. "Early recruitment to a prison career," Lång says, is the biggest problem in penology:

> You should never put a young person in prison during his teens. A teenager is growing. His relations to the social environment, his

relation to the opposite sex or also to some of his own sex — all these are very sensitive periods in the life of a man. They're often male, these people who are staying in prisons. And I think that we destroy the entire life of people when we incarcerate them at an age under twenty. And we can also see it the other way: If you have a late incarceration, the possibilities that these persons can leave the career is much greater. The earlier you are putting a youngster into closed institutions, the bigger is the possibility and the risk that he will never leave the career. In the age from perhaps twelve, fourteen up to nineteen, we are shaping the part of the population which is staying with the criminal justice system to the end of their life . . . Everyone who is staying with us as a recidivist must have had a first time. And when you slow down the early recruitment, you also have a later second visit; you are slowing down the pace of recidivism.[31]

After 1980, with incarceration increasing almost everywhere in the Western world, Finland's falling prison rate made it something of an odd sock. Lång is disturbed by what is happening elsewhere and calls American criminal policy, in particular, a scandalous instance of "decivilization."

We are destroying the solidarity which should inform every state. People in a society should have a solidarity with the system; but, if you have to use violence or very heavy police and army machinery to keep it going, then those who are controlled have no common interests with that society. They can really go against it. I think that one reason why today we have to listen to fairly uncivilized speeches about the criminal justice system is fear of what they in the last century called the criminal classes. We are shaping criminal classes because we have a surplus population, to which we haven't given any positive social tasks. They are just there to be controlled.[32]

K. J. Lång's generation is now nearing retirement. It remains to be seen whether its policy of reducing imprisonment will be altered by the next generation, whose progress through the civil service they have, in a sense, blocked. Meanwhile, Finland's continuing decarceration illustrates what a compact elite with a coherent policy can accomplish. Most Western countries in recent years have seen a pronounced "democratization" of crime policy. What the *vox populi* has generally demanded is harsher punishment. Finland stands out against this tendency and highlights its risks. A rational crime policy depends on the maintenance of a denser, more complex understanding than a punitive policy does. In the volatile atmosphere of political debate under conditions of instant publicity, comforting simplicities are more apt to prevail. Finland so far has sheltered its policy from political or journalistic attack and kept it in the hands of experts. The example should interest Canada, which is currently exposed both to an American-style populist clamour for harsh punishment and to a growing consensus in the judiciary, the National Parole Board, the csc, and the civil service in the departments of Justice and the Solicitor General that the country has to begin climbing down from the shelf of a high imprisonment policy while there is still time. One does not have to endorse elitism per se to see that reform becomes very difficult when policy is made subject to the whims of instant opinion.

All the evidence presented in this chapter points to the fact that prison rates in many countries could probably be safely and quickly reduced by a half to two-thirds within the framework of existing justice institutions. Finland, starting in the late sixties from a rate slightly in excess of Canada's today, has done just that during the last generation. Judges like Cunliffe Barnett have shown that many people can be kept out of prison by calling on other community resources. Pioneers in deinstitutionalization like Jerry Miller have demonstrated the potential of individualized, noncustodial sentencing plans. And communities like Genesee County have proven the feasibility of keeping their jail rates at half that of neighbouring counties, while at the same time improving conditions for victims, offenders, and citizens. All have stood against the tide and indicated what is possible when courageous and enlightened leadership is available.

14

SHAME OF DOING AMISS

S hame is a powerful emotion. John Locke wrote in the seventeenth century: "The smart of the rod, if shame accompanies it not, soon ceases, and is forgotten, and will quickly, by use, lose its terror . . . Shame of doing Amiss and deserving Punishment is the only true Restraint belonging to Vertue." But shame can also have the opposite effect. As I have emphasized again and again in this book, the existing system of criminal justice fails as a correctional system because of the way in which it rejects and stigmatizes the offender. The ostracization is so total, and the stigma so hard to erase, that the offender is pushed to invert the standards by which he has been condemned and claim his offence as his honour — like the Pennsylvania lifer in Chapter 12 who told Howard Zehr, "What gave me respect is what you would think should give me shame." Avoiding this counterproductive confirmation of criminal identities is central to the new approaches described in the last three chapters; all of them try to open a path of possible rehabilitation to the offender by converting guilt to obligation. The theory underlying these attempts to shame without stigmatizing and correct without provoking counterviolence has been set out by Australian criminologist John Braithwaite in his book *Crime, Shame and Reintegration*.[1] Braithwaite's book is one of the most frequently cited among those exploring alternative modes of crime control. Both its influence and the cogency of its argument make it worth dwelling on for a moment here.

Braithwaite argues that "potent shaming directed at offenders is the essential condition for low crime rates." But he also specifies that, for shaming to have this effect of controlling crime, it must be what he calls "reintegrative shaming." A crucial distinction has to be made, he says, between this positive form of shaming and disintegrative, or stigmatizing, shaming, which works to reinforce antisocial identifications.

> Reintegrative shaming means that expressions of community disapproval, which may range from mild rebuke to degradation ceremonies, are followed by gestures of reacceptance into the community of law-abiding citizens. These gestures of reacceptance will vary from a simple smile expressing forgiveness and love to quite formal ceremonies to decertify the offender as deviant. Disintegrative shaming (stigmatization), in contrast, divides the community by creating a class of outcasts. Much effort is directed at labelling deviance, while little attention is paid to de-labelling, to signifying forgiveness and reintegration, to ensuring that the deviance label is applied to the behaviour rather than the person, and that this is done under the assumption that the disapproved behaviour is transient, performed by an essentially good person.[2]

Reintegrative shaming will almost inevitably be the prevailing form of social control in close-knit societies where people confront each other on a relatively equal footing. Among the aboriginal people on Canada's West Coast, an offender, and those responsible with him, could be released from guilt by hosting what was called a Shame Feast, an institution that is now being revived by the Gitksan and Wet'suwet'en people as part of their Unlocking Aboriginal Justice program. A spontaneous occurrence of what Braithwaite calls a "ceremony to decertify deviance" is described in Chapter 12 by Howard Zehr in the mediation case in which the foreman of the vandalized factory improvised a ceremony involving a meal and the burning of the contracts of reparation once the vandals had successfully fulfilled the conditions imposed on them. Braithwaite argues that "the nub of deterrence is not the severity of the sanction but its social embeddedness; shame is more deterring when administered by persons who continue to be of importance to us; when we become outcasts we can reject our rejectors and the shame no longer matters to us."[3] In other words, it is through social relations that can be broadly described as of the community type rather than the contractual type, that effective, nonpunitive social control is exerted.

Repressive social control, on the other hand, almost invariably involves some form of disintegrative shaming, and therefore defeats its own purpose. Imprisonment is a case in point. "Prisons," Braithwaite writes, "are warehouses for outcasts; they put problem people at a distance from those who might effectively shame them and from those who might help reintegrate them. Imprisonment is a policy for breaking down legitimate interdependencies and for fostering participation in criminal subcultures."[4] What is needed instead are expressive ceremonies in which every bond that still ties the offender to family, friends, and community is mobilized, and the moral and pedagogical power that is uniquely embodied in the victim is invested in the offender's reintegration.

Until now, Braithwaite says, the science of criminology has generally disregarded the superior effectiveness of correctional approaches that call in the offender's social ties rather than cut them off. The general tendency of academic criminology has been to "professionalize, systematize, scientize, and decommunitize justice" — to disable the very mechanisms that are most likely to correct offenders. He points out, for example, that the United States, which has "spent lavishly on criminology" and produced a good half of the world's influential criminologists, has, at the same time, a rate of imprisonment far in excess of any other Western country except Russia. Braithwaite stops short of claiming a direct causal connection, but says that this fact certainly makes him wonder whether developments in the science of criminology have not "tended to further debilitate the social response to crime, rather than to strengthen it."

Even what Braithwaite calls criminology's "liberal permissive" strand, which has recognized disintegrative shaming clearly enough, has not been able to get out of this bind. As early as 1938 American criminologist Frank Tannenbaum noticed that, once delinquents have been labelled, all subsequent efforts at reform seem only to produce a perverse reinforcement of the label's power. This was a helpful observation, as far as it went; but, unfortunately, Tannenbaum and his successors in this "labelling perspective" recognized no limits to the operation of this power.[5] They simply described a vicious circle: crime could not be denounced without labelling, and labelling, like a new species of original sin, inexorably perpetuated the evil. The result, in Braithwaite's words, was "a debilitating nihilism," which tended to unnerve society's response to delinquency. Inevitably, such an approach produced a backlash among those not educated enough to deny the commonsense assertion that crime is a free infliction of real injuries for which someone must finally be held responsible, not just the insidious working out of society's power of ascription. Braithwaite's distinction between two types of shaming gets liberal criminology out of this bind by allowing it to take up what is valuable from the labelling perspective and dispense with what is problematic. Reintegrative shaming, by its power both to confront and then to "decertify" deviance, takes the sting out of labelling without rendering the community powerless to name its ills.

The capacity to shame without casting out is a feature of what Braithwaite calls "communitarian societies." The outstanding example among economically developed countries is Japan. Japan's economic profile would lead us to expect a high rate of crime and a high rate of imprisonment. Instead we find just the opposite: a rate of imprisonment of 37 per 100,000 (lower almost by half than the lowest rates in Europe), and a rate of registered crime that is a small fraction of that in any other industrialized country.[6] The United States has 205 armed robberies per 100,000 of population; Britain has 50; Japan has less than 2.[7] This rate, moreover, has dropped consistently since World War II, while crime rates in all economically comparable countries have risen. These remarkable results have been produced by a communitarian preference for correction over punishment. They precisely illustrate Braithwaite's hypothesis that the effectiveness of sanctions depends not on their severity but on their social embeddedness. For that reason, I would like to look further into the Japanese example.

Japan's criminal justice system dates from the period at the end of the nineteenth century when the country adopted a modern Western constitution. Its legal institutions are based on predominantly German models. But, within this Western shell, a quite un-Western way of doing things has evolved, particularly since World War II. The difference begins with proactive policing, which operates within a powerful consensus favouring public order and decorum. John Charles, a British expatriate living in Tokyo, has given this half-sardonic, half-admiring description.

> Grassroots police work [involves] helping drunks to throw up in the gutter and getting them to their train, telling feuding couples to cool it, and keeping a weather eye open for anything "unusual." Tokyo bobbies are information gatherers, the eyes and ears of the establishment. For this reason bicycles are still more in evidence than cars. Gangs of idle teenagers are routinely approached and cajoled about the anxiety and shame their loafing must be bringing to their families. Instead of a chorus of raucous defiance . . . the officers are listened to with bowed heads and shuffling feet. More amazing still is the reaction accorded the volunteer "watch committees" of elderly ladies who patrol the streets and tick off miscreants . . . Armed with bags of uplifting literature, they venture into noisy back alleys only to emerge triumphant and unscathed. This is not so daring as it sounds: most Japanese will scratch their heads if asked to name any "unsafe areas."[8]

American legal scholar John Haley, who directs the Asian Law Program at the University of Seattle, reports that "in a very large number of cases involving minor offences . . . where the police have discretion, they simply don't report the crime or the offender to the prosecutor."[9] When a charge is laid, prosecutors exercise similarly broad discretion as to whether to proceed. At each step in the criminal justice system, Haley says, there is an expectation that guilty persons will "confess, show remorse, make some contact with anyone who has been victimized by their offence, and negotiate . . . a reparation with the victim that is to the victim's satisfaction. The victim then will respond, in many cases, with a formal letter to the judge or the prosecutor or the police that the victim has been satisfied, and essentially pardons the offender."[10] Prosecutors suspend prosecution, according to Haley, in one-third of all cases. Some cases are prosecuted in the public interest, even where the offender is remorseful and has contacted the victim; but, in such cases, the judge is apt to suspend execution of the sentence.

The pressure to settle, rather than persist in, disputes operates together with civil habits of apology, reparation, and reintegration to produce Japan's very low jail rate. In Western societies, since the Middle Ages, criminal justice has consisted in satisfying the demands of the state — crime has been defined as a violation of the king's peace — and restoring the injured dignity of the law through punishment. In Japanese society, where social harmony receives the main emphasis, satisfaction of victims is crucial:

> Reparation will be what the victim believes are the appropriate things for the offender to do. This will always include an apology. It will always include the offender's admission that they've done something wrong and their expression of remorse for having done that. And then it will ordinarily include a reparation which can be a monetary payment, or it may be a monetary payment coupled with some expectation that the person will do some service for the

community. But there will be some conduct on the part of the offender which shows the offender has taken responsibility for what they've done. In cases of property crime, if it's a theft, for example, the property will always be returned or its value provided to the victim.[11]

Japanese criminal justice, in John Haley's view, has a clear and consistent purpose: to correct the behaviour of offenders. The rationale for imprisonment in other industrialized countries, as Thomas Mathiesen has argued (see Chapter 5), is often markedly unclear and incoherent. The correction of offenders depends, first, on an acknowledgement of accountability, and, second, on a practical way of discharging the account. It also depends on the initiative of family, friends, and community; and the formal system, accordingly, fosters this initiative, rather than depressing it by putting system objectives first. American community organizer John McKnight has argued that a rough inverse proportion exists between formal and informal institutions: the more the maintenance of society is taken over by professionals in law, medicine, education, social work, and the like, the less vibrant will be those informal ways of coping that professional interventions replace.[12] Japanese society seems to have a firmer grasp on this relation than Western societies, which generally fail to ask what is suppressed, hidden, or replaced when professional treatment is intensified. Those who direct Japan's criminal justice institutions apparently recognize that imprisonment is a blunt and destructive instrument, necessary as the state's ultimate sanction, but likely in most cases to lead to denial of responsibility and a defensive formation of criminal subcultures, which foster recidivism. Consequently, it is applied as sparingly as possible; instead, "enormous attempts are made to ensure community involvement with the criminal justice system to ensure that the community will re-integrate an offender who is correctable."[13]

John Haley's study of Japanese legal institutions is called *Authority Without Power: Law and the Japanese Paradox*. The paradox lies in the way a weak state generates a strong social order. The Japanese are not in themselves more docile or more pliable than other peoples: wars of imperial aggression, the considerable amount of gangsterism and racketeering in present-day Japan, and the well-publicized, quasi-military pitched battles that have been fought over the Narita airport all argue against the hypothesis that Japanese citizens are peace-loving paragons.[14] The secret of their low crime rate lies in the way a weak legal order came to "rely increasingly upon community consensus and the viability of the sanctions the community already possesses. To the extent that legal sanctions are weak," Haley writes, "their validity depends upon consensus, and thus as 'living' law, they become nearly indistinguishable from nonlegal or customary norms."[15]

The explanation of why the contemporary Japanese legal order has reinforced community norms rather than replacing them with legal rules is to be found in Japanese history. For most of this history, Japanese society has been largely composed of autonomous villages. They were incorporated in larger political and military orders, but they remained for the most part self-governing. The mobilization of the whole community, which rice cultivation demanded, strengthened their solidarity. Central institutions of governance, meanwhile, remained weak and limited in comparison with their Western counterparts. From these conditions emerged the Japanese paradox. When a Western-style constitution was adopted at the end of the nineteenth century, the new state gained legitimacy only as it accommodated and cooperated with communal and customary practice. A unique hybrid resulted.

The continuing authority of community norms was also fostered by the Japanese philosophy of law. In Japan, law never acquired the moral force it did in the West. Law conferred legitimacy, but legal rules were understood as political, rather than ethical, commands. In the West, Haley says, moral and legal norms were "coexistent." The obvious fact that laws *are* political commands did not escape Western jurists, but what made laws just in Western eyes was their sanctification by an embracing divine order. The eighteenth-century English jurist William Blackstone begins his *Commentaries on the Laws of England* by defining law as a rule of action prescribed by a superior to an inferior, but then goes on to say that, since man stands precisely in this relation to God, the law of nature that commands him to conform to his maker's will stands above human law.[16] The Utilitarian philosophy, which arose in the later eighteenth century, represented a radical break with this tradition. "There are no such things as any 'precepts' . . . by which man is '*commanded*' to do any of those acts pretended to be enjoined by the . . . law of nature," Jeremy Bentham roundly declares. "If any man knows of any let him produce them."[17] Utilitarianism, however, produced a very partial and incomplete revolution in jurisprudence; and, even where it did take hold, it was often joined in a confused way to older moral and metaphysical rationales for punishment. It remains a common assumption in Western societies that whatever is morally wrong ought to be illegal, and whatever is illegal is *ipso facto* also morally wrong.

In Japan, laws might enforce moral norms, but they were not understood as expressions of a universal moral order, as they were in the Western tradition. Haley explains:

> Japan is one of the few countries in the world which historically has not developed or been deeply influenced by a belief system that claims universality. Very few Japanese that I'm familiar with historically or in terms of individual acquaintances accept the idea of an overriding set of principles or standards that have universal application over time. The Japanese are far more contextual. They accept that there are standards that apply in certain situations but not in others, that the way we should behave is determined by the communities in which we operate, rather than as a result of the existence or belief in the existence of an overriding, universally applicable standard of behaviour, which each community ought to follow.

As a result, it is much easier for Japanese to separate law from morality. Legal rules are instruments of state control. These are rules made by legislatures or judges or administrative officials imposed to maintain order in society. It's not moral or immoral to obey or disobey legal rules. The legal rules may reflect the values and the norms of the community or they may not. There's a separation of law and morality that also is reinforced by Chinese legal tradition, which I think saw law as separate from morality. Legal rules may incorporate or represent moral rules, but legal rules weren't in themselves moral rules.[18]

Japanese culture, formed in the a-theistic milieu of Buddhism, did not anchor law in the divine. This left morality more or less identical with custom and community interest. The caricature of the East as the civilization of *rite*, and the West as the civilization of *right*, has its point. The emphasis on right in the West produced an image of justice as God's implacable demand for vengeance against evildoers, but it also produced the view that our Creator endowed us with inalienable rights and an unimpeachable dignity. Conversely, in the East, the emphasis on rite defended community from state encroachment, but also endowed community consensus with an authority against which there was no ready appeal.

This brings up the most commonly voiced criticism of any appeal to Japan as a model for Western criminal justice reform: Japan's civil peace, it is said, is purchased only at the price of oppressive conformity. It's easy to applaud a society of 100 million people served by only 15,000 lawyers, say the critics, but there are costs Westerners would never accept: living in what one cynic calls "the friendly neighborhood police state."[19] John Haley, without denying that Japanese society can be oppressively conformist, argues that the difference between Japan and Western societies does not prevent our learning from Japan. Japan has been absorbing and assimilating Western ideas and institutions for more than a century without loss of its fundamental character. Could Western countries not reciprocate? Haley's argument is as follows:

Japan, in this area, is relevant only as an example of a national system that applies some very basic principles in their criminal justice system that are not in themselves Japanese. What the Japanese are doing has nothing to do with being Japanese. The way it works, the fact that it's so easy to do in Japan, has cultural props. But the principles that are applicable here are not unique to Japan at all.

We do exactly the same thing in our families, we do it in our own communities. When people do things that are wrong, we expect that they will accept responsibility and acknowledge that they've done something wrong and then we expect them to begin to correct their behaviour. And once they've begun to do that, if they belong to our communities, whether it's a family or whether it's the firm, at the workplace, any situation in which we have ongoing relationships with the person who is a wrongdoer, as they are corrected, we welcome them back. We say, "Hey, you were drinking last year and you've stopped drinking. You were on drugs, you've stopped using drugs. You had difficulty controlling your temper, you went out and got some treatment. Or I helped you get some treatment. And now you're on the road to recovery. It doesn't mean that you don't make mistakes, that you don't ever commit the wrong again. But you're making efforts, and we're not going to throw you out of the house, we're not going to send you out on the streets, we're not going to fire you from your job, because we have this ongoing, continuing relationship with you." And in the process, the person is corrected. We do it with our children, we do it with our friends, we do it in our churches. We do it within any of the cohesive communities that we have in which we understand that we have relationships.

Almost all of our crime problems are problems that occur within the society where communities have broken down, where these social structures — whether it's family, whether it's a church community, whether it's a workplace community or whether it's a territorial community, like a town or a neighbourhood — have all broken down, and we are acting as autonomous individuals without the support systems that really make us social beings as opposed to individuals.[20]

John Braithwaite also argues against the idea that the conform-
ism of Japanese society undercuts the viability of communitarian
crime control in the West. To imagine that an achievement like
Japan's can be purchased only at the price of diminished personal
liberty, he says, supposes "some sort of hydraulic relationship
between rights and duties." This mistaken view belongs to a
tradition in criminology that has seen a high crime rate as the
cost of a free society and implied that

> a political choice has to be made between rights and duties; we can
> choose Tokyo with its emphasis on duty and neglect of rights (and
> with its consequently low crime rate and stultification of diversity),
> or we can choose New York with its cultivation of rights and neglect
> of duty (and with its crimes and artistic and intellectual ferment).
> Yet with this formulation there is never an explanation of why there
> should be a negative correlation between cultural emphases on rights
> and duties. It is not at all clear that there are not or cannot be
> societies with both a strong cultural emphasis on duties and a strong
> emphasis on rights.[21]

There is no reason in principle, Braithwaite says, why a society
employing a moralizing rather than a repressive form of social control cannot direct this control to more individualistic ends. Why
not a society that is dutiful in its defence of the individual, or
that uses shame in furtherance of diversity rather than against it?
This is not to say that Braithwaite views shame as an entirely
beneficent power. "By increasing the capacity of societies to
shame," he acknowledges, "we will increase the extent to which
the power of shaming can be harnessed for both good and ill.
Shaming can be used to stultify diversity [and enforce] the
tyranny of the majority." He only argues that this is not an
inevitable result of moving to a more communitarian orientation.
Classical sociology, with its sharp distinction between the traditional and the modern, tended to portray progress from more
simple, solidarity-based forms of society to more complex and

differentiated forms as a zero sum: what was gained on the one hand was lost on the other. Braithwaite disputes the inevitability of this progression. According to him, neither freedom and solidarity, nor rights and duties, need be traded against each other.

There is no society so atomized that it does not preserve a "core consensus" that compliance with criminal law is an important goal. Nor is there any society in which most families, neighbourhoods, and workplaces don't get along by accommodation rather than exclusion. This creates a sufficient basis in all contemporary societies for the devolution of some of the state's sanctioning power to those communities with the power to exercise it effectively. But what is needed for this to happen, Braithwaite argues, is "a comprehensive theory of criminal justice." He, and a philosopher colleague, Philip Petit, have tried to provide this theory in a companion work to *Crime, Shame, and Reintegration*, titled *Not Just Deserts: A Republican Theory of Criminal Justice*.[22]

Criminal justice practice, Braithwaite and Petit argue, is currently founded on a mixture of incoherent principles and disarticulated systems, which is why criminology is vexed by endless inconclusive debate. One of the ways in which this incoherence is manifested is in the constant displacement of problems from one subsystem of criminal justice to another. For example, in Canada, when citizens' organizations like CAVEAT place ads on billboards and in national magazines arguing that "our justice system is allowing too many violent offenders on the streets to murder and brutalize," the parole board gets nervous and tightens all parole eligibility, with the result that prisons become more crowded and consequently more tense. In the United States, the prison overcrowding created by a flood of petty drug offenders has resulted in earlier release for violent offenders, a displacement in the opposite direction. Either way, the intended effects are overwhelmed by consequences that are unforeseen and unintended. Incoherence is also evident in the inconsistent rationales for punishment that are put forward by sentencing judges, and the

inconsistent reactions with which the public greet these decisions. (Chapter 3 discusses this problem of incoherence with
specific reference to Canada's Young Offenders Act.)

According to Braithwaite and Petit, the fundamental reason for
this constant displacement of problems among the institutions
of criminal justice is that these institutions are being asked to do
something of which they are incapable. The parole board, to go
back to my earlier example, does not have the ability to make
the citizens safer. It can do nothing but shift the problem to
some other jurisdiction. Most criminal justice agencies are not
sufficiently embedded in their society to be able to exercise the
sanctioning power they have been given effectively, and so they
can only tinker and temporize. They have the power but lack the
capability, while communities find themselves in the opposite
condition — they have the capacity but lack the authority.

Braithwaite and Petit believe that this problem can only be
addressed through a reordering of the relations of state and
community in crime control. This reordering is already happening in a few places, in a piecemeal way, in the community
initiatives described in the preceding chapters. Japan provides an
example of how a state can fulfill its own proper purposes by
magnifying citizen initiative rather than depressing it. What
Braithwaite and Petit have contributed is a sense of how new
modes of crime control relate to broader currents in political
philosophy, and of the necessity of a vibrant common life if moral
authority is ever to supersede repressive power in the field of
criminal justice.

ON CIVIL SOLUTIONS

It is commonly assumed that criminals form a special class of people whose conduct justifies a special, and rather exceptional, reaction. In this chapter, I explore the contention of Dutch criminologist Louk Hulsman that this assumption, despite its commonsense appearance, is actually nothing more than a well-entrenched fantasy and that, consequently, the world would actually be better off without a separate system of criminal justice. Hulsman is professor emeritus of law at Erasmus University in Rotterdam and, formerly, a senior official of the Dutch Ministry of Justice. As a justice official, he trained police and judges, drafted legislation, directed public prosecutors, oversaw prisons, and played a part in the remarkable reduction in imprisonment that the Netherlands effected between 1955 and 1975.

As an academic criminologist, Hulsman has become a leading member of the international movement for penal abolition. He argues that it is only as an artifact of the criminal justice system that we perceive criminal conduct to be a consistent phenomenon or criminals to be a consistent class:

> Within the concept of criminality a wide range of situations are linked together. Most of these, however, have separate properties and no common denominator: violence within the family; violence in an anonymous context in the streets; breaking into private dwellings;

completely divergent ways of receiving goods illegally; different types of conduct in traffic; pollution of the environment; and some forms of political activities. Neither in the motivation of those who are involved in such events, nor in the nature of the consequences, nor in the possibilities of dealing with them (be it in a preventive sense, or in the sense of the control of the conflict) can any common structure be discovered. All that these events have in common is that the criminal justice system is authorized to take action against them. Some of these events cause considerable suffering to those directly involved, quite often affecting both perpetrator and victim. Consider, for example, traffic accidents, and violence within the family. The vast majority of the events which are dealt with by criminal justice, however, would not score particularly high on an imaginary scale of personal hardship. Matrimonial difficulties, difficulties between parents and children, serious difficulties at work, and housing problems will, as a rule, be experienced as more serious both in degree and duration. If we compare criminal events with other events, there is — on the level of those directly involved — nothing intrinsic which distinguishes those "criminal events" from other difficulties or unpleasant situations. Nor, as a rule, are they singled out by those directly involved to be dealt with in any way which differs radically from the way other events are dealt with. It is therefore not surprising that a considerable proportion of the events which would be defined as "serious crimes" within the context of the criminal justice system remain completely outside that system. They are settled within the social context in which they take place (the family, the trade union, the associations, the neighborhood) in a similar way as other "noncriminal" conflicts are settled. All this means that there is no *ontological reality* of crime.[1]

Denying the ontological reality of crime directs attention to "the forms of social and cultural organization" that bring it into being and give it the appearance of uniform and consistent reality. Criminal justice procedure, Hulsman believes, reconstructs reality in an unusual way. First it focuses on a narrowly defined incident — the crime. Then it seeks an individual to whom blame can be attributed. The incident, the perpetrator, and the victim, if there is one, are all withdrawn from their context and frozen in the arrangement that constituted the crime. Everything will be judged on the basis of what happened at that moment, regardless of what subsequently occurs.

What mainly has to be decided about the crime is its blameworthiness, or where it fits in "the hierarchy of gravity." To a considerable extent this grading takes place "in a separate universe determined by the structure of criminal justice itself." This separate universe is a theological relic, "a true copy of the doctrine of 'the last judgement' and 'purgatory' developed in certain varieties of western Christian theology"; this part of Hulsman's theory is discussed in Chapter 7. The precisely measured period for which a sinner must burn in purgatorial fire to atone for his sin is the archetype of the carefully graded correlation between offences and jail terms that are found in present-day criminal codes. In both cases, the consequences follow from the definition of the act, and that definition is made by an infallible judge and his priestly intermediaries, without reference to how anyone actually experienced that act. The omniscient power that laid bare the hearts of sinners and read there a true record of their deeds is preserved in the pretension of criminal courts.

Criminal justice categories and procedures abstract from social life to such an extent that they end up constituting what Hulsman calls a "fictitious interaction" between "fictitious" persons. The powers possessed by diagnostic categories in medicine or academic disciplines in schooling are roughly analogous. Once a disease is diagnosed, protocols concerning both its treatment and its social reception tend to suppress its more concrete and situated meaning within the curriculum vitae of the sufferer. So it is with crime. Once an event is isolated, named, and treated as a crime, the social resources that might otherwise produce a solution are demobilized. It is pulled into a self-contained, quasi-theological professional sphere where the application of a definitive name fully determines the outcome.

These operations can be observed at work in the weak position of victims in the criminal justice system. Victims are the closest thing this system has to actual clients, but they are without power to direct the proceedings taking place on their behalf. Once a complaint has been lodged, the victim remains in the case only in the instrumental role of witness. The bills of victims' rights that have been adopted in various North American jurisdictions alter this situation somewhat by expanding the rights of victims to information, compensation, and a voice in court; but I'm not sure that they fundamentally alter the structural position of victims in Hulsman's terms. The secondary position of the victim is still very clear, for example, in policies requiring police to lay charges in domestic assault cases regardless of the victim's wishes. Women refusing to testify against their partners in such cases have been found to be in contempt of court.

In the same way that it sidelines victims, the criminal justice system also limits the personal responsibility of its functionaries through an extreme division of labour. The judge who preaches personal responsibility from the bench will probably never again see the person to whom his homily is addressed. The offender is also prevented from taking responsibility. No apology, however contrite, and no restitution, however generous, can save him from the degraded identity assigned him by the court. He is unable, as Hulsman's countryman Herman Bianchi has said, to contribute to his own "social salvation."

Because of its self-contained and self-serving character, the current cultural organization of criminal justice projects a distorted image of social life — "a bad fantasy," Hulsman calls it. The abstraction and isolation of crime from the tangle of meanings and relationships that comprise its real social situation produces an easily manipulated commodity. Thin and unrealistic constructions of the events constituting crime will tend to suggest equally unrealistic responses to these events. Appropriation of social problems by criminal justice agencies tends to inhibit learning and disable regenerative responses in the concerned community. These negative effects of criminalization as a way of addressing social problems, in Hulsman's view, argue for alternative forms of social control wherever possible. Such alternatives range from changes in the physical environments where unwanted events occur to changes in social relations. In one of his essays, for example, Hulsman cites a project he and his academic colleagues undertook in association with the neighbourhood association in the city of Dortrecht. In this neighbourhood, "part of the population felt seriously menaced by other groups . . . [and] the quality of life deteriorated. This gave rise to numerous claims of criminalization and extensive dramatizing press coverage. The increased police activity . . . of a criminalizing and surveillance type . . . made the situation worse. People started to leave the neighbourhood." A researcher, working under the auspices of the neighbourhood committee, undertook an inventory of the different "tribes" in the area and how they interacted. Each group was characterized according to its own evaluation, so that, for example, those who were perceived by others as hardened and dangerous criminals were called "the strong men." Each group's view of the situation was solicited in open-ended interviews. The researcher then produced an anthropological map of the district and found that uncontained conflict — and subsequent criminalization — occurred where groups lacked "overlapping lifestyles," i.e., a set of shared experiences leading to a *modus vivendi*. This finding resulted in recommendations that promoted more social contact between the various tribes. Greater mutual understanding led to a reduction in problems and an end to the migration of residents out of the area.[2]

This example indicates Hulsman's preferred approach to alternatives: he would rather look for alternative forms of social control than alternative ways of administering criminal justice. "Alternatives to criminal justice," he says, "often take place in a context in which the presuppositions of criminal justice . . . are not really challenged. In most of these discussions, the existence of crime and criminals is considered a given natural fact, and not the outcome of selective defining processes which are also open to social choice."[3] This is self-defeating, in Hulsman's view, because it reinforces the very assumptions that block possible solutions.

One such assumption is the belief that crime and moral evil are identical. This belief, as John Haley points out (see Chapter 14), has long been characteristic of Western societies and has produced the view that whatever is wrong should be illegal and whatever is illegal must also be wrong. An example of this belief in action is the current criminalization of drug abuse. It is obvious that trying to control the consumption of proscribed drugs through the criminal justice system has been an expensive, destructive failure that has fostered evils far worse than those it was supposed to eliminate. Nevertheless, the war on drugs continues, sustained not just by the many vested interests it has brought into being, but by the underlying popular belief that penalization of drug use, however futile, is a moral duty. Hulsman's approach would not be to seek alternative approaches to reducing drug crime, but to question the criminalization of drugs.

When criminalization itself is questioned, the whole horizon changes, and alternative modes of social control become visible. Immoderate, socially destructive drug use could potentially be limited in many ways — depenalization alone would already remove a great deal of its glamour and cachet, thus likely reducing demand — but these possibilities cannot emerge without the prior recognition that law and morality are distinct. Law, in Hulsman's eyes, is conventional. It may indict things that are not wrong and fail to indict things that are wrong. Some business practices that are entirely legal may still be deeply immoral, while some actions that are illegal, like acting in contempt of court to protect a confidence, might still be moral. There is, of course, considerable overlap between the categories of crime and moral evil; but distinguishing between them, Hulsman believes, would expand the repertoire of social control far beyond what is contemplated when alternatives are sought only within the horizons of criminal justice.

In a talk he gave to the International Conference on Prison Growth in Oslo in April of 1995, Hulsman proposed the substitution of "civil solutions" for many of the problems now addressed by the institutions of criminal justice. He used the term "civil" in its full range of meanings, evoking civility, civilization, and the involvement of civilians; but he also meant to say that civil law ought to be preferred to criminal law, wherever possible. To illustrate he cited research he and his colleagues at Erasmus University had carried out. Beginning in March of 1984, they followed the cases of a group of women who had been threatened and harassed by former partners, sometimes in ways eligible for serious criminalization. These women had been dissatisfied with the behaviour of the police, or the results of other criminal justice interventions on their behalf, and had been persuaded by feminist lawyers to take civil action against their tormentors. Through the use of civil summary procedures a woman could seek an injunction prohibiting the man from entering the area where she lived. The research showed that women who took this route were more satisfied with the results than they had been with criminal action. Hulsman cites three main reasons. First, it is "a low cost, easily understandable, quick, and flexible procedure," which leaves the woman in control while still addressing her perception of threat. Second, it changes her status from victim to plaintiff. "From a pitiful, humiliated, dependent state she becomes an active party, a claimant in a civil law case. By doing this she shows not only the one who threatens her, but also herself and the outside world, that she has her own life and her own identity, and that she is able to draw her own line . . . This alone increases her defensibility."[4] Finally, this way of proceeding also brings publicity. In the case he studied, "feminist lawyers made deliberate use of this publicity to bring attention to the problem of sexual violence, and to show the world and other women that it is really possible to draw the line and make an end to this problem."[5]

Substituting civil procedures for criminal prosecution offers a promising avenue for reform, but Hulsman believes finally that no ready-made formula exists for alternative crime policies. Moreover, he sees a danger in academics trying to invent such a formula. Like Foucault, he holds that the intellectual should not assume the part of the prophet who tells people what to do and "prescribes for them frames of thought, objectives, and means which he develops in his head, working in his study surrounded by his tools — the traditional way in which many criminal law academics have worked."[6] Instead, he believes scholars should attempt to reveal how the current institutions actually work, and how they got the way they are, in order to allow people to modify them and find new paths. Faithful to this aim, he has tried to show that, in its present cultural and social organization, criminal justice reifies crime, overemphasizes the isolated offender, focuses too narrowly on blame allocation, and derives from a "last judgement" view of the world. The alternative begins with a historically informed exploration of this mode of thought. A new approach to what Hulsman, with deliberate neutrality, calls "problematic events" will take shape only as "we free ourselves from the idea that the extremely diverse situations which are criminalizable have something in common." As this happens, he believes that it will become possible to mobilize a variety of existing social resources in the interest of civil solutions.

16

CIRCLES OF SUPPORT

In Chapter 7, I presented the thesis of British theologian
Timothy Gorringe that the Christian doctrine of atonement
has had a formative influence on Western thinking about punishment. According to Gorringe, mainstream Christianity interpreted this doctrine as justifying harsh punishment for crime by
showing that God himself had required the sacrifice of His son
as satisfaction for the sins of the world. However, there has also
been within Christianity an interpretation of the Atonement that
runs counter to this dominant tradition. It was first enunciated
by Peter Abelard only a few years after Anselm of Canterbury
proposed that Christ's crucifixion should be understood as vicar-
ious satisfaction for the wrong mankind's disobedience had done
to God. "How cruel and wicked it seems," Abelard wrote in his
Commentary on Paul's letter to the Romans, "that anyone should
demand the blood of an innocent person as the price of anything,
or that it should in any way please him that an innocent man
should be slain — still less that God should consider the death
of his Son so agreeable that by it he should be reconciled to the
whole world."[1] He goes on to put forward an alternative position,
arguing that redemption is not achieved by a token traded against
God's wrath but by the inspiring power of Christ's example.

> In that his son has taken upon himself our nature and preserved
> therein in teaching us by word and example even unto death — he
> has more fully bound us to himself by love; with the result that our

hearts should be enkindled by such a gift of divine grace, and true
charity should not now shrink from enduring anything for him . . .
everyone becomes more righteous — by which we mean a greater
lover of the Lord — after the Passion of Christ than before, since a
realized gift inspires greater love than one which is only hoped for.
Wherefore our redemption through Christ's suffering is that deeper
affection in us which not only frees us from slavery to sin, but also
wins for us the true liberty of sons of God, so that we do all things
out of love rather than fear.[2]

Gorringe traces this "exemplarist view of the atonement" from
Abelard down to the present day. He finds it in the Renaissance
humanism of Erasmus and Socinus, and in Anabaptists like
Thomas Munzer, who argue that "the remission of sins occurs
without any punishment being exacted." It carries on in the
seventeenth century in the inner light tradition of the Ranters,
Diggers, and Quakers, and is powerfully present in the late
eighteenth and early nineteenth centuries in the poetry and
prophecy of William Blake. Blake was aghast at the processions
of the condemned up Tyburn Road to the gallows, and his
prophetic books refer again and again to "Tyburn's bloody tree."
He believed that the understanding of God as iron law, which
underwrote the bloodlust of Britain's criminal code, was completely at odds with scriptural Christianity, and he often parodied
this God who was, for him, nothing more than "an allegory of
kings and priests," his heavens "writ with curses from pole to
pole." "Man," said Blake, "can have no idea of anything greater
than man, as a cup cannot contain more than its capaciousness."
Therefore, God can appear to us only as "the divine humanity"
we see in Jesus, who is "a friend and brother" and not "a God
afar off." The sanguinary God represented in satisfaction theory
is an abstraction, "an abominable void . . . brooding secret in his
hills of stored snows." Belief in this celestial tyrant produces "the
Druid temples dropping with Blood," by which Blake symbolized
the unquenchable vengeance of Britain's "Bloody Code." "Every

Religion that preaches Vengeance for Sin is the Religion of the Enemy and the Avenger, and not the Forgiver of Sin, and their God is Satan."[3]

One could cite other examples since Blake of this counter-tradition — Hastings Rashdall, writing in 1925 on *The Idea of Atonement in Christian Theology*, echoed Blake's portrait of bloody Druid rituals when he described satisfaction theory as "at bottom a survival of primitive modes of thought"[4] — but what I want to point to here is its renewal in the movement for "restorative justice" among Christians today. As Christianity's official position has weakened, and it has become once again a religion that must be chosen rather than inherited, a more subversive and more biblical teaching on justice has moved from the peace churches into the mainstream denominations. An example is the Church Council on Justice and Corrections, a consortium of the major Canadian churches, which has become in recent years a penetrating critic of Canadian penal policy, as well as a clearinghouse for alternatives.[5] One of the leaders in this movement has been Pierre Allard, a Baptist minister who joined the CSC in 1972 as chaplain of Archambault Penitentiary near Montreal and today heads its Chaplaincy Department. He says that the turning point in his ministry came when he became a victim of crime himself. Since joining the CSC at Archambault and then moving on to the Dorchester Penitentiary in New Brunswick, he had been an advocate for prisoners. Then, one March morning in 1980, he received a phone call from the RCMP informing him that his brother had been found lying frozen in a field outside Montreal, brutally murdered.

> It changes your world, because then you are part of the harm that is being done. It was a spiritual crisis for me because I had been going to churches and to any group that invited me and challenging them to develop better approaches to prisoners and to not forget them. Out of sight, out of mind — to try to fight that saying. And then I felt the anger myself, and I wanted to hit back.

And I remember going to the funeral for my brother in Quebec City. And my older brother, who does not necessarily share my religious conviction, just before we went into the church — we were going to carry the casket — he really became very angry, and he said, "We have no guts. We're going into a church to pray to a God I don't even believe in. If we had any guts, we wouldn't be here, in the church; we would be in the bars in Montreal trying to find out who did it and do the same things to them." And there was very much part of me that identified with that.

But we went through the funeral, of course, and then I went back to my church, which was behind the walls of Dorchester Penitentiary at that time. And I remember, in the middle of the night as people were sleeping, sitting alone in that chapel and looking at a Cross that one of the inmates had made and starting to cry like a baby. For me, they were healing tears. And I never looked back on that.

They have never found the people who killed my brother, but I did not want those people to be executed like my brother had died. I wanted them to come to discover life the way I see life. Because if people saw life the way I see life, they would not take another life. So, there was a deep, deep yearning that said, "I wish and pray to God that they would come to see life the way it is." And that's been a desire that I've pursued and carried in my heart.[6]

Pierre Allard's words recall Abelard's in their discovery of Christ's passion as overflowing love rather than the discharging of a debt. Once his own heart had changed from thoughts of revenge to thoughts of reconciliation, he began to see this same movement mirrored in the Christian Bible. The Bible, on one level, is a virtual catalogue of crimes. In the very first generation of Adam and Eve's descendants, Cain murders his brother Abel. Moses commits murder. David indulges his adulterous love for Bathsheba by ordering her husband to be "set . . . in the forefront of the hottest battle," where he is killed. Even God is stirred to vengeance by the wickedness of His people. But through all this runs the promise of deliverance, which is prepared in the priestly and prophetic books and fulfilled in the New Testament. Jesus is presented as the innocent sacrifice who ends the need for sacrifice forever, the scapegoat who turns the very idea of the scapegoat inside out. "Repay no one evil for evil," Paul wrote to the Romans, "but overcome evil with good." This was the faith of the early church, but it began to be corrupted when the Emperors Constantine and Theodosius conferred civil authority on Christian bishops and the church began to emerge as "the new Rome." The Reformation, when it came, reformed many things but produced, as we have already seen, an even more bloodthirsty account of justice than had prevailed in the medieval church.

What is required today, Allard thinks, is an understanding that the practice of ostracization and stigmatization that began in the monastery and eventually produced the modern penitentiary "goes completely against what [offenders] need. They don't need isolation. They need a new community." Without one, they will be consigned by default to "the community of crime." Prison consolidates this community by cutting offenders off from regular society and by habituating them to the ersatz society of the prison. The stigma becomes a badge of belonging, the regimentation a substitute for self-control. Like any impressive experience, prison produces camaraderie among those who have shared it; and this camaraderie, Pierre Allard says, extends beyond the prison walls.

> Although many guys at times are well intentioned and mean well when they come out and they don't want to go back into that, unless they have created new social bonds and a new community, if they don't have a new community to go back to, they're going to go back to the old community of friends. Because there's such a need for each one of us to belong somewhere.
>
> I say jokingly at times that I dream of the day when, at the gate of a penitentiary, there's going to be a yellow bus, a Sunday School bus, full of people from a church, saying, "Hi, Joe. Welcome back. You're going to have to do your part. But as far as we're concerned, we're

going to offer you a lot of friendship, we're going to support you."

Instead he gets out of there, he's alone. Where does he go? He hits the tavern. The guys see him. They hug him. They treat him to women, song, and dance. And they're so happy to see him, and they call him by name and he feels that he has returned. And they treat him like this for a few weeks, and then they say, "Well, you know, Joe, now it's time you go back to work." He hates it and he loves it. He knows what it means. He doesn't want to go back to jail, but he also knows that what he's going to start doing now will bring him back.

I don't want to be simplistic, but I have come to realize that it's not our individual efforts that are going to make a big difference; it has to be the impact of a community of faith on a community of crime, because these people need a new community.[7]

Because the ministry of reconciliation Pierre Allard preaches depends as much on what happens after people leave prison as it does on what goes on within the walls, he has established within the csc the institution of community chaplaincy. Community chaplains help ex-offenders establish themselves; they also work with the families of those who are inside. Baptist minister Hugh Kierkegaard has been a community chaplain for the csc in Toronto since 1992, and it has made him aware, he says, of how the stigma of the prison spreads to the families of offenders as well.

The stigma they carry — not because they've done something wrong but simply because they love someone who has done something wrong — the stigma they carry for that is a very debilitating thing. We have families that come to us from churches, and we say, "Have you talked with anybody in your church about this?" "We can't talk about this, they wouldn't understand." The woman who says, "My son is working out of the city now, he has a job out of the city." She tells her friends that because she knows that they wouldn't understand if she explained to them that he's awaiting trial in a detention centre and is probably going to be sentenced to four or five years in the federal system. And there's an incredible amount of pain that comes with that. In essence, they're victims, unseen victims, of the way that we do justice.[8]

At the moment, a lot of the hostility, rejection, and contempt that society feels towards prisoners is concentrated on those who have been convicted of sex crimes, and particularly pedophiles. In recent years a number of such men have been driven out of communities in which they tried to settle after being released from prison. Manitoba and Saskatchewan have passed laws authorizing police and prison officials to divulge information about "high-risk" criminals released into the community, and Ontario has introduced legislation along the same lines.[9] Restrictive "peace bonds" have been issued against pedophiles under Section 810 of the Criminal Code, which allows a judge to impose "reasonable" conditions on persons from whom an injury can be plausibly anticipated. The federal government even went so far as to announce its intention to amend the Criminal Code to allow electronic monitoring of "potential high-risk offenders" regardless of whether they had been charged or convicted of an offence. This proposal was later scrapped, not reportedly because of the violation of civil rights but because of the anticipated expense.[10]

The horror and contempt that any form of pedophilia currently inspires has prompted some Christians to try to realize Pierre Allard's vision of "the impact of a community of faith on a community of crime" by forming support groups around feared ex-prisoners. One such case involves Wray Budreo, a man with a number of convictions for offences against children, who was released from the Kingston penitentiary after being held until the end of his sentence. (The csc, in many cases, prefers to begin a "structured release" after two-thirds of the sentence has been served, since this allows cautious supervision of the offender's return to the community. But it has been forced to hold most pedophiles until "warrant expiry" because of the public outcry that now greets any early release.) Budreo attempted to settle in Peterborough but his house was put under a virtual siege by protesters and reporters. He escaped to Toronto. There, csc community chaplain Hugh Kierkegaard and a number of like-minded colleagues stepped in and established a "circle of support":

> Our involvement began as we realized that he was here in the community to stay, he had nowhere else to go . . . If we chased him out of this community, chances are [things] would just go from bad to worse . . . The chances of someone re-offending go up when they're isolated from community, when they are afraid, and when they are driven back to old coping mechanisms, for instance, drinking or substance abuse. So, there's a balance to be struck here, and, if we work with these individuals in community and we hold them accountable and we build some structures to receive them, then they're not isolated, they're not alone, and they're not driven back to old coping strategies, because they have the support in the community that allows them to cope in new ways.[11]

At first the members of the circle of support were in daily contact with Budreo. "Every day somebody would go and see him," Kierkegaard says, "go have coffee with him, go visit, talk." They helped him find a place to live, and they mediated between him and other agencies, like the police and the media. They saw themselves both as advocates for Budreo and monitors for the community — "a real balancing thing," Kierkegaard says. As time went by, and the publicity died down, contact didn't have to be quite as frequent; but the circle has been maintained since late 1994 and so far Budreo has stayed out of trouble.

One of the members of this circle is Sally Boyles, the rector of Holy Trinity Anglican Church in downtown Toronto and a former prison chaplain at the Vanier Institute for Women. She thinks that the panic provoked by pedophiles in recent years reflects an absence of personal connections.

Some people in the neighbourhood need to get to know this person and to ask the questions that scare them the most and keep asking those questions until they have some satisfaction, because I think that a great deal of fear goes away if you understand a person better and you know their habits. And I don't think there's anything wrong with asking those difficult questions. When I say this person should be allowed to live safely in a neighbourhood, the neighbourhood should also be allowed to live safely with this person. And so, I'm not in [favour of] easy reintegration at all but to have some people who will take up the cause of this person and begin to help the community name what measures have to be in place to help this person live safely there.

When I was a little girl, I lived in a very tiny community, and everyone knew that there was someone in town who loved peeking in windows. I don't think, as a child, it hurt me to know that I was to keep my blind pulled in my bedroom. And as far as I know, that person never went to jail, but there was also no one in town who didn't know that person's tendency. We could say that we should be so safe that I wouldn't have to think of that, but it strikes me that that leaves me out of relationship with that person, and that person, indeed, had mental challenges. And so, it is prudent that we, with many more resources to begin with, have to do some caring towards that other person.[12]

The alarm that spreads around sex offenders, and pedophiles particularly, is often unconstrained by any relationship through which the feared person can either be understood or controlled. Without direct knowledge it is easy to impute a subhuman character to the offender and to exaggerate the danger he poses. "One of the things that we do know about sexual offending," Hugh Kierkegaard says, "is that the vast majority of sex offenders are someone that the victim knows quite well. They're not strangers, they're not people in the community who go around and prey."

As I have already said, the number of sex offenders held in Canadian prisons has increased dramatically in recent years.

According to an article that appeared in *Maclean's* in 1995, "about 5,000 of the 23,000 convicts in the federal corrections system have sex crimes on their records."[13] It has been suggested that this increase represents a change in attitude towards sexual offenders as much as an increase in the frequency of sexual deviance. However, this does not necessarily mean that things now punished were formerly tolerated; they may, rather, have been subject to informal controls. Like Sally Boyles, Hugh Kierkegaard can remember how such controls worked in the case of someone he knew growing up — in his case, in Saint John, New Brunswick, during the 1950s:

> That individual, who would have been in his early twenties at that point, was developmentally delayed, smoked big cigars, and rode around on his bicycle. We'll call him Frankie. We were told as children, "You can say hi to Frankie, but don't you ever talk to him or don't you ever go anywhere with him." And so, we didn't. And the parents and everybody in the neighbourhood made sure. There was a kind of an unwritten social contract in our neighbourhood that Frankie was a part of the community, and he was allowed to be there and live with his parents in the community, but it was implicit to the contract that he was not to deal with the children in the community.
>
> I've thought about that story a lot in the last year. It may be a little idyllic. But how do we create that kind of community or recreate that kind of community where these people are allowed to live among us in a way that recognizes the potential harm that could be done but also recognizes that they probably are people that have been harmed as well? They were offended against before they became offenders, and perhaps there was nobody there to protect them or to speak on their behalf when they were being offended against. How do we create the kind of community that allows them to live in the community with accountability but also with the recognition that they're somebody's son or daughter or brother, they're not a stranger from outside, they're one of us? That seems to me the challenge that we're facing here, working with warrant-expiry sex offenders, and it's

a challenge not only to the way we view offenders but the way that we understand community.[14]

Another attempt to build a circle of hospitality and support around a released sex offender occurred in Hamilton, but it was attended by a lot more controversy than had been the case in Toronto. It began when Charlie Taylor was released at warrant expiry from Warkworth Penitentiary after serving a seven-year sentence for sexual interference with boys between the ages of eight and ten, his fourth conviction on such a charge. Taylor is a man of limited intelligence, and the prison psychologist was worried about what would happen to him. He appealed to Harry Nigh, the Mennonite pastor of Welcome Inn, a combined Mennonite church and community centre in a low-income section of east Hamilton, and the former director of M2W2, an organization that connects prisoners with people on the outside willing to visit and support them. He was a friend of the psychologist's and had known Charlie Taylor in prison. He agreed to help Taylor get settled in Hamilton. The Hamilton police, as the law now requires, had been notified of Taylor's release, and Nigh made his involvement known to them.

> Two detectives met with me, and I just said, "I just want you to know that we're here and that we want to provide support for Charlie." They said, "We don't want him here. We want him to go to Burlington. We want him to go to any other community, but we don't want him here. We've got a file here from the institution saying he has a 99 percent chance of re-offending."
>
> Within our local community in Hamilton, there had been a recent case of a man who had escaped from Hamilton Psychiatric Hospital. The police had made a decision not to inform the public immediately, and, within a matter of hours, he had sexually assaulted a young boy, and they had taken an awful lot of bad publicity about this. So, they were very gun-shy about another pedophile coming back into the community.[15]

In Charlie Taylor's case the police decided they would inform the public. Already burned by the previous incident, their concern had intensified when they were told by the prison authorities that the drug therapy intended to reduce Taylor's sex drive had been discontinued because it had caused life-threatening blood clots. The release of his name, picture, and criminal record touched off a major panic. A bold front-page headline in the *Hamilton Spectator* called the street on which he settled "The Street of Fear." The story went on to describe a frightened citizen photographing a suspicious-looking man in a parked car, who turned out to be a photographer from the *Spectator*. The neighbourhood was leafleted by concerned citizens, and Charlie Taylor's picture was posted on every lamppost. Harry Nigh was caught unawares in the centre of a firestorm.

> The school department people issued a photograph and details about Charlie, warning the children. Every child in the Hamilton-Wentworth region received this on his desk. It came on the desk of my son, who was, at that point, in grade four, and he said, "Oh, I know him, he was at our place for supper last night." We were really glad that it was at the end of the school year because the kids wanted to know. And I was terrified because I knew the kind of publicity that can be generated in this way. I thought we might end up with pickets out in front of our house.
>
> The police also decided that Charlie was a significant danger to re-offend because of the termination of the drug treatment program, and they decided to keep him under twenty-four-hour surveillance. So, for six weeks, he was under constant, twenty-four-hour surveillance, front and back at his house. And that opened up a whole range of other realities, such as taking food in to him, making sure that he was provided for, because he was scared to go out on the street. Every street post had his photo on it, and people were up and down looking for him. He couldn't go out. If he did go out, people actually ran from him on one occasion. He was kind of like a captive here in his own house, under house arrest. There was one episode, almost like

Beverly Hills Cop, where he went out with coffee to give to the undercover police who were watching him, and they said, "Oh, you shouldn't be out here. You're not even supposed to know we're here." That was kind of his nature. This lasted six weeks, at enormous cost — over $300,000 we have been told — for this surveillance to happen.[16]

In the midst of all this, Harry Nigh organized a circle of support for Charlie Taylor. It functioned, like the circle in Toronto, as both support and monitor. Members of the circle helped Taylor with practical things like furniture and food during the period he was under seige; but they also confronted him at times when they thought his behaviour was getting a bit risky. On occasions when they thought he might be "losing it a bit" and a show of authority might be helpful, they asked the police to step in. One woman from Nigh's congregation who joined this effort got him a cat, something Nigh says he would never have thought of but which has been "life saving." Nigh also invited his congregation to take Taylor in.

I went back to my church and said, "What do we do? Do you want to accept Charlie into our congregation? You know who he is, and you know all about him." We had two meetings. Everyone spoke and expressed their fears and expressed their hesitations. And unanimously the church said we will accept him. And, I think, partly it's the character of our community here, because it's low-income folk, and a lot of them have known institutionalization of various forms in their lives. One woman said, "If Jesus hadn't accepted me, where would I be? So, how can we say no to Charlie?" So, he came. We said yes to him.

In the face of the hostility of the community and the fear of the community, we, as a church, also decided to have a welcoming party for him on a Sunday evening. It was one way of saying to him we accept and adopt you with all of the difficulties that you bring to us. We welcome you as a brother and as a person in God's image.

Charlie actually invited the police to come to the party too, and they came. Actually, one of the officers came at 10:30 at night. He came up the back steps. He said to him, "Charlie, I'm really sorry. We wanted to come earlier, but we were afraid the press would be here." The police officer who was the liaison is a tremendous person, who built a relationship of trust with Charlie. He became part of our circle of support meetings. He would come and listen.[17]

Harry Nigh does not claim that their circle of support is a perfect arrangement. When he first met with angry citizens who did not want Charlie Taylor in Hamilton, they asked him whether he was prepared to "take responsibility" for Taylor's actions. They wanted to know, in effect, whether Nigh could guarantee that Taylor would not re-offend. He answered that he and his friends could not take responsibility in that sense, but that he thought it was more dangerous for all concerned to have Taylor isolated than to have him befriended. He recognizes and respects "righteous anger" about the violation of children, and he has taken every precaution to ensure that Taylor not be left alone with children; but he thinks that communities should be capable of a more creative response than ostracization in such cases. As it is now, one rather simple, childlike man with a sexual attraction to children seems able to paralyze an entire community with fear. One detective sergeant in the Hamilton police told Nigh that, in the year after Taylor got out of prison, 10 percent of his time was taken up with this one case. The street where Taylor lived was deserted and callers from as far away as Toronto were contacting the Hamilton police claiming to have seen him. The circle of support mobilizes the community in a more helpful way while still "provid[ing] for security as well as some insight into what's going on."[18]

One of the Hamilton citizens opposed to Taylor moving there was Stella Woock, a retired nurse. She had been active in the local Neighbourhood Watch organization, and in attempting to drive prostitutes out of the district by publishing the licence-plate numbers of their customers. She was also a member of a municipal working group on "the Integration of High-Risk Offenders in the Community," a team involving police, politicians, and community representatives. She worked extensively with children through Sunday school and boys' and girls' clubs. As soon as she heard Taylor was coming to Hamilton, she guessed that he would choose her downtown neighbourhood; when she was proved right, she immediately set about organizing the information campaign that blanketed the area with posters and leaflets. She received "letter after letter after letter," all expressing fear and disgust.

Harry Nigh urged Stella Woock and her neighbours to go and talk to Taylor and get to know him. "I know you're angry, I know you're distraught about the children in your neighbourhood," she remembers him saying, "but wouldn't you be willing to come and meet him?" She asked five different people to come with her to speak to him, "and all but one of them wanted to beat him up." So she decided to meet with him on her own in order to impress on him how strongly the neighbourhood felt and how angry they would be if anything happened to their children. The meeting took place in a doughnut diner and ended with an exchange of phone numbers. She saw him a number of times after that and once helped him out when he needed to take his cat to the vet. She found that there was "something personable" about him; but she never changed her view he should be permanently incarcerated in the interests of public safety. He eventually stopped calling her when he learned that she had told the *Hamilton Spectator* that he was a dangerous man. She insists that it's true.

He is a dangerous man. He's lethal to kids. And the bottom line is there is no cure for this, so he's an accident waiting to happen. He will strike again, he will. And, I think, if people realize that, then these persons should be deemed high-risk offenders and not be allowed out. This is my personal opinion. When children are involved, it's time we, in the public, stood up and spoke. Instead of just the police and the social workers and the authorities speaking out, we need to have a say too.[19]

Where Stella Woock and Harry Nigh differ is not on the question of whether pedophilia can be "cured." Both subscribe to the broad consensus on this point, which a former counsellor in a halfway house for sex offenders puts in this way: "Experts often disagree on the degree to which therapy and treatment for sex offenders reduce recidivism, but there is virtual unanimity on the fact that they're not ever going to lose their propensity for sexual assault — much the way many reformed alcoholics struggle with the desire to drink for the rest of their lives."[20] They disagree, rather, over how to respond to the presence among us of distorted and broken people, people who, as Hugh Kierkegaard says, were often "offended against before they became offenders." The priority that Woock gives to the interests of children leads her to place Charlie Taylor outside the margins of acceptable community, despite the sympathy she feels for him as a person. It makes her willing to countenance permanent confinement and the huge costs it would entail on the basis of apprehended risk. Harry Nigh believes that Taylor's circle of support has shown that a more resilient and more creative response is possible. It cannot offer a guarantee, but it can give scope to prudence as well as charity, and it does leave the door open to redemption.

We came out of church one Sunday, and we were standing around talking, as we always do here. And across the street, a man started screaming. Right over there, he started screaming at Charlie at the top of his lungs, "You get out of here. I'm going to kill you. You're not wanted in this community." And he was very drunk. And we were galvanized. You can imagine. At the top of his lungs. People were coming out in the houses around. And it was just the kind of experience that we had feared all the way along was going to happen. "I'm going to shoot you," he yells. This man was a single parent, living with two young kids. And I said to Charlie, "You get home."

And so, he got on his bike and hightailed it off.

And I went over to talk with him, and he was very drunk. I stood on the steps, and there was a lot of beer bottles around. And he said, "I don't care if they come and get me. The Creator will take care of my children." And so on. "You know what he's done. He's a child molester. He is not wanted in this community."

Our people went home scared, and we were just praying. What was going to happen next? Charlie called his police contact, and they went and talked with the man. But the next morning I came, and he called me over. His name was John. And he said, "Pastor, can I see you for a minute." He said, "I want to apologize to you and your people for what I did yesterday." And he started talking to me, and I started talking and asking some questions and realized here was a man who was living alone with his two kids. But he was also a man, as he talked to me, who had been a victim himself of abuse at the St. John's Training School. He showed me a letter. He had just gotten this letter: $28,000 settlement for the abuse that he had suffered. He was a man who had a scar on his stomach where he had tried to take his life dealing with this kind of anguish. I said, "John, why don't you come on over. We've got programs for your kids. You're welcome to come on over too."

And next Sunday, he was in church with his two kids. My friend Charlie was too scared to come back, he wasn't there that Sunday. Two weeks later, they both met in the foyer of the church. They shook hands, apologized to one another, made a reconciliation. One of our people at church said, "Harry, if you had told me that a week later this guy would be sitting in church, I would never have believed it. That blows my mind." That made two of us.

But it seems to me that, in a microcosm, if people can somehow bridge those gaps and begin and talk to one another, that the levels of fear can be reduced and people can see one another as people.[21]

Charlie Taylor has lived in Hamilton since 1994 and has begun to make connections in the city. In October of 1996 he was brought into court on a charge that he had violated the peace bond against him by babysitting his neighbour's children, but the charge was thrown out in early 1997. Harry Nigh believes that the woman with whom Taylor shares his flat was always present when Taylor was with these children and that nothing untoward occurred. Stella Woock says that one of the children told her she had been improperly touched. The case is murky, but Taylor's acquittal in a hostile climate argues strongly for his innocence. He continues to have daily contact with someone from the circle of support. Other circles for feared released prisoners have also been established. As of June 1998, according to Hugh Kierkegaard, thirteen such circles were operating in Toronto, and six more across the country.

There is considerable political pressure in Canada at the moment to offer communities additional protection against "high-risk offenders." "Unless we do something about this population, *notwithstanding their rights*," Alan Markwart, a senior policy adviser to the attorney general of British Columbia, told the *Globe and Mail* in 1995, "we run the risk of eroding public faith in the justice system to the point of a public overreaction as extreme as [in] the United States." Bending the concept of rights nearly to the breaking point, he went on to say that the civil rights of potential offenders had to be weighed against "the rights . . . of future victims."[22] Canada already has a law mandating a separate proceeding following a conviction through which the Crown can have someone declared a dangerous offender, and therefore held indefinitely. Since the law was passed in 1977, 178 people have been so designated. Ten of them have already died in jail, and only four have been paroled.[23] To this existing power of indefinite detention, the Reform Party would now like to add the power to detain people deemed likely to re-offend once their sentences are complete, and has introduced a bill to this effect in the House of Commons. The bill cannot be passed without government support, but, as discussed in Chapter 3, it did add to the political pressure that induced then Justice Minister Allan Rock in the fall of 1996 to introduce the controversial measure

I mentioned earlier, authorizing electronic monitoring of those judged to present a high risk. This proposal has now been withdrawn, reportedly because of its excessive cost, but anticipated improvements in monitoring technology could lead to its reintroduction. A Colorado parole officer, writing in *The Futurist* a few years ago, claimed that by 2001 "electronic supervision incorporating radio monitors, fuzzy logic, and medical implants" will be capable of providing sensitive chemical control of offenders by means of microprocessors that recognize an offender's "aberrant phases" and cause an implant to release drugs that "selectively tone down criminally sanctioned behaviours."[24]

Canada's Dangerous Offender Act grants our judiciary draconian powers to make a prospective judgement about a person, rather than just denouncing his acts; but it at least follows a trial that is based on these acts. The Reform bill, and the government's aborted electronic tracking proposal, take a further step by adding new sanctions to an already completed sentence based on judgements of potential. These measures would involve punishing people for things they haven't yet done, which almost certainly violates Canada's Charter of Rights, as well as pushing the prison into the notoriously difficult business of trying to make authoritative judgements about risk.

Circles of support cannot precisely be called a solution to this dilemma. They depend too much on faithful and virtuous action to be treated as a model, or blueprint. Models and blueprints belong to the world of risk assessment and zero tolerance, in which a solution to our vulnerability can be engineered. But they do address the dilemma by showing that making people safe "in a new community" can sometimes be an alternative to electronic surveillance or permanent incarceration. What Harry Nigh calls "seeing one another as people" is the essence of the idea. Charlie Taylor was brought out of the terrifying isolation and contempt belonging to the category "child molester," into a new community. And through that community, he became visible as a person.

This is precisely the direction in which Pierre Allard wants to reform the Christian perspective on criminal justice. It is easy, one could even say natural, to feel that those who have done cruel and depraved things deserve nothing from us. The scandal of Christianity is Christ's assertion that those who are in prison are his brothers. One of the ways in which Pierre Allard, together with his wife Judy, have tried to foster a similar sense of kinship between Christ's modern followers and the incarcerated of today is by bringing visitors into prisons:

> Judy and I were among the pioneers in bringing people inside jail, ordinary people, people who sat in churches and had never thought they would ever go in a prison. Well, we brought an awful lot of them through the years. And I would say, in 99 percent of the cases after people had been there once or twice, they always came and said, "Pierre, I never thought it was like this." And what had happened was that all the exemplification they had in their minds or the mental images they had of the prisoners — and I did not ask them what they were, but now they had been completely broken down. Why? Because they had met human beings.
>
> I'll always remember one lady who had raised eight children as a widow. She had to raise them all. Her husband died on the birth of the eighth one. And finally she called me, and she said, "You know, I've been resisting for two years. I feel I should go. But what can I bring?" I said, "Look, you've raised eight children. That's a great preparation to come to prison." So, after we did the clearance and all that, Elsie came one night, and I could just see how nervous she was. And we sang and shared. And then when we broke for coffee, I just saw one guy taking a beeline toward her. She was really nervous, she kind of backed off. And he went to her and said, "Look, you remind me so much of my grandmother." And then the ice was broken, and she's followed that guy now for about fifteen years.
>
> It's that human character. It's not trying to say, "Hey, they have not done it." It's that, whatever they have done, there is still a spark of the Divine. However ugly the image is of God, however broken

it is, we must try, with determination and courage and with faith and hope, to find that little corner and try to spark it for greater renewal.[25]

Pierre Allard's emphasis on getting past "whatever they have done" is Christianity, not sentimentality. His years in prison have often brought him into brutal confrontation with the reality of evil. He insists only that evil is not the ultimate reality. A story he told me from his days at Archambault testifies to this faith:

> My wife and I walked into Archambault Penitentiary. And I don't want to dramatize here, David, but I guarantee you, when we walked in that penitentiary that night, we just sensed there was a presence of evil. There was something just different. And just as we went in, about forty guys came down to the chapel area. And as we went to begin the group, one guy turned to Judy, and he said, "There's a knife in the air, and it's going to fall at this very minute." And at that very minute, one inmate on the range was opening up the brains of Leopold Dion, who had killed some children in the Quebec area, and was saying that he was Lawrence of Arabia and splattering his brain all over the place and singing about it and yelling about it. I had to go and be part of that situation.
>
> For me in many, many ways, some situations in crime are so ugly, so scary — they have a depth of depths that is very scary for us. And to know that Jesus walked through those Valleys of Death and emerged on the other side in the Resurrection, I think, can give a vision and a strength to a prison chaplain and those involved in criminal justice to continue going on so that good can triumph over evil. This is, for me, the key verse for our ministry: Romans 12:21 — "Don't let evil triumph over you, but triumph over evil with good."
>
> Christianity should be the most realistic faith, in a sense, because it does not deny evil. It recognizes the reality of evil, it recognizes how ugly is all the damage that evil is and does. But at the same time, it is not afraid of penetrating that world of evil and saying, with God's help and in Jesus, we can triumph. The entering of evil without

fear can only — in my perspective and in my own ministry, I don't dare approach it without Christ's strength and Christ's presence.[26]

What Pierre Allard calls Christianity's realism about evil has been one of the strengths of the movement for restorative justice. Evil is an absence, a terrifying lack, like "the Nothing" that eats away at the edges of the world in Michael Ende's *The Neverending Story*. Imprisonment can only displace, or postpone, its effects. Pierre Allard and his colleagues have actually addressed the neglect that underlies crime. Without minimizing or arguing away people's fears, they have tried to supply, in a practical, nonideological spirit, the things that are missing, like community support for threatening ex-prisoners. They have shown, I think, that only a willingness within the community to face up to evil can finally replace reliance on imprisonment.

17

JUSTICE AS SANCTUARY

In the year 927, King Aethelstan, the Anglo-Saxon ruler of England, granted to the Minster of Beverley, in Yorkshire, the privilege of sanctuary. The Minster was a monastery church, and the king's proclamation meant that within the vicinity of the monastery, including the town of Beverley, anyone fleeing vengeance would be safe from arrest or seizure. Several signposts outside the town indicated the distance a fugitive needed to travel to reach the sanctuary; another milestone marked his arrival. Records from the fifteenth century, during the tumultuous period of the Wars of the Roses, show that about 200 people a year found sanctuary in Beverley, most because of manslaughter. Refugees could stay in Beverley for one month, so long as they were willing to try to settle their differences with whomever was after them. During this period, they were considered guests, and sat at table with the canons of the Minster. If no settlement was reached by the end of this month, they were allowed a second month's stay, but they had to take their meals in the kitchen. If negotiations were still unsuccessful, fugitives were required, during their third month of residence, to begin working for their keep. Finally, if an agreement still remained out of reach, they were either put on a boat for the Continent, granted safe conduct to some other refuge, or, occasionally, permitted to remain at the Minster as contributing members of the community.[1]

The right that King Aethelstan conferred on Beverley can be traced back to the earliest recorded civilizations. The temples of Egypt, Greece, and Rome sheltered fugitives. In old Israel, the Law of Moses required that there be three cities where anyone who had killed without premeditation could find refuge (Deuteronomy 19). During the Middle Ages, every church was a sanctuary, and the right was sometimes extended, as in Beverley's case, to whole towns. Even after the Reformation, when this right was withdrawn from churches, sanctuary towns continued to exist in parts of northern Europe right up to the end of the eighteenth century.

The right of sanctuary was significant for two main reasons. First, it was a safe place from which an offender could sue for a settlement. As such, it was the cornerstone of a system of justice in which crime was still regarded as a matter between citizens, and not necessarily the affair of the state. Second, it recognized that there are many types of law, all existing together in a crazy quilt of overlapping jurisdictions. William Blackstone, in his *Commentaries on the Laws of England*, lists as many as ten different kinds of law that prevailed simultaneously in the England of his day. He includes, among others, natural law, divine law, the law of nations, the common law, the local customary law, ecclesiastical law, and the law merchant.[2] Sanctuary was an element of divine law that superseded other bodies of law in certain special places. The existence of such places recognized an irreducible difference between the laws of God and the laws of man, and gave both their due. No single procedure could answer all circumstances.

Dutch criminologist Herman Bianchi, whose work on the history of crime and punishment was introduced in Chapter 7, argues in his book *Justice as Sanctuary* for a return to this view of law, and for a reinstitution of sanctuaries.[3] Contemporary Western legal institutions are often presented as having been selected and tested during a long evolution. This view holds that whatever was discarded or fell into disuse must have shown itself unfit. Bianchi turns this prejudice on its head and argues that, during the development of modern criminal law, our understanding of justice has actually been depleted. We have lost precisely the two elements embodied in the right of sanctuary: the possibility of the offender initiating a settlement, and the sense that there is always more to justice than can be realized within a single perspective.

How this happened is described in detail in Chapter 7, but I will summarize it here briefly as a basis for my discussion of Bianchi's conception of justice as sanctuary. According to Bianchi, the predominance of punishment over restoration in the Western account of justice grew out of the eschatological and other-worldly dimension of medieval Christianity. St. Paul's letters to the first Christian churches preach "the ministry of reconciliation" as a form of practical, embodied communal life; but, by the end of the first millennium, justice had come to be understood more as the maintenance of a metaphysical order than as a way of living together. Scholastic theologians arranged law in a hierarchy in which human law reflected natural law, which in turn reflected divine law. This arrangement made the enforcement of law at the same time a reinforcement of cosmic order, and so gave judges tremendous confidence and authority. Law ruled the church, and justified the church's rule. As national states emerged they took over the power of prosecution that the church had pioneered and employed it for their own edification and aggrandizement, as the church had first done. As heresy had been to the church, Bianchi says, crime became to the state.

Secular law retained the impress of its ecclesiastical origins even as it gradually lost any religious inspiration. When Luther burned the books of canon law and asserted that the church ought to be an "invisible, apolitical, alegal" community, the idea of the church as a clerically ruled legal order passed over into the state.[4] With the Enlightenment, and the transformation of Nature from created order to rational construct, the idea that human law is subsidiary to divine law and natural law began to fade altogether. "The law of nature," Bianchi says, "lost its character of a belief system. More and more it developed into a rationalistic method of finding new law. Towards the end of the eighteenth century the overall confidence in rational legislation had grown so far as to make it unimaginable that any secular legislation could ever be against nature."[5]

The loss of natural law as a vital ground for enacted law left Western societies with a rootless, and consequently somewhat fantastic, confidence in legislative pronouncement. Enactment of new laws came virtually to define government, and people began to believe that "law, if well-given, well-observed and well-enforced, will lead directly to the ideal state." This utopian belief produced "an excessive confidence in the human ability to institute just legislation." The eclipse of natural law also led to another "weird consequence": At the very moment when the "natural" and inalienable rights of man were being proclaimed, a "legal" institution was being devised that could suspend these rights. "If natural and given law have become identical," Bianchi writes, "an appeal to natural law as a corrective for given laws is no longer possible."[6]

A second consequence of the secularization of law was that it lost its foundation in an explicit account of justice. After the Enlightenment, "discussion of the idea of justice [became] nearly extinct in the West." It was assumed that "any law should in principle be considered good if properly handed down by a formal legislator." Bianchi finds this notion unsustainable. "Justice and law," he says, "cannot be conceived of as separate or different or antagonistic. Law is impossible without a well-conceived idea of justice."

The divorce of law and justice has produced what Bianchi calls "a consensus model" of criminal justice. Society, according to this model, is the product of a social contract, or prior agreement among the citizens, and society's legal/judicial subculture is the unproblematic agent of their common will. Legal institutions speak for society, and the survival of society is seen as the highest possible good. When judges remark from the bench, as they frequently do, that such and such a punishment is intended to send a message to society, they perfectly embody this view. Ethical accord among the citizens is taken for granted, and the offender's good is subordinated to the general good. This model produces a sense of the solidarity of the good citizens against the "bad" citizens and can be seen at work in ideas such as "the war against crime."

Opponents of this consensus model sometimes propose as an alternative a *dissensus* model of criminal justice. According to this model, the consensus the criminal law claims to embody is actually the cloak of class rule. There are, in fact, fundamental and irreconcilable differences within societies; therefore, the citizens will never agree on a set of general norms. Those who view criminal justice in these terms often see crime as a misguided political response to conditions of oppression. They point out, correctly, that unprosecuted white-collar crime costs society vastly more than the petty street offences that make up "the crime problem."[7] And they deny that any common interest unites the powerful and privileged dispensers of justice with the unfortunate persons whom they imprison.

Bianchi admits that this view of crime is pertinent but argues that, in the end, opposing dissensus to consensus only splits the truth in two. The idea of consensus papers over the unequal distribution of power; the idea of dissensus denies the universality of certain norms. To overcome this contradiction, he proposes a third way: an *assensus* model of crime control. Crime, in this model, is neither to be excused as a displaced form of class conflict nor punished as a violation of an imaginary consensus. Rather it is to be seen as a breach between people that needs to be made good.

The term "assensus" Bianchi derives from John Henry Newman, the Victorian theologian who left the Church of England to become a Roman Catholic and eventually a cardinal. Newman, in his book *An Essay in Aid of a Grammar of Assent*, asked himself,

"How is the truth of Christianity to be conveyed to those who have not experienced it?" Dogmatic apologies for Christianity, he noted, often gained "notional assent," but he wanted to know how real assent — substantial understanding involving the whole person — was to be achieved.[8] As an admirer of Newman, Bianchi noticed the parallel with criminal justice. Criminal proceedings compel an offender to give notional assent to justice by enforcing his conformity to its requirements, but they do not call forth real assent. Bianchi's assensus model is a framework for pursuing real assent to justice in the case of criminal conflicts.

A philosophy of assensus, in Bianchi's view, demands a reinterpretation of the often unconscious religious ideology that permeates the present system of punitive justice. He recognizes that "Christian doctrine is the root of so much evil in the history of crime control that many people would prefer to clear the crime-control system of all traces of religious abuse." But he argues that, since "humankind is, after all, *homo religiosus*," and crime control "has always been based on religious belief," it is better to make conscious use of religious principles than to ignore them. He writes,

> When, in my [earlier] book on the ethics of punishing, I described the distorted Christian roots of the punitive model, I made an important discovery. If these same Christian principles, along with others from Biblical sources, were interpreted correctly, they would offer a remarkable body of sensitizing concepts useful in building a new model of crime control much more just than our present system.[9]

So Bianchi set out to reappropriate biblical principles, rescuing them from the burden of mistranslation and misconception with which they had become encumbered. He was assisted in this task by Martin Buber's modern German translation of the Hebrew Bible. Buber originally undertook this massive project together with Franz Rosenzweig in an attempt to free the book's original voice from national, literary, and historical encrustations. Work began in 1925 and ended only in 1961, four years before Buber's death and many years after Rosenzweig's. This new translation revealed a conception of justice very much at odds with the criminal justice practices that developed in Europe after the thirteenth century.

Buber attempted to convey the sense of *tsedeka*, the Hebrew word usually translated as "justice," by finding or coining three modern German words: *Bewahrung* (genuineness and substantiation), *Bewahreitung* (confirmation of truth), and *Befreiung* (liberation and release from guilt)."[10] The term substantiation suggested that "justice is known by its result, just as the tree is known by its fruit." Justice is not the righting of an abstract balance, or a sacrifice intended to restore a cosmic order, but what is enacted and made manifest in the response to wrongdoing.

> *Tsedeka* has been accomplished . . . if no one has been given a stone for bread; if people have not been appeased, cajoled, or placated with empty and unreliable promises; or if people have not been deluded with false hopes never to be substantiated. This means by implication that human beings can never decide upon their own righteousness, never confirm their own authenticity. The conclusion is up to the others concerned: they will establish their judgement. As such the concept is other-oriented.[11]

Confirmation of truth, Buber's second rendering of *tsedeka*, yields a dialogic, as opposed to a yes-or-no, objective, version of truth. Aristotle and, later, Aquinas, insisted that something was either true or not true. "*Tertium non datur*" — there is no third possibility. Buber uncovered a different account of truth; one that was *relational*, without necessarily being relative or subjective. Truth must be grasped whole, as truth-in-action, not divided along a subjective-objective or relative-absolute axis. "What-actually-happened" and "what-it-meant" must be allowed to interpenetrate. Sincerity, reliability, and commitment are as much a part of the nature of truth as conformity to facts. Bianchi says,

If, during the war, you were hiding Jews in your home and a German knocked on the door and said, "Do you have Jews?" of course, you said "No." It was a lie; but it was, in fact, the truth because you were protecting someone with your truth. You did truth to a Jew hiding in your house.[12]

Release from guilt, Buber's third and final rendering of *tsedeka*, treats guilt not as an ineradicable stain but as an opening to a solution. The present justice system, Bianchi says, does the opposite. He compares it to the hidden God of Calvinism:

> The suspect [is] punished and . . . left at the incomprehensible and mysterious mercy of the criminal court, but nevertheless must accomplish works of gratitude, that is, forced labour without salvation. For the punitive organization that we have constructed since [Calvin's time] behaves like a god in heaven. Whatever offenders may offer as good works, whether they be remorseful, repentant, or willing to do their utmost to repair the harm caused, that can never contribute to their social salvation. On the contrary, once found guilty, they are lost and in a shameful way, left entirely to the tender mercies of prosecutors and judges. What these authorities have to offer is not acquittal but stigmatization for life.[13]

Justice as *tsedeka* allows guilt to modulate into indebtedness. It consists, in Bianchi's summary definition, in "incessant diligence to make people experience the genuine substantiation of confirmed truth, rights, and duties and the eventual release from guilt."[14] *Tsedeka*, in this sense, is "diametrically opposed to the Western model of justice."

> Its most striking contrast to traditional Western justice is the implied priority given to results over intentions. In a *tsedeka* model the act of justice is judged by its result, just as the tree is known by its fruit . . . it is unimportant whether it be a lovely tree or a crooked one, a substantial, solidly constructed, and well-administered legal

system or a flimsy one; the only concern should be whether it generates the results we expect. In this model, a legislator, just like a tree planter, must consider in advance how to secure the promised result. Moreover, the result must be in accord with the intent. If the result is not in accord with the promise, it is not just a failure of administration but much worse: justice has not been done.[15]

Enlightened by the window Buber had opened for him on the Jewish Bible, Bianchi came to see that what Christianity had received from Judaism, and what had still been luminously present in the teachings of Jesus, was an understanding of law very much at odds with the received Western sense of the term. Torah, the Mosaic law, as Buber presents it, is the expression of a living will with which people are free to enter into a relationship, not a net of rules demanding blind obedience. Even the Ten Commandments, according to Buber, should not be understood as an impersonal code but as a statement of the conditions of a personal relationship addressed by an "I" to a "Thou." To keep the law is to dwell in this relationship, and to restore it when it has been violated.

Criminal justice, as it is currently practised, lacks any substantial conception of justice. It presents, in George Bernard Shaw's cruel but apt caricature, "the grotesque spectacle of a judge committing thousands of horrendous crimes in order that thousands of criminals may feel that they have balanced their moral accounts."[16] The procedures by which the offender is condemned and punished offer him no living example of justice. Imprisonment is just in theory, unjust in practice.

The solution to this dilemma, in Bianchi's view, lies in the establishment of an alternative mode of justice based on the principles of *tsedeka* and assensus. This second track would operate alongside the existing system, rather than replacing it. Bianchi finds precedents for his proposal in the multiple conceptions of law that existed before the triumph of the unitary modern state. "The usual and time-honoured solution to the problem of legal imperfection," he writes, "was the presupposition of two legal systems, existing and operating side by side . . . one human . . . and the other . . . exercised by God or . . . based on the law of nature."[17] In Augustine these two systems take the form of two interpenetrated "cities," the city of God and an earthly city, which operate simultaneously. The relationship between the two is *dialectical* rather than *dualistic*. Indeed, Augustine was the great enemy of the dualism of the Manichaeans, who divided the cosmos into antagonistic realms of dark and light. A dialectic relation, on the other hand, supposes interdependence.

> It means that regarding the testing of truth, metaphysical contradictions, and opposing social forces, one side cannot be understood or even exist without the other side. A difficulty or incongruity in one system can be counterbalanced by the other system. It is an interaction of systems, just as there is an interaction of individuals. Nothing can be explained, nothing understood, without taking the dialectic opposite into account. Dialectic is the necessary and indispensable condition for all knowledge, for all justice and fairness, and for all equity and decency.[18]

To function, this double system of justice would require the reinstitution of the right of sanctuary, allowing offenders immunity from prosecution so long as they were pursuing a settlement. Should a reconciliatory approach fail, or were either victim or offender unwilling to attempt it, the hostile procedure of the criminal law would remain available. Renewal of this right would be critical to this assensus mode of dispute settlement in several respects. First, it would frustrate and moderate the victim's desire for revenge by temporarily blocking it. Second, it would create a space not permeated by hostile authority, from which offenders could pursue their duty of redress with dignity. And, finally, the existence of sanctuaries would signify the ultimate primacy of justice as love in at least one phase of the doubly constituted justice system that Bianchi proposes.

What modern sanctuaries might look like remains to be seen. In some respects they would resemble prisons, since their perimeters would probably have to be guarded. But they would have the crucial difference of preserving the initiative of both offender and victim. This does not necessarily mean that everyone who committed a wrong would be able or willing to find a way out of the trouble, nor that every victim would be responsive. But it would mean that if there *were* a way out, if confirmation of truth and release from guilt were a possibility, then this opening to the good would not be wasted.

At present, as a story Bianchi told me illustrates, such openings can only be thrown away.

> There were two boys in Amsterdam, two brothers of eighteen and nineteen years old. And they held up a cab driver and tried to get his money. The man defended himself, and so they kicked him with their boots in such a way that the man ended up in wheelchair. These boys were not that intelligent [and had seen a lot of violence on television that seemed not to permanently injure anyone] and they thought that if you kick a man in his loins, he just gets up . . . So they were in prison awaiting their trial and they repented. They said, "My God, what have we done, what have we done? How stupid we were. And the poor man."
>
> So their attorney [who had been a student of mine] said to them, "Well, write him a letter and offer him something." So they wrote a letter, saying, "We are willing to take care of you for twenty-five years. We'll make a contract." The man was thirty-six years old, not married, will never get married in a wheelchair, will be living from social assistance for the rest of his life. Awful. So they offered to take care of him for twenty-five years.
>
> No answer. The attorney said, "Write him again." They wrote him a second time. Then the man had been thinking, had been discussing it with other people. And some friends said to the cab driver, "Why don't you accept it? Accept it. They will do their utmost to make your life bearable." So, he wrote back, "Okay, I accept."

That was brought before court. [The boys' attorney summoned me as witness and] I said, "This is divine justice. Do it." "No," said the public prosecutor, "all these boys attacking cab drivers have to learn a lesson." So they must go to prison for eight years, and after that they can take care of the cab driver.[19]

The boys did go to prison; and, predictably, when they got out, they felt that they had already suffered enough and were no longer willing to look after the cab driver. The case goes to the heart of what Bianchi thinks is wrong with a one-track system of justice: it insists on punishment even where a settlement satisfactory to the parties is available. How much goodwill is wasted in this way, how many enemies are created unnecessarily, is impossible to know. The only way to find out would be to create the parallel system of restitution-based justice that Bianchi proposes.

Bianchi's proposal for a dual, or dialectical, system of justice distinguishes him from other penal abolitionists. Those who call for the complete elimination of prisons, he says, accuse him of being like a pacifist who still wants to allow a little war. His answer is that the need for prisons can never be completely eliminated under contemporary circumstances. The monks of Beverley, when confronted with a fugitive who could not, or would not, settle the case against him, could always put him on a boat to the Continent. The native people of North America could banish those who would not cooperate from their communities. Today, in a worldwide society linked by high-speed travel and instant communication, no "out there" remains. Some system of confinement and control for those who remain deaf to justice is, therefore, imperative.

I have never been so stupid as to think that we will ever be able to get rid entirely of a punitive system of criminal law . . . We should offer all criminals without any exception the possibility of redressing the harm they've done . . . [But] if you offer that many times, and if they continue to refuse and stand in the evil they have done, then

. . . we use a prison, because we can no longer send them into the forest, we can no longer send them into the desert. Well, we have a desert; that's a prison.[20]

Imprisonment, in Bianchi's estimation, can be restricted but not entirely eliminated. However, if imprisonment were restricted, as he proposes, to the dangerous and the uncooperative, and only for as long as they remained dangerous or uncooperative, he supposes that "Holland . . . would no longer have 12,000 people in prison but perhaps 1,000."

When the French Revolution administered the *coup de grâce* to the already almost extinct right of sanctuary in 1792, the founders of the new republic argued that this right would not be required in future, since the law itself would henceforward be a sanctuary for all.[21] This promise has not been fulfilled. A uniform system of justice applying the same procedure in all criminal cases has actually done great harm by undermining other modes of conflict resolution. To the sum of existing hostilities has been added the hostility produced by the alienating procedures of the criminal law.

The double system of justice that Bianchi proposes would eliminate this unnecessary harm. Access to assensus procedures would ensure that every alternative has been exhausted before someone is given up to the anomie of the prison. If neither the offender's victim(s), nor his family and friends, nor the chance to make amends, can turn him around, or if the opportunity is manipulated or abused, then the other system would be available. We know that there are those who are, in a phrase I quoted earlier from Simone Weil, "so estranged from the good that they seek to spread evil everywhere"; and we must suppose that not all can be reclaimed by a more accommodating style of justice.[22] But what we do not know is how many enemies are made by applying the hostile procedure of the law where it is not required, and how many offenders might return to "confirmed truth . . . and duties" if given a chance. A double system would allow this test to be made.

PRISON IS NOT THE
ONLY PUNISHMENT

Penal Violence and Alternatives
in Poor Countries

So far in this book I have emphasized the dramatic increase in imprisonment in many Western countries during recent years, and the urgent need for alternatives to stem this growth. In this chapter I briefly examine the situation of non-Western countries that cannot afford to expand their prison systems, indeed that can barely afford decent maintenance for the prisoners they already have. Alternatives are as urgently necessary in these countries as they are in wealthier states, but for different reasons. In poorer countries, the main issue is prison conditions, rather than prison growth.

Raúl Zaffaroni is a professor of law at the University of Buenos Aires and an activist in the international movement for penal abolition. In the past he has been the attorney general of the Argentine state of San Luis and a federal judge. The problem of penal power in Latin America, he says, is not primarily a question of prison numbers, but of "the general violence of the penal system."[1] The size of Latin American prisoner populations has generally remained constant — in Argentina, for example, the rate of imprisonment per 100,000 was 88 in 1906, 100 in 1972, 90 in 1980, and 83 in 1995. The current level is higher than that of the Netherlands and the Scandinavian states, but lower than in Britain, Germany, or Canada.

What Zaffaroni means by the general violence of the penal system is illustrated by some research he and his colleagues carried out under the auspices of the Costa Rica–based Inter-American Institute of Human Rights. Focusing on the period between 1977 and 1987, their study showed that the tendency for Latin American states to oscillate between democracy and dictatorship is partly generated by the power of the police. "The discourse of dictatorship," he says, "is law, security, order." When the grip of dictatorship relaxes, there is at first a heady effusion of human-rights rhetoric. This alarms the police, who interpret it as a threat to their considerable power, which sometimes even exceeds the army's. Human-rights talk also threatens the livelihood of the police insofar as it denounces corruption, which generally provides what Zaffaroni calls "a complement of salary" for Latin American police officers. In other words, salary levels are predicated on its availability in the same way that a waiter's wages presuppose tips. Against these threats the police mobilize a law-and-order campaign and "project into society an image of civil war." This involves the execution of "little thieves" and the planting of weapons beside them, as well as honouring any police casualty with the pomp due a hero fallen in war. Between 1982 and 1987 in Buenos Aires, Zaffaroni says, 750 people were killed by the police. In São Paolo, Brazil, during the same period 2,384 persons were killed; and the rise and fall in the frequency of these killings appeared to have a clear strategic relationship to elections and other political events the police had an interest in influencing.

Not all fourteen countries Zaffaroni and his colleagues studied conformed exactly to this description; Argentina, Brazil, and Venezuela supplied the archetype, while Mexico, Uruguay, and Costa Rica were exceptions. But the phenomenon was generally constant enough to be called a pattern. Within this pattern of uncontrolled police power, imprisonment is just one aspect of penal violence. The same people liable to be selected for imprisonment are liable to be selected for execution on the street. Those who do go to prison often face horrendous conditions and considerable danger of disease, as well as violence from guards and other prisoners. A new Human Rights Watch study of prison conditions in Venezuela cites official statistics showing 207 prisoners killed and 1,113 injured in Venezuela in 1996 alone.[2] Prison conditions, therefore, rather than numbers as such, are generally the most serious concern.

Zaffaroni says that inadequate budgets and untrammelled penal power cause Latin American prisons to deteriorate into three types. The first type is the hell on earth described in the cover copy of the Human Rights Watch report mentioned above: "overcrowded, understaffed, physically deteriorated, and rife with weapons, drugs, and gangs." The second type is the more convivial form that Zaffaroni calls a ghetto. This is a prison that has also escaped public control but is not sealed to the outside, so its porous boundaries permit economic and social relations to develop with the surrounding society. Zaffaroni cites a large prison of this kind in La Paz, Bolivia, where families move in with inmates, inmates go out to sell their manufactures, and the whole set-up resembles a poor neighbourhood as much as a prison. The third type is a "hotel," where "the budget of the prison is complemented by the contributions of the distinguished guests." When these contributions are redistributed, conditions improve. Zaffaroni says that there are now a number of Latin American prisons of this type.

It is not easy to recognize a worthwhile public purpose in any of these three remarkably different cases. All show a deterioration towards alternative styles of self-government — reign of terror, self-sufficiency, and plutocracy — in which penal power has escaped juristic direction or purpose and become, in effect, a law unto itself. Deteriorated prisons defy the law they are ostensibly intended to uphold and enforce; and, if, as Zaffaroni argues, penal power is only justified insofar as it vindicates the rule of law, then imprisonment under current Latin American fiscal and political conditions is self-defeating. It reflects only the hegemony of a violent and self-interested police power, not the disinterested dominion of law.

The futility of imprisonment has also been recognized by Julita Lemgruber, the former director of Brazil's second-largest prison system in the state of Rio de Janeiro, and a friend and colleague of Raúl Zaffaroni's. As a graduate student in sociology, she studied the women's prison in Rio and published a book about it. Then she became an assistant to the director of Rio's seventeen prisons, leading to her appointment as head of the system in March of 1991. As soon as she took office, she set about reducing violence and corruption. At the first reported violent incident, she went directly to the prison and talked to the guards.

> I said, "I think you haven't understood that this is a new adminis-tration, and we won't stand for this." And so this guard got up and said, "Okay, Mrs. Lemgruber, we dance as the music goes." Those were his words, we dance as the music goes. Before nobody cared if we beat the prisoners; now you are saying that you don't want this, so we have to dance to your music.[3]

It turned out to be not quite this simple, and some guards remained implacable enemies throughout her tenure, but she did succeed during her four years in office in considerably reducing violence in Rio's prisons. Lemgruber's theory was that violence breeds violence; and that if she could reduce the brutality of the staff to the inmates, the violence of the inmates to each other would abate as well. It worked. During the four years prior to her appointment, there had been seventy-nine murders in Rio's prisons; during her four-year tenure there were eight.

The second item on her reform agenda was to reduce corrup-tion. In a prison, she says, nothing happens during the day when the administration is there. The action takes place at night. So she arranged for directors of prisons to make unexpected visits at unaccustomed hours. For the first time, guards who had sold escapes to prisoners were arrested and successfully prosecuted. Two of the convicted guards had received $40,000 for arranging for a well-known drug dealer to walk unmolested out the front door of the prison in a guard's uniform.

Lemgruber was proud of these reforms; but she says that, in the end, her experience running Rio's prisons only confirmed conclusions she had reached years before when she was doing her graduate research:

> When I was studying this women's prison, I would go there twice, sometimes three times a week, and I would sit and talk to those women. And, if you go to prisons, you don't have to [conduct a] study to be convinced that that thing doesn't work. You see the suffering, you see how it destroys families, how it destroys personal histories. You don't have to theorize, you just have to live the day-by-day lives of those people who are there, who are telling you the stories of what happened to them because they went to prison — not because they committed a crime, but because they went to prison . . . So, after four years of all this fighting and I-can-do-this-I-can-do-that, I'm more than ever convinced that, no matter how much you work, no matter how much you change, prisons will always be the same. Even if you run a prison with all the money you can have, even if you offer everything you can think of, you'll never change a person by depriving this person of their liberty . . . Only very violent people should be sent to prison.[4]

In Rio the problem of violence is real and pressing — Lemgruber says that she doesn't stop at red lights at night for fear of being robbed, or even having her car stolen — but, even so, she estimates that for Brazil as a whole nonviolent offenders make up about half of the prison population. In one case that she came across in the women's prison, a woman was sentenced to three years' imprisonment for stealing two packages of disposable diapers. "How Much Would You Pay for Two Packs of

Disposable Diapers?" was the headline of the article she wrote for the newspaper comparing the cost of the imprisonment to the cost of the diapers.

Taking into account the cost of imprisonment, its ineffectiveness as an anti-crime measure, and the brutalizing cruelty of Brazil's prisons — fifteen of Rio's thirty-eight prisons have less than one square metre of space for each of their current prisoners — she believes that there is a cogent case for alternatives to imprisonment in Brazil. As a special assistant to Rio's secretary of justice, she is now working on identifying and implementing these alternatives. Brazilian law already allows noncustodial sentences, she says, but judges are reluctant to give them. Some of the difficulties are practical; without a parole or probation service to supervise community sentences, judges cannot be assured they will be executed. Lemgruber is now trying to organize a corps of social workers that could exercise the necessary supervision. But attitudes are even more important:

> The judges are not using the law at their disposal because they're not used to using it. There is not a culture of alternatives; there is the culture of the prison. We must change this culture. We must show them that other kinds of punishments are punishments also. Prison is not the only punishment.[5]

Reforms of the kind Julita Lemgruber is trying to bring about in Rio de Janeiro are being supported in a number of other poor countries by Prison Reform International, an organization founded in 1989 to fight for decent prison conditions, a reduction in the use of imprisonment, and "the use of constructive noncustodial sanctions which encourage social reintegration whilst taking account of the interests of victims."[6] The executive director is Vivien Stern, an Englishwoman who also heads the National Association for the Care and Resettlement of Offenders, Britain's largest organization representing the interests of prisoners and ex-prisoners. Vivien Stern generalizes from the arguments made by Raúl Zaffaroni and Julita Lemgruber to the hope that countries that can't afford decent prisons will lead the way in devising alternatives. One of the first projects Prison Reform International supported was a scheme to help establish community service as an alternative to prison in Zimbabwe.

Zimbabwe has all the problems of a typical African country: overcrowded prisons, lots of people in prison because they couldn't find the money to pay a fine equivalent maybe of $10, no other way of dealing with offenders and no tradition, since colonialism, of dealing with offenders other than by sending them to prison. But in terms of the development process, a prison is a monstrous waste of money, a creator of illness, a creator of dependent wives and children that the state is not prepared to keep, and a drain on development and on the country's resources.

The Zimbabweans were interested in finding another way, and leading people in the Zimbabwean criminal justice system worked with us and the European Union, who provide the money through us. There's now an extremely successful community-service scheme going in Zimbabwe, which has already diverted about 4,000 people from the prison system. The community-service scheme is a model for Africa, because it's very low in its use of resources, and it makes a very recognizable contribution to the benefit of the community by putting people to work in community organizations that have very little money. Organizations that look after disabled children or look after the elderly and have to run these services on a shoestring can get free workers from the community-service scheme.

And it seems to have taken root very well in the African context, where prisons were, after all, imported by colonialists. They were not an African idea. They don't fit with the African idea of justice, which is very much based on restitution. Community service fits very well. And we're very hopeful that the model of community service that we've been able to support and work on with the Zimbabweans will be adopted in other African countries. The European Union is interested in seeing it replicated, and we're hopeful of getting the money to replicate it now in four neighbouring countries. So, the Zimbabweans, who've worked on this and have a very clear idea how to do it, will be able to go to countries around and help their colleagues there to set up similar schemes. And eventually it could become a major part of criminal justice systems in Africa. Many people would not go to prison who now go to prison, and the amount of suffering, death, and poverty that could be saved by that development is measurable and substantial.[7]

Vivien Stern sees great promise in the fact that imprisonment as a punishment for crime is an institution with very shallow roots in African soil. Just how shallow, she says, was brought vividly home to her during a visit to a prison in the southern African state of Malawi.

I addressed a meeting of 900 prisoners, all sitting on the floor, discussing with me, with maybe three or four officials there. Nothing's locked. The wall is something that even I, who am not athletic, could climb over. They all stay there more or less, and they don't riot, and they don't mutiny, and they live more or less as the prison expects them to live. So, you have to ask yourself, Is this a prison in the conventional sense? Because these people stay there, and they obey the rules more or less. They protest ferociously about the appalling treatment, but they accept the legitimacy of what's being done to them. So, if you don't need security and if you don't need high walls and if you don't need to lock anything, why are they having what we would call a prison in the first place? Clearly there's something wrong with the concept, something completely alien in the concept that enables you to have something called a prison but which has hardly any security and where any child could climb over the wall. If there is, in the African tradition, an acceptance of the legitimacy of punishment in that way, then the scope for a different form of punishment that's not based on the European, nineteenth-century idea of a prison is very, very promising, and we ought to be able to think of another way: Why aren't these people working in some way in their villages, in some way maintaining their families and making another form of restitution to whoever it was they stole from or whatever it was they did? Because clearly they're not a security risk in any sense that we understand, and they might as well be growing their own food rather than having the government struggling to feed them and failing to do so.[8]

Stern, who has had lengthy experience with British prisons, says that what she observed in Malawi was utterly unlike anything she had seen at home.

Very few people locked up in a British prison accept the legitimacy of what's done to them. They think that it was unfair, the trial was probably unfair, they got a harsher sentence than the person who was doing it with them; it was all the fault of their upbringing anyway; and rich people steal a lot of things and don't get into prison, it's only the poor who get into prison. There's a whole complex of ideas which make the British person in prison often feel that it's completely illegitimate that they're there and that their role is to try and get one up on the system. That's the normal culture of prisons as we know it, except in Africa, where there was no evidence that this was the way it worked at all and where there was a completely different set of relationships I observed between the prisoner body and the staff body. The staff felt a respect, if I can use that word, a respect for the prisoners and a deep shame at the way they had to keep them: the rags that they were wearing, the poor food, the lack of medicines, the disgusting huts that they were all sleeping in, with about twelve inches per body. There was a community of shame and of survival that bound the staff and the prisoners together in a way that you certainly wouldn't see in the West.[9]

Stern's experiences in Malawi led her to wonder whether the habit of imprisonment, acquired during colonialism, might not be obscuring other and better possibilities. In the solidarity between staff and prisoners and in the vividness of their shame, she could see the outlines of older communal institutions of punishment and restitution. These institutions, in her view, will be easier to restore in Africa, where the cultural habits that would sustain alternatives remain vital, than in Western countries, where the prison has a deeper hold on the social imagination. Nevertheless, to her mind, the times demand alternatives in Western countries as well:

> We went through a phase where we tried to make prisons much more humane: large numbers of staff, relationships between staff and prisoners, a place which was therapeutic and educational and a place where the emphasis was on good relationships and human development. And there were, under that idea, some very humane prisons. Denmark, for example, springs to mind. The Netherlands went through a phase of very humane prisons. I fear that phase is ending. With the pressures on expenditure, the lack of faith in helping human beings to be better, the temptation will be to use incarceration in what one has to call a concentration-camp model: Keep people locked up as cheaply as possible for as long as you feel they might do something nasty to someone else, which is why, I think, we need to think very quickly about another model. And that's why I'm very excited about what's happening in Africa.[10]

Vivien Stern hopes that countries like Zimbabwe and Malawi can take the lead in prison reform, showing Western countries the way. Terrible prison conditions create a strong spur to action. Money is not lacking, since alternatives on the whole can be cheaper. What is mainly needed, Stern thinks, is support and encouragement for new thinking, and that's what PRI is now trying to provide.

IV

Conclusion

"Do I desire the death of a wicked man?" says the Lord YHVH.
"Don't I want him to repent of his wickedness and live?"

Ezekiel 18:23

A TURNING POINT?

In the first part of this book, I sketched the reasons why the number of prisoners has increased so substantially throughout the Western world since 1980. I also noted the disturbing fit between large prisoner populations and an emerging order that is variously described as postmodern, global, consumerist, etc. The character of this new order is still uncertain — like the old story of the elephant examined by several blind men, the names it attracts vary with the parts of it being examined — but, whether it is called the end of history or the new age, most observers agree on some of its more obvious attributes: anxiety about livelihood, unprecedented mobility of people and capital, dissensus about appropriate public behaviour, increase in the number of economically superfluous people, and unprecedented media intensity. These conditions magnify fear and enhance the importance of rituals of containment and reassurance. Imprisonment is such a ritual. It may be manifestly ineffective in controlling misbehaviour or making society safer, but it makes a compelling dramatic tableau of crime punished, order restored, and conformity justified. This symbolic function makes it very likely to increase in the face of social turbulence, as of course it has.

The nature of modern criminal justice institutions has amplified the surge in prison numbers. These institutions are based on a philosophy epitomized by Henry Brougham, a Whig legal

reformer and Lord Chancellor of England, in this description of
the duties of a lawyer he made in 1820:

> An advocate, by the sacred duty which he owes his client, knows in
> the discharge of that office but one person in the world, that client
> and none other. To save that client by all expedient means — to
> protect that client at all hazards and costs to all others and among
> others to himself — is the highest and most unquestioned of his
> duties; he must not regard the alarm, the suffering, the torment, the
> destruction which he may bring upon any other.[1]

Brougham's statement is a vivid, even shocking, portrayal of
justice as the product of a great machine. A lawyer is not to think
of the common good, but only of the specific interest he represents, even if that interest should bring "torment and destruction" on others. The sanctity of his contract with his client
becomes for him the highest good. The only justice that can be
hoped for is the justice that will result from the faithful execution
of all contracts. Just as Adam Smith's invisible hand orchestrates
economic justice when each obeys his own interest, so the adversarial system of law is presumed to arrange the best possible
outcome through the competition of blind interests.

This philosophy is an empty shell — a procedural framework
and nothing more. It guarantees rights and upholds the social
contract by which citizens have made obedience to law a matter
of their own self-interest; but it is mute on the substantive
questions of what justice finally is or why we should love it.
George Grant speaks of "the terrifying darkness that has fallen
on modern justice"; modern liberalism has multiplied rights
without finally being able to say what it is about human beings
that makes them inherently worthy of rights.[2]

The institutions that have developed within this conception of
justice are designed to determine by scrupulous trial the exact
degree of the offender's guilt and then to make him suffer in the
same degree. This is both their glory and their weakness. They

contain few resources with which to address the crisis of the expanding prison. They have no mandate to make peace, discover the underlying sources of trouble, restore the dignity of victims, or offer offenders some practical means by which their offences can be made good. They will, therefore, tend to address perceived breakdowns in the social order by mechanically increasing levels of imprisonment. This makes them unsatisfactory instruments for addressing certain kinds of social upheaval. Nevertheless, they continue to be used in this way. Political reaction generally follows established pathways, and imprisonment is a well-trained cultural reflex. Increasing it is the line of least resistance for judges, legislators, prison administrators, and parole officials faced with public outcry about crime.

Against these compelling reasons to expect that large concentrations of prisoners will be a regular feature of the new social landscape can be set two opposing arguments. The first, as I hope I have demonstrated in Part III, is the existence of effective, affordable alternatives that do much less social damage. The second is public recognition of the futility and counterproductivity of imprisonment as a correctional institution. I believe this recognition is widespread, even though it may often be overpowered by the desire for vengeance or masked by fears that there is no other realistic way to contain criminality. Jerry Miller's story in Chapter 13 of the relocation of the four hundred juveniles held in the maximum-security Camp Hill prison in Pennsylvania during the 1970s is, in this respect, a parable: when his diagnostic experts were given no alternative they judged that 95 percent of these boys ought to be in secure settings; but, when workable alternatives were presented, they then judged that only forty of the four hundred needed to be in custody. Public views of imprisonment depend on the context in which they are formed. Because the prevailing context in the West today is a feeling of insecurity, continuously aggravated by a pattern of media crime reporting skewed towards exceptional cases, there is undoubtedly a lot of superficial support for current policies of mass imprisonment. Nevertheless, I think it possible that within the murky mixture of emotions with which the public confronts issues of crime and punishment, there is both a bad conscience about the institution of imprisonment and an incoherent, unformed hunger for more satisfying modes of justice. As the default mode of enforcing law and maintaining order, imprisonment continues to expand; but it does not necessarily convince. Its rationales have grown thin and threadbare, and even its supporters advance few positive claims for it beyond the necessity of impounding enemies.

Imprisonment as the expected punishment for most criminal offences is less than two hundred years old. The practice gained currency towards the end of the eighteenth century, when the old armamentarium of punishment began to seem inhumane and ineffective. Canadian criminologist Greg Smith, in an essay on the decline of public physical punishment in London between 1760 and 1840, has examined the movement of opinion underlying this change in the preferred mode of punishment. For example, he quotes a commentator who styles himself "Philanthropos" writing in the *London Magazine* for June of 1767:

> It is not the Intenseness of Pain that has the greatest Effect on the Mind, but its Continuance; for our Sensibility is more easily and more powerfully affected by weak but repeated Impressions than by a violent but voluntary Impulse . . . The Death of a Criminal is a terrible but momentary Spectacle, and therefore a less efficacious Method of deterring others than the continued Example of a Man deprived of his Liberty.[3]

Imprisonment was introduced as crime's regular reward, Smith argues, because, in the context of changing sensibilities and changing forms of life, it was seen to "work" as punishment in a way that spectacular and theatrical displays of violence no longer did. Two hundred years later, a prison sentence is the standard means by which justice is seen to be done, but its plausibility as a punishment that "works" is waning.

A retributivist theory of justice insists that the scandal of crime deserves a precise and measured response; this insistence, in my view, is the bedrock that remains when other, more doubtful, rationales for imprisonment are scraped away. Imprisonment may not deter crime or rehabilitate offenders; but it does show that evil has its deserts, and provides a scale on which it can be measured. Denying these deserts deprives the social world of its proper moral proportions. The measure of what a criminal act deserves might be arbitrary, but if it is at least consensual and consistent, the order of justice is symbolically repaired and the harm acknowledged. Punishment, says CAVEAT founder Priscilla de Villiers, represents a "drive to restore the orderliness of life [and] a need to rebuild the reasonableness of daily existence."[4]

But, as we have seen, imprisonment purchases reassurance and a restored sense of moral proportion at tremendous cost. This is retributivism's predicament. Crime must be answered in a convincing way; but imprisonment can accomplish this purpose only by generating new injustices. This predicament could be sidestepped so long as belief in an autonomous "system of law" seemed to remove judgement from human hands, but I do not think it can be sidestepped any longer. There *is* no frictionless medium in which retributive pain can be unproblematically delivered. Imprisonment is not just a neutral system of moral accounting; it is a violent ritualization of power, and, as such, it produces effects that undermine and overwhelm its capacity to represent justice.

This is the crossroads at which Western criminal justice systems now stand. They have inherited a procedural account of justice that proliferates rights but has nothing to say about what justice actually is; a retributivist theory of punishment that satisfies the public cry for the restoration of moral order, but degenerates into pure revenge in the absence of a convincing mode of punishment; and a prison system, based on a mishmash of incoherent and unbelievable principles, that in reality does little more than warehouse the problem. Persistence in this status quo, once its ideological veils have come off, will lead to a further expansion of the penal complex that Nils Christie calls gulags Western-style, and introduce an uneasy edge of bad faith into its operation. The alternative is to begin to rethink the whole question of crime and punishment, and to rediscover the exigent but always unfinished question of justice.

This rethinking, as I have tried to indicate, is already well under way, and is being fed from a variety of sources previously suppressed or sidelined by the professional monopolies that comprise the criminal justice system. Christians have begun to criticize the retributive strand in their tradition and reclaim the "ministry of reconciliation" that St. Paul preached to the Corinthians. Aboriginal cultures have renewed the practice of what John Braithwaite calls "reintegrative shaming" and are now hybridizing this practice with Western-derived procedures. Disillusioned communities have seen how the criminal justice system, by appropriating conflict, steals the very means by which community is created. A "sea change in political rationality" has unseated "society" as the genesis, victim, and avenger of crime, and substituted the concrete social relations involved in restoring victims and holding offenders accountable. And a number of worried professionals, in both the academy and the criminal justice system, have publicly expressed their fears that, without reform, an ever-expanding prison system will eventually incubate new forms of totalitarianism.

In Canada, during the last few years, alternatives have begun to achieve a level of acceptance that has surprised, and even worried, some of their supporters. Wayne Northey has just retired after eight years as editor of *Accord*, "a Mennonite Central Committee publication for VictimOffender [*sic*] Ministries," which has been one of the main voices of the movement for restorative justice. When he began, he writes in a valedictory editorial,

> many of us committed to this vision felt a little like speed boaters
> out on the ocean . . . trying to attract the attention of the big

government ocean liners [and] often despair[ing] that they would ever notice us. The day came, however, when our little boats were nearly displaced in the ocean liners' wakes. As we recovered, we were shocked to see emblazoned on their sides beyond our dream: "RESTORATIVE JUSTICE."[5]

Northey goes on to worry that this may prove to be a "Judas embrace." But he says, nevertheless, that during his tenure he has seen "government officialdom at every level embrace the new vision of Restorative Justice."

The first sign that the federal government was taking the problem of the rise in prison populations seriously came with the report of the Sentencing and Corrections Review Group in 1995. This group included the commissioner of the CSC, John Edwards, the chairman of the National Parole Board, Willie Gibbs, and the deputy ministers of the Justice and Solicitor General's departments. It was convened by the government to make recommendations after it was revealed that Canada's prison population had grown by about 30 percent since 1985 and might grow, according to CSC projections, by 50 percent more over the next decade.[6] The group's report made it clear that the present situation was unsustainable: "Continuing to do business in the same way will inexorably lead to further crowding and degraded prison conditions, program effectiveness and security measures . . . The current strategy of heavy and undifferentiated reliance on incarceration as the primary means of responding to crime is not the most effective response in many cases, and is financially unsustainable."[7]

By the time of this report, Solicitor General Herb Gray had already told the House of Commons Justice Committee that his government was prepared to work with the provinces to devise alternatives to incarceration for offenders posing no threat to public safety.[8] The main fruit of this commitment so far has been the addition of what are called conditional sentencing provisions to the Criminal Code. Under the Code's new Section 742.1,

approved in the fall of 1996, offenders are allowed to serve
sentences of less than two years "in the community" so long as
this "would not endanger [its] safety." A recent decision of the
Ontario Court of Appeal interprets this new law quite broadly
and opens the way for its wide application. In a forty-five-page
judgement, released in April of 1997, the court argued that
community safety can be interpreted to include the danger
that the offender will himself be harmed and rendered more
dangerous in prison. Parliament, the judgement affirmed,
"clearly intended . . . to encourage courts to reduce reliance on
imprisonment as a response to crime."[9]

The government has also given a nod to crime prevention by
creating a $32 million fund for this purpose. The amount repre-
sents approximately one percent of the annual $3 billion budget
for police, courts, and prisons. According to the *Globe and Mail*,

> It will be up to each community to apply for funds under the pro-
> gram . . . More than 50 percent of the $32 million . . . will be used
> to establish crime-prevention councils. The councils will bring to-
> gether police and those responsible for housing, social services,
> public health, recreation and schools to decide on a common strategy
> . . . Programs for young people are the priority for the fund [but] the
> government also wants to direct money toward aboriginal commu-
> nities and making Canadian streets safer for women . . . A new
> national crime-prevention centre, headed by former Toronto mayor
> Barbara Hall, will decide who gets the money.[10]

The effect of this crime prevention initiative remains to be
seen. Conditional sentencing, likewise, is too new to assess its
impact on the rate of imprisonment. The most recent prison
figures from Statistics Canada indicate a slowing of growth to 1
percent between 1996 and 1997, but this change is not necessarily
connected with federal policy initiatives.[11] At the time of writing,
several hundred conditional sentences have already been handed
down, some in cases that would generally be perceived as serious.

In May of 1997, an Ottawa judge gave a community sentence to a woman convicted of manslaughter in the shooting death of her violent common-law husband. Noncustodial sentences have also been given in cases of dangerous or impaired driving resulting in death, as well as of fraud and sexual indecency. Several of these cases have been appealed by the Crown, and a supplementary amendment has been added to the original conditioning sentencing provisions, instructing judges to consider the principle of deterrence as well as public safety where a community sentence might be contemplated. The amendment apparently resulted from fears in the Justice Department that some judges were interpreting the new law too liberally.[12]

Four days after this amendment came into effect, in May of 1997, Mr. Justice Forestall of the Ontario Court's General Division indicated his determination to continue giving conditional sentences in serious cases when he handed down a noncustodial sentence in the case of a St. Catharines man whose drunken driving had killed two people. The offender was ordered to do 240 hours of community service over eighteen months, surrender his driver's licence for four years, undergo counselling, and spend 75 hours over the next two years making presentations to students on the consequences of drinking and driving. On the same day in Winston-Salem, North Carolina, a man facing similar charges was given two life sentences after a jury rejected the prosecutor's argument that he should be executed.[13]

While the federal government, and the courts, have been taking these preliminary steps towards reducing imprisonment, the provinces of Quebec and New Brunswick have also announced policies of decarceration. Acting in marked contrast to Ontario's moves to increase imprisonment and make its prisons cheaper and more alienating (discussed in Chapter 3), Quebec's public security minister, Robert Perreault, released a report in April of 1996 that called for the closing of as many as six of the province's prisons, and a reduction in prison numbers of 13 percent. Noting that in recent years registered crime had been falling in Quebec while imprisonment had increased by 7.5 percent annually, the report argued that Quebec's "challenge consists of changing our treatment of criminality through incarceration and repression to a system based on prevention, resolution of conflict, and the use of incarceration only for individuals who pose a threat to the population's security." Through these measures, the government of Quebec also hopes to save $16 million a year.[14] New Brunswick has gone even further, promising a reduction of 25 percent in jail capacity. "When we examined those who were in provincial institutions, we found that 86 percent had been previously sentenced for other offences, so we know that it is not a deterrent to put them in jail," said New Brunswick's solicitor general Jane Barry. The province intends to direct most of the $5.4 million annual saving to community-based rehabilitation and the hiring of additional probation officers. The executive director of the New Brunswick branch of the John Howard Society, Brian Saunders, says that he has been surprised at the lack of negative reaction from citizens. He attributes the calm public response to the effective way in which the Solicitor General's Department made the case for reform.[15] Well-publicized scandals involving the sexual abuse of prisoners at provincial institutions may also have generated public disaffection with provincial prisons.

Alongside these government initiatives, there are signs of what Dutch criminologist Willem de Haan has called "the politics of bad conscience," both within the institutions of criminal justice and among the country's intelligentsia more generally. In March of 1996, Ontario Provincial Court Judge David Cole told a conference in Toronto that "a surprising number of judges feel that much of [the] processing and reprocessing of social misfits does very little to prevent or control crime." He cited a dozen recent decisions in which judges had expressed doubts about the usefulness of imprisonment.[16] The generally conservative *Globe and Mail* has also spoken against routine use of incarceration. "Prison should be a last resort," urged a *Globe* editorialist in February of 1996. "[It should be] imposed not as a reflex, but out of necessity. Incarceration should be avoided where possible because (1) it is tremendously expensive and (2) it often creates not a reformatory for offenders but a hothouse for budding criminal minds."[17]

During his recent three-year term as commissioner of the CSC, John Edwards was a spokesman for this skeptical reductionist point of view within the federal civil service. I met with Edwards in Ottawa shortly after the Sentencing and Corrections Review Group, of which he was a member, made its report in favour of alternatives to imprisonment. He told me:

> I think it's deep in our culture at the present time that most people who run into reasonably serious trouble with the law should be tossed in jail. And that, I think, applies to Crown prosecutors. It probably applies even to defence attorneys, who say to themselves, "Well, my client, having had a series of break-ins, the issue is one year or two years." And so, people are tending to think in terms of incarceration in certain circumstances as a matter of course. It's not just our judges; it's a state of mind that permeates the criminal justice system. And the kind of thing that I think is important to try and explore is, why has that habit become so entrenched and what can we do about it?
>
> One of the reasons it's become entrenched is that the criminal justice system does not have the time to do what many people in the system would like to do, which is to evaluate an offender from the point of view of what will help that offender find a useful life. They don't have time. It's basically a rapid-fire, heavy-caseload sausage factory, where cases come in and the more quickly they are resolved, the better; which often means that there's a plea bargain quickly determined by defence and prosecutor. The defence may say three years, the prosecutor says five years, they compromise on four years, go to the judge, the judge says fine and moves on to the next case. That decision on four years' incarceration costs the taxpayer an enormous amount of money. But they didn't consider that.
>
> At the same time, they may have done terrible damage to family

connections and what have you, when there might have been, if there had been a thorough evaluation of the person, there might have been a more humane and certainly more cost-effective means of ensuring correction; i.e., a solution within the community.[18]

Edwards expressed doubts about most of the standard rationales for imprisonment. He said that the only reason that made solid sense to him was the need to keep certain dangerous people under control, in some cases temporarily, in others permanently. "But the proportion of people who must be in jail for long periods of time," Edwards said, "is very, very small in my judgement." He discounted the idea that prison is a deterrent to crime on the grounds that conscious, accurate calculation is not usually involved in the acts for which people are sent to prison.

> A lot of offences are carried out under the influence of drugs or alcohol or something of this kind. A lot of it's impulsive-type activity . . . If they feel that they have very little hope in life, if they are poorly educated, unable to get employment, they've got a drug habit or what have you, they may feel a compulsion that far overpowers any deterrence that might be at the back of their minds.[19]

Edwards also depreciated the role of imprisonment in the correction of offenders. Rehabilitation, he said, "is easier to achieve in the community than in prison." It's hard to inculcate prosocial behaviour in an essentially antisocial environment; hard to teach self-control to people subject to rigid external control; and hard to help captives learn how to live in freedom. Among the commonly expressed rationales for imprisonment this leaves only retribution. Edwards acknowledged an instinctive desire for vengeance but said that, even so, it is remarkable how little imprisonment really satisfies this appetite.

> If you take someone who's done something terrible and throw them into jail, even if it's fifteen years later, if the word gets out that they're

going to be released on parole, the same people who were damaged by the original offences are immediately up in arms, saying, "This is terrible. We can't have this person coming out." The truth is, in many of these cases, I believe, the jailing of someone has not resolved or even come close to resolving the fundamental problem, and that is the need to heal the community for the damage that was done. Putting someone in jail doesn't seem to heal. All it does is delay or put in cold storage the problem until the individual is coming out again.[20]

Based on his view that incapacitation is the only indisputable foundation for imprisonment, and that only a small minority of current prisoners justify this treatment, Edwards suggested that Canada has considerable scope to reduce imprisonment. Approximately two-thirds of Canadian prisoners — 80 percent of provincial inmates and 20 to 30 percent of the federal total — are currently being held for nonviolent offences.[21] There is no reason in principle, he said, "why [Canada] should have higher rates of imprisonment than the Netherlands or Finland," countries with less than half our current levels. The crucial first step in building down the prison system, Edwards argued, will be to refuse to build it up. "Build it and they will come" seems to be the rule in prison construction, as judges sentence up to the capacity of the system.

There's no necessary connection between building more and reducing overcrowding. You may in fact just get more people coming into the prisons. We're even worried now about the small women's prisons that we're building across the country. Some judges are saying that, if they don't have to send an offender away thousands of miles to the Prison for Women in Kingston, they may be more inclined to give prison terms in their province.[22]

John Edwards resigned in April of 1996 in response to criticisms of the csc by an official inquiry into an incident at the

Prison for Women in Kingston. Prisoners were strip-searched by members of a male riot squad from the nearby Kingston Penitentiary and left in bare cells for twelve hours covered only by paper smocks. Justice Arbour of the Ontario Court of Appeal found that the treatment of several of the prisoners involved "extreme force and terror" and was "cruel, inhumane, and degrading."[23] In the days leading up to this incident, the prisoners had attempted escape, threatened the lives of guards, and thrown urine at them. Edwards had no direct involvement in the incident — the decisions were made locally — but he resigned as a matter of honour and was succeeded by Ole Ingstrup. Ingstrup had also been Edward's predecessor and mentor, and his views are broadly similar to those I have quoted here. For example, he told an international symposium held in Kingston in March of 1998 that "those working within the prison system are obliged to step forward and tell the world that prison is a costly and often destructive response to social ills."[24]

I have dwelt on my interview with John Edwards at some length both because I find it striking that the head of Canada's prison system would admit to such misgivings about the efficacy of imprisonment, and because I believe he speaks for a substantial body of thoughtful opinion in Ottawa. A reduction in the prison population continues to be the policy of the federal government. Speaking in Edmonton in January of 1998, Solicitor General Andy Scott committed himself to a continuation of his predecessor's policy of working with the provinces to reduce prison numbers and promised revisions to the Corrections and Conditional Release Act that would help bring about this reduction.[25] However, it remains to be seen whether this policy is the beginning of a new way of doing things, or just a marginal reform intended to prevent the system from growing out of hand. As I have said, imprisonment is a well-conditioned reflex, which gives the institution a decided political advantage whenever the climate of public opinion heats up on the subject of crime. Imprisonment, as the habitual, expected response to crime, is self-justifying; alternatives require explicit justification, often on the basis of unfamiliar first principles. Consequently, any sustained revolution in criminal justice will demand considerable intellectual courage, social imagination, and political leadership.

Governments in Canada are currently sending out contradictory messages on this topic, with some provincial governments promising to get tougher, some to adopt alternatives, and others talking out of both sides of their mouths at once. Finding ourselves at a crossroads, we appear to be emulating Stephen Leacock's famous horseman and riding off in all directions. I don't want to try to guess at the future; but I think it's clear that certain conditions will have to be met if the elements of a new vision as described in Part III of this book are to cohere into a workable, publicly acceptable, system of crime control. So I will conclude by setting out those conditions, as I see them.

It needs to be said, first of all, that many of the causes of rising imprisonment, and, therefore, its solutions, lie outside the ambit of the criminal justice system. Crime is certainly magnified and manipulated by criminal justice systems, but it usually begins in circumstances of poverty, joblessness, family breakdown, sexual violence, drug addiction, and neighbourhood abandonment. The situations that reach the criminal courts may already have been botched beyond remedy. All that a more wholesome and peace-oriented mode of justice can do in such cases is reduce collateral damage and remove unnecessary barriers to regeneration.

It is also important to recognize that many of the problems currently addressed within the institutions of criminal justice could be handled better outside these institutions. As Louk Hulsman has said, it is often better to seek alternative forms of social control than alternative ways of administering criminal justice. For example, if drugs were decriminalized, and the damage they do contained by other means, a quarter to a half of all new recruits to the prison system would be eliminated at a stroke. Communities would have to find ways of dealing with unwanted drug consumption, but they would be free of the far worse fallout of the war on drugs. The black market would collapse and, with it, the reign of terror resulting from the battle for control of this market. Entrepreneurial energies now misdirected by the perverse incentives of this market could be applied to the economic regeneration of deteriorated urban districts. The racism that has flourished under the cover of the drug war would be undercut, and so would the romantic counterculture of crime that has grown up in response to this racism. According to black American scholar Gerald Early, the commercial expression of this counterculture through rap music and its associated styles of dress and personal bearing now distorts the aspirations of black people by "exploit[ing] the image of the black male as outlaw and deviant, to titillate the white suburban mind and to give black culture, for the black consumers of the product, some supposedly subversive, radical edge."[26]

A second of many possible examples of how crime could be combatted outside the parameters of the criminal justice system is through a socially based movement for disarmament. Weapons don't commit crimes, but their availability at crucial moments can make existing violence much more lethal. The Board of Education in the Toronto district of Scarborough has recently demonstrated the possibilities of this approach. A two-year campaign to disarm students, backed by the threat of immediate expulsion, resulted in a drop of more than half in weapons-related offences, and a reduction in serious incidents involving threats or assault with a weapon from thirteen a month in 1993 to just over one a month in 1997. Of 193 students suspended after being caught with a weapon, only two re-offended; and of the 42 finally expelled, more than half finally earned re-admission.[27]

When it comes to alternatives within the criminal justice system, I think a critical starting point has been established by Herman Bianchi. His dual, or dialectical, system outlined in Chapter 17, would put a form of justice based on restoration, restitution, and settlement alongside the existing prosecute-and-punish mode. Crimes could be followed up using either track, depending on the disposition of victims, offenders, and public authorities. A renewed right of sanctuary would allow an offender to initiate action on his own behalf rather than leaving him entirely at the mercy of the court.

This proposal has three great strengths. First, it would give alternatives independent standing and thus help to shield them from co-optation and degradation by a system with which they are incompatible. Second, it would prevent alternatives from becoming mere supplements, used only to clean up the easy cases at the margins of the system and having little effect on the treatment of the main body of cases. (A good example of this phenomenon is the way authorities have limited victim-offender mediation to relatively minor matters in many jurisdictions.) And, finally, a dual system would limit criminal trials to cases in which they are actually necessary. At the moment we have no clear idea how much of what is now adjudicated on hostile, adversarial principles could actually be dealt with within the horizons of Bianchi's definition of justice as *tsedeka*: "incessant diligence to make people experience the genuine substantiation of confirmed truth, rights, and duties, and the eventual release from guilt." A dual system, as I said earlier, would allow us to find out.

I have tried to suggest at various points in this book that present-day criminal justice practices have deep roots in Western culture. It may be, as Harold Berman suggests, that in a civilization "whose images of community have been above all religious and legal . . . the connection between the religious metaphor and the legal metaphor has [now] been broken."[28] But even so, our practices retain the imprint of their origins. We may now live without faith, but we still live in the husks of what faith has made. Developing new institutions in these circumstances will require patience, tact, and a sensitive registration of our civilization's ambivalent legacy. Easy, one-sided criticism of modern liberal societies will not necessarily improve their prospects. It is entirely possible, as George Grant points out, that if modern technological societies abandoned their liberalism "they might fall to something lower" rather than rising to new heights.[29]

This danger persuades me that alternative ways of doing justice ought to follow, rather than precede, a careful and balanced critique of existing ideas. It is true, of course, that the commerce between ideas and practices runs both ways, and that experiment can help to produce a new way of thinking. But even so, I fear the adoption of alternatives as technical improvements rather than as elements of a more encompassing vision. Mark Umbreit and Howard Zehr, the American pioneers of victim-offender mediation whose work is discussed in Chapters 10 and 12, have recently expressed their worries along these lines. They argue that the current vogue for alternatives, if rushed and oversold, could easily end up producing assembly-line restorative justice. They point, for example, to the training manual used by Real Justice, the organization in Bethlehem, Pennsylvania, that is introducing Wagga Wagga–style family group conferences to North America. It inculcates a principle it calls KTSS: "keep to the script, stupid." This principle suggests that the technique itself, and not the participants, are what do justice. It raises the spectre of a mechanical and ultimately authoritarian process in which both victim and offender enact scripted roles. Umbreit and Zehr also ask whether, "because the FGC model is so closely linked to early intervention by police or school officials (partic- ularly the Australian model developed in Wagga Wagga), it could easily fall prey to the frequent and well-documented American pattern of new and alternative juvenile justice programs taking the easy cases, many of which would have dropped out of the system in the first place." Altogether these criticisms reflect a well-founded fear of what will happen if family group conferenc- ing is taken as a cheap, easily replicated panacea, rather than as a confirmation of the principle that lasting justice must fully engage the energies and resources of those who are directly involved.[30]

The justice initiatives I have described in this book represent a way of approaching conflict rather than a set of techniques that can be applied willy-nilly. They cannot simply be taken over by overtaxed justice systems as a ready-made answer to crowded courts and overcrowded prisons. "If the wrong man uses the right means," runs an ancient Chinese saying, "the right means work in the wrong way."[31] Technique matters, but only in the context of a guiding orientation. Restorative justice, Howard Zehr recently wrote, is still "a seedling" that is "young and insecurely rooted." Adopting its methods prematurely without adequate preparation can lead to both co-optation and disillusionment. How many reforms are adopted in half-baked form, and then denied more serious consideration because they have already "failed"? "The dangers should not obscure the promise," Zehr continued, but it is should be recognized that "innovations in entrenched systems such as criminal justice are often . . . diverted from their original visions. Terms are watered down: old approaches are justified with new concepts; programmes are instituted without the necessary value base, with the result that they do not work, or have unintended negative consequences."[32]

Dave Worth (whose work in victim-offender mediation is discussed in Chapter 12) has also reflected on the dangers of a facile faith in alternatives. Our practices follow our beliefs, he says, and we cannot expect fundamental change until many more come to see justice not as the mechanical application of laws but as the personally suffered experience of a dynamic, never-ending quest for the substance of peace and right relationship.

> When you talk to the people in the system, they say, "If you give us a few more policemen or a few more judges or a few more lawyers or a few more jails . . ." or you talk to the people in the alternative system, and they say, "Oh man, a few more halfway houses. Give us a few more victim-offender reconciliation programmes. Give us a few more of this or that . . ." I'm convinced that's not it at all. Those are important because they're symbols and they're experiments.

They're pushing the boundaries of what is actually possible. But what really has to happen is we have to change our belief system. We've got to go down to the root of the thing, and we have to decide some day what really is the appropriate response to a violation. What is it that we want?

And basically we still believe in the old vengeance model. We still believe in retribution. You mess with me, I'm going to mess with you. And I'm probably going to hit you harder than you hit me, because then I think somehow that's making justice, or at least, if not justice, I'm getting it back. And ultimately that's death. We've seen it in the big picture. And this is the link, for us as Mennonites with the question of war. It's the same response. If somebody hurts me in the international scene, then what we do is we get a bigger army, and we go beat them back. If somebody creates a small atomic bomb, we make a bigger one. You mess with us, you blow one city up, we'll blow your whole country off the face of the Earth. And we are applying the same war mentality against the problem of crime. You hear it: it's a war against crime.

Well, war doesn't work. It doesn't bring peace and harmony to anybody. It brings more pain and suffering. Take a look around the world today. Is the war machine working? I don't think it is. Take a look around the world today and the problem of crime. Is the war mentality working? It's not working. And so, we've got to go back to the roots of our understandings of what is wrong with crime and what is our response.[33]

A spirit of expediency and haste poses a related threat to the growth of a new practice of justice. In Ontario in 1990, 50,000 criminal charges were withdrawn by prosecutors or thrown out of court after the Supreme Court of Canada ruled there had been undue delays in hearing the cases. In its ruling, the Supreme Court established a cutoff period of eight months. According to the most recent report of the provincial auditor, Ontario currently has 224,000 Criminal Code cases pending in its courts, of which 70,000 are more than eight months old.[34] British

Columbia is also facing a big backlog. These circumstances may create tremendous pressure to find alternative ways of dealing with court cases, and this temptation to do the right thing for the wrong reasons poses a threat to the integrity of "seedling" practices. Each of the alternatives described in Part III matured at its own speed in its own proper place. Each expresses some particular local or personal genius. Such examples have the capacity to inspire and even to suggest valid general principles, but none are blueprints or techniques that will survive transplanting to a place where the ground has not been prepared. There is a world of difference between adopting new practices on their demonstrated merits and mechanically implementing "alternatives" for some expedient end, unconnected to justice, like economizing on expensive court proceedings or reducing overcrowding in prison.

Another challenge that alternatives to imprisonment will have to overcome if they are to move from the margins to the mainstream is the charge that they do not constitute serious sanctions, but are just a form of what Dietrich Bonhoeffer calls "cheap grace." If they are perceived by a substantial section of the public as a failure of nerve within the justice system, they are likely to produce a political backlash that will further polarize an already polarized society. Whether or not this happens depends partly on belief, as Dave Worth points out; but it depends also on enforcement. To win public respect, conditional sentences will have to be executed with the same stringency as prison sentences. I know of no studies yet on the supervision of conditional sentences. But I am aware of certain problems in the supervision of community service assigned to young offenders. In Toronto, for example, some agencies deputed by the courts to oversee community service recognize what they call "socialization" as a way of discharging community service hours: I have even heard of volleyball qualifying. If such practices were to accompany a wide-scale application of conditional sentencing, they would soon bring this new measure into public contempt. The example of Genesee County, on the other hand, proves that community service can be made a credible and demanding alternative to incarceration. The key is cooperation between the justice system and the community agencies supervising community service, and the threat of incarceration in cases where the privilege of community service is abused.

Finally, I want to point to the danger of jumping, in Herman Bianchi's words, "from the frying pan of repressive justice into the fire of professional and bureaucratized dispute settlement." Many of the alternatives I outline in Part III require the mobilization of a community. Family group conferences, sentencing circles, victim-offender mediation, noncustodial court sentences, reintegrative shaming — all depend, in one way or another, on using social ties and civil habits to control crime. Only effective expressions of community can bring the formal justice system back within its proper limits and end the imprisonment explosion. For this to happen, there must continue to be a community — a distinct social sphere in which relationships of a noneconomic and nonprofessional kind predominate — and it must enjoy a certain sovereignty vis-à-vis formal institutions of justice. If the professional agents of the formal system become the organizers and shapers of the community response to crime, the notion of community will lose its meaning and whatever vitality remains to it. For there to be what Braithwaite and Petit call a "republican practice of crime control," there must first be a *res publica* — a public thing. Community-based criminal justice alternatives are some of the most impressive new shoots of civic life, but they will continue to flourish only so long as they remain expressions of citizenship, rather than paid professional service.[35]

We live today under conditions of rapid verbal inflation. New words and concepts quickly puff up as they gain currency in the mediasphere and, as they enlarge, their use as prestigious fetishes tends to eclipse the fact that they lack any precise reference. Professor Uwe Poerkson of the University of Freiburg calls these verbal amoebas or shapeshifters "plastic words."[36] Such words have been so thoroughly cleansed of all real meaning that they denote nothing — only a mist of positive connotations remains. These terms are thus ideal professional resources: they say "experts at work" without conveying anything precise. The word "community" has, to some extent, already suffered this fate. Terms like "restorative" or "healing justice" are not yet well known enough to have had this happen, but it is quite possible that they too will eventually become the disguises of new professional interests.

I have no wish to end on a sour note. But I am mindful of a warning George Grant issued to a teach-in on revolution at the University of Toronto in 1965. Beware "easy hopes" and "dangerous dreams," he told his audience, for "if people have vast expectations about a society such as ours, they are going to be disappointed." Moral commitment is too precious not "to be put into the service of reality."[37] I believe the new directions I have traced in this book are both real and promising; but for their promise to be fulfilled, each will have to remain faithful to its particular genius, and not be drawn into false hopes and rhetorical distortions. The threat of gulags Western-style and the promise of alternatives both have grounds within the emerging order. I am too old to be optimistic, but still young enough to be hopeful.

NOTES

Introduction

1. Cited in John Braithwaite, *Crime, Shame and Reintegration* (Cambridge, UK: Cambridge UP, 1989) 179.

2. Cited in Andrew Rutherford, *Prisons and the Process of Justice: The Reductionist Challenge* (London: William Heinemann, 1984) 8.

3. Osborne (1859–1926) chaired the New York State Commission on Prison Reform. He began his tenure by living for a week under an assumed name at Auburn Prison. He later became warden of Sing Sing and created a Mutual Welfare League to foster self-government among prisoners.

4. Eric Schlosser, "More Reefer Madness," *Atlantic Monthly* Apr. 1997: 90–102.

5. Kirk Makin, "Early Release Law a Failure, Study Says," *Globe and Mail* 14 Oct. 1997.

6. Norval Morris and David J. Rothman, introduction, *The Oxford History of the Prison* (New York: Oxford UP, 1995) xii. Cited in Marc Mauer, *Americans Behind Bars: U.S. and International Use of Incarceration, 1995* (Washington, DC: The Sentencing Project, June 1997) 11. This and other Sentencing Project publications are available from The Sentencing Project, 918 F St. NW, Suite 501, Washington, DC 20004, USA.

7. Nahlah Ayed, "Penitentiaries Hiring 1,000 Officers," *Globe and Mail* 24 Apr. 1998.

8. David Cayley, "Prison and Its Alternatives" (Toronto: CBC Radio, 1996) 49. Transcript of a series broadcast on *Ideas*. This, and the transcript of the 1993 series "Crime Control as Industry," are available from CBC Transcripts, Box 500, Station A, Toronto, ON M5W 1E6.

9. See *Deschooling Society* (1971), *Tools for Conviviality* (1973), *Energy and Equity* (1974), and *Limits to Medicine* (1976).

10. Cayley, "Prison and Its Alternatives" 2.

11. Kirk Makin, "Inmate Programs Questioned," *Globe and Mail* 20 Nov. 1997.

12. *Globe and Mail* 31 Mar. 1995; Rob Tripp, "What's the Real Cost of Punishment?" *Toronto Star* 13 Jan. 1997: A11.

13. Fox Butterfield, "Crime Keeps on Falling, but Prisons Keep on Filling," *New York Times* 28 Sept. 1997: Section 4.

14. Louk Hulsman, unpublished interview, Oslo, 30 Apr. 1995.

15. Marc Mauer, *Intended and Unintended Consequences: State Racial Disparities in Imprisonment* (Washington, DC: The Sentencing Project, Jan. 1997) 5–6.

16. Nils Christie, *Crime Control as Industry: Towards Gulags Western-Style*, 2nd ed. (New York: Routledge, 1994) 13.

17. *Ruffin v. The Commonwealth of Virginia* (U.S. Supr. Ct., 1871). Quoted in Austin McHugh, *Christian Faith and Criminal Justice* (New York: Paulist Press, 1978) 47.

18. Jeremy Bentham, "Utility and Punishment," *Philosophical Perspectives on Punishment*, ed. Gertrude Ezorsky (Albany: State University of New York Press, 1972) 56.

19. Christie, *Crime Control* 117 and 88.

20. Nils Christie's paraphrase of Foucault in *Crime Control* 82. See also Michel Foucault, *Madness and Civilization* (New York: Pantheon, 1965).

21. Braithwaite, *Crime, Shame* 116.

22. Cesare Beccaria, "On Crimes and Punishments," *Theories of Punishment*, ed. Stanley Grupp (Bloomington: Indiana UP, 1971) 126.

23. Herman Bianchi, *Justice as Sanctuary* (Bloomington: Indiana UP, 1994) 17.

24. Kirk Makin, "Courts in Tatters, Judges Say," *Globe and Mail* 17 Nov. 1997: A1.

25. Barry D. Stuart, "Building Community Justice Partnerships: Community Peacemaking Circles, A Description of Yukon Experiences," unpublished draft paper, Whitehorse, Aug. 1996.

26. Rosemary Couch and Barry Stuart, "Recidivism and Community Justice in Kwanlin Dun," unpublished paper. Cited in Stuart, "Building Community Justice" 27.

Chapter 1: The Expanding Prison

1. David Cayley, "Crime Control as Industry" (Toronto: CBC Radio, 1993) 2. Transcript of a series broadcast on *Ideas* in March 1993. This, and the transcript of the 1996 series "Prison and Its Alternatives," are available from CBC Transcripts, Box 500, Station A, Toronto, ON M5W 1E6.

2. Cited in Cayley, "Crime Control as Industry" 2.

3. Cited in Cayley 2.

4. Quoted in Jerome G. Miller, *Search and Destroy: African-American Males in the Criminal Justice System* (New York: Cambridge UP, 1996) 137.

5. Louk Hulsman, unpublished interview recorded at the International Conference on Prison Growth, Oslo, 30 April 1995.

6. Louk Hulsman, "Criminal Justice in the Netherlands," *Delta: A Review of Arts, Life and Thought in the Netherlands* 1974. Cited in Christie, *Crime Control* 43.

7. Cayley, "Prison and Its Alternatives" 12.

8. John Edwards (former CSC commissioner), unpublished interview for "Prison and Its Alternatives."

9. Cayley, "Prison and Its Alternatives" 22. See also Maeve McMahon,

The Persistent Prison? Rethinking Decarceration and Penal Reform (Toronto: U of Toronto P, 1992).

10. Report of the Presidential Commission on Law Enforcement and the Administration of Justice (1967). Quoted in Andrew Rutherford, *Transforming Criminal Justice* (Winchester, UK: Waterside Press, 1996) 19. I draw extensively on Rutherford's analysis in the following pages.

11. Rutherford 22.

12. Rutherford 25.

13. Rutherford 29.

14. Rutherford 65.

15. Rutherford 62.

16. Rutherford 70.

17. Rutherford 71.

18. Rutherford 82 (note).

19. Robert Martinson summarized a lot of this research in a 1975 survey article in *The Public Interest* (35: 22–54) called "What Works: Questions and Answers About Prison Reform."

20. A recent article in *The New York Review of Books* suggests that the big increase in crime that was registered in the United States in the late 1960s and early 1970s had a lot to with the introduction of the 911 emergency call system. Up to this point, says James Lardner, major American cities had tended "to grossly underreport their crime statistics." With the 911 system, "the act of reporting became easier for the public and the act of suppressing statistics became harder for the police."

21. M. J. Crozier, S. P. Huntington, and Joji Watanuki, *The Crisis of Democracy: Report on the Governability of Democracies to the Trilateral Commission* (New York: NYU Press, 1975).

22. Cayley, "Prison and Its Alternatives" 13.

23. Cayley, "Crime Control as Industry" 15.

24. Cayley, "Prison and Its Alternatives" 13–14.

25. Unpublished interview with Johannes Feest.

26. These figures, and those that I subsequently cite regarding the disproportionate impact of the criminal justice system on black Americans, come from Tracy Huling and Marc Mauer, "Young Black Americans and the Criminal Justice System: Five Years Later," published by The Sentencing Project, 918 F St. NW, Suite 501, Washington, DC 20004 USA.

27. Kirk Makin, "Black Imprisonment Trends 'Shocking,' Says Racism Report," *Globe and Mail* 16 Jan. 1996: A1.

28. Huling and Mauer 11.

29. Miller 82.

30. Huling and Mauer 10.

31. Huling and Mauer 10.

32. Timothy Appleby, "Top Court in U.S Links Race to Crime," *Globe and Mail* 16 May 1996.

33. *Bureau of Justice Statistics Bulletin*, August 1995.

34. Huling and Mauer 1.

35. Miller, *Search and Destroy* 7–8.

36. "As It Happens," CBC Radio, 23 Jan. 1996; *National Review*, Jan. 1996.

37. Cayley, "Prison and Its Alternatives" 12–13.

38. Christie 41–42.

39. Unpublished paper for the International Conference on Prison Growth, Olso, 28 Apr. 1995.

40. George Gerbner and Larry Gross, "Living with Television: The Violence Profile," *Journal of Communication* 1976. Cited in Mathiesen 7.

41. James Curran, "Communications, Power and Social Order," in Michael Gurevitsch *et al.*, eds., *Culture, Society and Media* (London: Methuen, 1982). Cited in Mathiesen 7–8.

42. Rutherford is a former official of the British prison service who now writes on British penal policy. In what follows, I have drawn extensively on his account of this period in his new book, *Transforming Criminal Justice*.

43. Cayley, "Prison and Its Alternatives" 12.

44. John Braithwaite, *Crime, Shame* 116.

45. Rutherford, *Transforming Criminal Justice* 101.

46. Figures cited by Andrew Rutherford in a presentation on "The Problematic Relationship Between Crime and Imprisonment" to the International Conference on Prison Growth in Oslo, Apr. 1995.

47. Rutherford, *Transforming Criminal Justice* 128.

48. Cited in Cayley, "Prison and Its Alternatives" 16.

49. Rob Tripp, "High Cost, Little Protection," *Toronto Star* 12 Jan. 1997: F7.

50. Tripp F7.

51. Jim Bronskill, "Crisis Feared as Prisoner Levels Grow," *London Free Press* 4 Dec. 1995: A1.

52. Hamilton journalist Kevin Marron has told the story in a book called *Fatal Mistakes: How a Senseless Murder Led to the Creation of* CAVEAT (Toronto: Doubleday, 1993).

53. Neil Boyd, "First Degree Murderers and the 15-year Window," *Globe and Mail* 30 Mar. 30 1996.

54. Kevin Marron, *The Slammer: The Crisis in Canada's Prison System* (Toronto: Doubleday, 1996).

55. Alana Mitchell, "Mother's Protest Swells to Gain Rock's Attention," *Globe and Mail* 19 Feb. 1996: A5.

56. Ross Howard, "Olson Causes Families More Anguish," *Globe and Mail* 11 Mar. 1997: A8.

57. "CBC Radio News," 8 p.m., 4 May 1997.

58. Kirk Makin, "Olson Scenario Puts Rock in a Hard Spot," *Globe and Mail* 12 Mar. 1996: A5.

59. Celeste McGovern, "Crime and No Punishment," *Western Report* 8 Jan. 1996: 18–22.

60. Cited in Andrew Coyle, *The Prisons We Deserve* (London: Harper-Collins, 1994).

61. *Simone Weil: An Anthology*, ed. Sian Miles (London: Virago, 1986) 123.

62. Alexander Solzhenitsyn, *The Gulag Archipelago* (London: Fontana, 1974) 168.

Chapter 2: Crime Control in the United States

1. Donatella Lorch, "Incarceration-Minded Meet to Buy Cells, Razor Wire and More," *New York Times* 23 Aug. 1996.

2. Edward Walsh, "Strapped Small Towns Try to Lock Up Prisons," *Washington Post* 24 Dec. 1994: A3. Quoted in Jan Elvin, "'Corrections-Industrial Complex' Expands in U.S.," *National Prison Project Journal* 10.1 (Winter 1994–95): 1–4.

3. "Prison Population Boom," *Globe and Mail* 8 Aug. 1997: A8.

4. See especially Andrew von Hirsch, *Doing Justice: Report of the Committee for the Study of Incarceration* (New York: the Committee, 1976).

5. Beccaria, "On Crimes and Punishments" 135.

6. Cited in Cayley, "Prison and Its Alternatives" 9.

7. H.B. no. 106, Mississippi Legislature; S.B. no. 2005, section 28, (1), Mississippi.

8. Al Bronstein, from an unpublished talk at International Conference on Prison Growth, Oslo, 28–30 April 1995, and "Crime and Punishment in America," PBS, 13 Jan. 1997.

9. James S. Kunen, "Teaching Prisoners a Lesson," *New Yorker* 10 July 1995.

10. "States Seek to Recover Prison Costs by Making Inmates Pay," *Globe and Mail* 8 July 1996.

11. "Virginia OKs Tougher Sentences, Ends Parole in Landmark Bill," *Criminal Justice Newsletter* 3 Oct. 1994: 5.

12. Miller, *Search and Destroy* 128–31.

13. Cited in Cayley, "Prison and Its Alternatives" 8.

14. "Status Report: State Prisons and the Courts, January 1, 1995," *National Prison Project Journal* 10.1 (Winter 1994–95): 5.

15. *Austin v. Pennsylvania Department of Corrections*, 90–7497 (U.S. Distr. Ct. of Eastern Pennsylvania).

16. News release, U.S. Senate Judiciary Committee, 27 Sept. 1995.

17. Bronstein, unpublished talk recorded at the International Conference on Prison Growth, Oslo, 29 April 1995.

18. Cited in Christie, *Crime Control* 88–89.

19. *Madrid v. Gomez*, C90-3094-TEH (U.S. Distr. Ct. for Northern California). See also Jenni Gainsborough, "Court Decides Landmark Class Action

Case in Favor of Pelican Bay Prisoners," *National Prison Project Journal* 10.1 (Winter 1994–95): 13–14.

20. "Alcatraz of the Rockies Quietly Opens for Business," USA *Today* 13 Dec. 1994.

21. "Violent and Irrational — And That's Just the Policy," *The Economist* 8 June 1996: 25.

22. Nils Christie, cited in Cayley, "Prison and Its Alternatives" 4.

23. Cited in Cayley, "Prison and Its Alternatives" 2.

24. Miller, *Search and Destroy* 2.

25. Campaign for an Effective Crime Policy [CECP], "The Impact of 'Three Strikes and You're Out' Laws: What Have We Learned?" Sept. 1996. Available from CECP, 918 F St. NW, Suite 505, Washington, DC 20004, USA Tel: (202) 628-1903, Fax: (202) 628-1091.

26. Richard C. Reuben, "Get-Tough Stance Draws Fiscal Criticism," ABA *Journal* Jan. 1995: 17.

27. Fox Butterfield, "Tough Law on Sentences Is Criticized," *New York Times* 18 Mar. 1996.

28. CECP, report.

29. "Crime and Punishment in America," PBS documentary, 13 January 1997.

30. Peter Moon, "Jail-for-Life Policy Negates Value of Prison Reforms," *Globe and Mail* 26 June 1995: A8.

31. See Jerome G. Miller, *Last One Over the Wall: The Massachusetts Experiment in Closing Reform Schools* (Akron: Ohio State UP, 1991).

32. Cited in David Cayley, "Beyond Institutions" (Toronto: CBC Radio, 1994) 16–17. Transcript of a series broadcast on *Ideas*, 16–17 March and 23–25 March 1994.

33. Cited in Cayley, "Prison and Its Alternatives" 6–7.

34. Cited in Cayley 7.

35. See James Traub's profile of DiIulio, "The Criminals of Tomorrow," *New Yorker* 4 Nov. 1996 50–65; and John DiIulio, "Prisons Are a Bargain by Any Measure," *New York Times* 17 Jan. 1996.

36. There has been a continuing debate in the United States about the costs averted by imprisonment. The hypothetical statistics that are employed are based on disputed estimates of what offenders would have done, had they been at large. Criminality is a taken-for-granted quantum in the discussion. What this overlooks, as Robert Martinson has pointed out, is that imprisonment doesn't just avert crime, it also fosters it. "A particular pox should be visited upon those who support mandatory incarceration on the basis of questionable assumptions about how many crimes are 'saved' by incarceration," Martinson writes, "when they do not make similar estimates of the numbers of crimes contributed as a result of damage done to the offender by imprisonment." "Is the Treatment of Criminal Offenders Really Necessary?" *Federal*

Probation 40 (Mar. 1976): 4, cited in Miller, *Last One* 139.

37. Cited in James Traub, "The Criminals" 51.

Chapter 3: Perception and Reality in Crime Policy

1. "Preventing Youth Crime," *Globe and Mail* 17 Dec. 1996.

2. Henry Hess, "Juveniles Climbing Robbery Charts," *Globe and Mail* 16 May 1996.

3. Elaine Carey, "The Truth About Our 'Rising' Youth Crime Rate," *Toronto Star* 18 May 1996: A1.

4. Kirk Makin, "MPs Question Ontario's Hard Line on Youth Crime," *Globe and Mail* 4 June 1996: A5.

5. Julian Roberts, *Public Knowledge of Crime and Justice: An Inventory of Canadian Findings* (Ottawa: Canada, Justice Department, 1994).

6. Alana Mitchell, "Views on Crime Distorted, Study Says," *Globe and Mail* 31 Dec. 1994: A1.

7. For an example of public opinion on this issue, see Lee Lamothe, "Getting Away With Murder," *The Next City* (Fall 1996): 57–63.

8. "Young Offenders Need Programs, Not Just Prison Sentences," *Vancouver Sun* 2 Aug. 1995.

9. Heino Lilles, cited in Cayley, "Prison and Its Alternatives" 36.

10. Heino Lilles, "Canada's Young Offenders Act: Some International Perspectives for Reform," submitted to the House of Commons Standing Committee on Justice and Legal Affairs, Feb. 1995: 10–11.

11. Cited in Cayley, "Prison and Its Alternatives" 37.

12. Max Gluckman, *Essays on the Ritual of Social Relations* (Manchester, UK: Manchester UP, 1962).

13. Cited in Cayley, "Prison and Its Alternatives" 36–37.

14. Cited in Cayley 39.

15. Cited in Murray Campbell, "Electronic Anklets to Replace Province's Halfway Houses," *Globe and Mail* 4 Oct. 1995.

16. Graham Stewart, Ontario Director of the John Howard Society, cited in Rob Tripp, "What's the Real Cost of Punishment?" *Toronto Star* 13 Jan. 1997: A11.

17. See also Thomas Claridge, "Bail Funds for Needy Won't Be Renewed," *Globe and Mail* 17 Jan. 1997.

18. Kirk Makin, "Ontario Cancels Cost-Effective Bail Plan," *Globe and Mail* 18 Jan. 1997.

19. Martin Mittelstaedt, "Ontario to Build Super Prisons," *Globe and Mail* 13 Sept. 1996: A1.

20. Richard Mackie, "Youth Detention Centres to Go Private," *Globe and Mail* 6 Feb. 1998: A6.

21. Ingrid Peters Derry, "Boot Camps," *Accord* 13.3 (Feb. 1995): 4.

22. Patricia Meade, cited in Brian Laghi, "Young Offenders Learn Basics at Camp" *Globe and Mail* 12 Feb. 1996.

23. Martin Mittelstaedt, "Violent Young Offenders Will Be Sentenced to Boot Camp," *Globe and Mail* 30 Aug. 1996: A3; Ijeoma Ross, "Ontario Gives Company Contract to Run Young Offenders Boot Camp," *Globe and Mail* 30 May 1997.

24. Ross Howard, "Youth Rehabilitation Loses Priority," *Globe and Mail* 3 June 1994: A1.

25. See Hugh Winsor, "Dangerous Offenders Face More Jail Time," *Globe and Mail* 10 May 1995; and "Tracking Bracelets Too Costly," *Globe and Mail* 6 Mar. 1997.

26. Tim Harpur, "Jailing Youth a Waste, Justice Minister Says," *Toronto Star* 21 Nov. 1995: A13.

Chapter 4: Rituals of Repression

1. The Sentencing Project, information flyer.

2. Zygmunt Bauman, "From Welfare State into Prison," unpublished paper for the International Conference on Prison Growth, Oslo, Apr. 1995.

3. Zygmunt Bauman, *Intimations of Post-Modernity* (London: Routledge, 1992) xi.

4. Cited in Cayley, "Prison and Its Alternatives" 17.

5. Bauman, "From Welfare State into Prison."

6. Pierre S. Pettigrew, notes from speech to a conference on "Accelerating Rural Development in Africa," Airlie, Virginia, 23 Sept. 1996: 2.

7. Bauman, "From Welfare State into Prison" 7.

8. Bauman, *Intimations* 220.

9. John Kenneth Galbraith, *The Culture of Contentment* (New York: Houghton Mifflin, 1992).

10. Bauman, cited in Cayley, "Prison and Its Alternatives" 18.

11. Zygmunt Bauman, *Modernity and the Holocaust* (Ithaca, NY: Cornell UP, 1989) 86.

12. Zygmunt Bauman, *Life in Fragments: Essays in Post-Modern Morality* (Oxford: Blackwell, 1995).

13. In what follows, I am following either an unpublished text of Illich's remarks to the International Conference on Prison Growth, Oslo, Apr. 1995, or Cayley, "Prison and Its Alternatives" 45–48.

14. Jean Pierre Vernant, *Myth and Thought Among the Greeks* (1965; New York: Routledge and Kegan Paul, 1983) 309.

15. Cited in Vernant 315.

16. Cited in Cayley, "Prison and Its Alternatives" 47.

17. Cited in Cayley 47–48.

18. Fyodor Dostoevsky, *Crime and Punishment*, trans. Michael Scammell

(New York: Washington Square Press, 1966) 435–36.

19. Cited in Cayley, "Prison and Its Alternatives" 41.

20. Thomas Mathiesen uses the term "Fiasco" in his *Prison on Trial* (London: Sage Publications, 1990).

Chapter 5: Something Must Be Done

1. Mathiesen, *Prison on Trial* 54.

2. Schlosser 90–102.

3. Anthony Doob, "Punishment in Late Twentieth Century Canada: An Afterword," *Qualities of Mercy: Justice, Punishment and Discretion*, ed. Carolyn Strange (Vancouver: UBC Press, 1996).

4. Cited in Mathiesen 81.

5. *The Collected Dialogues of Plato*, ed. Edith Hamilton and Huntingdon Cairns (Princeton: Princeton UP, 1961) 263.

6. Cited in *Philosophical Perspectives on Punishment*, ed. Gertrude Ezorsky (Albany: State U of New York P, 1972) 107.

7. *Simone Weil: An Anthology* 122.

8. C. S. Lewis, "The Humanitarian Theory of Punishment," *Theories of Punishment*, ed. Stanley Grupp (Bloomington: Indiana UP, 1971) 301–8.

9. *Simone Weil: An Anthology* 94–95.

10. *Simone Weil: An Anthology* 122–24.

11. Cited in Herman Bianchi, *Justice as Sanctuary* 32.

12. Cited in Cayley, "Prison and Its Alternatives" 29.

13. Lloyd W. McCorkle and Richard R. Korn, "Resocialization Within Walls," *Annals of the American Academy of Political and Social Science* 293: 88. Quoted in Mathiesen, *Prison on Trial*.

Chapter 6: The Real World of Imprisonment

1. All quotations on this and following pages are from Jim Cavanagh's autobiography in "Prison and Its Alternatives" 49–53.

2. All quotations from Monty Lewis are taken from "Prison and Its Alternatives" 53–56.

3. Monty Lewis and Joanne Jacquart, *The Caper: The Monty Lewis Story* (Fredericton: Cons for Christ, [no date]). Available from Cons for Christ Ministry, Inc., P.O. Box 3414, Postal Station B, Fredericton, NB E3A 5H2.

4. Cited in Cayley, "Prison and Its Alternatives" 92.

5. Harry Nigh, unpublished interview, fall 1995.

6. Cited in Cayley, "Prison and Its Alternatives" 92.

7. Cited in Cayley 56–57.

8. Cited in Cayley 57–58.

9. Dennis Cooley, "Prison Violence in the Correctional Service of Canada: An Analysis of Security Incidents and Cross-Jurisdictional Data," Correctional

Service of Canada, Research and Statistics Branch, 1990.

10. Dennis Cooley, "Criminal Victimization in Male Federal Prisons," *Canadian Journal of Criminology* (Oct. 1993): 479–95.

11. G. Sykes and S. Messinger, "The Inmate Social System," R. Cloward *et al.* (eds.), *Theoretical Studies in the Social Organization of the Prison* (New York: Social Science Research Council, 1960) 6–9.

12. Dennis Cooley, "Social Control and Social Order in Male Federal Prisons," a thesis submitted to the Faculty of Graduate Studies in partial fulfillment of the requirements for the degree of Doctor of Philosophy, Department of Sociology, University of Manitoba, Winnipeg, 1 April 1995. 140 & 162.

Chapter 7: God Is Himself Law

1. Bianchi, *Justice as Sanctuary* 9.

2. Bianchi 12–13.

3. Harold J. Berman, *Law and Revolution* (Cambridge, MA: Harvard UP, 1983) 54–55.

4. Berman 77–78.

5. Berman 94.

6. Berman 96.

7. Berman 113.

8. Peter the Lombard, *Sentences* (1150). Cited in Berman 593–94, n. 21.

9. Berman 200.

10. Berman 208.

11. Berman 183, in a paraphrase of Aquinas.

12. Berman 171.

13. Berman 171.

14. Berman 171.

15. Hulsman, cited in Cayley, "Prison and Its Alternatives" 40.

16. Gerald McHugh, *Christian Faith and Criminal Justice* (New York: Paulist Press, 1978) 22–23.

17. Ivan Illich, unpublished talk, International Conference on Prison Growth, Norwegian Academy of Science and Letters, Oslo, 29 Apr. 1996.

18. *Codex Theodosius* XVI. I. 2., cited in McHugh, *Christian Faith* 16–17.

19. Bianchi 16–17.

20. Timothy Gorringe, *God's Just Vengeance* (Cambridge, UK: Cambridge UP, 1996) 27.

21. Berman 177.

22. Cited in Gorringe 94–95.

23. Cited in Gorringe 101.

24. Cited in Gorringe 95.

25. Cited in Gorringe 138–39.

26. Cited in Gorringe 165.

27. Gorringe 197.

28. Gorringe 23–24.

29. Berman 181.

30. Cited in Berman 521.

31. Cited in Berman 536.

32. Berman 558.

33. Berman 562.

34. Berman 198.

Chapter 8: A Perpetual Solitude and Seclusion

1. Cited in Thorsten Sellin, "Dom Jean Mabillon: A Prison Reformer of the Seventeenth Century," *Journal of Criminal Law and Criminology* 17:589–90.

2. Cited in Sellin 584.

3. Cited in Sellin 584.

4. Cited in Sellin 585.

5. Cited in Sellin 586–87.

6. Cited in Sellin 583.

7. Cited in Sellin 587.

8. Pierre Allard, "Statement of the Correctional Service of Canada Values and a Biblical Perspective for the Role of Chaplain," presented to the Northern Baptist Theological Seminary, 1986:47.

9. Michael Ignatieff, *A Just Measure of Pain: The Penitentiary in the Industrial Revolution, 1750–1850* (New York: Columbia UP, 1978) 11.

10. Ignatieff 38.

11. Ignatieff 39.

12. Beccaria, "On Crimes and Punishments" 126.

13. Beccaria 119.

14. Beccaria 126.

15. Beccaria 126.

16. Beccaria 130.

17. Bentham, "Utility and Punishment" 62.

18. Bentham 57.

19. Bentham 58.

20. Bentham 61.

21. Bentham 56.

22. Ignatieff 88.

23. Barnard Turner and Thomas Skinner, *Account of the Alterations and Amendments in the Office of Sherriff* (no pub. 1783) 23. Cited in Ignatieff 88–89.

24. Ignatieff 15.

25. Braithwaite, *Crime, Shame* 116.

26. Raúl Zaffaroni, unpublished interview, Oslo, 30 Apr. 1995. For more on La Paz and Third-World prisons, see Chapter 18.

27. Ignatieff 42.

28. Cited in Ignatieff 124.

29. Cited in Ignatieff 130.

30. Ignatieff 5.

31. Ignatieff 5.

32. Michel Foucault, *Discipline and Punish: The Birth of the Prison* (1975 [French]; New York: Vintage, Vintage Books, 1979) 200.

33. McHugh, *Christian Faith* 37.

34. Pierre Allard 49.

35. Cited in Ignatieff 212.

36. Ignatieff 212.

37. Zygmunt Bauman, *Freedom* (Milton Keynes: Open UP, 1988) 18.

38. *Ruffin v. The Commonwealth of Virginia* (U.S. Supr. Ct., 1871) quoted in McHugh 47.

39. Bianchi 95.

Chapter 9: A Sea Change

1. Quoted in David Cayley, "The Politics of Information," CBC Radio, 22 May 1983. See also Gaye Tuchman, *Making News* (New York: The Free Press, 1978).

2. My narrative here generally follows criminologist Maeve McMahon's presentation in "Prison and Its Alternatives" 20–22.

3. Roger Caron, *Go Boy: Memoirs of a Life Behind Bars* (Toronto: McGraw, 1978) 230–32.

4. Maeve McMahon, *The Persistent Prison?* 15.

5. Cited in Maeve McMahon, "Critical Criminology and the Problem of Power," *Xponica/Chroniques* 9: 1–20. (Komotini, Greece: Thrace University).

6. Foucault, *Discipline and Punish* 227.

7. Foucault 227–28.

8. Foucault 224.

9. Foucault 223.

10. Foucault 222.

11. David Garland, *Punishment and Modern Society* (Chicago: U of Chicago P, 1990) 131.

12. Stanley Cohen, *Visions of Social Control: Crime, Punishment and Classification* (Cambridge, UK: Cambridge UP, 1985) 10.

13. McMahon, "Critical Criminology" 6.

14. James Miller, *The Passion of Michel Foucault* (New York: Anchor, 1996) 228.

15. McMahon, "Critical Criminology" 6.

16. Janet Chan and Richard Ericson, *Decarceration and the Economy of Penal Reform* (Toronto: Centre of Criminology, University of Toronto, 1981).

17. Cited in Cayley, "Prison and Its Alternatives" 22–23.

18. McMahon, "Critical Criminology" 3.

19. Andrew Rutherford, *Prisons and the Process of Justice: The Reductionist Challenge* (London: Heinemann, 1984).

20. McMahon, "Critical Criminology" 13.

21. Cayley, "Prison and Its Alternatives" 33–34.

22. Cayley 34.

23. Pat O'Malley, "Criminology and the New Liberalism," 1996 John L. L. Edwards Memorial Lecture at the U of Toronto Centre of Criminology, 12 January 1997. All subsequent quotations are from the text of this lecture which is available at http://www.library.utoronto.ca/www/libraries_crim/centre/lecture.htm

24. Richard Neely, *Take Back Your Neighborhood: A Case for Modern-Day Vigilantism* (New York: Donald Fine Inc., 1990).

Chapter 10: Crime Control and Community

1. Berman 77–78. The passage is cited in full in Chapter 7.

2. Bianchi, *Justice as Sanctuary* 117.

3. Rudyard Kipling, "Recessional Hymn for Queen Victoria's Diamond Jubilee."

4. Nils Christie, "Conflicts as Property," *The British Journal of Criminology* 1 (Jan. 1977).

5. Christie, "Conflicts as Property" 8.

6. Cayley, "Crime Control" 23.

7. Cayley 23.

8. "Municipal Mediation Boards, An Alterative to Prosecution: An Overview of the Norwegian System" (Oslo: Royal Norwegian Ministry of Justice and Police, 1992).

9. Peter McAloon, "New Zealand Justice and Family Group Conferences," *Accord* 13 (3 Feb. 1995) 6. (*Accord* is a publication of the Mennonite Central Committee Canada, P.O. Box 2038, Clearbrook, BC V2T 3T8.)

10. Marie Sullivan, "New Zealand Adopts Maori-Based Restorative Justice Practice," presentation at a conference held in Saskatoon, March 17–18, 1995, as reported in *Restorative Justice: Four Community Models* (Clearbrook, BC: MCC Canada Victim Offender Ministries, 1995) 9. Available from Mennonite Central Committee Canada; see note 9.

11. Lilles, "Canada's Young Offender's Act" 21.

12. Sullivan 11.

13. Cayley, "Prison and Its Alternatives" 64.

14. Cayley 65.

15. Cayley 65.

16. Lilles 30.

17. Lilles 30.

18. Sullivan 22.

19. Lilles 33.

20. Mark Umbreit and Howard Zehr, "Family Group Conferences: A Challenge to Victim-Offender Mediation?" *Accord* 15 (2 August 1996) 1.

21. Cited in Cayley, "Prison and Its Alternatives" 74.

22. Cited in Cayley 75.

23. Cited in Cayley 67.

24. Cited in Cayley 75–76.

25. "Native Justice an Alternative to Jails, Says Judge," *The Chronicle Journal* [Thunder Bay] 7 Dec. 1997.

26. Barry D. Stuart, "Building Community Justice."

27. *R. v. Moses*, 71 C.C.C. (3d). 247 (Y.T.C.), 199.

28. This and all subsequent quotations from Harold Gatensby can be found in Cayley, "Prison and Its Alternatives" 82–84, or are taken from unpublished sections of the interview with Gatensby recorded for that program.

29. Rosemary Couch and Barry Stuart, "Recidivism and Community Justice in Kwanlin Dun," unpublished paper cited in Stuart, "Building Community Justice" 27.

30. Stuart, "Building Community Justice" 87.

31. Cited in Cayley, "Prison and Its Alternatives" 84.

32. Rupert Ross, *Dancing With a Ghost: Exploring Indian Reality* (Markham, ON: Octopus Publishing Group, 1992) 11ff.

33. Stuart 222.

34. Stuart 126.

35. Stuart 92.

36. Stuart 51.

37. *Satisfying Justice* (Ottawa: The Church Council on Justice and Corrections, 1996) v.

38. Stuart 33.

39. Stuart 35.

40. Stuart 93.

41. Stuart 5.

42. Judge J. de Weerdt refers to this sentence in *R. v. Ootova*, N.W.T.J. No. 118, Nos. CR01379 and CR 01380 (26 Sept. 1991).

43. Joan Ryan, *Doing Things the Right Way: Dene Traditional Justice in Lac La Martre, N.W.T.* (Calgary: U of Calgary P / Arctic Institute of North America, 1995).

44. Deborah Wilson, "Indian Band Paving New Road Back from Despair," *Globe and Mail* 3 Jan. 1994.

45. Hollow Water First Nation, "Community Holistic Circle Healing: An Approach," unpublished paper (Hollow Water, MB: 18 Aug. 1990) 2.

46. "Community Holistic Circle Healing: An Approach" 2.

47. "Community Holistic Circle Healing, Position on Incarceration," 20 April 1993, unpublished paper, available from Hollow Water First Nation, Hollow Water, MB ROE 2E0.

48. Cited in Cayley, "Prison and Its Alternatives" 86.

49. "Community Holistic Circle Healing: Position on Incarceration" 5.

50. Cited in Cayley, "Prison and Its Alternatives" 86.

51. Rupert Ross, *Return to the Teachings: Exploring Aboriginal Justice* (Toronto: Penguin Books, 1996).

52. Cited in Cayley, "Prison and Its Alternatives" 87.

53. Peter Moon, "Natives Find Renewal in Manitoba Prison," *Globe and Mail* 20 July 1995: A1.

54. Kirk Makin, "Prisons Expect More Aboriginal Inmates," *Globe and Mail* 19 Feb. 1998.

55. Peter Moon, "Natives Deserve Own Laws, Report Says," *Globe and Mail* 24 Feb. 1996.

56. "Toward Native Justice," editorial, *Globe and Mail* 24 Feb. 1996.

57. Shafer Parker Jr., "Segregated but Equal," *Western Report* 8 Jan. 1996, 22.

Chapter 11: Rights and Reservations

1. Ross 58–59.

2. See, for example, Isaiah Berlin, *Four Essays on Liberty* (Oxford: Oxford UP, 1969), or Lewis, "The Humanitarian Theory."

3. Teressa Nahanee, "Taking the Measure of Self-Government: For Native Women It's a Bad Deal," *Compass* Nov.–Dec. 1992: 17.

4. *R. v. Curley, Nagmalik, and Issigaitok* N.W.T.R. 263 (T.C.), 1984.

5. *R. v. Qavavauq*, N.W.T.J., no. 44, no. CR 00619, 1989.

6. *R. v. G. (A.)*, N.W.T.J., no. 1172, 1990.

7. Canada, *Minutes of Proceedings and Evidence of the Standing Committee on Justice and Legal Affairs*, House of Commons, no. 85 (28 Feb. 1995): 13.

8. Mary Crnkovich's detailed report on the case appears in *Inuit Women and Justice: Progress Report Number One* (Ottawa: Pauktutit, 1931).

9. Cited in Cayley, "Prison and Its Alternatives" 87.

10. Cited in Cayley, "Prison and Its Alternatives" 87.

11. "The Role of the Victim in the Criminal Justice System — Circle Sentencing in Inuit Communities," unpublished report prepared for the Canadian Institute for the Administration of Justice Conference, Banff, Alberta, 11–14 Oct. 1995.

12. *The Inuit Way* (Ottawa: Pauktutit, [no date]) 17.

13. Cited in Cayley, "Prison and Its Alternatives" 88.

14. The case is discussed in "Prison and Its Alternatives" 88 and in Canada, *Minutes of Proceedings* 14.

15. Cited in Cayley, "Prison and Its Alternatives" 88–89.

16. Cited in Cayley 89.

17. Cunliffe Barnett, "Circle Sentencing, Alternative Sentencing," presentation to National Conference on Alternative Justice Dispute Resolution, Native Community Law Office Association of British Columbia, 24–25 Feb. 1995. For more on Barnett's experiences, see Chapter 13.

18. Barnett cites *R. v. Howard*; CA014152, 12 Dec. 1991.

19. *R. v. Boyd*, Quesnel Registry #16524, 11 Oct. 1994.

20. See Shafer Parker Jr., "A Year at the Lake," *Western Report* 19 June 1995: 32–36.

Chapter 12: From Guilt to Obligation

1. Cited in Cayley, "Prison and Its Alternatives" 60.

2. Cited in Cayley 60.

3. Cited in Cayley 60.

4. Cited in Cayley 67.

5. Thomas Hobbes, *Leviathan* (New York: E.P. Dutton & Co., 1950) 266. Cited in *Philosophical Perspectives on Punishment*, ed. Gertrude Ezorsky (Albany: State U of New York P, 1972) 3.

6. Cited in Cayley, "Prison and Its Alternatives" 69.

7. Eric Gilman, "Reflections on the September 1996 Victim-Offender Mediation Association Conference: Growth and Challenge, Hope and Fear," *Accord* 15 (3 Jan. 1997) 6.

8. *Satisfying Justice: A Compendium of Initiatives, Programs, and Legislative Measures* (Ottawa: The Church Council on Justice and Corrections, 1996) 10–13.

9. Tim Roberts, *Evaluation of the Victim-Offender Mediation Project, Langley, B.C., Final Report*, (Victoria, BC: Focus Consultants, 1995).

10. Rev. David Gustafson, "Victim-Offender Mediation and Reconciliation: Towards a Justice Which Heals," address to the third International Prison Chaplains' Association Conference, Aylmer, Quebec, 18–23 Aug. 1995: 12.

11. Gustafson 13–14.

12. Gustafson 14.

13. Gustafson 15.

14. Cited in Cayley, "Prison and Its Alternatives" 52.

15. *Satisfying Justice* vii–ix.

16. Howard Zehr, *Changing Lenses* (Scottsdale, PA: Herald Press, 1990) 63.

17. Cited in Cayley, "Prison and Its Alternatives" 67.

18. Cited in Cayley 85.

19. Cited in Cayley 68. The state of Pennsylvania is one of a handful of American states that mandates life without parole for first or second degree murder. Howard Zehr has recently published *Doing Life* (Intercourse, PA: Good Books, 1996), a book of photographs and interviews with Pennsylvania lifers.

Chapter 13: Working Within the System

1. Cited in Cayley, "Prison and Its Alternatives" 80.

2. Cited in Cayley 80–81.

3. Cited in Cayley 81–82.

4. *R. v. Loran Victor Cahoose*, before the Honourable C. C. Barnett, Anahim Lake, BC, 17 June 1996.

5. Cited in Cayley, "Prison and Its Alternatives" 89.

6. Cited in Cayley, "Crime Control as Industry" 12.

7. Miller has related his experiences as Massachusetts' Commissioner of Youth Services in *Last One Over the Wall: The Massachusetts Experiment in Closing Reform Schools* (Columbus, OH: Ohio State UP, 1991).

8. Cited in Cayley, "Beyond Institutions" 6.

9. Cited in Cayley 6.

10. Cited in Cayley 6–7.

11. Cited in Cayley 8.

12. Cited in Cayley 9.

13. Cited in Cayley 10.

14. Cayley, "Prison and Its Alternatives" 35.

15. Cited in Cayley, "Beyond Institutions" 17–18.

16. Cited in Cayley 18.

17. Miller, *Search and Destroy*. His footnote cites Robert Vintner, Theodore Newcomb, and Rhea Kish, eds., *Time Out: A National Study of Juvenile Correctional Programs*, (Ann Arbor, MI: National Assessment of Juvenile Corrections, the University of Michigan, Jun. 1976) 236, 294 n. 44.

18. Cited in Cayley, "Prison and Its Alternatives" 70.

19. Cited in Cayley 70.

20. Cited in Cayley 71.

21. Cited in Cayley 71.

22. Judge Graney's sentence was passed on 25 May 1984, and reported in the *Batavia Daily News*.

23. The story was related to me by Dennis Wittman, and also reported in *The Christian Science Monitor*, 24 Jun. 1986.

24. Cited in Cayley, "Prison and Its Alternatives" 71–72.

25. Cited in Cayley 72.

26. Cited in Cayley 73–74.

27. Cited in Cayley 74.

28. Christie, *Crime Control* 51.

29. Quotations from K. J. Lång, where not otherwise noted, are drawn from an unpublished interview recorded at the International Conference on Prison Growth, Norwegian Academy of Science and Letters, Oslo, 30 Apr. 1995.

30. Christie, *Crime Control* 52.

31. Cited in Cayley, "Prison and Its Alternatives" 24–25.

32. Cited in Cayley 26.

Chapter 14: Shame of Doing Amiss

1. Braithwaite, *Crime, Shame.* (See Introduction, note 1.)
2. Braithwaite 55.
3. Braithwaite 55.
4. Braithwaite 179.
5. Frank Tannenbaum, *Crime and Community* (New York: Columbia UP, 1938). Cited in Braithwaite 17.
6. Nicholas Kristo, "Why Japan Wins the War on Crime," *Globe and Mail* 26 May 1995.
7. John Charles, "Mr. Walkabout," *The New Internationalist* 282 (Aug. 96): 28.
8. Charles 28.
9. Cited in Cayley, "Prison and Its Alternatives" 42.
10. Cited in Cayley 42.
11. Cited in Cayley 43.
12. See David Cayley, "Community and Its Counterfeits," *Ideas*, 3, 10, 17 Jan. 1994 (transcript available), CBC Radio, 1994, my profile of John McKnight, and his book, *The Careless Society: Community and Its Counterfeits* (New York: Basic Books, 1995).
13. Cited in Cayley, "Prison and Its Alternatives" 44.
14. Jeff Sallot, "Japanese Policemen, Hoods Learn to Live and Let Live," *Globe and Mail* 25 Nov. 1995.
15. John Haley, *Authority Without Power: Law and the Japanese Paradox* (New York: Oxford UP, 1991) 169.
16. Cited in Gorringe, *God's Just Vengeance* 14–15.
17. Cited in Gorringe 15.
18. Cited in Cayley, "Prison and Its Alternatives" 440.
19. Charles 18.
20. Cited in Cayley, "Prison and Its Alternatives" 45.
21. Braithwaite 158.
22. John Braithwaite and Philip Petit, *Not Just Deserts: A Republican Theory of Criminal Justice* (Oxford, UK: Clarendon Press, 1990).

Chapter 15: On Civil Solutions

1. Louk Hulsman, "The Abolitionist Case: Alternative Crime Policies," *Israel Law Review* 25 (3–4, Summer–Autumn 1991).
2. Hulsman 706–7.
3. Hulsman 694.
4. Hulsman 705.
5. Hulsman 705.
6. Hulsman 708.

Chapter 16: Circles of Support

1. Gorringe 109.

2. Gorringe 110.

3. William Blake, *Jerusalem* book 2, plate 52, *The Complete Poetry and Prose of William Blake*, ed. David V. Erdman (New York: Anchor/Doubleday) 201.

4. Cited in Gorringe 212.

5. The Church Council on Justice and Corrections is a coalition of eleven churches founded in 1974. See especially its publication *Satisfying Justice: A Compendium of Initiatives, Programs, and Legislative Measures*, available from 507 Bank St., Ottawa, ON K2P 1Z5.

6. Cited in Cayley, "Prison and Its Alternatives" 90–91.

7. Cited in Cayley 92–93.

8. Cited in Cayley 93.

9. "Bill Targets High-Risk Criminals," *Globe and Mail* 11 Dec. 1996: A10.

10. "Tracking Bracelets Too Costly," *Globe and Mail* 6 Mar. 1997.

11. Cited in Cayley, "Prison and Its Alternatives" 94.

12. Cited in Cayley 94.

13. Paul Kaihla, "Sex Offenders: Is There a Cure?" *Maclean's* 13 Feb. 1995: 57.

14. Cited in Cayley, "Prison and Its Alternatives" 94–95.

15. Cited in Cayley 95.

16. Cited in Cayley 95.

17. Cited in Cayley 95–96.

18. Cited in Cayley 97.

19. Cited in Cayley 97.

20. Gordon Laird, "Deviant Justice," *This Magazine* Jul.–Aug. 1996: 35–39.

21. Cited in Cayley, "Prison and Its Alternatives" 98.

22. Ross Howard, "High Risk Inmates Cause Concern," *Globe and Mail* 24 Apr. 1995.

23. Kirk Makin, "The Plight of Canada's Dangerous Offenders," *Globe and Mail* 20 Jul. 1996.

24. Max Winkler, "Walking Prisons: The Developing Technology of Electronic Controls," *The Futurist* Jul.–Aug. 1993: 34–36.

25. Cited in Cayley, "Prison and Its Alternatives" 98–99.

26. Cited in Cayley 98–99.

Chapter 17: Justice as Sanctuary

1. The first paragraph of Chapter 17 paraphrases Bianchi, *Justice as Sanctuary* 141–42.

2. Berman, *Law and Revolution* vii.

3. The book was first published in the Netherlands in 1985 as *Gerechtigheid als Vrijplaats*.

4. Berman 29.

5. Bianchi 94.

6. Bianchi 94–95.

7. Ruth Morris, Harry Glasbeek, and Dianne Martin, *We're Being Cheated! Corporate and Welfare Fraud: The Hidden Story* (Toronto: Rittenhouse, 1987). Available from 736 Bathurst St., Room 213, Toronto, ON, M5S 2R4. The authors estimate the cost of tax evasion and employment insurance fraud at $20 billion annually, and welfare fraud at $500 million, then point out that 80 percent of welfare fraud convictions result in jail sentences, as opposed to only 13 percent for tax and EI fraud. They also estimate that the amount of corporate theft is about ten times as great as the amount of street theft. See also Braithwaite and Petit, *Not Just Deserts* 186 ff. They argue that the number of serious white-collar crimes in the community is so vast that "to mobilize criminal enforcement against even the tiniest proportion of them would bankrupt the wealthiest of governments."

8. John Henry Newman, *An Essay in Aid of a Grammar of Assent*, cited in Bianchi 84.

9. Bianchi ix.

10. Bianchi 175, n. 15.

11. Bianchi 23.

12. Cited in Cayley, "Justice as Sanctuary" (Toronto: CBC Radio, 1997) 8. Transcript of broadcast from *Ideas* 27 Oct., 3, 10 Nov. 1997.

13. Bianchi 41.

14. Bianchi 48.

15. Bianchi 19.

16. George Bernard Shaw's introduction to S. and B. Webb, *English Prisons Under Local Government* (London: Longmans, 1992) liv. Cited in Gorringe 234.

17. Bianchi 90.

18. Bianchi 91.

19. Cited in Cayley, "Justice as Sanctuary" 17–18.

20. Cited in Cayley 18.

21. Bianchi 144.

22. *Simone Weil: An Anthology* 94.

Chapter 18: Prison Is Not the Only Punishment

1. All quotations from Zaffaroni are taken from the unpublished transcript of an interview recorded at the International Conference on Prison Growth, Oslo, 30 Apr. 1995.

2. Human Rights Watch/Americas, *Punishment Before Trial: Prison Conditions in Venezuela* (New York: Human Rights Watch, 1997) 2–3.

3. Julita Lemgruber, unpublished interview recorded at the International Conference on Prison Growth, Oslo, 28 Apr. 1995.

4. Cited in Cayley, "Prison and Its Alternatives" 32.

5. Cayley 38.

6. Prison Reform International, *Annual Report 1994* (London, UK: Penal Reform International, 1994) 6. Available from 169 Clapham Rd., London SW9 0PU, UK.

7. Cited in Cayley, "Prison and Its Alternatives" 30.

8. Cited in Cayley 30–31.

9. Cited in Cayley 31.

10. Cited in Cayley 31.

Chapter 19: A Turning Point?

1. This statement is used as an epigraph to David Ricardo Williams's *Just Lawyers: Seven Portraits* (Toronto: U of Toronto P, 1995). The source is not given.

2. See George Grant, *English-Speaking Justice* (Toronto: Anansi, 1975) and David Cayley, *George Grant in Conversation* (Toronto: Anansi, 1995) chapter 6.

3. Greg T. Smith, "Civilized People Don't Want to See That Kind of Thing: The Decline of Public Physical Punishment in London, 1760–1840," *Qualities of Mercy: Justice, Punishment and Discretion*, ed. Carolyn Strange (Vancouver: UBC Press, 1996) 26.

4. Joe Woodward, "The Quality of Mercy Is . . . Ambiguous," *Western Report* 6 Nov. 1995: 34.

5. Wayne Northey, "Looking Back and Looking Forward," *Accord* 17.1 (Feb. 1998) 1–2.

6. "Ottawa Aims at Cutting Prison Populations," *Globe and Mail* 31 Mar. 1995; Rob Tripp, "What's the Real Cost of Punishment?" *Toronto Star* 13 Jan. 1997: A11.

7. Canada, Sentencing and Corrections Review Group, *Rethinking Corrections*, discussion paper (Ottawa: 1995).

8. "Ottawa Aims at Cutting Prison Populations," *Globe and Mail* 31 Mar. 1995.

9. Thomas Claridge, "Court Re-affirms Conditional Sentences," *Globe and Mail* 12 Apr. 1997: A3.

10. Anne McIlroy, "War on Crime to Target Young," *Globe and Mail* 1 June 1998: A1.

11. Kirk Makin, "Prisons Expect More Aboriginal Inmates," *Globe and Mail*, 19 Feb. 1998.

12. Pauline Tam, "Conditional Justice: Officials Try to Curb Use of Sentencing Option," *Ottawa Citizen* 12 May 1997: D1; see also Gord Henderson, "House Arrest Makes Mockery of Court System," *Windsor Star* 3 May 1997; and David Roberts, "Manitoba Set to Appeal Ruling Involving 13-Year-Old Girl," *Globe and Mail* 8 June 1997.

13. "U.S. Man Gets Life in Drunk-driving Death of Teens," *Globe and Mail* 7 May 1997.

14. Rhéal Séguin, "Quebec Launches Prison Reforms," *Globe and Mail* 3 Apr. 1996.

15. Kevin Cox, "Penal Reforms Draw Little Reaction in New Brunswick," *Globe and Mail* 10 June 1996: A2.

16. Kirk Makin, "Judge Questions the Value of Prison Sentences," *Globe and Mail* 5 Mar. 1996: A6.

17. "Imprisoned by Inertia," *Globe and Mail* 7 Feb. 1996.

18. Cited in Cayley, "Prison and Its Alternatives" 26–27.

19. Cited in Cayley 27.

20. Cited in Cayley 27.

21. The two-thirds figure was arrived at by taking John Edwards's information that 80 percent of federal prisoners and 30 percent of federal prisoners are sentenced for nonviolent crimes and applying it to 1994–95 Statistics Canada's totals of 13,948 federal prisoners and 19,934 provincial prisoners.

22. Cited in Cayley, "Prison and Its Alternatives" 28.

23. Jeff Sallot, "Corrections System Head Resigns," *Globe and Mail* 2 Apr. 1996: A1.

24. Kirk Makin, "Incarceration Rates Too High, Official Says," *Globe and Mail* 17 Mar. 1998.

25. Eoin Kenny, "Solicitor General Wants Fewer Inmates, More Crime Prevention," *Toronto Star* 3 Jan. 1998.

26. Gerald Early, "Whatever Happened to Integration?" *Atlantic Monthly* Feb. 1997: 105.

27. Henry Hess, "Tough Stand on Weapons Pays Off," *Globe and Mail* 8 Sept. 1997: A6.

28. Berman vi.

29. Cayley, *George Grant in Conversation* 149.

30. Umbreit and Zehr 1.

31. *The Secret of the Golden Flower: A Chinese Book of Life*, trans. Richard Wilhelm (1931; New York: Harcourt, Brace, 1962) 83.

32. Howard Zehr, "Restorative Justice Hits the Big Time: But Will It Remain True to Its Vision, Values?" *Accord* 15.2 (Aug. 1996): 1.

33. Cited in "Prison and Its Alternatives" 62.

34. Richard Mackie and Kirk Makin, "Ontario Court Delays Reach Crisis Point," *Globe and Mail* 26 Nov. 1997: A8.

35. The best extended treatment of this theme that I know of is John McKnight, *The Careless Society: Community and Its Counterfeits* (New York: Basic Books, 1995).

36. See Uwe Poerkson, *Plastic Words: The Tyranny of a Modular Language*, trans. Jutta Mason and David Cayley (University Park, PA: Pennsylvania State UP, 1995); or, for a short digest of the argument, David Cayley, "Plastic Words," CBC Radio, *Ideas*, 4 Feb. 1993. The idea of plastic words as verbal amoebas comes from Ivan Illich.

37. Cayley, *George Grant in Conversation* 23.

INDEX